Project Arcade
Build Your Own
Arcade Machine

Project Arcade
Build Your Own Arcade Machine

John St.Clair

Wiley Publishing, Inc.

Project Arcade
Build Your Own Arcade Machine

Published by
Wiley Publishing, Inc.
10475 Crosspoint Boulevard
Indianapolis, IN 46256
www.wiley.com

Published simultaneously in Canada

ISBN: 0-7645-5616-9

Manufactured in the United States of America

10 9 8 7 6 5 4 3

1B/SQ/QU/QU/IN

For general information on our other products and services or to obtain technical support, please contact our Customer Care Department within the U.S. at (800) 762-2974, outside the U.S. at (317) 572-3993 or fax (317) 572-4002.

Wiley also publishes its books in a variety of electronic formats. Some content that appears in print may not be available in electronic books.

Library of Congress Control Number: 2004103159

WILEY

Credits

Executive Editor
Chris Webb

Development Editor
Scott Amerman

Production Editor
Gabrielle Nabi

Copy Editor
Publication Services

Editorial Manager
Kathryn A. Malm

Vice President and Executive Group Publisher
Richard Swadley

Vice President and Publisher
Bob Ipsen

Vice President and Publisher
Joseph B. Wikert

Executive Editorial Director
Mary Bednarek

Project Arcade cabinet artwork by
Tom Van Horn

Project Coordinator
Erin Smith

Graphics and Production Specialists
Carrie Foster
Jennifer Heleine
Mary Gillot Virgin

Quality Control Technicians
John Greenough
Andy Hollandbeck
Susan Moritz
Angel Perez
Brian Walls

Permissions Editor
Laura Moss

Media Development Specialist
Kit Malone

Book Designer
Wiley Composition Services

Proofreading and Indexing
Publication Services

*This book is dedicated to my wife, Kristi, and my children, Kayci, Isaac, and Sebastian,
without whom my life would not be complete.*

*I'd also like to dedicate this book to my parents, Ed and Liliane,
and brothers Don and Andy, who inspire me.*

Acknowledgments

I'd like to thank my wife for her support and love while I wrote this book, and for doing the job of two parents so that I *could* write it. I can't imagine life without you by my side. I want to thank my kids, Kayci and Isaac, for their understanding and for being willing to do without daddy while I was working on the project. I'd also like to officially welcome Sebastian to the world, who managed to be born somewhere in the middle of all the paperwork and carpentry. Glad you're here, little guy! Finally, I'd like to thank my parents and brothers for their support and encouragement, and my in-laws Don "Cappy" and Jeannie Oakley for the same. (Thanks for the hands-on help, Cappy!)

I'd like to also thank my friends Mark and Michele, who were willing to drop everything and come up to help when I got myself in a bind. You can't ask for truer friends. I'm thankful as well for the encouragement and support of my boss, Ed Morrison, who was as excited as I was about the whole thing.

I'd be remiss not to mention the folks who turn ideas into books—my editors Scott Amerman, who kept the book and me on target; Chris Webb, who believed in the idea to start with; Laura Moss, for taking care of the details so I could stick to my writing; and everyone else at Wiley Publishing who helped make this book a reality. Thanks, everyone. I hope I didn't drive you nuts!

Special thanks go out to all the people who helped turn my Web site from a simple little one-page affair five-plus years ago to the community it is today, which ultimately led to the book in your hands now: Jay "planetjay" Wilkinson, in particular, for doing so much to help keep things running behind the scenes, Tom "Tom61" White for doing much the same, and Michael "JustMichael" Horton, Kevin "SirPoonga" Jonas, and Matt "Nivo" Nivison for helping run the message forums.

Another round of appreciation goes to Andy Warne, Kelsey Schell, Howard Casto, Tom Van Horn, Robin Merrill, Dave Hagstrom, and Zonn Moore, for providing technical expertise, feedback, and proofreading of book material. Also to Sean "LuSiD" Hatfield for donating his plans for the project, and a big thank-you to everyone else who allowed me to include their projects and material in the book!

I'd also like to give a shout out to all the chat-room and message-board regulars, whose contributions are too numerous to mention and are found throughout this book. Also, a big kudos and thanks to all who have documented the construction of their own Project Arcade machines. Thanks for being part of everything, ladies and gents!

Yes, it's a bit sappy, but I mean every word. Without everyone here, this book wouldn't be nearly as good as I hope you'll find it to be.

Contents at a Glance

Contents

· ·

Part III: Hooking Things Up Under the Hood — Time to Trick the Computer   157

Chapter 17: Buying Your Way to Gaming Nirvana **405**

Chapter 18: Online Places to Go **417**

Appendix A: Where to Find Arcade Parts for Your Project **447**

Appendix B: The Great Debate—Preserving Versus
MAMEing the Past **451**

Appendix C: What's on the CD-ROM **453**

Introduction

Gotcha! As soon as you picked up this book, you started a journey toward absolute game-playing Nirvana! You might be a classic arcade-loving child of the 1980s, or perhaps an enthusiast of more recent, modern arcades. Remember playing *Pac-Man* at the local convenience store, or *Street Fighter* at the mall's arcade? Whatever caused this book to catch your eye, I'm betting that somewhere down the line the thought of owning one of these machines has crossed your mind. Wouldn't it be great to have your favorite arcade machine in your own den or recreation room? Imagine your friends' reactions when they encounter this treasure from their past in your home. This is definitely high on the "wow" factor! The problem is, though, that it's just one game. Sooner or later the thrill wears off, and it starts to gather dust.

No problem—as an arcade enthusiast, you're probably also a game player at home. If you haven't found them on your own yet, you'll discover through this book the joy of playing near-perfect replicas of your favorite games on your computer. The first time you play *Pac-Man* on your computer, the "wow" factor is back! Between commercial and shareware re-creations of classic and modern arcade games, and the thousands of unique games developed for the computer, there's a neverending variety to suit everyone. However, sooner or later you'll realize that playing *Pac-Man* with the keyboard lacks something. It just isn't the same as steering around the maze with a genuine ball-topped arcade joystick.

So—you can own your own arcade machine at home (this book will give you some pointers on that), and you can play thousands of games on your computer (we'll get you started on that, too), but both fall short of that perfect arcade experience. Wouldn't it be great if you could combine the two? Wouldn't it be great if you could . . . build your own arcade machine? Imagine an arcade machine with that perfect combination of joysticks, buttons, and trackballs running all your favorite games. Picture it painted to match your decor, with your favorite game characters decorating the sides and a lit marquee at the top saying "My Arcade!" Wouldn't that be awesome? This book will show you how. Congratulations—you've started down the road to game-playing Nirvana!

About This Book

This book is a culmination of five years of research into the subject of interfacing genuine arcade controls to computers. It is a polished and portable companion to the author's Web site, the Build Your Own Arcade Controls FAQ (BYOAC), located at www.arcadecontrols.com/. Most of the research and information for this book came from the Web, and I'll refer to various sites throughout. Access to the Internet is useful and recommended; however, it is *not* required. Everything you need to get started is right here.

This book is meant to be read from start to finish in order. I've kept the technical jargon and theory to a minimum, providing just enough background information to understand the direction we're heading when it comes time for the hands-on material. For those who are interested in a deeper understanding of the theory behind these projects, I've included pointers to more information where relevant.

This book will take you step by step through the process of designing and building your own arcade machine. You'll be able to begin immediately after the first chapter; you'll have the gratification of watching your design take shape as you proceed through the pages. In fact, one common trap is getting to the point where the machine is playable before it's totally finished and getting lost in the game play. One day you'll realize it's been weeks since you've actually worked on it because you've spent all your time playing, even though it's held together with string and chewing gum! That's not a problem though: The book will be waiting for you when you're ready to pick it up again.

We'll take a couple of side trips along the way. I discuss building a standalone desktop arcade control panel (arcade controls minus the cabinet) for those who want the experience but don't want to dedicate the space. I also cover hooking up game console controllers to your computer, such as the Nintendo 64 or Playstation game pads, for those who feel that they provide the best game-playing experience. Finally, for those who think the building part is beyond them (it's not, by the way), I'll point out and review some of the various commercial products you can buy. There is something in this book for everyone!

Assumptions

I'm assuming you have access to a computer. The majority of the computer-related material is PC-centric, but enough of it applies to Macintosh computers that Mac enthusiasts can successfully use this book to build an arcade machine as well. I'm not assuming you have any electronics or carpentry expertise. Depending on the path you take as you build your machine, you may gain those skills, but it's possible to build the entire thing with off-the-shelf parts. If you do decide to take the more advanced route (and I recommend it), I'm assuming you're willing to learn as you go. Most of all, I'm assuming you're ready to have fun!

Things You'll Need

- **Plans:** You'll need a set of plans to work from. Plans for upright arcade cabinets are included on the companion CD-ROM. You can use or modify them as suits you. I'll also show you where to find other plans on the Internet, and I'll give you suggestions should you choose to draw your own.

- **Computer:** A fairly modest computer will allow you a good classic arcade game experience. Depending on what you want to play, even an old 486 or Pentium-class machine can play a slew of great, albeit older, games. To play more recent games, you'll want at least a Pentium III– (or better) class machine. Specific requirements will depend on the software you want to play. Macintosh users will find that similar factors apply. Whatever you have available for this project will work fine to start with. You can always upgrade later if you discover you can't run the games you want to play.

- **Software:** The software that makes everything work comes from a variety of sources. Some of it can be had for free, and some of it has to be purchased. Where possible, the necessary software has been included on the companion CD. The software behind this hobby is updated frequently, however, and you should consider downloading updated versions of whichever software you choose to use. Links are of course provided. Software will be covered in great detail in Chapters 13 and 14.

- **Tools:** Odds are, you already have many of the necessary basic set of tools. Screwdrivers and a drill will meet the need for those of you who want to build a cabinet from off-the-shelf parts, while woodworking tools will be required if you want to build it all from scratch. I'll discuss tools more in Chapter 2 when I cover the anatomy of an arcade cabinet. Unless you're planning a lot of woodworking in your future, this is a good time to find a friend or relative with a workshop that you can borrow.

- **Budget:** Budget requirements will vary depending on what you're trying to accomplish. Desktop arcade control projects will average $200 to $300, while full-sized arcade cabinet projects can run $500 to $1,500 or more! The nice thing is that, with proper planning, you can start small and inexpensively and work your way up to bigger projects as your budget allows. For instance, you can start with a desktop arcade control panel that can later be incorporated into a full-sized arcade cabinet. Factors such as whether you need to purchase a computer and tools will obviously have a significant effect on your overall budget.

- **Space and Time:** No, this isn't a *Star Trek* reference. Space and time required for a project like this are often overlooked but are clearly worth some consideration. It *is* possible to complete a project like this in a weekend, but the more likely scenario is that you'll work on it in bits and pieces over the course of a couple of months. One truism is that a project like this is often never "finished"—there's always another tweak or upgrade to try. With this in mind, where you build your project becomes important. If you're going to tie up your garage for a month or two, you might want to check with your spouse first!

 Don't fall into the trap that one unfortunate fellow did. He spent months building an absolutely gorgeous custom arcade cabinet, only to discover it was too wide to fit through the doorway of his basement once completed. I'm not certain how that was resolved, but there's definitely a lesson to be learned there!

How This Book Is Organized

In this book, you'll find chapters spread across five parts. Each part covers a different theme, and each chapter is broken down into sections covering the chapter's subject. The parts and chapters are laid out in a sequence designed to walk you through the process of building an arcade machine in a logical order. You'll probably be happiest browsing the contents of the entire book, and then diving in to Chapter 1.

Part I: Playing Your Games the Way They Are Meant to Be Played — with Arcade Controls

The two chapters in this part get you started on your project. You'll start by exploring the different kinds of projects you can build. In Chapter 2 you'll pick a design and come up with a plan, and then you'll jump right into the actual construction.

Part II: Designing and Building Your Dream Arcade Control Panel

Part II is where it starts to get really fun. Chapters 3 through 5 cover the different kinds of joysticks, buttons, trackballs, and other arcade controls you can include in your arcade machine. Chapter 6 covers designing the control panel and installing the controls you've chosen. It's starting to look like a real arcade machine now!

Part III: Hooking Things Up Under the Hood — Time to Trick the Computer

Part III is the most "techie" part of the book. These four chapters describe how to make the computer think a joystick and trackball are really a keyboard and mouse. Chapter 7 briefly covers some theory, and Chapters 8 and 9 cover using the keyboard port and mouse port, which is how the majority of these projects are done. The last chapter in this part, Chapter 10, discusses several other clever methods people have found to connect arcade controls to a computer, including the USB port for plug-and-play connections.

Part IV: Putting Together the Final Pieces

Part IV is the capstone of the project. Chapters 11 and 12 discuss sound systems and monitor options, respectively. Chapters 13 and 14 go over software, configuring your system for the ultimate game-playing experience, and installing the computer in the arcade cabinet. Finally, Chapter 15 covers the miscellaneous odds and ends that will enable you to turn your creation into your idea of the perfect arcade machine: artwork, the marquee, and so on.

Part V: Like the Concept but Not Sure You Have It in You?

This part covers subjects for those of you who aren't quite sure you can or want to build an arcade machine. Chapter 16 points out troubleshooting tips and where you can go to get help when stuck. Chapter 17 covers the various products you can purchase, from arcade cabinet kits to outright arcade cabinets, and it includes several reviews. Chapter 17 also briefly covers using game console controllers (such as the Nintendo 64 or Sony Playstation) on your computer, with do-it-yourself information included on the companion CD-ROM. Finally, Chapter 18 will introduce you to a few arcade cabinet and controller projects to inspire you and show you places to go online for more information.

Appendixes

Every ExtremeTech book has them, and this one is no exception! Handy information is gathered in this section, including where to find arcade parts for your project. There's also an interesting debate presented on whether to preserve or "MAME" an arcade machine. Feelings on this subject run deeper than you might think!

 The book's companion CD-ROM winds up with a clickable glossary of terms you'll encounter as you read.

Conventions Used in This Book

Throughout the book, you'll find highlighted text where I point out cautions, cross-references, notes of interest, and helpful recommendations, as well as mention what's included on the book's companion CD-ROM. Specifically, five types of highlighted pointers appear:

 These give you valuable information that will help you avoid disaster. Read all of these carefully!

 These are pointers to other areas in the book or sites on the Internet where you can find more information on the subject at hand.

 These are recommendations of best-practice methods and superior products or tools to use.

 These pertain to items of interest related to the subject at hand. Although you can safely skip these, I recommend that you read them at your leisure. They'll help you to be a better arcade-machine builder!

 These refer you to valuable information, links, software, illustrations, and more that is included on the companion CD-ROM to this book.

Playing Your Games the Way They Are Meant to Be Played — with Arcade Controls

Picking Your Path to Game-Playing Nirvana

I remember vividly the feeling I had when I realized I was really going to do this—that I was really going to build my own home arcade cabinet! I didn't really have any idea how I was going to get there, but I knew that if others could do it, then I could, too. All I needed to do was pick my goal, plan out the steps, buy a few things, and then I'd have my own arcade cabinet. Nothing to it, right? Well, of course, there were a few minor details along the way, like actually building the thing. Still, after dreaming about it for well over a year, there I was, finally getting started! Now it's your turn. I'll walk you through the process from beginning to end, starting with goal setting and planning in this chapter. Are you ready? I almost envy you for just starting the book—for you, the magic is just beginning!

Where to Start? Finding Your Muse

The hardest part of any project is deciding where to start. It's tempting to jump right in and start hammering and sawing, but a bit of homework now will pay off in the end. Before you start on your own project, you should devote some time to browsing the examples of those who have gone before you. At the time of this writing, there were over 775 examples of arcade projects listed on the Build Your Own Arcade Controls Web site (also known as BYOAC) and on the companion CD-ROM for you to see.

 Cross-Reference It's a fact of life on the Internet that very little stays the same. By the time this book makes it into your hands, many of the project examples included on the CD-ROM will have been updated, and many more will have been added. Be sure to visit the examples page on the Build Your Own Arcade Controls Web site, located at www.arcadecontrols.com, for the latest and greatest!

Some projects are works of art, and some only a parent could love, but all have one thing in common: Each was lovingly put together by its creator and might have a feature or two you wouldn't have thought of and won't be able to live without once you've seen it. The bar has been raised many times during the five years I've been involved in this hobby. It's unusual to have a month go by without some project inspiring me to bigger and better things in my own endeavors.

As meaningful as every project is to its owner, in every field there are examples that stand out from the rest. In Chapter 18, you'll find several arcade cabinet and desktop arcade control projects to inspire you. Although it's worthwhile to browse all the example projects available, doing so can literally take days! If you're looking to fast-track the inspiration process, skip ahead to Chapter 18 and read through those.

| Tip |

Now would be a good time to get out a notebook and start jotting down ideas as they come to you during this process. The number of possibilities in this kind of project can be overwhelming, so good organization from the start will help. Be sure to include the address of any project's Web site that you make note of. When it comes time to implement the ideas from your notes, you'll want to be able to quickly find the site again to check up on the finer details.

Choosing Your Goal

By now you're probably beginning to realize that there is no one model of what an arcade machine is. As you browse through other people's projects, you'll encounter upright arcade cabinets, sit-down cocktail cabinets, desktop arcade control panels, and contraptions that defy description. How do you decide where to begin? I'll describe each of these in the sections that follow, and include pictures to help you make some decisions. Start by asking yourself the questions found in Table 1-1.

Table 1-1   Questions to Ask Yourself

Question	Point to consider
Are you looking to recapture the full arcade experience?	Nothing brings you back to the arcade like a full-sized upright arcade cabinet.
Want the arcade experience but need a spouse's approval?	Consider a sit-down cocktail cabinet that doubles as a piece of fine furniture. Okay, I admit calling it fine furniture may be a stretch, but a cocktail cabinet can blend into the decor nicely.
Do you have the time, skills, and patience to build a full cabinet?	If not, a desktop arcade control panel may be for you. They are comparatively small and not too difficult to make.

Question	Point to consider
Do you want to start small and work your way up?	Start with a desktop control panel that can be incorporated into an upright cabinet later.
Is space at a premium?	With a little ingenuity, you can make a countertop arcade cabinet like those you'd find at a tavern.
Do you just want to plug in a game console controller and start blasting away?	For about $30, you can build an interface that will allow you to hook up your favorite controller to your computer.

Take a few minutes to assess your personal situation. Do you have a limited amount of time to devote to the project, or are you in it for the long haul? Where will you put your creation when completed? Be thinking of considerations such as these and the questions in Table 1-1 as you go over your project options.

Building a desktop arcade controller

A desktop arcade controller takes the control panel from an arcade machine and adds a box around it to hold it and protect the insides (see Figure 1-1). The top panel holds the joysticks, buttons, and other arcade controls. Inside the box are the underside of the controls and the electronics needed to interface the controls to the computer. The back of the control panel has a hole or holes for the cables that hook into the computer.

FIGURE 1-1: Several commercial desktop arcade controllers.
Photo courtesy of Hanaho Games, SlikStik, and Xgaming, Inc., respectively.

What are the benefits of a desktop arcade controller?

Building a desktop arcade controller is a good project for those with a more casual interest in game playing. You get the benefits of playing with real arcade controls without having to lose floor space in the house. I keep a small one-player unit on my desk for when I get that gaming bug, and I slide it out of the way when I want to work. Not only do desktop arcades save space, but you also do not have to dedicate an entire computer system for game playing. They are also portable for those times when you visit arcade-deprived friends.

Warning! Visiting friends with your contraption or letting them play at your house can have one side effect: Shortly after playing, the question "How can I get one of these?" will come up. This is your cue to tell them where they can purchase a copy of this book. By no means should you allow them to borrow your copy. You will need it when you begin your next design!

Desktop arcades are also easier to build than full-sized arcade cabinets, but they can still contain the same mixture of arcade controls. Although the design and layout work is the same, the woodworking is much simpler and you don't have to worry about the audio and video systems.

What are the drawbacks of a desktop arcade controller?

Desktop arcade control setups have a couple of downsides. For one, you lose your desktop space. Wait—wasn't I just praising these units as a way to save space? Well, yes, but it's relative. You're not dedicating floor space, but you are giving up workspace. Even the smaller one-player units can measure a foot and a half wide by a foot deep, and the larger units can be 2 to 3 feet wide—that's a lot of desk space to give up!

After the initial thrill of playing wears off, the realization will set in that you're still in front of a computer screen. Playing a game with real arcade controls on your desktop is definitely fun, but it's not quite an arcade cabinet. If you're trying to recapture the feel of an arcade, you'll want the arcade cabinet atmosphere as well as the controls. Don't get me wrong—I think a desktop set is a project worth building, and I believe I'll always have one on my desk. It's just no substitute for the real thing.

Some arcade game collectors will scoff at calling a home-built arcade cabinet *the real thing.* There's actually a bit of controversy on the subject, with valid points on both sides of the debate. You'll find more on this topic in Appendix B.

Building an arcade cabinet

An arcade cabinet is essentially a box containing the monitor, speakers, arcade control panel, and miscellaneous electronics that make an arcade game work. In our case, the miscellaneous electronics include a computer that runs the whole operation. Many variations of arcade cabinets can be found. The following descriptions cover the most popular (see Figure 1-2).

FIGURE 1-2: A variety of different arcade cabinets. From left: Upright, countertop, and cocktail.
Photo courtesy of Jeffrey Allen, Oscar Controls, and Game Cabinets, Inc., respectively.

Upright arcade cabinets

You're probably most familiar with the stand-up, *upright* arcade cabinet seen in arcades and convenience stores everywhere. They typically stand about 6 feet high and have 19- or 25-inch monitors, though later models can have much bigger monitors. These cabinets will support up to four players easily, depending on the design of your control panel. There is also a variation of the upright cabinet called a *mini*, which is a scaled-down version with a smaller monitor and cabinet that usually supports only one or two players. Roughly two-thirds of the build-your-own cabinets made are uprights.

Cocktail arcade cabinets

You're likely to have spotted the *cocktail* arcade cabinet also. They are popular in arcades, and for some reason pizza parlors tend to favor them as well. These units are about 4 feet by 4 feet square and about 3 feet high. The monitor rests face up in the middle of the cabinet with players looking down on it as they play. These cabinets are usually limited to two players sitting opposite each other and taking turns. About one-third of the build-your-own cabinets are cocktail cabinets.

Cockpit arcade cabinets

A *cockpit* arcade cabinet (not shown in Figure 1-2) is a full-sized enclosure with a seat included as part of the cabinet. There are fewer of these than the other types of cabinets made, presumably because of the sheer size. They typically take up the space of two or more upright arcade cabinets. These are usually one-player machines, though I have seen at least one two-player unit. I am aware of only a small number of cockpit cabinets that have been made by the build-your-own crowd.

Countertop arcade cabinets

The last main variation of the arcade cabinet is the *countertop*, or *bar-top*, model. These machines are not much bigger than a set of desktop arcade controls, primarily being taller and deeper to house a small monitor. You will typically find these machines in taverns and bars, hence the name bar-top. They are most popular for trivia and puzzle games (like Tetris). Again, only a small handful of these cabinets are made by folks who try their hand at an arcade cabinet.

What will you gain by building an arcade cabinet?

Building an arcade cabinet has to be the most rewarding variation of this hobby you can find. It's as close to the real thing as you can get without putting a full arcade into your basement. Depending on the type of cabinet you make, you can get a full-sized arcade control panel with genuine arcade controls custom-designed for the type of game play you're after. Add a monitor shrouded in darkness that minimizes distractions and a moderate sound system, and you can immerse yourself in the arcade experience. There's also plenty of space available to have such fancy things as removable steering wheels, sophisticated speaker systems, and four-player panels.

You can also customize your software setup to hide the fact that the brain behind your arcade cabinet is a computer. With a combination of a front-end menu system and an arcade-themed background and sounds, it's possible to completely disguise the non-arcade origins of your creation. Throw in a working coin door and you'll begin to believe you're standing in front of a real arcade machine — one that can play an unlimited number of games! I'll go through all of this in later chapters.

An arcade cabinet is also much easier to share with your friends, particularly if it has a two- or four-player control panel. Add music jukebox software (see Chapter 11, "Audio — Silence Isn't Golden"), and your legally-obtained collection of music files, and you've got an entertainment centerpiece for your next party that will be the envy of your friends. If you have the time and resources, building an arcade cabinet is definitely the way to go!

What are the drawbacks of an arcade cabinet?

Building an arcade cabinet is more of an effort than building a desktop arcade controller. They are also more expensive, running anywhere from the $500 range for a small project to $1500 or more for the mother of all arcade machines. Arcade cabinets also tend to suffer from *feature creep* as they are being constructed, turning a simple project into a mammoth (and more expensive) one. This may not necessarily be a bad thing, but it does tend to be wearing on your family members' patience.

Arcade cabinets can also occupy a significant amount of floor space, and unlike desktop arcade controls, they cannot be put away when not in use. They also require dedicating a computer system solely for their use in most cases, although a couple of folks have managed to make do with external laptops or shared computers. Assuming you'll be dedicating a computer to the project, you'll need to factor in the cost of any computer components you need to buy for the cabinet.

Tip

If you own a computer, the odds are that you've upgraded at some point and have an older computer lying around. These computers make excellent starting points for arcade cabinet projects. They will limit you to somewhat older games because of hardware requirements, but there are still hundreds of games that are great additions to an arcade cabinet. Using an old computer also makes an excellent bargaining point when trying to convince a reluctant spouse. You can always upgrade computer parts once the cabinet is built.

Buying your way to gaming Nirvana

For every build-your-own project in this book, there's an already-made solution you can buy instead. Since I became involved in this hobby, a variety of vendors have cropped up who are eager to sell you what you're looking for. They can be sorted into two categories — small shops building products in their garage and large operations that have added new product lines. I'll present a look at offerings from both types of vendors in Chapter 17, "Buying Your Way to Gaming Nirvana."

The smaller shops tend to come and go, although a few have stood the test of time. These vendors are usually much more willing to customize their products to your design than are the larger operations. They also tend to offer better customer support, because the person you contact for assistance may also be the person who built your product in the first place. They tend to have slower shipping times, however, due to the realities of being a smaller operation, and are often more expensive.

The larger operations have the benefit of mass production, financing, and a distribution infrastructure such that they can get their products to you faster than the smaller vendors. Their product lines are fixed, however, and they are less likely to be willing to customize a solution for you. At least one large vendor has been known to do customizations, so it never hurts to ask. Support from a larger company can be hit or miss, with some vendors providing faster and better support than others. Pricing should also be lower from a larger vendor.

What do you gain by buying?

If you've got the money but not the time or patience to build your own, buying a pre-made product can be a great solution. You'll get a professionally made piece of gaming equipment that's attractive and comes with a warranty. If it stops working, there is someone you can go to who's responsible for getting you back in business. Depending on your access to tools, and factoring in what your time is worth, it may actually be cheaper to purchase rather than build your dream arcade machine.

What do you lose by buying?

Although it *can* be less expensive to buy rather than build, that's not often the case. If you already have access to the tools needed and have the available spare time, you will probably find it cheaper to build rather than buy. There's also the flexibility of being able to customize every facet of your design. Finally, there's a level of satisfaction with being able to say "I built it!" that you obviously won't get with a purchased product.

 If you decide to buy rather than build, take some time to do a bit of research first. Log on to the Build Your Own Arcade Controls message forums (`www.arcadecontrols.com`) and the alt.games.mame newsgroup (`http://groups.google.com/groups?q=group:alt.games.mame`) and ask for opinions on any products you are considering. Also, pay by credit card if you can, and insist that your card not be charged until the product is shipped.

 Although we try to keep the Build Your Own Arcade Controls message forums family-friendly, an occasional bad apple can slip through. The alt.games.mame newsgroup is an unmoderated Internet newsgroup that is not owned by anyone, meaning people are free to speak their mind as they see fit. You get straightforward opinions, but the language can be *colorful* at times.

Thinking point

Take a moment to stop now and think about what we've covered so far. If you're planning to jump right in, you should try to make some decisions based on the above material and narrow the scope of what you're attempting to create. Do you know what type of project you want to undertake? Have you assessed the time and money you can devote to the project? Are you going to build or buy? As you begin to pick a plan, buy materials, and lay out your designs, you'll begin to limit the number of changes you can make midstream. By no means is change impossible, but it does become inconvenient in terms of time and expense. If you're planning to read the book through first and then begin your project, you can safely postpone thinking at this point!

Plan, Plan, and Then Plan Some More

So where do you go from here? As a friend of mine is fond of saying, "Proper planning prevents poor performance!" You need to make a few decisions before you proceed. There's a bit of the chicken-and-egg syndrome coming up. It's hard to make planning decisions without knowing more about the various options available, but I've tried to gear this book toward your being able to jump right in without having to read it through first. In the next few paragraphs, I'll point you toward later chapters for additional information or inspiration for planning purposes.

However, if you'll trust me, there's already a plan in place over the course of the book. When all is said and done, you'll end up with a nice two-player upright cabinet ready to play. If that's the route for you, you can skim over the next piece and then jump in to Chapter 2.

Deciding to build or buy

At this point, I hope you have a general concept in mind for the kind of arcade machine you want. This would be a good time to consider the build-or-buy decision. You may wish to skip ahead to Chapter 17 to browse through the various commercial offerings to see if one of them will fit the bill. Don't forget to factor the costs of buying against the time and costs of building.

Planning for controls and interfaces

I'll go over the various controls and interfaces in detail in Chapters 3 through 10. Still, you should be able to make some preliminary choices now. How many players do you want your cabinet to support? If you're just starting out, a two-player cabinet is probably your best bet. However, if you have a favorite four-player game (and three friends who you know will come play), then a four-player cabinet might be your goal. You don't really need to make any decisions regarding the interface just yet, other than planning to leave some space in your control panel for it. Figure about a 4-inch by 6-inch area inside the control panel for the interface.

Cross-Reference An interface in this case consists of the electronics or other device used to connect the arcade controls to the computer—something that translates the signal that the arcade controls generate to something the computer understands. This topic is covered in detail in Chapters 7 through 10.

Picking software

Most of this area can be left until much later in the building process. However, at this point you should consider a few things that can make a difference in how you proceed. If you want to play a particular game, think about the kind of controls it may require. For instance, if the newly re-released Centipede is your cup of tea, you'll need to plan for a trackball. The majority of games will run fine with a couple of joysticks and a bunch of buttons, but do consider any particular game favorites before you start building.

The second software consideration that may alter planning is the operating system choice. This will primarily affect your interface decisions. Almost every interface option will function in a Microsoft Windows or MS-DOS (or MS-DOS-compatible) environment. If you're planning to use Linux or a Mac, however, then you'll need to investigate the interface's requirements before you proceed. Also bear in mind that more computer games are written for the Windows platform than any other. Arcade cabinets have been made with both Linux- and Macintosh-based systems, but unless you have a specific reason to do otherwise, running a Microsoft operating system will be your best (easiest) choice.

Note My recommendations have nothing to do with the capabilities of Linux and Macintosh. I'm a big Linux fan, using it both personally and professionally. I also have a lot of respect for the Macintosh and its capabilities. Please don't flood me with e-mail pointing out the error of my ways regarding my operating system choice. Constructive criticism is, of course, welcome!

Figuring your budget

Now is the time to decide how much you're willing to spend on this project. This, as much as anything else, will determine what kind of project you're able to build. Planning for the mother of all arcade machines on a limited budget may be an exercise in frustration. However, with some careful thinking, you can lay the infrastructure for your dream machine and build it up slowly. A two-player panel now can be swapped out for a four-player panel later, when you have the financing to buy all the required parts. A low-end computer can be upgraded to a high-end computer later. About the only choice that's not alterable is the physical construction of the cabinet. For instance, you might only be able to justify buying a 19-inch monitor at the start, but have a 25-inch monitor in mind down the road. In that case, be sure to build the cabinet wide enough to support the larger monitor later!

Putting it on paper

A goal without a plan is but a dream. A plan is only as solid as the paper it's committed to. Now that we've hit the end of the chapter, take the time to write down any thoughts and decisions you've made. Be sure to keep references noted as well, such as page numbers or Web site addresses for later referral. This may save you frustration in the long run. Continue this habit as you proceed through construction.

As a side note, near and dear to my heart is the creation of Web sites. If you know about creating Web sites, or even think you might want to learn, consider keeping a construction diary. Take plenty of pictures as you go and accurate notes. This will not only help you if you need to refer back for any reason, but, if you put it up on a Web site, might just also be the inspiration for the next person who decides to build his or her own arcade machine!

Tip Start a separate sheet of paper devoted to your budget. Keep track of every single expense so you can keep an eye on the bottom line. It's amazing how quickly those quick trips to the hardware store for a few screws can start to add up. Of course, if you're hoping to hide the evidence from a spouse, this step is *not* recommended!

Summary

You have a lot of choices ahead of you, all of which lead to guaranteed fun! An upright, cocktail, or countertop arcade cabinet will make a great addition to a family room or game room. If space is at a premium, you might choose a desktop arcade controller. Whichever you decide upon, proper planning will help ensure success. Whether you choose to build an arcade cabinet or a desktop controller, or buy your way to gaming fun, this book will guide you along the way!

Speaking of plans, that's just one of the things I'll cover in the next chapter, where you get to jump right in and start building your arcade cabinet. The magic's starting, so let's go!

Building Your Arcade Cabinet

Wow, I built that! That's the first thought that ran through my head when I finished putting together the arcade cabinet I'm about to show you how to build (see Figure 2-1). After all the work, trips to the hardware store, and admittedly some amount of frustration, I could finally see the project taking shape before me. It's an awesome feeling getting there, and you're about to begin!

Although it may be tempting to jump right in, this is one chapter you should read once the whole way through before beginning to build. Pay close attention to the parts and tools needed — nothing is more frustrating than being on a roll and then having to interrupt what you're doing to run to the store. Take your time with this chapter. The work you put into it will be the foundation for the rest of your project.

FIGURE 2-1: Your goal—the completed arcade cabinet shell.

Anatomy of a Cabinet

You'll find there are several different models of arcade cabinets, but they all have a set of characteristics in common. I'll cover the basic anatomy of an arcade cabinet, using an upright arcade machine as my example, but the explanation applies equally well to other types of cabinets. Refer to Figure 2-2 as you read through the descriptions.

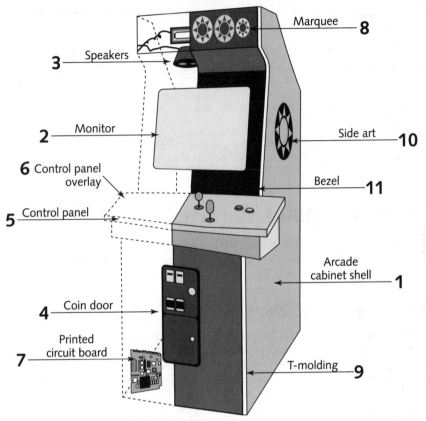

3 — Speakers

2 — Monitor

6 Control panel
overlay

5 — Control panel

4 — Coin door

7 — Printed
circuit board

Marquee **8**

Side art **10**

Bezel **11**

Arcade
cabinet shell **1**

T-molding **9**

FIGURE 2-2: Anatomy of an arcade cabinet.

1. **Arcade cabinet shell**. The wooden shells that make up the cabinets come in a variety of shapes and sizes.

2. **Monitor**. Every cabinet has a monitor. Monitors are typically 19 or 25 inches in size, with later-model arcade cabinets having much bigger monitors.

3. **Speakers**. The sound system of the arcade cabinet.

4. **Coin door**. A metal door on the cabinet where players insert money or tokens to be able to play the game.

5. **Control panel**. The panel where the various controls for the game are mounted.

6. **Control panel overlay**. The artwork covering the control panel, often covered by a clear protective covering made from a variety of materials.

7. **PCBs**. The computer boards inside the cabinet that make the game work. You'll be using a real computer in place of the PCBs.

8. **Marquee**. The sign at the top of an upright arcade cabinet, usually backlit.

9. **T-molding**. A strip of plastic (usually) that is mounted in a groove around the edges of an arcade cabinet. The T-molding is both decorative and protective.

10. **Side art**. The artwork that decorates the sides of a cabinet. Sometimes side art is painted; other times it is a vinyl sticker.

11. **Bezel**. A shroud around the monitor covering the gap between the sides of the monitor and the sides of the cabinet, intended to hide the insides of the arcade cabinet.

Determining the Things You Need

Before you can begin, you'll need to make a few quick decisions. Are your skills up to the task? What kind of wood are you going to use, and which plans will you follow? This section will help you answer those questions and get started.

Assessing your woodworking skills

The good news is that you do not have to be a master carpenter to build an arcade cabinet. In fact, I won't make any *serious* effort to teach you proper woodworking skills at all! I can safely say that your woodworking skills are as good as if not better than mine, because I didn't have any when I started. I was about as far from a woodworking expert as you can be and still have opposable thumbs! Fortunately, if I can build an arcade cabinet, anyone can! (Yes, you too.)

If your woodworking skills are better than mine, you may very well find areas where you might want to do something a little differently than I've shown. That's OK! As you work through the plans, you should feel free to make changes as you see fit. The important thing to remember is that as long as the construction is sturdy, your only goal here is to put together a cabinet that makes *you* happy. When all's said and done you'll have made a cabinet of your very own!

Choosing the wood

Your first decision will be what kind of wood to use. You've got several options, and it's not feasible to cover them all here. However, most arcade cabinets are built from one of three varieties of wood: plywood, particleboard, and MDF. Each has its pluses and minuses. Your determining factors should be weight, suitability for painting or staining, and how difficult it is to work with a particular choice of wood.

Plywood

Plywood is manufactured by laminating thin sheets of wood together. They are laid together with the grain of the sheets at 90 degrees to each other, which provides the plywood with its strength. There are many different grades of plywood, rated by their strength and appearance.

The various grades fall into two main categories: plywood intended for construction, and plywood intended for display. Obviously, plywood meant for display is the best kind for an arcade cabinet.

When you're working with 4 × 8 sheets of plywood, the wood is stronger along the axis that lies parallel to the grain of the top sheet of wood, typically along the 8-foot length. Use this to your advantage when using plywood in your cabinet. For example, if making a 2-foot by 3-foot base, making sure that the 3-foot section is cut from the 8-foot side will give you a slight strength advantage over orienting it the other way. It's not a major advantage, though, so it's OK to orient your pieces in different directions to take maximum advantage of the available wood.

When shopping for plywood for a cabinet project, you should consider the type of finish you're going to use. If you are planning to laminate the cabinet, then the finish of the plywood is not critical. If you intend to paint or stain the cabinet, then you should look for sanded plywood where one face has been prepared for painting or staining. Be sure the plywood you're using has totally dried before applying a finish, or the look of the finish may be altered as the wood continues to dry.

Plywood has the advantage that it's not as heavy as some of the other wood choices, and it has a nice grain pattern if you are considering staining. Damage during construction can be repaired with wood putty, although that makes staining difficult. The wood putty area will probably have a different appearance from the surrounding wood when stained. Some of plywood's drawbacks are that the wood can warp (it's sometimes difficult to find plywood at lumber stores that's perfectly straight) and it can be difficult to rout a groove in the edge. If you are planning your cabinet to appear as a piece of furniture, this is the choice for you. Many arcade cabinets have been built from plywood.

Particleboard

Particleboard is a wood product made by mixing sawdust with industrial glue. It is intended for furniture, countertop construction, and so on. The surface is rough and is best covered with a laminate of some kind. Painting or staining particleboard is not recommended. You *can* paint particleboard successfully, but it requires a significant effort to sand the surface smooth enough for a quality paint job.

Particleboard won't bow or warp like plywood, but it will absorb liquid and swell up if wet. Particleboard is often confused with OSB (oriented strand board), which is made of wood chips and glue. The difference is the size of the particles mixed with the glue to make the wood; however, the information here applies equally well to both. Problem areas during construction can be repaired with wood putty as for plywood, but because you'll be finishing with a laminate or painting, it's easy to hide.

Particleboard is strong enough for cabinet building, but due to its properties it is not well suited for the task. Few build-it-yourself arcade cabinets have been made from particleboard.

Medium-density fiberboard

MDF stands for medium-density fiberboard, which is similar to particleboard in that it's made from wood fibers and glue. However, the fibers in MDF are very small. This gives MDF a smoother texture than particleboard and plywood, and makes it easy to paint. Because it has no grain, you won't want to stain it. MDF is a very sturdy wood with a hefty weight, and is designed for furniture, shelving, cabinetry, and the like. These qualities make it perfect for a project such as an arcade cabinet. Like particleboard, however, it will swell up with water, so make sure you keep it dry until painted!

MDF is probably the easiest wood choice to work with and the most popular among arcade machine builders. It cuts, drills, and routs very easily, and it is fairly inexpensive. Like the other wood choices, problems are easily repaired with wood putty and will be invisible when painted. Its biggest disadvantages are the weight and the vulnerability to water. There's also some thought that the adhesive in the wood fibers can be tough on your tools. Finally, dust from MDF and similarly manufactured woods is particularly bad to breathe. Because of this, some wood shops won't cut MDF for you. Proper eye protection, breathing masks, and adequate ventilation are strongly recommended when you are working with MDF.

When cutting through MDF, you should go a little slower than you would go through other wood such as plywood. Because of its composition, MDF can gunk up your tools and you will start to burn the wood from friction instead of cutting it. Keeping your work area clean will help. Be sure to let the tool do the work and avoid the tendency to "help it" with pressure. In fact, during construction of the cabinet featured in this book, I broke one tool (a hole saw) by ignoring this advice!

There is a hybrid wood called MDO (medium-density overlay) made from plywood with a sheet of MDF covering it. This gives it the strength and weight of plywood with the smooth texture of MDF. This type of wood is more expensive and difficult to find than the other types mentioned but makes an excellent alternative for cabinet construction. There is another alternative called melamine, which is MDF covered with a formica-like substance. This material is a little harder to work with, as the covering can chip, but it is another alternative to straight MDF.

Because of its suitability for this kind of work, the Project Arcade cabinet is built from $3/4$-inch MDF. The same thickness of plywood or MDO will work just as well as the MDF, and you can even choose to use a different thickness of wood, although that will require adjusting some measurements of the plan. The control panel top is the exception to this rule, being made from a $5/8$-inch piece of hardwood. I'll cover the details later in the book, but the $5/8$-inch wood was chosen to accommodate a $1/8$-inch layer of Plexiglas covering, bringing the total to $3/4$ inch.

MDF is more durable than particleboard and somewhat less durable than plywood. It's easier to work with than the other wood choices, and easier to repair with wood putty when you need to do so. However, any of the wood choices presented here will work, and ultimately it comes down to what you are most comfortable or willing to work with. Most arcade cabinets are built from MDF.

Choosing a cabinet plan

Many plans are available on the Internet for you to follow when building an arcade cabinet (see Table 2-1). You can use some for free, while others must be purchased. You can also easily roll your own by taking a tape measure to a friendly arcade and making notes. However, you'll have to make some educated guesses on the insides of the cabinet this way, and not all arcade operators will tolerate someone poking around their cabinets. Plans exist for upright arcade cabinets, cocktail table cabinets, countertop cabinets, and sit-down cockpits.

Of the approximately 800 arcade cabinets listed in the BYOAC database, the most popular plan by far is an upright cabinet by Sean Hatfield, better known online as LuSiD's Arcade Flashback. Sean's plans have been included on the companion CD and are the plans used in the pages that follow. These plans will lead to the cabinet shown at the beginning of this chapter in Figure 2-1. If you are looking for a different style of cabinet, investigate the plans in Table 2-1.

 Cross-Reference

Because of the rapidly changing nature of the Internet, if you can't find the Web site links that follow, visit this book's Web site for updated links (www.projectarcade.com).

Table 2-1   Various Arcade Cabinet Plans

Plan	Location	Description
LuSiD's Arcade Flashback	http://www.lusid.net, and on CD	An upright arcade cabinet suitable for a 25-inch monitor, and the basis for Project Arcade.
1UP's Pac-MAMEA	http://www.1uparcade.com/	An upright arcade cabinet with rotating control panels featuring different control sets.
ArcadeParadise	http://www.arcadeparadise.org/downloads.html	An upright arcade cabinet.
Frostillicus's plans	http://arcade.tomvanhorn.com/	An upright arcade cabinet featuring a rotating control panel with multiple control sets.
GameCab	http://www.gamecab.com/	Countertop cabinet plans and desktop joystick console plans.
GameCabinets Inc.	http://www.gamecabinetsinc.com/	GameCabinets, Inc. sells detailed upright, cocktail, and cockpit cabinet plans. Full-sized cutout templates are also available. You saw one of their cabinets in Figure 1-2.

Continued

Table 2-1 *(continued)*

Plan	Location	Description
Jeff's Ultimate MAME* Arcade Machine	`http://www.webpak.net/ ~jmcclain/mame/index.html`	An upright arcade cabinet.
JelloSlug's Arcade	`http://www.jelloslug.mamehost .com/`	Plans for a cocktail cabinet.
MAMEROOM	`http://www.mameroom.com/,` and on CD	MAMEROOM.COM sells very detailed upright, cocktail, and cockpit cabinet plans. Full-sized cutout templates are also available.
MAMEstation	`http://www.mamestation.com/`	An upright arcade cabinet.
Massive MAME Project Plans	`http://www.mameworld.net/ massive/How-to/Cabinet_Plans/ cabinet_plans.html`	As of this writing, there are six plans for a variety of upright, cocktail, and cockpit cabinets.
MiniMAME	`http://www.minimame.com/`	A half-sized upright arcade cabinet.
Oscar Controls Gotham Cabinet	`http://www.oscarcontrols.com/ unnamed/`	An upright arcade cabinet, featuring separate upper and lower assemblies for easy transport.
Oscar Controls Happy Hour Bartop MAME	`http://www.skum.org/bartop/ downloads.htm`	A countertop mini arcade cabinet.
Scott's Unicade	`http://home.austin.rr.com/ shumate/unicade/design.htm`	An upright arcade cabinet.
Supercade	`http://www.cybercoma.com/ supercade/design.shtml`	An upright arcade cabinet with a unique two-level control panel.
Taz's MAME cabinet	`http://mywebpages.comcast.net/ pmailley/index.html`	A two-piece showcase style cabinet. There is a pedestal for the controls in front, and a large screen behind.
Thorn's Mortal Kombat cabinet	`http://mywebpages.comcast.net/ sugg3d/MAME/CabinetSketch.html`	An upright arcade cabinet patterned after the Mortal Kombat series of cabinets.
VectoRaster Project	`http://www.pcreliability.com/ vectoraster/`	An upright arcade cabinet.

* MAME stands for Multiple Arcade Machine Emulator, and I'll be covering it in Chapter 14.

On the CD
The links in the table and every other link in the book are also included on the companion CD-ROM for your convenience so you don't have to type them in.

Making your own plans

Got a yearning to roll your own? Designing your own cabinet can be fun and exciting, and I have a few suggestions if you'd like to try it. First, look over other people's arcade cabinets if you haven't done so yet. Take note of the features they have that you'd like to include in your cabinet. Do you want to incorporate a rotating control panel? Perhaps a custom-sized monitor is in order? Don't forget to plan for accessibility into the cabinet for later maintenance. As you pick the features you'd like for your cabinet, be sure to pay careful attention to stability. These cabinets are usually big and heavy, and they tend to take a small amount of abuse from enthusiastic play. It would be horrible to have a cabinet fall apart and possibly hurt someone during an otherwise fun-filled evening.

Once you have your basic design down on paper, run it by a few folks for opinions. The message boards at the Arcade Controls Web site (www.arcadecontrols.com/) are an excellent resource for this. There are a lot of people there who will have the right kind of experience and enthusiasm for your project. Don't be surprised if you pick up a few good pointers and possibly requests for copies of your plans when finished! You did intend to share, didn't you?

Getting Ready to Build Project Arcade

Ready to begin? Great! If you'll be using the LuSiD plans included on the CD-ROM, the rest of this chapter applies directly to you. If you've decided to use another set of plans, much of the following will still apply in general terms, such as the various construction tips. Either way, you should read through the rest of this chapter first, then put the book down and start making your masterpiece!

Setting up shop

The first thing you need to do is to decide where your mad-scientist laboratory will be. You should pick an area with adequate ventilation for dust and paint fumes, such as a garage or open basement. If you're lucky enough to have a workshop, so much the better! Because I was writing this book while building my cabinet, I decided to set up shop in my study to avoid frequent trips back and forth. This was my first mistake! It worked very well for writing, but it will be months before I get the dust out of everything! My next cabinet project will be built in the garage. (Oh yes, a lot of people find this to be like eating potato chips. You can't stop at just one!) In fact, when it came time to paint Project Arcade, I did move it into the garage.

The place you choose should also have enough room to work in. The side panels for this project are over 6 feet tall, and you'll need to be able to lay them down as well as stand them upright. Also, don't forget your cabinet's final destination. The final assembled cabinet will be 34 inches wide at the control panel. This is too wide to fit through some doors. You can plan for this eventuality, however, by not attaching the control panel until the cabinet has reached its final home. That will make the width of the cabinet only 27.5 inches, which will just fit through most household doors. Finally, don't forget the weight of the cabinet. These things are heavy; if you're building it in the basement and intend to house it in the upstairs game room, be sure you have someone who can help you maneuver it up the stairs without injuring anyone. If getting to the game room from the work area will be a problem, you'll need to rethink where you're building the cabinet.

Going over the plans

If you have access to a printer, now would be a good time to print out the plans included on the CD-ROM. You'll need to have Adobe Acrobat Reader installed on your computer to do so. It's also included on the CD-ROM if you need it. You *can* refer to the plans in Figure 2-3, but you'll probably be happier with your own printouts, as they'll be much larger. You'll be able to mark them up without writing in the book, conveniently take them with you to the hardware store, and so on.

Each square on the plans is 1 inch. The various parts of the cabinet are laid out on the three sheets to take maximum advantage of the space available. Each part is labeled and has the dimensions included. The dimensions assume that you will be using $3/4$-inch wood and a monitor 26 inches wide or smaller. Bear in mind that a monitor is measured diagonally, so a 27-inch monitor will be approximately 25 inches wide. Also, if you intend to use $5/8$-inch wood, two pieces will need to be modified. The *cabinet front coin door* will need to be 25 by 30 inches, and both *CP box–side* pieces will need to be $14^1/4$ inches wide. To change the width of the cabinet to accommodate a larger or smaller monitor, change all 26-inch edges accordingly.

Note   Remember that I elected to use a $5/8$-inch piece of wood for the control panel top for the Project Arcade cabinet. You can cut out the $3/4$-inch control panel top shown in the plans if you're not planning to use a Plexiglas overlay (see Chapter 15, for more information) or if you want a practice panel (recommended).

Obtaining tools and supplies

The goal of this section is to get you everything you'll need with as few shopping trips as possible. You'll probably still have to run out for that "little extra something," but this will be a good start. This section concentrates only on what you'll need to do the woodworking and painting to build the cabinet. Materials needed for the rest of the project, such as joysticks and buttons, are presented later in the book.

I'll start with a look at the tools you'll most likely need. The tools in Table 2-2 are the ones I used to build the Project Arcade cabinet, and are the tools most often used by people who build their own cabinets. If you are planning to build only one cabinet, you might want to consider borrowing or renting tools instead of purchasing them. Bear in mind, however that depending on the tool needed, decent quality can sometimes be purchased for about the same cost as renting.

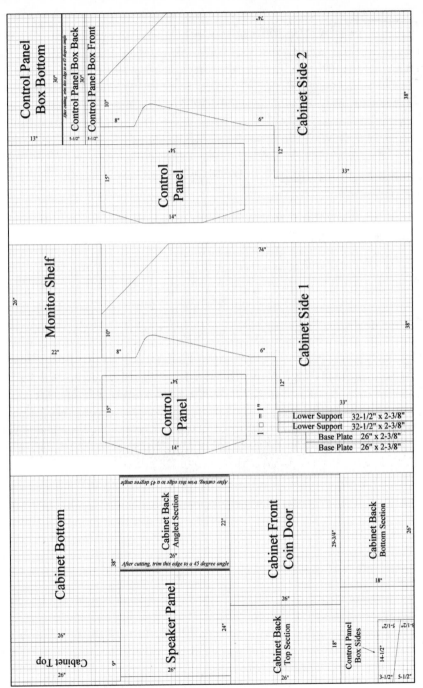

FIGURE 2-3: The Project Arcade/LuSiD–based plans.

Table 2-2   Tools You Will Need

Tool	Purpose
Circular saw	You'll want a good circular saw to make the majority of your cuts as you cut out the pieces.
Jigsaw	You'll need a jigsaw to make curved cuts and to cut out holes for speakers and a coin door.
Table saw	You might want a table saw to make a few 45-degree angle cuts. This can be done with a good circular saw or jigsaw as well. I would not recommend purchasing a table saw just for this project.
Drill	A drill is a necessity. You'll use it to pre-drill your screw holes, and to make holes in your control panel to mount joysticks, buttons and the like.
1⅛-inch spade bit	Most arcade controls mount in a 1⅛-inch hole. Spade bits are a better choice than a hole saw for creating the holes in your wood when using MDF, because the hole saw can gum up and start to burn the wood.
1⅛-inch forstner bit	A forstner bit is similar to a spade bit, but meets the wood at 90 degrees instead of at an angle like a spade bit. Forstner bits are somewhat slower to use than spade bits, but create perfect circles every time and work very well with Plexiglas. A forstner bit is *highly* recommended!
1⅛-inch hole saw	Hole saws are good choices for working with Lexan or Plexiglas control panel covers.
Countersink bit	To get that nice, smooth finish to your wood, you'll use this bit to countersink your screws.
Power screwdriver	You'll be much happier with a separate power screwdriver or second drill than having to constantly switch bits on your primary drill. You can, of course, elect to use manual screwdrivers instead.
High-speed rotary tool	A high-speed rotary tool, such as a Dremel, is something you do not necessarily need but might find handy. They work well for grinding down and fixing small areas. I used mine repeatedly for fine-tuning my cabinet.
Router	You'll find the router to be one of your most versatile tools. You'll use it to rout out areas for joystick mounting and to cut the groove in your edges for the T-molding.
Slot cutter bit	You'll need a slot cutter bit for your router to make the groove for the T-molding. Usually a 1⁄16-inch or 3⁄32-inch size will do, but size may vary depending on what T-molding you purchase.
Sander	An electric sander is another item you should consider but can do without in a pinch. If you're willing to trade elbow grease for electric power, you can sand by hand instead of with a sander. You're likely to end up doing a fair share of sanding, so a sander is recommended.

Tool	Purpose
Hot glue gun	A hot glue gun is optional but recommended.
T-square	Perfect 90-degree angles are easier to achieve with a T-square.
Level	You'll want to make sure all the parts are level as you assemble them.
Straightedge	A good metal straightedge will help you make perfect cuts. Hardware stores sell them in varying lengths up to 8 feet.
Sawhorses/ workbenches	You'll need a couple of sawhorses or workbenches to hold your wood while you work on it. Because of the size of the cabinet sides, three are recommended.
Clamps	Unless you have more than two hands, you'll want to pick up at least four clamps to hold pieces still while you work on them. Look for clamps that have rubber shoes to protect the wood.
Paint	A gallon of paint should suffice for painting your arcade cabinet.
Primer	To prepare the cabinet for painting.
Painting supplies	Drop cloth, two rollers, mixing sticks, and one or two paintbrushes.

You'll also want a good set of expendable supplies on hand as you build your cabinet (Table 2-3). A good rule of thumb is to pick up more than you think you'll need. There's nothing quite as annoying as having to interrupt a project in the middle because you're short on supplies. Be careful with your wood as you take it home. The plans call for using the sheets of wood all the way to the edges, so take care not to gouge the edges as you transport them.

Table 2-3   Supplies You Will Need

Item	Purpose
Wood	Three sheets of 4-foot × 8-foot MDF in ¾-inch thickness unless you've chosen to use another type of wood for the cabinet. You'll also want one 4-foot strip of 2-inch × 2-inch lumber as well. *Optional:* A small sheet of ⅝-inch (34 inches × 18 inches) for the control panel top.
Screws	An assortment of ½", ⅝", 1", 1⅛", 1¼", 1½", and 2" screws of the same thickness, #8 recommended. Wood screws or drywall screws work well.
L-brackets	Six 2½-inch and four 2-inch L-brackets.
Shelf brackets	Four good-sized (9 inches or so) shelf brackets.
Cabinet hinges	Optional. These will be used to hinge the cabinet front for access if you so choose. You'll need cabinet hinges designed for recessed doors, sometimes referred to as European cabinet hinges.

Continued

Table 2-3 *(continued)*

Item	Purpose
Surface bolt	Optional. If you elect to hinge the cabinet front, you'll use the surface bolt to lock the cabinet front in place.
Velcro	One roll of Velcro.
Grommet sleeve	A grommet sleeve like those used in computer desks, 1½ inches to 2 inches in size.
Glue sticks	At least one package of glue sticks suitable for wood use for your hot glue gun.
Wood putty	One container of wood putty to fill countersink holes and repair blemishes.
Sandpaper	Sandpaper of various grits for different parts of the job. A rough grit will be good for sanding down imperfections, while a fine grit will be used when painting.
Miscellaneous	Pencils, good erasers, rulers, tape measures, and other common household items will come in handy during construction.
Protective gear	Pick up good-quality protective gear for your ears, eyes, and breathing. Be sure to include protective gear for your assistant as well if you have one.
Casters	Four casters with a wheel depth of 3 inches (2 inches will do in a pinch).

Beginning Construction

It's about time to fire up some power tools! I'm assuming at this point that you've made your first shopping trip and have set up shop in an adequate area. You should have your protective gear available and your tools and supplies ready to go. Ready to start?

Tip   Are you planning to document your project as you go? Now's the time to start! Get that camera ready, and watch out for dust. As you work with the wood, fine particles of dust will go everywhere. Keep your camera inside a case or otherwise protected in between pictures.

Drawing and cutting out the plans

I'll get you started with laying out your construction plans on your sheets of wood. Take a good look at your wood before you begin to sketch the plans out. Is one edge in better shape than another? Check it with your T-square and level. Is the edge genuinely straight, or is it angled? Making sure now will help in the long run. If your first edge is not straight, and you base the rest of the edges and measurements on it, then the rest of your pieces may end up incorrectly proportioned, causing you problems as you begin to assemble.

Caution

From here on out, always keep one eye out for safety. Building an arcade cabinet is a lot of fun—it would be a shame to ruin that by getting injured or even killed in an accident. Working with power tools requires a certain amount of respect for the tool. Always follow the instructions included with the power tool for proper use and care. Routers can get away from you, power saws can kick back at you, improperly grounded tools can shock you, etc. Better to be slow and safe than hasty and hurt.

Don't forget to decide on the width of your cabinet before you start drawing and cutting. This decision should be based on the size of the monitor you intend to put in it. If you already know which monitor you plan to use, you can adjust the dimensions of the plans to accommodate it. If you don't know, then the width of the cabinet as designed is a good size for most needs, suitable for a 26-inch-wide display, which will accommodate a 27-inch monitor (monitors are measured diagonally). Even if you know you're intending to use a smaller display, such as a 19-inch, you should consider not reducing the width of the cabinet. This will allow you room to grow should you decide to upgrade to a larger display at a later time.

One thing you should think about as you begin is wood loss due to cutting and other imperfections. An average circular saw blade is $1/16$ inch wide. If you have two pieces drawn out back-to-back sharing a common edge, and you cut perfectly down the middle, then you are reducing both pieces by $1/32$ inch. As a practical matter, this small amount of loss will not matter in assembly. If, however, you cut to one side of the line instead of down the middle, you've introduced a $1/16$-inch variance to one piece and not the other. If you compound this by sanding or by error, you begin to introduce a discrepancy in size that may be visibly apparent during construction. Take care as you lay out and cut your pieces to avoid these issues.

Fortunately, wood is a forgiving medium. If you examine carefully the pictures taken of Project Arcade during construction, you may notice various edges that are slightly off. Sanding, wood filler, and the small amount of give that soft wood provides will take care of these things. When the project is finished, none of this will be noticeable. Don't let minor imperfections during construction discourage you. Remember, there are only two things you have to accomplish in this project. First, it has to be appealing to you (and perhaps a spouse) only. Second, it has to be safe and structurally sound. Other than that, beauty truly is in the eye of the beholder. That said, take your time and some care, and you'll create a work of art guaranteed to provide hours of fun!

There are a few tips to think about while laying out, cutting, and assembling your wood.

- Measure twice (or more!) and cut once. As my father-in-law often says, "No matter how many times I cut the wood, it's still too short!"

- When measuring distances for lines, use several tick marks. Two tick marks are all that's required to make a line, but three or more will help ensure that your line is straight instead of angled.

- This is a good time to call in favors with your buddies and get one to help you. Some of the construction can be heavy or awkward, and a helper can be invaluable. A lot of folks will build two cabinets at a time, one for them and one for their buddy.

- Have your helper double-check your measurements and lines. It's easy to overlook a problem with something you've been working on for a while, which someone with a fresh perspective might see. I had numerous measurements that were somewhat off, and at one point we discovered we had incorrectly measured a cabinet side that was a whole 2 inches short. Imagine our distress if we had cut that before we caught the error!

- Never assume that measurements from the store are accurate. Sometimes a 4-foot × 8-foot board isn't really 4 feet × 8 feet. In the case of Project Arcade, the MDF sheets purchased were actually 49 inches wide. There is some methodology in the wood industry where measurements aren't always as labeled. A stick of 2-inch × 2-inch wood is actually 1.5 × 1.5 inches, for instance. If in doubt, measure.

- As you draw out and cut the wood, label each piece. This will make it much easier to assemble the pieces later!

- When you have two pieces that are opposite sides of each other, clamp them together and make sure of a close match, sanding away minor differences. The cabinet sides and the control panel box sides are identical opposite pieces.

- When choosing a saw blade, bear in mind that a finer-toothed blade will produce smoother cuts, although at a sacrifice in speed.

- Before you begin to cut, take an unused section of wood and do a test cut. This will let you make sure your tools and you are both working properly!

- When sawing, cut through the end of the wood. If you stop at the end, you might jerk the tool up, causing imperfections at the end of the cut. Continue your cut past the end of the wood to ensure a smooth cut all the way through.

- Check your cuts from a couple of angles. Sometimes cuts that aren't quite straight can be seen from one angle but not another.

- Use your straightedge and clamps for as many cuts as possible. Freehand where you have to, but take the guesswork out of the process when you can.

- When attempting to blow away sawdust, remove your mask first! Much productivity was lost in laughing when my father-in-law got this backward.

The first sheet of wood

Go ahead and lay out the first page of the plans with the rectangular shapes on your wood and proceed to cut them out now. My father-in-law (Cappy) was my able-bodied assistant for this part of the project. You can see our first sheet laid out in Figure 2-4. These cuts are fairly straightforward and make a good start to the project. If you are using a different thickness of wood, you'll need to adjust the cabinet-front coin door piece slightly. If you are using ⅝-inch board, for instance, it'll need to be 26 × 30 inches instead of 26 × 29 ¾ inches. There are two sections that might need further comment.

FIGURE 2-4: Drawing out the first sheet of wood.

Cabinet back angled section

The cabinet back angled section has two edges that need 45-degree angles. These are the longer 26-inch edges, although you may have modified the length. Start by cutting them straight as normal. Then when you have the piece separated you can cut the edges to 45 degrees. This can be one of the more difficult cuts to make, and is a good candidate for a table saw if you have one. We made it using a jigsaw with a 45-degree angle setting. By no means should you attempt to freehand this cut. It's easy to slip and make mistakes and possibly get injured. In Figure 2-5, you can see where we used our jigsaw in the 45-degree angle setting, with a straight board clamped down for our guide.

I found it helpful to draw out the 45-degree angle as a reference before we began the cut. You don't need a protractor for this if you remember basic math. There's a special triangle called an isosceles right triangle, or a 45-45-90 triangle. This is a triangle that has a 90-degree angle and two 45-degree angles. The special property of this triangle is that both legs of the 90-degree angle are the same length. If you look at Figure 2-6, you can see how we take advantage of this. Because our wood is $3/4$ inch thick, if we mark a point $3/4$ inch along the edge of the wood and connect this to the corner of the board, we automatically make our 45-degree angle. If you make these measurements on both corners of the 26-inch edge and then connect a line on the bottom side from the inside angle identified by the arrow on both corners, you have a handy guide to verify your 45-degree angle during and after the cut. Repeat this on the other 26-inch edge, making sure both cuts angle down to the same side of the board as shown in Figure 2-6.

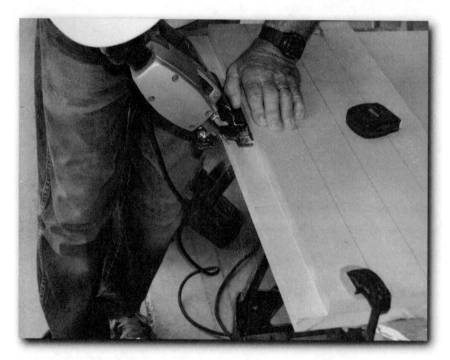

FIGURE 2-5: Making the 45-degree angle cut.

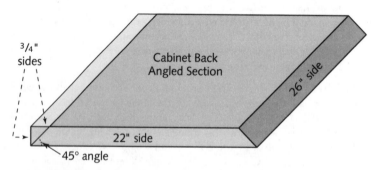

FIGURE 2-6: Cabinet back angled section with 45-degree cutout on left and right edges.

Control panel box sides

The length of the control panel box sides will need to be modified if you are using a different thickness of wood than the 3/4-inch wood used in Project Arcade. If you are using $^5/8$-inch wood, reduce the length from $14^1/2$ inches to $14^1/4$ inches. The control panel box sides should be identical when both are cut out. These will be the left- and right-hand sides of the control panel box, with the taller edges to the back. The control panel will sit on top of these, angling down toward the player. To make sure these are identical, use the technique of clamping them together and sanding down any minor differences. If there are major differences, then something has gone wrong.

The degree of slope of the control panel top is a matter of personal preference. The taller $5^1/2$-inch edges are designed to fit properly onto the arcade cabinet and should not be modified. However, the smaller $3^1/2$-inch edges can be modified if desired. Some people prefer more or less slope to their control panel for personal comfort. You might consider making a mockup before proceeding too much further. Using Styrofoam, cardboard, or scrap pieces of wood, you can experiment with different slopes until you find one you're happy with. You will need the control panel top from one of the next two pages of plans for your experimentation. Be careful — your arcade controls extend below the control panel top as well as above, so you cannot reduce the $3^1/2$-inch edges too drastically. Different controls have different sizes, so I cannot give you a precise minimum height. However, you are unlikely to reduce it far enough to cause problems because the angle will become uncomfortable.

The second and third sheets of wood

You're one-third of the way there! This would be a good time to take a short break and think about any issues you ran into on the first sheet. If you're having any problems with tools or the environment you're working in, you should solve them before beginning the next two sheets. This would also be a good time to reaffirm your assistant's devotion to the project (he or she might need a bigger bribe by now).

The pieces on the second and third sheets of wood are a bit more complex due to angles, but laying them out and cutting them is still a straightforward matter. You'll notice there are two control panels shown. Only one is needed for the project. The other is extra, and can be used for a swappable control panel or a spare, or you might choose not to cut it out at all. There is also some extra space left over on the two sheets. Save these pieces, as you will be able to use them later as shims, supports, or spare wood to fix misshaped pieces. Remember that for the Project Arcade cabinet, I elected to use a separate $^5/8$-inch sheet of hard wood instead of the MDF. There are a few pieces that need further elaboration.

Control panel box back

The control panel box back will need to have one 30-inch edge cut at an angle. The exact angle necessary will vary depending on the slope you have given the control panel box sides. You can measure it to match exactly once you have all the pieces cut out, and then cut the angle precisely. However, to do so you need to have a saw that will let you do precise angles. Many jigsaws or circular saws will only do straight and 45-degree angle cuts. Fortunately, the angle of this cut is not critical. It's only important that the back of the box does not interfere with the control panel top's ability to lie smoothly on the control panel box sides. You can accomplish this with a 45-degree angle cut. Use the same techniques presented in the cabinet back angled section presented a little earlier.

Cabinet sides 1 and 2

Cabinet sides 1 and 2 are the trickiest pieces to lay out and cut. The straight and angled sides are not too bad, though they are long. The hard part comes when drawing and cutting the curved shape toward the top left of the piece. This piece is purely cosmetic, and you may elect to simply continue the lines that precede the curve, meeting them at an angled point instead of a curve. Doing so will have no detrimental effect on the cabinet.

If you decide to go with the curved look (which I think looks better), you can make it easier on yourself by drawing out a grid on your wooden sheet. Consult Figure 2-7 as you follow these instructions. Begin by drawing out the rest of the cabinet side, except for the two lines that meet in the curved area. Extend the 8-inch top section down an additional 5 inches in a dotted line. Draw another 6-inch dotted line at a right angle as shown. Fill in a lightly drawn 1-inch grid, making a rectangle of the two sides.

From the top left corner of the cabinet side, mark a spot that is 4 inches to the right and 10 inches down. This is point D. One inch to the left of the bottom right of the grid is point C. Now draw a solid line from point A to point D. Draw another solid line from point B to point C. This gives you the two angled lines leading into the curved section. Following the plans, you can now sketch the curve between points C and D. The exact shape of the curve is not critical, as it is for appearances only.

Once you have drawn and cut out one cabinet side, lay this piece on top of the next sheet as we have done in Figure 2-8. Make sure the corner, bottom, and back sides are square and clamp the two sheets together. You can now draw a perfect match of the curved area on the second sheet!

Preparing for the next step

Congratulations, the bulk of the cutting is now behind you! During assembly you may make a variety of small cuts, but you now have all the major components for your cabinet almost ready for assembling. Before you start assembling your pieces, however, you should take one last look over them to make sure they are all square and level. Double-check the measurements as well. Anything that's slightly off can be sanded to correct it. If any major problems exist, you should consider cutting out a replacement piece, even if it means a trip to the store for another sheet of wood. You're going to have this cabinet for a long time, so there's no reason to live with a major defect!

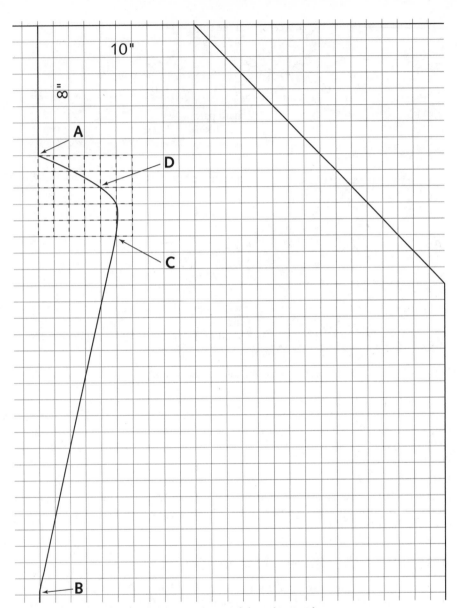

FIGURE 2-7: Exploded view of the curved area of the cabinet side.

FIGURE 2-8: Using one cabinet side as a template for the second.

A power sander may come in handy here, but there's a quick and easy alternative for this first round of sanding. Take an unused block of wood and wrap a sheet of rough-grit sandpaper around it. As you can see in Figure 2-9, you now have a sanding block suitable for quick work on uneven areas.

Next take the pieces that are opposite sides of one another and clamp them together. Go over them carefully to make sure all the sides match up and are smooth. Clamping them together makes it easy to smooth out any uneven spots. The pieces to do this to are the control panel box sides, and the cabinet sides.

Assembling the Project Arcade cabinet

It's time to turn that pile of wood into something resembling an arcade cabinet! I'll cover the various stages of assembly in the pages that follow. However, as you assemble the pieces, there are some common basic construction techniques you should use. Keep them in mind as you go, as I won't be emphasizing them when I describe the assembly. Also, don't forget to keep on measuring twice before you do any final fittings, and to use help if you have it.

FIGURE 2-9: The sanding block makes quick work of a small variance in this cut.

I used a couple of methods to fasten pieces of the cabinet together. Where possible, I avoided drilling through the outside of the cabinet to minimize screw holes needing touch-up. Any screws on the outside of the cabinet sides should be countersunk. If you are covering with a laminate of some kind, you can countersink the screws flush with the wood. If you are going to paint or stain, you should countersink your screws by $1/4$ inch or so. Be careful not to go too far into the wood; remember, it's only $3/4$ inch deep! You'll be filling in the screw holes with wood putty, but that's a cosmetic fix, not a structural one. The size of the screw will depend on the specific area being connected, but I recommend using a consistent width of screw such as a #8. This will let you drill all your holes with the same bit, varying only the length of the screw used. I used $1/2$-inch, $5/8$-inch, 1-inch, $1^1/8$-inch, $1^1/4$-inch, $1^1/2$-inch, and 2-inch screws on the Project Arcade cabinet. Drywall screws are an excellent choice for this, as are regular wood screws. You'll also want properly sized nuts and flathead machine screws (the kind with blunt tips, not pointed) to fit your casters. Screws $1^1/4$ inch to $1^1/2$ inch will do fine.

The size of your drill bit should be just a tiny bit smaller than the threads of your screws, to allow them to grab the wood without splitting it. MDF can split easily, so pre-drill all your holes and avoid powering screws into the wood. Mark your drill bit with a permanent marker as a depth guide when you're pre-drilling holes. When you use a power screwdriver to put in the screws, ease up on the speed when the screw is almost completely in to avoid stripping out the wood.

Another technique I used often in constructing Project Arcade was to attach cabinet sections together with strips of wood at the joints. Cut some of the scrap wood into 1¹/₂-inch to 2-inch square strips of wood (or buy a length of 2-inch × 2-inch lumber), and then cut them down to various lengths as needed. After carefully measuring where they should go, use your hot glue gun to glue them into place. The hot glue helps structurally, but more important, it lets you position the piece where it goes when you cannot reach the area with a clamp. You'll have about 15 to 20 seconds to fine-tune the positioning before it grabs, and you should hold it for another 30 seconds or so. After that, you'll put screws through the wood strip into the cabinet side from the inside. With the right-size screws, you'll get a nice secure platform to mount your cabinet sections to without having to drill from the outside. Place your cabinet pieces onto the wooden-strip platform, and drill down into the 2-inch strips, taking care to make sure these screws will miss the screws holding the strips to the cabinet sides. Consult the various figures that follow for a better picture of this technique.

Tip

Ask just about any carpenter which holds better, wood glue or screws, and you'll almost always be told wood glue. That wasn't the answer I expected, but it is consistently repeated. I decided to hedge my bets, and glue *and* screw where it made sense. Use wood-glue sticks in your hot glue gun.

One last thought you should consider before beginning assembly concerns the groove for your T-molding. It may be easier for you to cut the groove in the edge of your pieces before they are assembled. As we built Project Arcade, we elected to cut the groove after assembly, and it was not terribly difficult. In hindsight, I'd suggest cutting the groove before assembly just for convenience. A variety of methods can be used to cut the T-molding groove. The hands-down best way is to use a three-wing slot cutter bit for your router, as pictured in Figure 2-10. The router rests flush on the side of the board, with the depth of the router set so that the cutting blade of the bit sits perfectly in the middle of board's edge. Use the same depth (it won't be in the middle) to cut the ⁵/₈-inch control panel top if you choose the thinner board, because the total size of the board with Plexiglas cover will still be ³/₄-inch. The size of the cutting bit will depend on the T-molding you purchase. Most ³/₄-inch T-molding requires a ³/₃₂-inch bit, which is difficult to find. The CD-ROM material for Appendix A lists a couple of sources for these and other bits. Some people have resorted to using a Dremel tool with a variety of bits. This is *not* recommended. It is slow and difficult, and the results are questionable. High-speed rotary tools like the Dremel are fine for small areas, but are not good choices for long cuts like the T-molding groove.

Caution

Warning! Routing out the T-molding groove will produce a tremendous amount of dust—as much if not more than the original sawing. Do not forget your safety gear, particularly your breathing mask. If you're planning to assemble inside, you might want to do your T-molding groove outside. I certainly wish I had!

FIGURE 2-10: A ³/₃₂-inch slot cutter bit ready to cut some grooves.

Starting with the base

The logical way to start building your arcade cabinet is from the bottom up. You'll begin by building the base of the cabinet. For this step, you need the two lower supports, front and back baseplates, cabinet bottom pieces, and the casters. Begin by laying out the supports and baseplates on the cabinet bottom as shown in Figure 2-11.

The baseplates sit flush with the edges of the base, while the lower supports fit snugly in-between them. When positioned equally, there are approximately 2 inches between the sides of the baseplates and the sides of the cabinet base. The lower supports should be positioned equally, approximately 4 inches from the edges of the cabinet base. Draw lines around the edges of the baseplates and supports, and then remove them. Now drill several holes through the cabinet base matching up with the position of the baseplates and lower supports. I used three screws for the baseplates and five for the lower supports. Be careful not to drill through the material under the cabinet base! Use a workbench or piece of scrap wood underneath as a buffer.

FIGURE 2-11: Preparing the underside of the cabinet base.

Once you have all the holes in the cabinet base pre-drilled, use your hot glue gun to glue the baseplates and lower supports back onto the cabinet base. Be sure to avoid getting glue into the screw holes. Let everything set for a few moments, then carefully turn the cabinet base assembly over. Pre-drill back through the cabinet base into the baseplates and lower supports, and then insert the screws. Two-inch screws will work here, and because this is inside the cabinet you'll only need to countersink the screws flush with the cabinet base. Once all the pieces are attached, inspect the four sides of the cabinet base. If either of the supports or baseplates extends beyond the edge of the cabinet base, sand it down until they are flush.

Turn the assembly back over, and position the casters on the cabinet base as shown in Figure 2-12. If you are using 2-inch wheels, you'll need to first cut and glue into place a piece of adequately sized scrap wood to give the wheels enough height to extend past the baseplates and supports as shown in the figure. Without the extra shim for height, 2-inch wheels will just barely pass the baseplates and supports and will not work well at all. Be sure to position the casters such that you have enough room to position your drill to reach all the screw holes. If you position the caster too close to the support boards, you may have difficulty getting your drill into position for the inside corner's screw. You'll be using the flathead machine screws and nuts to fasten the casters to the cabinet base. Mark the screw holes for all four casters, then remove the casters and pre-drill their holes. Use a drill bit the same size as the machine screws, as it is the nuts that will secure them and not the threads in the wood. Flip the cabinet base onto its side, and thread a machine screw through the cabinet base and caster. Tighten a nut onto the screw, and then do the same for the next three screws. Repeat for all four casters. Put the cabinet base back down and verify with your level that the cabinet base is in fact level. If it is off level you'll need to identify why and correct it before proceeding with the rest of the assembly. Congratulations, you've completed the first step of assembly!

FIGURE 2-12: The assembled cabinet base with casters.

Sides

Ready for the next step? A helper will come in handy for this one, as well as a 26-inch-high card table or workbench. In this step, you'll be attaching the two cabinet sides to the cabinet base. This is a critical step! If the side panels are not put on perfectly square to the base, then the rest of the pieces will be similarly off and give you problems. Take your time to do this step right.

Begin by placing the cabinet base assembly on its 38-inch side, with your helper or table positioned behind the top of the cabinet base. Place your first cabinet side down on the cabinet base, with the bottom of the cabinet side flush with the bottom of the baseplates. When finally assembled, from the side you should not see the cabinet base assembly at all (Figure 2-13). The top of the cabinet side will rest on the table, or in a pinch you can brace some of the other 26-inch-high pieces of wood under the cabinet side top. Place your level on the cabinet side in various spots, and adjust as needed until everything is perfectly level. Once the bottom and the left and right sides of the cabinet side and cabinet base are square, clamp the cabinet side to the cabinet base lower supports, as shown in Figure 2-13.

Make one last check with the level, and then mark your spots to drill your screw holes. You'll want to make sure your first screw along the 38-inch side starts at least an inch from the edge, to allow room for your T-molding groove. If it is too close to the cabinet side edge, the screw will go through the space the T-molding groove occupies. Don't forget the T-molding on the back side of the cabinet if you've extended it that far as well. Five evenly spaced screws through the cabinet base and one in each of the baseplates will give plenty of support to allow the rest of the assembly. Make sure you adequately pre-drill and countersink these screws, and don't attempt to power them in. You are going into the $3/4$-inch edges of the cabinet base and baseplates, and they will split if you are not careful.

With your helper, carefully rotate the cabinet around so it is resting on the newly installed cabinet side, and repeat the above process with the second cabinet side. Once both sides have been attached, you should be able to carefully stand the cabinet up on its base and leave it freestanding. It's beginning to look like an arcade cabinet now!

FIGURE 2-13: Making sure the cabinet base and cabinet side are square.

For added stability, add L-brackets to the cabinet sides on both the top and underside of the cabinet base. First take a reading with your level on the sides of the cabinet, down toward the cabinet base in a few spots. Are the sides level vertically? Because there is nothing connecting them at the top, there may be a bit of play, throwing off the level, but it should be pretty close to the mark. If it is noticeably off, you may need to adjust the screws going into the baseplates slightly. If your baseplates were not exactly the right size, then having a tight fit to them may be introducing a slight angle to your cabinet sides. Better to have the screws into them be slightly loose than to introduce stress into the cabinet construction with a slight angle. Once you're satisfied the sides are level, install three of the $2^1/2$-inch L-brackets on each cabinet side on the top, as shown in Figure 2-14. Space the two end brackets a few inches in, with the third bracket square in the middle. Remember, you're drilling into $3/4$-inch MDF, so use $1/2$-inch or $5/8$-inch screws.

FIGURE 2-14: Carefully place the L-brackets so as to not interfere with other screws already in place.

Now carefully lay the cabinet down on its back, and install two 2-inch L-brackets as shown in Figure 2-15. The L-brackets will go halfway between the baseplate and the front edge of the cabinet base. Once again, make sure you are not encroaching on the space required for the T-molding groove. Finally, with the aid of your helper, rotate the cabinet so that it's lying on its front. Repeat the bracket installation on the back side in the same manner. Stand the cabinet back up, and you're done — you now have a solid foundation for the rest of your cabinet construction!

FIGURE 2-15: Installing the L-brackets on the underside.

Top, back, and speaker shelf pieces

You're now ready to tackle the top, back, and speaker shelf pieces of the cabinet. For this step, you need the cabinet top, cabinet back angled section, cabinet back top section, cabinet back bottom section, and the speaker shelf. You'll also be using 2-inch square strips of scrap wood as supports. From here on out, unless otherwise stated, all cabinet pieces will be mounted so that they are recessed $3/4$ inch from the edge of the cabinet sides. Begin by drawing a line $3/4$ inch from the edge of the cabinet sides on the inside surfaces of the cabinet sides at the back, angled, and top sides of the cabinet. Make sure this line is precise, as it will be your guide for placing the top and back pieces.

Cabinet back bottom section

Using the guide lines, set the cabinet back bottom section into position. Place four clamps to give the section something to rest against without moving, as shown in Figure 2-16. If the sides of the cabinet are not meeting flush with the cabinet back bottom section, use a couple of pieces of scrap wood as temporary supports against the sides.

FIGURE 2-16: The cabinet back bottom section ready for the next step.

Now take a couple of 8-inch sections of 2-inch scrap wood, and glue them to the cabinet sides so that they fit snugly against the cabinet back bottom section. Do not glue them *to* the cabinet back bottom section. Make sure with your level that the strips and the cabinet back section are vertical before the glue sets. Remember you only have about 15 seconds to position the strips before they set. After the strips have set up for a minute, remove the clamps and back bottom section. Pre-drill and screw three screws through the strips into the cabinet side. Remember to mark your drill bit depth and use appropriate-sized screws so that you do not drill through the outside of the cabinet sides. With the strips now firmly in place, you can reposition the cabinet back bottom section and fasten it onto the strips with four screws on each strip. Make note of the placement of the strip's screws first so that you don't drill the cabinet back screw holes in the same spot. Because these screws are in the back, they'll only need to be countersunk flush with the cabinet back section. When complete, it should look like Figure 2-17.

FIGURE 2-17: The cabinet back bottom section securely fastened into place.

Tip

From here on out, I won't go into specific detail on how to fasten pieces together. All steps use similar techniques. Pre-drill your holes, mark your drill bits appropriately, and make sure your screw lengths are such that they will not go through to the outside of the cabinet. Screws in the back and top will only need to be countersunk flush to the cabinet. Glue the 2-inch mounting strips to the cabinet sides, and once they are positioned correctly, further fasten them to the cabinet sides with screws. Position your screws in the strips such that you can fasten the back and top pieces onto them with those screws going between the strip screws in an interlocking pattern. Do not glue the back and top pieces onto the strips; this way you can remove them later if need be for repair and maintenance.

Cabinet top

Next you'll be setting the cabinet top section into place. You should have a line ³/₄ inch below the top of the cabinet sides, and another ³/₄ inch from the front of the cabinet top. Draw another line ³/₄ inch below the top line. Now take 8-inch sections of the 2-inch support strips, and fix them into place flush with the second top line with glue and screws as done previously. Use your level to make sure they're straight before they set. Also, make sure the front of the strips are about ¹/₂ inch back behind the front vertical line. Now take your cabinet top section and screw it into the support strips as shown in Figure 2-18.

FIGURE 2-18: The cabinet top securely mounted into place.

Speaker shelf

You have a couple of options for the speaker shelf. Ultimately you need two cutouts in the speaker shelf for your speakers to rest in. If you already have the speakers you plan to use, you can mark and cut out the holes now. You have approximately 6 inches from the front edge of the speaker shelf in which you can make your speaker cutouts. Anything further back and you run the risk of having your speaker cutout resting partially outside your monitor glass and partially inside (which will cause problems).

The other alternative is to mount the speaker shelf without speaker cutouts. This lets you assemble the cabinet and determine the exact fit of various components before placing the speaker cutouts. That in turn ensures proper placement of the speaker cutouts, but does make it more cumbersome to cut the holes later. However, because the top and back angled panels can be removed, providing access to the speaker shelf, this is not terribly difficult. Cutting the speaker holes later is the method we used for Project Arcade. If you're planning to cut them now, jump ahead to Chapter 11 and read the section on speakers before proceeding.

Begin by drawing a line that continues the top (horizontal) angle of the cabinet side that leads into the curved area. Clamping your straight-edge firmly against the angled portion will let you easily continue the line to the back of the cabinet side. The precise angle is not critical, so long as it is approximately the same as the angle of the cabinet side piece. Now draw a line parallel to this line ³/₄ inch higher. This top line represents the bottom of the speaker shelf. Fasten one 16-inch-long or two smaller 8-inch support strips flush along the bottom of this top line to support your speaker shelf. Make sure your support strips do not come any closer than 1¹/₂ inches to the front of the cabinet sides, and no further back than 24 inches along the angled line. Now mount your speaker shelf onto the support strips. It should look something like Figure 2-19. Make sure the speaker shelf is level from left to right.

FIGURE 2-19: The speaker shelf mounted into place.

Cabinet back angled section

You're getting close! Next you'll be tackling the cabinet back angled section—the piece that rests against the cabinet top and follows the angled back of the cabinet sides. Begin by drawing a line ³/₄ inch below and parallel to the angled section of the cabinet back if you haven't already done so. Mount a couple of 8-inch support strips midway along this line, with the top of the support strips flush with the line. Test-fit the cabinet back angled section, checking to see if the 45-degree edge of the section fits flush with the cabinet top section (Figure 2-20). If not, consider doing a bit of fine-tuning with sandpaper before fastening the section to the support strips. The fit is not critical, as it will not be seen by anyone, but if there are gaps then light from the marquee may escape out of the top of the cabinet. If minor sanding doesn't resolve the fit, you can fill it with wood putty, though that means you can't remove that section later.

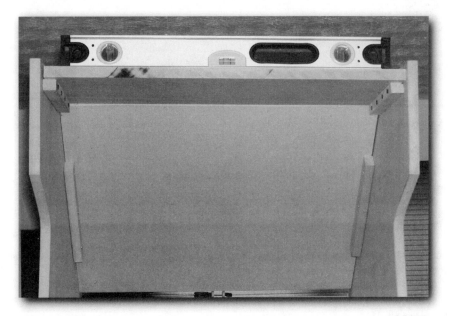

FIGURE 2-20: The cabinet back angled section in place (speaker shelf removed for photo).

Cabinet back top section

You're now down to the last three sections of the cabinet! Next you'll attach the cabinet back top section. Begin by following the now-familiar routine of attaching two support strips $^3/_4$ inch in from the back edge of the cabinet, approximately 4 inches below the cabinet back angled section. Don't forget to verify that they're level vertically before the glue sets. Now place the cabinet back top section against the support strips, and hold it in place with clamps. Two clamps will act as a temporary support shelf for the section, while the top two clamps will help hold it snug against the support strips as shown in Figure 2-21. Check the fit against the 45-degree angle of the angled back section, and fine tune with sandpaper if necessary. A perfect fit here is not vital, but you'll have the same consideration with light escaping through gaps. Once you're satisfied with the fit and placement, fasten the cabinet back top section to the support strips.

FIGURE 2-21: From the back: The bottom two clamps hold the weight, while the top two clamps press the back against the support strips in front.

Monitor shelf

You'll want to take some extra care with the monitor shelf. Monitors are the heaviest part of a cabinet, and they can implode if they fall. For that reason, the mounting technique for the monitor shelf is a bit different from the rest. The monitor is also one of the main ways you interact with the cabinet. You should make sure that the monitor is mounted at an angle (normally about 15 degrees) and far enough back in the cabinet that the viewing is comfortable. I'll show you how to mount the monitor shelf in such a way that it should accommodate almost any monitor. You may have to do some creative engineering once you have your specific monitor chosen, however, adding a brace, shim, or bracket as seems appropriate. Just be sure that any method you use keeps the monitor securely and safely fastened. Don't forget to account for the possibility of laying the cabinet down. A monitor that is secured from sliding forward or backward can still tip and crash if it is not mounted properly and the cabinet is tipped at an angle.

Start by drawing a line horizontally along the cabinet sides, $34^1/_4$ inches from the cabinet base. This will place the monitor shelf slightly below the top of the control panel. Take a 1-foot section of 2-inch × 2-inch lumber, and mount it with glue only so that the top of the support strip is flush with the $34^1/_4$-inch line. The support strip should be mounted approximately 6 inches back from the front edge of the cabinet side. *Do not screw in the support strips from the inside.* Take extra care that the support strips are level. Before the support strips have completely set up, gently place the monitor shelf on top of them and check the level once again. If the shelf is off level in any way, fine-tune the support strips as needed until the shelf is perfectly level. Now remove the shelf.

Next place your straight-edge along the bottom of the support strip, and make a mark on the front and back *outside surface* of the cabinet side coinciding with the straight-edge. Move the straight-edge to the top of the support strip and mark the outside of the cabinet side again. Lightly draw lines connecting your marks on the outside of the cabinet sides. Mark a point along both lines 6 inches and 18 inches from the front edge of the cabinet; this tells you where the support strip is from the outside of the cabinet. Now pre-drill three 2-inch screw holes into the support strip from the outside of the cabinet, countersinking about $1/4$ inch into the wood. Screw in the 2-inch screws, and complete the procedure for the other side of the cabinet as well. Place your shelf back on the support strips, and check the level once again. Make adjustments as required.

Assuming all is good to this point, position the monitor shelf so that the front edge is flush with the front of the cabinet. The glass covering the monitor will eventually rest on the monitor shelf about $3/4$ inch from the front of the cabinet. Remove the shelf, apply glue to the top of the monitor shelf supports strips, and firmly press the monitor shelf into place, taking care to properly position it flush with the front of the cabinet. Allow it to set for a couple of minutes.

Now take your shelf brackets, and mount them to the cabinet sides and underside of the monitor shelf in the front and back on both sides. Be sure the brackets are flush against the monitor shelf and cabinet sides. Use a good $1/2$-inch or $5/8$-inch wood screw to fasten the brackets to the wood. Your monitor shelf is now complete and should look like Figure 2-22.

FIGURE 2-22: The monitor shelf (from underneath), mounted and ready for use.

Cabinet front coin door

You've made it to the last piece of the cabinet! After installing the cabinet front coin door, you will have completed the cabinet construction. The cabinet front coin door has a couple of options to choose from. You can elect to make it a permanently fastened piece or have the front piece hinged for access. You can also have it be a solid piece of wood or put a coin door in the middle of it. There are pros and cons to both sets of decisions.

Installing the coin door

Adding a coin door to your arcade cabinet is an extra touch toward arcade realism. You can even go so far as to make the coin mechanism generate credits when a quarter is inserted. Nothing makes it feel quite as real as hearing a quarter bounce around inside the coin box! It also makes a unique piggy bank or meter on the kids' playing time. Be careful, however — it's probably against local laws to charge people to play games without a license. Other than that, the one drawback of adding a coin door is that they can be pretty expensive. The Over/Under coin door from Happ Controls (the most popular model) will run you almost $90 new. Used models can be had for much cheaper but will usually need a bit of work to make them look nice. The Project Arcade cabinet was built with a working coin door.

If you elect to go with a coin door, your optimal choice is to center it in the cabinet front. Measure the width and height of the cabinet front and identify the center spot. Use that as your starting point to lay out the dimensions for the coin door hole. In the case of the Over/Under door, you'll need a mounting hole that's slightly over $7 \frac{1}{4}$ inches wide by $19 \frac{3}{4}$ inches high. The coin door has a lip that will extend $\frac{1}{2}$ inch past the edge of the mounting hole, so precise measurements are not critical. The corners meet in a 1-inch-radius curve. An easy way to cut out the hole for the coin door is to draw a rectangular box per the above dimensions centered in the cabinet front. Then make tick marks 1 inch from the corner on both lines at every corner, as you can see in Figure 2-23. Then use a 1-inch hole saw to cut holes in each corner matching up to the tick marks you made. From there, it's an easy cut with a jigsaw from hole to hole, and your coin door cutout is made. Test the fit, as you will likely need to sand and/or use the Dremel to fine-tune the dimensions. Once you've verified that the coin door will fit, remove it and place it aside. You won't be mounting it until after painting.

To hinge or not to hinge

If you hinge the cabinet front, it will provide convenient access to the computer system for upgrades and maintenance. You sacrifice a certain amount of arcade authenticity and cabinet stability by doing so, however. Instead of a perfectly sealed seam, there will be a slight gap between the door and the cabinet side. When building the Project Arcade cabinet, I determined that the utility of being able to access the computer from the front outweighed the drawbacks. Even if you choose otherwise, however, you still have access from the opening in the back. If you choose not to hinge the cabinet front, you'll use the same techniques as for the top and back pieces to mount the cabinet front $\frac{3}{4}$ inch in from the front of the cabinet. Also, if you do not hinge the cabinet, you might want to remove it once you've tested the mounting. That will make it easier to mount the control panel box and place your computer equipment inside the cabinet.

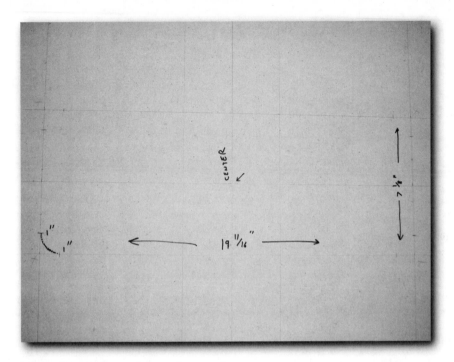

FIGURE 2-23: Marking up the coin door cutout.

If you elect to hinge the cabinet front, follow these steps. First, read the instructions on your hinge hardware and make sure you understand how it works. In the case of the hinges used for Project Arcade, the position of the door and the cabinet wall were opposite to the instructions included with the hinges. This made it necessary to reverse the hinges from the method shown in the instructions. To be sure of fit and function, you should use two pieces of scrap wood as tests before cutting into the cabinet. Once you're satisfied that the hinges you've chosen will work, go ahead and mount the cabinet front to the cabinet side as shown in Figure 2-24. Be careful as you mount the hinges, because you will be drilling into the cabinet side very close to the T-molding groove. If the spaces overlap it's not a disaster, but you'll have to cut a small notch out of the underside of the T-molding to accommodate the cabinet hinge.

Next you'll need a stop on the other side of the cabinet to prevent the cabinet front door from being pushed too far inward and ripping out your hinges. Cut a 2 1/2 -inch piece of scrap wood 29 1/2 inches long. Close the cabinet front so that it is square with the rest of the cabinet, and mark the edge where the stop will need to go. Mount the stop to the cabinet side with glue and screws as shown in Figure 2-25. This gives you a good sturdy stop for the cabinet front. This will also help minimize the appearance of the gap between the cabinet front and the cabinet side. The last step will be to install the surface bolt or other latching mechanism you've chosen to keep the cabinet front closed.

Way to go! You have completed the physical construction of your own Project Arcade cabinet. It's definitely time to reward yourself and your helper with an ice-cold beverage!

FIGURE 2-24: Cabinet front mounted with hinges with optional coin door cutout.

FIGURE 2-25: The cabinet front stop securely mounted to the cabinet side (looking from above).

Control panel box

After building the cabinet, putting together the control panel box is fairly easy. Begin by assembling the pieces you'll need — the control panel box bottom, back, front, and two sides, and the control panel top. You'll find it easiest to assemble this on a flat surface such as a card table. The construction technique used to assemble the box will be to first glue pieces together, and then countersink screws. The bottom of the control panel box front, back, and sides should be flush with the bottom of the control panel box bottom. In other words, they will not sit on top of the bottom piece. Start by attaching the front and sides to the box bottom with glue and screws.

You'll need a way to get the cables from the control panel box down to the computer. Using a hole saw, cut a hole in the middle of the control panel box back the same size as the grommet sleeve you purchased. Thread the sleeve into the hole, and then set the control panel box back aside.

Next you need a way to securely fasten the control panel top to the box while still allowing for removal for installation and maintenance of controls. A very easy way to do this is to use Velcro. Start by cutting a 1-inch-wide strip of scrap wood into eight 3-inch sections. Now place the control panel top on the control panel box assembly. The back should be flush against the box back, and the sides will overhang the box by an equal amount (should be 1¹/₄ inches). When you have the top in position, hold it onto the box with a couple of clamps. Reach inside the box from the back with a pencil, and draw a line on the top piece's underside along the front and side pieces (this is easier than it sounds). Remove the top piece. Your control panel box should now look something like Figure 2-26.

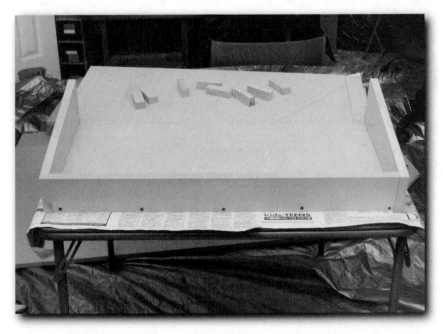

FIGURE 2-26: Partially assembled control panel box, with mounting pieces and marked top in the background.

Place two of the 3-inch strips onto the bottom of the control panel top, in the two front corners that you marked in the last step. Place another two strips about 2 inches from the back of the panel flush with the guide lines. Fasten the strips to the panel top with glue and screws, as shown in Figure 2-27.

Now cover the four mounting pieces on the control panel top with the soft part of the Velcro. Cover the remaining four strips with the rough part. The Velcro has a sticky adhesive side to mount it to the wood. To be extra sure, however, I recommend using two finishing nails on each piece to lend extra security to the Velcro. Sandwich one of the rough Velcro strips to each of the strips mounted to the control panel top, as shown in Figure 2-28.

Place the control panel top back on to the control panel box, making sure once again that the backs are flush and that the overhangs are equal on the left and right. Clamp it into place once more. Now reach inside the control panel box, and mark the positions of the second mounting strips. Make sure each is snug against the sides, repositioning them if necessary (Figure 2-29).

FIGURE 2-27: The control panel strips mounted to the underside of the panel.

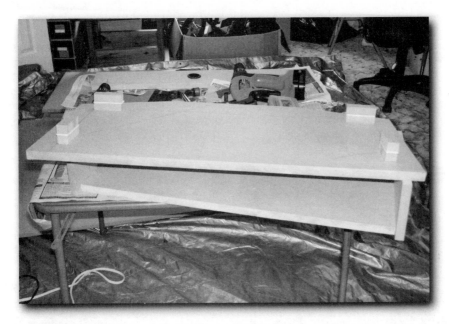

FIGURE 2-28: Mounting strips attached to one another on the control panel.

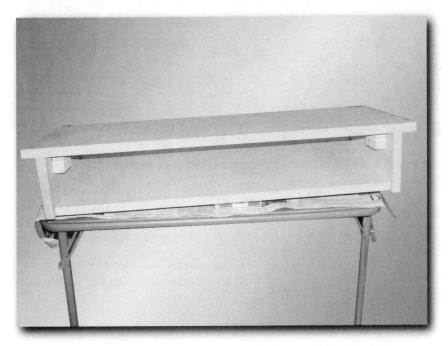

FIGURE 2-29: Looking into the back of the control panel box at the mounting strips.

Detach the mounting strips with the rough Velcro from the control panel top, and mount them to the control panel box using the marks just made. Be careful of your measurements; the Velcro can't hold if the two pieces can't reach each other. Better to be a tad too high than too low. Once the strips have been mounted, test-fit the control panel top to the box. You should be able to lift the entire box up by the control panel top only if the Velcro is working right. Once you're satisfied with the fit, remove the top and attach the control panel back with glue and screws. You've now completed the control panel box assembly (Figure 2-30). You won't be mounting it to the cabinet for now — that will come after the controls are installed and the cabinet is in its final home.

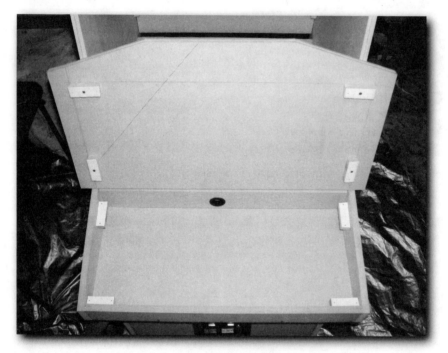

FIGURE 2-30: The completed control panel box ready for its arcade controls!

Painting the Project Arcade cabinet

You've reached the last section of Chapter 2! After all the work that went into the construction of your arcade cabinet, painting may be a bit anticlimactic. Painting is not particularly difficult. How much effort you put into it is entirely a matter of personal taste. I'll cover the recommendations for painting but won't go into too much detail. Just remember that the more effort you put into it, the better the finish will be.

Picking paint

You'll need a gallon of primer and a gallon of paint for your cabinet and control panel. The type of paint and primer is another personal preference, but there are some recommendations. The best choice for paint is a latex semigloss in whatever color you choose. A glossy paint will tend to show fingerprints and the like, while a flat paint doesn't quite have the appeal of a semigloss. You can get a better look with an oil-based paint if you prefer, but it is more difficult to work with and will take much longer to dry between coats. Use the right primer for your paint—water-based primer for latex and oil-based primer for oil-based paint. Raw primer will be white and will take several coats of paint to cover. You'll save yourself a few coats of paint if you have the paint store tint the primer with the color you're planning to use first.

Selecting your painting tools

There are four different methods commonly used to paint cabinets. The first is to simply purchase a few cans of spray paint and have at it. As a rule, almost every person who does this regrets it. The quality of the paint job from spray paint is poor. It will do in a pinch, but you're not likely to be happy with it.

The next method used by a few folks to paint their cabinets is to use a paint sprayer. You can get very nice results quickly by using a paint sprayer. However, a paint sprayer can be an expensive tool if you're not going to use it again. Also, paint spray sometimes can get away from you. Your spouse will not be happy if the family car and the arcade cabinet become matching accessories! Unless you already have a paint sprayer, it's probably not worth going this route.

Several folks have used paintbrushes to paint their cabinet. This works, but tends to be a bit slower than other methods. It is also harder to get a smooth finish with a paintbrush than it is with the next method.

The method you're most likely to be happy with is to paint the cabinet using rollers. Rollers will let you paint the cabinet quickly, and with overlapping strokes a smooth finish is easy to achieve. Spend a few extra dollars to invest in a high-quality foam roller. The cheap rollers you'll find at hardware stores tend to leave a textured finish behind, whereas the high-quality foam rollers give a smooth finish.

Preparing the cabinet

Before you can start painting, you'll need to prepare the cabinet. Begin by filling in any screw holes and blemishes with wood putty. Let the putty dry, and then sand the excess away for a smooth finish. Inspect the cabinet for any last blemishes or holes that need repairing. They may be hard to see now but will probably be glaringly obvious once painted. Take some time at this and have a second pair of eyes help you look it over.

Next carefully clean the entire cabinet. It's been ground zero to a variety of dust clouds, and is assuredly covered in dust even if you can't see it. Use a damp rag to clean the cabinet, and then make sure to let the cabinet dry completely before you begin. Be careful that you don't overdo the liquid on the cabinet—remember that MDF will swell up if it absorbs water.

Painting the cabinet

Make sure you are painting in an area with adequate ventilation and that you have proper breathing protection. Once the cabinet has completely dried, give it a coat of primer. You don't necessarily need to prime the entire insides of the cabinet, but some people recommend it to protect all the surfaces from the elements. It depends on the humidity of the area where you're going to keep the cabinet. If you're keeping it in a climate-controlled environment like a home, it's probably not necessary. You should, however, prime and paint a few inches into the surfaces that might show a bit of the inside, such as the monitor area and behind the gaps in the cabinet front. Let the first coat of primer dry according to the primer instructions, and then use a light-grit sandpaper to sand it down. Clean the cabinet again, let it dry, and then give it a second coat of primer, followed by a second sanding.

Once the primer is dry, switch rollers and give the cabinet its first coat of paint. Don't worry about the smoothness of this first coat. The object here is to cover the primer. Once the first coat is on, let it dry according to the manufacturer's instructions. For latex paint this is usually 4 hours, and for oil-based paint it can be as long as 24 hours. After the paint is dry, use a light-grit sandpaper to sand down the paint's rough spots until the side is smooth. This is where a power sander comes in handy — doing it by hand can be a lot of work. Be sure you are wearing your breathing mask; you do not want to inhale paint dust!

Once you've sanded down the paint, go over the cabinet again with a damp rag to remove the paint dust. Let it dry, and apply another coat of paint. Repeat the process of painting, sanding, and cleaning, each time using a finer grit of sandpaper. On the second and succeeding coats of paint, remember that a little paint will go a long way. Several thinner layers of paint will give you a better finish than a few thick layers. If you use these techniques, and vary the direction of your roller strokes, you'll soon have a beautifully smooth painted finish on your cabinet (Figure 2-31).

You've now gone from a pile of wood and tools to a fully constructed and painted arcade cabinet. All it needs now is some arcade controls and a few electronics to bring it to life. I'll be going over that in the next few chapters. Congratulations! You are well on your way to having your very own arcade machine!

FIGURE 2-31: Project Arcade, ready for the next step!

Summary

Wow, that was certainly a lot of work! You've managed to come a long way in just two chapters. From a pile of wood, you've put together the beginnings of your very own home arcade cabinet! Take some time now to go over the cabinet one last time before moving on. Check for stability, level, and paint finish. You can still make adjustments, but they'll get harder as time and your construction progresses. If everything's good, you're ready to move on.

Can you feel the excitement building? There's no doubt about it now — you're well on your way to arcade Nirvana! In the next few sections, you'll get to take a look at the various arcade components you can put into the cabinet. I'll start by introducing you to joysticks and pushbuttons next!

Designing and Building Your Dream Arcade Control Panel

Pushing Your Buttons and the Joy of Joysticks

What's your vision of the perfect arcade control panel? Does it have shiny red and blue pushbuttons? Bat-handled joysticks? Maybe you'd like a glowing trackball and polished silver spinner? Getting started is a fantastic feeling — you have a blank canvas (your empty control panel) in front of you, and you get to decide exactly what it's going to look like!

The possibilities are endless, and in the chapters to come I'll cover the majority of arcade controls you can use. Ultimately, everyone comes up with his or her own vision of what an ideal arcade machine should include. However, just about every control panel includes a good set of buttons and joysticks. That's what you will get started with in this chapter. There's a lot more to it than you might think!

Buttons, Buttons, Everywhere!

Kapow! Jump! Flap! Kick! No matter how you try, you'll find very few games that can be played without buttons — buttons to shoot and buttons to jump, buttons for flight or buttons to fight. Most games need buttons. Even the games that don't use buttons to play usually will use buttons to coin up the game and select the number of players. Also, if you're planning to go for the most authentic arcade feel possible, you'll want to do away with the keyboard altogether. To do that you'll need buttons to replace some of the keyboard's functions, such as a button to quit the game or a button to shut down the machine. In almost every kind of arcade machine, buttons play an important role. You can't start a game without a pushbutton. You can't jump, shoot, or punch without a pushbutton. Choosing the right kind(s) of button(s) therefore is important. By the time you finish this section you'll know more about buttons than you ever dreamed was possible.

Different types of pushbuttons

A look at one arcade parts vendor shows that it carries almost 40 kinds of buttons! Many of the differences are cosmetic — some buttons are round, some are square, etc. Some of the buttons are intended for specific purposes, such as *bet* for a poker game. In general, however, there are only two or three types of buttons you will be interested in for your arcade machine. Some of the different kinds of pushbuttons available are shown in Figure 3-1.

FIGURE 3-1: Many different pushbuttons.

Leaf switch or microswitch?

The first decision you'll need to make when choosing buttons is what kind of switch you want your buttons to use. The switch sits at the bottom of the button and is pressed when the button is pushed down, making contact with it. Pressing the switch is what activates the electronic signal telling the arcade machine a button has been pushed. There are two main switch types used in arcade machines: *leaf switches* and *microswitches*.

Leaf switch

Leaf switches consist of a small rectangular box of plastic through which two thin metal blades, or *leafs*, protrude. A short length of the metal lies on one side for connecting the wiring, while the main length of the metal lies on the other side underneath the button. The two leaf blades are usually a millimeter or two apart, with small nubs of metal facing each other beneath the button. When the button is pushed, the bottom of the button presses on the top leaf of metal, bending it down to make contact with the bottom leaf of metal, thus activating the switch. You'll find two types of leaf switches. Some are standalone mechanisms that are screwed into the bottom of the button holder, and some are built into the button holder directly. See Figure 3-2 for a close-up of leaf switches and comparison of the two styles.

FIGURE 3-2: Two different kinds of leaf switches.

The actual button for a leaf switch consists of a narrow plastic tube with a wide top, with a spring-loaded center piece that you press. There's a small clip at the bottom of the center piece that stops it from springing back out of the tube. Figure 3-3 shows two leaf buttons, one assembled and one disassembled.

The only other consideration for a leaf switch is the size. They come in two lengths — a shorter length for mounting in a metal control panel and a longer length for mounting in a wooden control panel. There is no functional difference between buttons of different lengths.

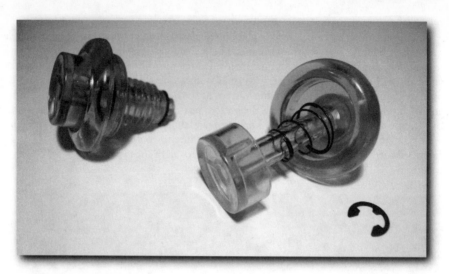

FIGURE 3-3: Assembled (left) and disassembled (right) leaf switch buttons.

Tip

Some leaf switch buttons are available in translucent colors. If that's your cup of tea, you can illuminate them from inside the control panel for a very cool retro effect!

Cross-Reference

For more information about using translucent buttons, refer to Chapter 6, "Building the Control Panel."

Microswitch

Microswitches work a bit differently from leaf switch pushbuttons. A microswitch pushbutton is a self-contained mechanism with three short blades of metal coming from the side and bottom and a tiny button on the top. The bottom blade is marked COM, and the two side blades are marked NC and NO. The finer details of wiring microswitch buttons will be covered in Chapter 7, "How It Works — Turning a Computer into the Brains of an Arcade Machine." For now, suffice to say that you'll be using the blades marked NO and COM, and not the blade marked NC. When the top of the arcade button is pushed, the bottom makes contact with the tiny button of the microswitch and presses it down, activating the switch. See Figure 3-4 for a look at a microswitch.

COM stands for Common, and this blade is always used. NO stands for Normally Open, and this blade is used when the button is up when not being used. NC stands for Normally Closed, and this blade is used when the button is pressed down when not being used. Arcade buttons are up when not in use, hence you'll use the NO and COM blades when wiring.

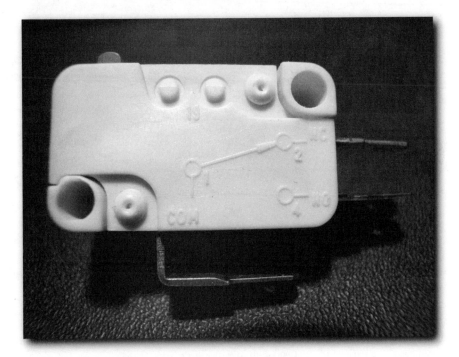

FIGURE 3-4: A close-up of a microswitch.

The actual pushbutton for a microswitch is similar to that of a leaf switch, except that the plastic tube is wide-bodied instead of narrow. The center piece is also spring-loaded but is held in place by two tabs of plastic instead of a clip. Figure 3-5 shows two microswitch buttons, one assembled and one disassembled.

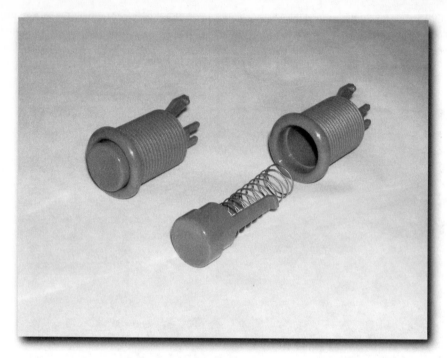

FIGURE 3-5: Two microswitch buttons: Assembled (left) and disassembled (right).

Choices

Whether to go with a leaf switch or a microswitch is a matter of preference and convenience. You can see a comparison of the two when idle in Figure 3-6.

Many arcade fans prefer the leaf style of switch for two reasons. First, the leaf switch buttons are quiet when pressed, unlike microswitches. Second, some people prefer the feel of a leaf switch button. Microswitch buttons make an audible click when pressed and typically do not have to be pressed down as far as a leaf switch button to make contact. Figure 3-7 shows a comparison of assembled leaf switch and microswitch buttons when pressed.

FIGURE 3-6: Assembled leaf and microswitch buttons when idle.

Whether you choose to use a leaf or microswitch button is entirely a matter of personal prefer-ence, as both function equally well. However, the choice may be made for you as a matter of availability. For some reason, presumably cost, as of the time of this writing manufacturers do not appear to be making leaf switch buttons anymore. It is possible to find leaf switch buttons, but you have to be willing to do some looking. See Appendix A for information on where to find leaf switch buttons and other hard-to-find parts.

The popular choice: microswitch buttons

Because of availability, most people will use microswitches. Even if you do use leaf switch but-tons, you'll likely use microswitch buttons for some of the administrative buttons, such as the *insert-coin* buttons and *player-1 start* button, saving the leaf switch buttons for game playing. Accordingly, there's still a bit more about microswitch buttons to tell you.

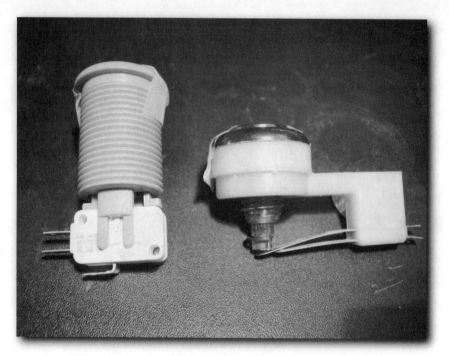

FIGURE 3-7: The same two buttons when pushed.

Pushbutton with horizontal microswitch

There are several styles of microswitch buttons available. The one shown in the previous figures is the *Pushbutton With Horizontal Microswitch* from Happ Controls, although this style is available from other manufacturers as well. The general consensus is that these are the best microswitch buttons to use for the action buttons of an arcade machine. These buttons are distinguished from other kinds of microswitch buttons by their concave button surface, and the microswitch is mounted horizontally under the button. Most players seem to prefer the concave button surface, and if you take a trip to an arcade you'll find that it's the most prevalent style.

Note   I will often refer to a part by its name from the Happ Controls company. This is a matter of convenience as Happ is the biggest supplier of arcade parts in the United States; however, it should not be considered an endorsement of Happ over another company. While building my own arcade machine during the writing of this book, I used parts from many manufacturers. Happ Controls is certainly a reputable vendor, but other vendors of arcade parts exist.

Cross-Reference   For a complete list of parts vendors, see Appendix A, "Where to Find Arcade Parts for Your Project."

Competition pushbutton

Another choice to consider is the *Competition Pushbutton* style shown in Figure 3-8. This is similar in construction to the *Pushbutton With Horizontal Microswitch* and has the microswitch mounted horizontally beneath it. The button surface is convex instead of concave, and hence has a slightly different feel. This is once again simply a matter of personal preference. Some people think it has a better response, while others simply can't get used to it.

FIGURE 3-8: The Competition Pushbutton with convex button surface.
Used by permission of Happ Controls.

Ultimate pushbutton with microswitch

The last of the pushbuttons most often considered for home arcade machines is the *Ultimate Pushbutton With Microswitch* (see Figure 3-9). This is similar to the *Pushbutton With Horizontal Microswitch* with the difference that the microswitch is mounted vertically beneath the button. Instead of the bottom of the button making contact with the microswitch's button, the pushbutton slides against the microswitch vertically, pressing the microswitch's button as is slides by. There are some people who prefer this style of pushbutton, but the general consensus is that this style is more prone to problems. If the part that slides against the microswitch wears away, or the button is not aligned correctly, you may experience intermittent *dead-button* syndrome.

Buttoning up the button choice

Although there are other kinds of buttons available for your project, it's best to limit your considerations to the choices enumerated previously. Other buttons may catch your eye because they are illuminated or have an interesting shape, but they are usually designed for nongame-playing uses or specific games such as gambling machines.

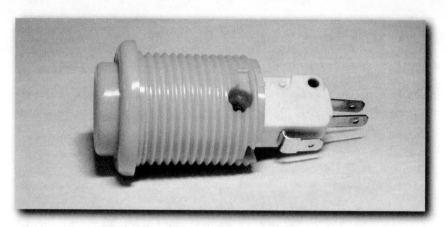

FIGURE 3-9: The Ultimate Pushbutton With Microswitch.
Used by permission of Happ Controls.

When purchasing buttons, be aware of what you're getting. Some vendors will sell pushbuttons without the necessary microswitches or leaf switches. This is not necessarily a deceptive practice, as these pushbuttons are typically cheaper than whole assemblies and are useful for arcade operators who buy parts in bulk for repair. You don't need to pay for a button *and* a microswitch if you already have a box of microswitches. Just be sure that what you're purchasing is clearly spelled out; if it's not, then ask.

Also be aware of the source of your buttons (and all arcade parts in general). Buttons from reputable arcade supply houses are generally all of good quality, but there are lower-quality look-alikes available. You may run into issues such as stiff springs and defects in the plastic, for instance. If in doubt, order a sample before placing a large order. Appendix A includes some (but not necessarily all) of the vendors known to provide quality products.

Joysticks

While there is general consensus on button choices, there is less agreement on what makes a good joystick. Once again you have many choices available to you (see Figure 3-10). I could fill pages and pages with information about different types of joysticks, and, well, because that's what you paid for, I'll do just that.

Types of joysticks

You have more choices for joysticks than for any other kind of arcade control. Although there are some 40 or more buttons available from one vendor, they all operate in essentially the same way, being some variant of a microswitch pushbutton. Joysticks, on the other hand, vary a great deal more from one model to the next. They vary by number of directions supported, type of switch used, type of interface supported, and physical shape. I'll introduce you to the more common choices in this section.

FIGURE 3-10: Some of the many different joystick choices available.
Used by permission of Happ Controls and Ultimarc.

Leaf vs. microswitch vs. optical

Joysticks have the same two options as pushbuttons — leaf switch and microswitch connections. There are also models that have optical interfaces, of which there are two styles. One style simply uses optics to register where you've moved the joystick, but still uses the same interfaces as the leaf and microswitch models. You are essentially using *optical switches* instead of the other two kinds. The Happ Controls Perfect 360 (see "Happ Perfect 360 Electronic") is one such joystick. The other kind of optical joystick is one that's purely optical. It uses optical switches and also requires a special optical interface. The Happ Controls Optical Rotary joystick is one such model.

Note   What's an optical interface? A computer mouse is an example of a device that uses an optical interface. When you move the mouse on the surface, the ball in the bottom of the mouse turns two spoked wheels inside the mouse body. There's one spoke for left-right movement and one for up-down movement. Optical sensors surround the spokes and register the change in the light as the mouse moves and the spokes turn — DARK-LIGHT-DARK-LIGHT, etc. The speed and direction of the spokes tell the computer where and how fast you're trying to move the mouse. We'll take advantage of this concept in the next chapter.

Which kind of switch type should you use? That's once again a personal preference. Choosing between the leaf switch and microswitch models involves the same considerations as choosing buttons. Leaf switch joysticks are generally thought to have a better feel and don't suffer from the clicking sound of microswitches, but unfortunately they are no longer made. There is a booming after-market in leaf switch joysticks, however, and they are not yet terribly difficult to find (see Appendix A). Optical joysticks, such as the Happ Perfect 360, are favored by some people but are generally not used due to their cost — they are typically three times the cost of the Happ Super joysticks.

Analog vs. digital

Which type of joystick should you use? Analog? Digital? Both have their strengths. The majority of joysticks you'll encounter for this project will be digital. They use switches, and switches are either pressed or not, on or off. They require some kind of digital interface to connect (see Chapters 7 and 8). The older PC joysticks, however, were analog. Instead of switches, they used *potentiometers* to tell where you were moving the joystick. A potentiometer is a small device that varies the amount of current flowing through a circuit depending on how the shaft of the potentiometer is turned. As you move the joystick, potentiometers in the joystick are turned, telling the computer you've moved the joystick. See Figure 3-11 for a look at an analog PC joystick. There are a few arcade analog joysticks, but there is little compelling reason to use them for your arcade cabinet. There is only a small handful of games that are meant for an analog joystick that won't work with a digital one.

Bats and balls

No, we didn't slip a section about baseball into the book. One of the immediate (and usually only) differences among joysticks that a casual game-player will notice is the physical handle. They come in four main shapes: bat-shaped handles, ball-shaped handles, flight-grip handles, and flare-type handles. See Figure 3-12 for the most common shapes.

The trigger-grip or flight-grip handles obviously are designed for specific types of games, such as flight simulators or *Zaxxon*. However, there is no functional difference between the ball- and bat-shaped handles. Once again it is entirely a matter of personal preference. I prefer the ball-shaped handles, but opinions seem to be split down the middle as to which is the better handle to use. The flare-type handle is usually used in specific games, such as the crane games in which the player steers a claw and tries to get a prize out of the bin. Flare-type joysticks are occasionally used as substitutes for the trigger-grip because they are less expensive and have a fire button on the top. They'll do in a pinch, but they're no substitute for the real thing.

Number of directions

Another way to distinguish joysticks from one another is by the number of directions they support. Most games are designed to be played with joysticks moving either in two, four, or eight directions (see Figure 3-13). Other types, such as 49-way joysticks, have been used, but typically the 2-way, 4-way, and 8-way joysticks will cover virtually anything you want to play. Several models of joysticks fall into the 2-, 4-, and 8-way categories.

FIGURE 3-11: A look inside a very disassembled analog PC joystick. Notice the potentiometers. This joystick will probably never get put back together!

FIGURE 3-12: From left to right, bat-shaped, ball-shaped, flare-type, and trigger-grip handles.

Used by permission of Happ Controls.

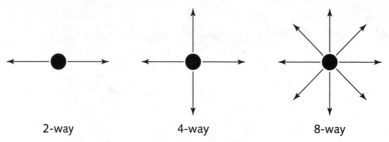

2-way   4-way   8-way

FIGURE 3-13: A 2-way, 4-way, and 8-way joystick layout.

Looking at Figure 3-13, you might think that you get the most versatility out of the 8-way joysticks, and for the most part you'd be right. If you have a joystick that can go UP, UP-RIGHT, and RIGHT, then it will work in a game that only needs UP and RIGHT, correct? Not always. Sometimes, a 4-way joystick is a better choice. For instance, consider *Donkey Kong*. In the game, you play Mario—a brave plumber running across horizontal girders (LEFT-RIGHT direction) and climbing ladders (UP-DOWN direction) in order to rescue the girl. Needing only LEFT-RIGHT-UP-DOWN directions, this game was sold with 4-way joysticks. Imagine playing with an 8-way joystick now. You are running as fast as your little pixilated legs can carry you from the flaming barrel on your left (Did I mention the barrels trying to run you over? You thought you had traffic problems!). Suddenly you come upon salvation in the form of a ladder to your right. When you start to climb the ladder, you want to be able to switch from moving right to moving up without hesitation as the flaming barrel tries to make your acquaintance. With a 4-way joystick and good timing, this isn't hard. However, you have an 8-way joystick. Trying frantically to hit the UP direction, you move the joystick from the RIGHT to the UP-RIGHT diagonal direction instead of straight UP. This leaves poor Mario standing still beneath the ladder while the flaming barrel barbecues him. Alas poor Mario, if only you'd had a 4-way joystick!

The same kind of reasoning applies with a 4-way joystick in an 8-way game. If you can only move UP-DOWN-LEFT-RIGHT, but you're flying a spaceship in a maze where you need to be able to go diagonally, sooner or later you'll smack into a wall and it's *game over*. As the saying goes, there's no substitute for using the right tool for the right job. Fortunately, in practice this doesn't seem to be as critical for 2-way games. Both 4-way and 8-way joysticks usually will suffice for 2-way games; though if you're trying to build a dedicated 2-way game machine, then, of course, you should try to find the right joysticks.

So what kind of joystick do you need to get for a multigame cabinet such as the one you're building now? The answer, of course, is both. I'll cover this in Chapter 6, "Building the Control Panel," but typically you'll end up with a couple of 8-way joysticks, with one 4-way joystick for games that need it.

Switchable joysticks

To further complicate matters, several manufacturers make joysticks that can be switched or converted from an 8-way to a 4-way joystick. Some require tools to convert them, typically just pliers to remove the retaining clip on the bottom of the joystick shaft. Arcade operators who buy joysticks in bulk and don't know if they'll be used in a 4-way or 8-way game typically use these. You might consider these if you are not totally sure if you'll want 4-way or 8-way joysticks.

Other types of 4-way/8-way switchable joysticks can be switched without tools. These typically have a lever or wheel on the base that can be moved by hand to convert from 4-way to 8-way. The drawback is that they require access to the bottom of the joystick, which is hidden by the control panel. You might consider these joysticks if you occasionally will want to switch from 4-way to 8-way and don't mind opening your control panel to do so. Some folks have been able to make use of these without opening their control panels by reaching in through the coin-door of their arcade cabinets.

There is an important consideration regarding joysticks that are switchable from 4-way to 8-way. Some methods, both commercial and homegrown, block the *functionality* of the diagonal directions but not the *physical* diagonal directions. One way they do this is with an actuator that fits over the end of the shaft. The bottom shaft of the joystick is too skinny to make contact with the switches. The actuator is a piece of plastic that fits over the shaft, thereby making it large enough to make contact with the switches when the joystick is moved. See Figure 3-14 for an example of an 8-way and a 4-way actuator.

FIGURE 3-14: A 4-way actuator (left) and an 8-way actuator (right).

The bottoms of the actuators are the same size, but the top is larger on the 8-way actuator than the 4-way. When the larger 8-way actuator is installed, the bottom of the joystick is big enough to press both the UP and RIGHT leaf switches far enough to make contact (see Figure 3-15).

FIGURE 3-15: Joystick with 8-way actuator making full contact on the diagonal.

However, when the smaller 4-way actuator is installed, the bottom of the joystick is only big enough to fully press the UP or the RIGHT leaf switch, but not both at the same time despite the fact that the shaft is pointed in the diagonal direction (see Figure 3-16). This means you could potentially find yourself with *dead-stick* syndrome when you attempt to hit the UP position but hit the UP-RIGHT position instead.

The more reliable design is to use a *restrictor plate*. A restrictor plate fits over the shaft of the joystick and physically restricts the stick from being pushed in the diagonal directions. See the next section for more on restrictor plates.

The last switchable design I'll present here is a clever design sold by Ultimarc (listed in Appendix A). Ultimarc has a model called the *E-Stik* that is a 4-way joystick that can be rotated 45 degrees. The nice part is that you do not have to access the bottom of the joystick to do so; a simple twist of the cover plate will switch it back and forth. This makes it an ideal joystick to use for games, such as *Q*Bert*, that require a 45-degree mounted stick. There are so few games requiring a 45-degree angled 4-way stick that it's hard to justify dedicating a stick for them. The E-Stik is a handy solution to that dilemma. Happ Controls sells a similar joystick, the *Universal*.

FIGURE 3-16: Same joystick with 4-way actuator failing to make full contact on the diagonal. Dead-stick syndrome!

Restrictor plates

As mentioned, a restrictor plate is a device that fits over the shaft of a joystick and *physically* restricts it from moving in diagonal directions, making an 8-way joystick a 4-way joystick. Some joysticks, such as the line of joysticks from Ultimarc listed later, come with restrictor plates built in to the bottom of the joystick. Simply turn a gear or move a switch and the restrictor plate rotates between 8-way and 4-way movement.

A company called Oscar Controls (see Appendix A) sells a line of restrictor plates as aftermarket add-ons for several models of joysticks. These restrictor plates sit on the top of the joystick instead of the bottom and are available in models that restrict movement to 2-way as well as those that restrict movement to 4-way. There is also a model that restricts movements to the diagonals for games like *Q*Bert*. There are two points to consider with these restrictor plates. First, the restrictor plates are visible on the top of the control panel (see Figure 3-17). Second, by default these restrictor plates are screwed into the panel (or a companion mounting plate, recommended) and are not quick-release. Mounting pins instead of screws can be substituted by request. Oscar Controls restrictor plates have been tested to work with Happ Controls Competition, Super, Perfect 360, and Ultimate joysticks, and older Wico leaf joysticks.

FIGURE 3-17: 4-way restrictor plates mounted on Happ Competition joystick.
Used by permission of Oscar Controls and Happ Controls, respectively.

Rotary joysticks

Rotary joysticks are like other joysticks in that they move in eight directions and work well in many situations. The extra trick of a rotary joystick is that the joystick handle will rotate clockwise and counterclockwise as well. There are a couple of games that use this feature, including *Ikari Warriors*. This feature makes it possible for you to aim your weapon while moving. A twist to the left while pressing forward, and your on-screen buddy aims to the left while going straight. These joysticks come in both optical and digital versions, requiring different interfaces. See below for a look at the Happ Controls Rotary joysticks.

A look at several different joysticks

In the next few pages I'll take a look at some of the many joysticks that are available for your project. It is by no means an attempt to cover every joystick. I have limited the scope to those joysticks that are frequently chosen by the arcade machine–building community and that are readily available for sale. For instance, the original Wico brand leaf joysticks are wonderful additions to a control panel. However, since they are no longer made and are difficult to find, I have not included them in this discussion. If you are fortunate enough to find them (I list possible sources in Appendix A), you should certainly consider trying them out.

Ultimarc T-Stik (Toggle-switch stick)

The *T-Stik* available from Ultimarc (see Figure 3-18) is a 4-way/8-way microswitch joystick with a bat-shaped handle. Industrias Lorenzo, a well-known arcade parts supplier, makes this joystick for Ultimarc. Industrias Lorenzo customizes the joystick to Ultimarc's specifications to tweak its performance and features for the home user. There is a small switch toward the bottom of the joystick that will rotate the built-in restrictor plate between 4-way and 8-way modes, allowing for tool-less conversion between modes. This makes the joystick a good choice if you want to be able to switch back and forth without opening your control panel, for instance through the coin-door.

The T-Stik does have one of the shorter shaft lengths of the joysticks presented here, which will require some attention when mounting in a wooden control panel. The shorter shaft length equates to a shorter throw on the joystick, which means a quicker response time. The shorter throw and a heavy spring contribute to a stiffer feel on the joystick, which some people prefer and some do not. The T-Stik gets positive reviews from visitors to the Build Your Own Arcade Controls (BYOAC) Web site. These joysticks, and all the ones that follow, unless otherwise specified, use microswitches.

FIGURE 3-18: The Ultimarc T-Stik.
Used by permission of Ultimarc.

The *T-Stik Plus* and the *T-Stik Plus Ball-Top* are two cousins to the original T-Stik joystick. They provide the same functionality of the original but add the ability to switch between 8-way and 4-way without requiring access to the underside of the joystick. You are able to switch modes by pulling up and rotating the stick until the switching mechanism engages. Once engaged, a twist to the left activates 8-way mode, a twist to the right activates 4-way. The T-Stik Plus is a bat-handled joystick with a single mounting length, while the T-Stik Plus Ball-Top is, appropriately enough, a ball-topped joystick with two shaft lengths available.

Note What is a joystick throw? It's the distance the top of the joystick can move before it stops. A short throw means a short distance before movement is registered and equals a quicker response. A longer throw means a longer distance and a slower response. Quicker response is not always preferred—for instance, when fine control is required, a longer throw may be the better choice.

Ultimarc E-Stik & Happ Controls Universal

The Ultimarc E-Stik and Happ Controls Universal are the same basic model made by Industrias Lorenzo, except Industrias Lorenzo customizes Ultimarc's E-Stik. This ball-top model has two unique features. For installation, it has a plastic cover plate that eliminates the need for a control panel overlay to hide the screws and mounting bracket. Also, as mentioned previously, the joystick can be rotated 45 degrees by twisting the cover plate or bottom, making it an ideal joystick for games, such as *Q*Bert,* that require a diagonally mounted joystick. This does take some attention when mounting (see Chapter 6, "Building the Control Panel").

The 4-way/8-way rotating gear on the bottom of the Ultimarc model of this joystick makes for an easy change between modes (see Figure 3-19), although the switch is not as easy to perform by feel as it is with the T-Stik. The Happ Controls Universal must be unscrewed to be rotated between 4-way and 8-way. Because of the longer throw of this joystick, in 4-way mode there is still a slight amount of diagonal movement possible. However, there is not enough movement allowed to reach the switches and register the diagonal direction.

Ultimarc J-Stik (Japanese) ball-top and oval-top

The Ultimarc *J-Stik* (see Figure 3-20) is the last of its joystick lineup and, like the others, it is 4-way/8-way switchable. This particular model is made and customized for Ultimarc by Sanwa, another respected arcade parts manufacturer. The J-Stik is available in either a ball-top or bat-shaped handle. It has a longer throw that has two settings, available by turning the restrictor plate over. The hole in the middle of the restrictor plate that the joystick shaft hits has angled edges. Flipped one way, the joystick shaft hits the top of the angled edge, making it stop slightly sooner than when flipped the other way, where it can be pressed all the way to the bottom edge of the restrictor plate.

The J-Stik uses the same rotating gear mechanism as the E-Stik and has the same considerations. It's easy to change between modes and, like the E-Stik, allows some travel in the diagonal directions before blocking contact with the switches diagonally. The joysticks are designed for metal control panels, but can easily be mounted to wooden control panels via a couple of methods (see Chapter 6, "Building the Control Panel"). The J-Stiks are also well thought of by the arcade machine–building community.

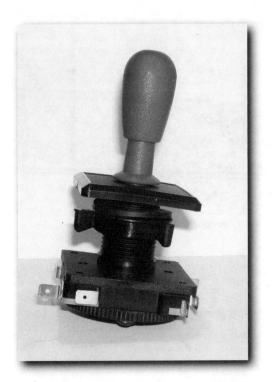

FIGURE 3-19: The Ultimarc E-Stik and its 4-way/8-way rotating gear.
Used by permission of Ultimarc.

Happp Competition

The Happ Controls Competition joystick (see Figure 3-21) is an 8-way microswitch joystick suitable for both wooden and metal control panels. The joystick has a square actuator, which makes it particularly easy to hit diagonals. This can be a blessing or a curse, as some users have reported accidentally hitting diagonals when they meant to go straight. This makes the Competition a poor choice for 4-way games. The Competition has a bat-shaped handle and a fairly long throw. This joystick can be ordered with a heavier spring, which is recommended by some users to improve the tactile feel. The Competition joystick is one of the less popular choices for joysticks in the build-your-own community, and it is primarily used by people who plan to play a lot of fighter games.

FIGURE 3-20: The Ultimarc J-Stik, side and bottom views.
Used by permission of Ultimarc.

FIGURE 3-21: The Happ Controls Competition joystick.
Used by permission of Happ Controls.

Happp Super

The Happ Controls Super joystick is a 4-way/8-way switchable joystick with a modified bat handle. The bat portion of the handle is shorter than other bat-handled joysticks (see Figure 3-22). The joystick is converted from 4-way to 8-way by flipping the actuator over, a process that requires partially disassembling the joystick. This makes the Super a good choice as a joystick to keep in stock to suit a variety of purposes, but not a good candidate for a control panel in which you want a single stick to play both 4-way and 8-way games. In 4-way mode, the actuator prevents the microswitches from being pressed when the joystick is moved diagonally but does not prevent the physical diagonal movement itself. This can lead to dead-stick syndrome if you inadvertently hit a diagonal when attempting to go straight.

The microswitches on the Super joystick have metal levers that are pressed by the joystick actuator, which then activate the microswitch buttons (see Figure 3-23, bottom view). Some users have reported trouble hitting the diagonals on this joystick, a glitch that can be fixed by bending the metal levers outward slightly. Be careful not to bend them too much or you will find yourself hitting diagonals accidentally. These levers make the stick tweakable to suit your individual preferences—a nice feature.

Happ dubs the Super its strongest (most durable) joystick, and it is the most popular choice among both commercial arcade panel vendors and those who build their own arcade machines.

FIGURE 3-22: The Happ Controls Super joystick.
Used by permission of Happ Controls.

Happp Rotary and Optical Rotary

There are two models of the rotary style joystick from Happ Controls. These joysticks are 8-way microswitch-based with a bat-shaped handle. The extra feature of these joysticks is that the handle twists for games that require aiming, such as *Ikari Warriors*. The Rotary model (see Figure 3-23) does this via a mechanical 12-position switch, while the Optical Rotary does the same via an optical interface.

Connecting these joysticks to your arcade machine requires a bit more work than other joysticks. The 4 microswitches connect in the same manner as other joysticks. The optical or 12-position switches require a different interface. Fortunately, a few methods for connecting these have been developed, some build-your-own and some ready to purchase off the shelf. See Chapters 8 and 9, "Using the Keyboard Connector for Arcade Controls" and "Arcade Controls Using the Mouse Connector," for options for connecting rotary and optical rotary joysticks.

These joysticks have a limited but enthusiastic fan base. If you are a fan of a game that uses one of these joysticks, then you'll be happy adding one to your project. Otherwise, they are probably not worth the extra steps and expense involved in connecting them.

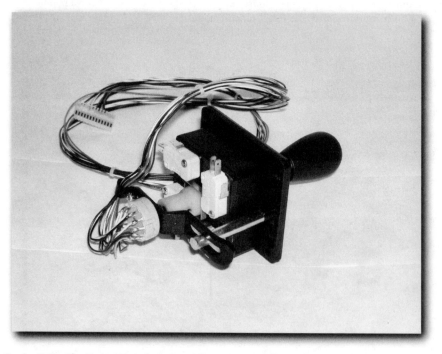

FIGURE 3-23: The Happ Controls Rotary (12-position mechanical) joystick.
Used by permission of Happ Controls.

Happp Perfect 360 Electronic

The Happ Perfect 360 joystick (see Figure 3-24) is considered the top of the crop of Happ Controls joysticks. It is similar to the Happ Competition and Super joysticks, with the bottom set of microswitches replaced with an optical sensor mechanism. The joystick is 4-way/8-way switchable by turning the actuator over. Like other actuator-based joysticks, the 4-way mode does not limit actual physical movement in that direction, allowing for dead-stick syndrome. However, the dead zone in 4-way mode is smaller in these joysticks than other 4-way/8-way sticks that use actuators instead of restrictor plates.

The photoelectric mechanism used in place of microswitches provides for clickless game play and precise control in both 4-way and 8-way modes. In place of the normal connection to the microswitches, there's a 5-volt (+5v) connection and a ground, and four individual connections for each direction. The 5-volt connection is something to remember when designing your control panel. There are many options for obtaining the 5-volt connection. See Chapter 7, "How It Works — Turning a Computer into the Brains of an Arcade Machine," for more details.

Because of the switchless interface, the Perfect 360 joysticks have a smooth feel and very precise control. These joysticks tend to be the hands-down favorite of those who try them, but are not as frequently used as the Super joysticks primarily due to the higher cost of the 360s. Fans of fighter games particularly favor them, and one popular hack of these joysticks is to replace the handle with a ball-top handle from old Wico leaf joysticks.

FIGURE 3-24: The Happ Controls Perfect 360.
Used by permission of Happ Controls.

GroovyGameGear.com's Omni-Stik Prodigy

GroovyGameGear.com (www.groovygamegear.com) is a recent entrant into the arcade joystick market with the introduction of its Omni-Stik line of joysticks. The Omni-Stik comes in two models, the basic *economy* model and the *Prodigy* model shown in Figure 3-25.

FIGURE 3-25: The Omni-Stik Prodigy.
Used by permission of IDVT Inc.

The joystick shaft of the Omni-Stik line is an interesting cross between a bat-shaped handle and a ball-top handle. The shaft has a taper like a bat handle but ends in a ball top. The basic Omni-Stik is switchable between 2-way, 3-way, 4-way, 5-way, and 8-way modes. Switching modes requires physical access to the bottom of the joysticks and some assembly, so it cannot be done on the fly. The Prodigy line is switchable between 4-way and 8-way from the top of the control panel. A small lever protrudes slightly above the mounting plate behind the shaft of the joystick. Rotating the lever left puts the joystick into 4-way mode; rotating it right puts the joystick into 8-way mode. The mounting plate that holds the joystick is a standard black-wrinkle surface with no screws showing, so it rests flush with the control panel top. The joysticks come in red, black, and blue models. Initial response to the Omni-Stik line of joysticks has been good.

Juggling joystick decisions

Suffering from information overload? Don't worry, it's mostly downhill from here. Joystick choice is probably the most agonizing decision you'll have to make. Although there are plenty of options to choose from in the next few chapters, none are as overwhelming as joystick choices. If you can't make up your mind, here are a couple of suggestions:

1. Hop onto the Build Your Own Arcade Controls (BYOAC) Web site at www.arcade controls.com, visit the message boards and chat room, and ask for opinions. Be prepared to discuss what your favorite games are and what kind of arcade machine you're trying to build.

2. If in doubt, choose a couple of 8-way joysticks (either the Ultimarc T-Stiks or the Happ Supers). Complement those with either a 4-way joystick (such as the Ultimarc E-Stik) or a switchable 4-way/8-way joystick (such as the Ultimarc T-Stik Plus or the GroovyGameGear.com Omni-Stik Prodigy). Bear in mind that once you've played with your arcade machine for a while, it's easy enough to swap joysticks.

Summary

Planning your control panel design can be a lot of fun. The biggest part of your control panel will be the buttons and joysticks. Buttons and joysticks distinguish themselves from one another by look and feel, and the types that you choose can have a real impact on how your arcade cabinet plays. Different buttons and joysticks lend themselves to different types of gaming (for instance, the 4-way versus 8-way games), and there really is no single right answer as to which ones to choose. Ultimately, it comes down to personal preferences (you'll hear that quite a bit in this book).

There's more to most arcade cabinets than just buttons and joysticks, though. Many really great games use unique controls, such as spinners and trackballs. That's what I'll introduce in the next chapter, "Taking Your Game Out for a Spin — Spinners and Trackballs"!

Taking Your Game Out for a Spin — Spinners and Trackballs

Picture yourself twisting a spinner to fly your ship wildly around a geometric field as you shoot down spikes. Or perhaps you're madly spinning a trackball across the screen dodging laser beams. These are things you just can't do with a keyboard or even a joystick. These kinds of arcade antics require something more. In this case, the right tools for the job happen to be the second most popular controls for arcade cabinets: spinners and trackballs!

What Do Spinners and Trackballs Do?

Spinners and trackballs are essentially two peas from the same pod, with similar functionality and characteristics (see Figure 4-1). By twisting the spinner or rolling the trackball, you control the movement of your character or ship in an arcade game. In the case of a computer-based arcade cabinet, you move the mouse cursor on the computer. That translates to proper control when playing a game that uses a mouse for onscreen movement. Games such as Tempest, Tron, Centipede, and Missile Command use spinners and trackballs for control.

FIGURE 4-1: Spinners and trackballs.
Used by permission of Oscar Controls, Happ Controls and SlikStik.

Spinners and trackballs are both optical devices. When the trackball is rolled or the spinner is spun, optical sensors detect the direction and speed of movement and send that information to their interface. Fortunately, computers already understand how to talk to optical devices. The mouse that you use on your computer is an optical device. This makes it very easy to connect arcade spinners and trackballs to a computer. Both typically connect to the computer in a similar fashion and to the computer both appear to be mice. All you need is an interface between the computer and the spinner or trackball to translate the spinner or trackball signal into a mouse signal. In a nutshell, there are two ways to do this. I'll go over interfacing spinners and trackballs in detail in Chapter 9, "Arcade Controls Using the Mouse Connector."

Spinner Choices

You'll find that spinners, whether homemade or purchased, all share a common set of characteristics. Starting from the top, they have some kind of knob that is used to grab and twist the spinner. The knob is attached to a shaft, usually by a setscrew in the knob that holds it tight. The shaft penetrates the control panel and ends in an encoder wheel that is mounted perpendicular to the shaft. The encoder wheel has teeth around the outer edge. The toothed edge of the wheel rides between two halves of an optical sensor on the interface board. It's not as complicated as it might sound, as you can see in Figure 4-2. As the spinner turns, the optical sensor sees the teeth of the encoder wheel flash by, telling the interface in which direction and how quickly the spinner is moving. Depending on the weight and size of the encoder wheel, an extra weight called a flywheel might be attached above or below it to provide extra heft and inertia to the spinner.

FIGURE 4-2: A typical spinner.
Used by permission of Happ Controls and Ultimarc.

Building your own spinner from scratch

One of the neater hacks you'll encounter while building your arcade cabinet will come from the people who build their own spinner controllers. It's one thing to take a manufactured arcade control part and find a way to interface it with a computer (which is impressive), but to take a handful of parts and build a spinner from them is the utmost in ingenuity. There are several methods for building a spinner from scratch.

A common issue to consider with all self-built spinners is the investment of time and money. At one time, purchasing a spinner and interfacing it with a computer was an expensive proposition, and building your own spinner was the only economical way to get one. Now, however, commercially made spinners for home-built arcade machines are available for as little as $48 (see *Purchasing an arcade spinner* in the next section). When compared to today's commercial spinners, a build-your-own spinner is primarily an exercise in fun for those who enjoy a clever hack rather than a great way to save money.

Note Throughout these paragraphs, the term *hack* refers to a clever use of an object or objects in a manner for which they were not originally designed. An example would be turning the guts of a hard drive into a spinner.

There are several build-your-own spinner plans available on the Internet. I've included a sampling below of a few popular and easy-to-follow guides. For a complete list, visit the spinner page on the Build Your Own Arcade Controls (BYOAC) Web site (`www.arcadecontrols .com/arcade_spinners.html`).

Twisty-Grip spinner

In 1998, a company called Retrosketch introduced a product line including a spinner under the name *Twisty-Grip*. The company has since abandoned production of spinners and has made the instructions for building them freely available online at `www.twistygrip.com/ spinners/spinners.htm`. The spinner can be made for about $78 in parts, as listed in the instructions, but with some creativity you should be able to drop that cost. Building this spinner will require using the insides of a mouse.

The plans for building the Twisty-Grip spinner are very detailed, including more than 100 pictures, and come with a parts and price list.

On the CD The instructions for building the Twisty-Grip spinner, as well as several of the following hacks, are included on the companion CD-ROM.

The QuickSpin arcade spinner project

The *QuickSpin* arcade spinner by Kendall Chun of Gearhead Labs is another build-from-scratch spinner. Designed for mounting directly into your control panel, it can be built for $30 to $40 in parts in a couple of hours. Instead of using mouse parts for its interface, the QuickSpin design connects to one of the several optical interfaces reviewed in Chapter 9, "Arcade Controls Using the Mouse Connector."

On the CD The plans for the QuickSpin are available on the companion CD-ROM and are also online at `www.gearheadlabs.com/spinner`.

Hard drive spinner hacks

The last homemade spinner design to consider is one in which you scavenge a dead hard drive for parts (see Figure 4-3). Hard drives consist of round platters mounted on a center core spinning at 5,400 revolutions per minute or faster. Because of the high speed and precision at which hard drives operate, their parts are particularly well suited for this kind of hack. Old hard drives are easy to find, and most use similar technology, so this hack is not difficult to reproduce. Several visitors to the Build Your Own Arcade Controls (BYOAC) Web site (`www.arcadecontrols.com`) have made hard drive–based spinners and documented their projects online.

One example of a spinner created with parts scavenged from a hard drive is featured on Doug Hansen's "Arcade Stupidity" at www.doughansen.net/arcade/spinner.htm and is included on the companion CD-ROM, along with well-documented instructions and two QuickTime video clips of the spinner in action. Don't let the name fool you; Doug's arcade cabinet is a project to be proud of!

The two videos of the hard drive spinner require the free QuickTime video player available from Apple at www.apple.com/quicktime. It is probably already installed on your computer.

FIGURE 4-3: The hard drive spinner hack.
Used by permission of Doug Hansen.

Purchasing an arcade spinner

You *could* build your own spinner, and doing so would certainly be within the spirit of this book. However, with so many other activities involved in creating your arcade cabinet, and the relatively low costs involved, you will probably be happier purchasing a spinner for your project. You have several choices.

Oscar Controls spinners

You will find many references to Oscar Controls (www.oscarcontrols.com) and their spinner products on the Build Your Own Arcade Controls (BYOAC) Web site and throughout the World Wide Web. The company is well regarded for the quality of their products and their customer-friendly technical support. Oscar Controls has several spinner products (see Figure 4-4) available for your home arcade cabinet — three spinner models, and six interchangeable spinner knobs. All of the Oscar Controls spinners use the same electronics and are compatible with multiple interfaces as covered in Chapter 9, "Arcade Controls Using the Mouse Connector."

FIGURE 4-4: Spinner products from Oscar Controls.
Used by permission of Oscar Controls.

Model 3 spinner

The *Model 3* is the workhorse of the Oscar Controls spinner lineup. Priced lower than the other two models, the Model 3 is a solid, reliable spinner that is available with or without a mounting plate. The mounting plate is an optional rectangular plate that mounts into your control panel from above and makes it a bit easier to install. Some people prefer not to have mounting plates covering the control panel artwork. The mounting plate makes no difference in the functionality of the spinner, so the choice of using or not using a mounting plate is mostly a cosmetic one.

The Model 3, like the other two choices from Oscar Controls, is priced without the knob for the top. This allows you to customize the look of your spinner with one of the six knobs available. Figure 4-4 in the preceding section shows the knobs available for purchase.

The Model 3 is a simple design, with a heavy-duty flywheel above a small encoder wheel (see Figure 4-5). Mounting the spinner in the control panel is very easy, requiring only a $^3/_8$-inch hole for the shaft and a couple of small screws underneath to hold the bracket in place. It will require just over $2^5/_8$ inches clearance from left to right under the panel and a mounting depth of $2^1/_{16}$ inches. This is the smallest footprint in the Oscar Controls spinners and makes it a good choice for tight quarters.

FIGURE 4-5: Model 3 spinner with *Discs of Tron* replica knob, no mounting plate.
Used by permission of Oscar Controls.

The spinner performed well in play testing. The heavy weight and small wheel give the spinner less sensitivity when you turn the knob, with a high degree of responsiveness (see the following sidebar for an explanation of sensitivity vs. responsiveness). This makes the spinner good for games needing fine control, but you'll want to boost the sensitivity for quick action games. More information on the Model 3 can be found at www.oscarcontrols.com/index_spinner.htm.

Spinner sensitivity

Sensitivity is determined by a variety of factors, including the mechanical components of the spinner, the electronics used to interface it, and software settings. This means that in a case in which the spinner's native physical sensitivity does not suit the game at hand, you can use software to adjust the sensitivity up or down. Some games are best played with less sensitive spinners, while others work better with highly sensitive spinners.

Playing a game with a spinner that is not sensitive enough will result in frustration as your game character inches slowly across the screen. Playing with a spinner that is too sensitive for a particular game is equally frustrating as your character ends up overshooting the mark. Unless you are designing a control panel specifically for one game (in which case you can pick a spinner with matching sensitivity characteristics), you will need to adjust sensitivity for one game or another.

There is a distinction between a spinner's sensitivity and its responsiveness. A spinner that has low sensitivity can still be highly responsive, meaning your on-screen character moves immediately when you turn the spinner. It just takes several turns to move your character across the screen because it is moving slowly.

The important thing to bear in mind is that low sensitivity is not a negative mark against a spinner. Low responsiveness certainly would be. Low or high sensitivity is only a matter of personal preference and should be considered in terms of the games you intend to play.

Vortex Spinner

If the Model 3 is the workhorse of the Oscar Controls line, the *Vortex Spinner* is its dragster (see Figure 4-6). The words that come to mind when attempting to describe this spinner are sleek and sexy. Okay, that may be a stretch, but the Vortex Spinner is a very well designed arcade component. It is an almost exact replica in both look and feel of the spinner controller from the *Tempest* arcade machine. The Tempest knob replica available separately from Oscar Controls makes a perfect companion for this spinner. The Vortex Spinner does not have a mounting plate option.

As with the Model 3, mounting the Vortex Spinner is very easy. It requires a single hole at least $5/8$ inch wide. The shaft of the spinner is only $1/4$ inch wide — the extra width of the hole is to accommodate part of the spinner mechanism under the control panel. The Tempest knob sits about $1/8$ inch above the control panel and completely hides the mounting hole. The underside of the spinner is mounted in a metal cage that attaches to the control panel with two screws. This cage requires a space approximately 5 inches by 4 inches under the control panel and a mounting depth of $1^7/8$ inches. The amount of space required may be a concern if you are trying to fit a spinner into a cramped control panel, so be sure to plan your layout carefully (see *Laying out your design* in Chapter 6, "Building the Control Panel").

FIGURE 4-6: The Vortex Spinner with the Tempest replica knob.
Used by permission of Oscar Controls.

The Vortex Spinner has a large encoder wheel, with a slightly smaller thin flywheel above. The large encoder wheel and lighter flywheel make this spinner very sensitive and responsive. In unscientific testing, the spinner progresses across the screen roughly 2 1/2 times as fast as the Model 3. Game play with the Vortex Spinner is excellent; it works extremely well in games requiring fast movement, and it also does a good job in games requiring fine control. You will probably end up tweaking the sensitivity in a handful of games. This spinner is my favorite of the Oscar Controls line. More information can be found at the Oscar Controls Web site: www.oscarcontrols.com/vortex.

Push/Pull spinner

If you have ever played the *Discs of Tron* arcade game, you'll be pleasantly surprised by the Oscar Controls Push/Pull spinner (see Figure 4-7). Like the Vortex Spinner, this model is a replica of an arcade original. It functions like a normal spinner but also adds the ability to pull up and push down on the knob, just like the arcade original. Doing so presses a leaf switch, making a connection as if another button had been pressed. There are a handful of games that benefit from a design like this. For instance, in *Discs of Tron* this feature was used to raise and lower aim when shooting. Complementing this spinner are two available knobs patterned after the *Discs of Tron* knob, in a metallic natural finish and anodized black.

FIGURE 4-7: Oscar Controls Push/Pull spinner with *Discs of Tron* replica knob.
Used by permission of Oscar Controls.

The Push/Pull spinner is the largest spinner presented in this section. It requires a 5-inch by 5-inch area beneath the control panel to accommodate the spinner mechanics, with a mounting depth of 4 inches. This is not a spinner that can be squeezed into a corner of a control panel as an afterthought! Mounting the Push/Pull spinner is straightforward, if a bit more involved than with the other two models. You'll start with a $^3/_8$-inch hole for the shaft and four smaller $^1/_8$-inch holes to screw in the frame. There are two metal bars $^1/_2$-inch thick that sit between the metal frame and the control panel bottom to provide proper spacing. Getting to the mounting screws requires holding the screwdriver at a bit of an angle, and installation of this spinner will be easier if it is done before any of your other controls are installed. A mounting and drilling template is available on the Oscar Controls Web site: www.oscarcontrols.com.

This spinner has the largest encoder wheel of all, measuring 4 inches across. Instead of the traditional flywheel, there is a barrel-shaped chunk of metal beneath the encoder wheel that houses the up/down mechanism as well as providing extra weight to the spinner. The Push/Pull spinner is as responsive as the other spinners sold by Oscar Controls, measuring somewhere between the Model 3 and the Vortex Spinner in terms of sensitivity. Game play with this spinner is good, with some software tweaking recommended in games requiring a high degree of sensitivity.

Although this may seem to be a niche market spinner, several people have used the up/down action functionality in a variety of ways. Because the up and down motions register as button presses, you can assign any function to them that you would a button. For instance, you might use the down motion of the spinner as a fire button in lieu of using a trigger-grip joystick to fire. One side note — because the spinner is meant to be moved up and down as well as spun, you should stick to the replica knobs instead of one of the others. Although all the knobs will fit, the inward slope on the bottom of the *Discs of Tron* replica knobs allows room for your fingers when it is pushed down, whereas another knob will not. Overall this is a very capable spinner for everyday playing, with the extra push/pull feature as a bonus. The Push/Pull spinner can be found at the Oscar Controls Web site: `www.oscarcontrols.com/index_pushpull.htm`.

SlikStik Tornado Spinner

You'll be a fan of the SlikStik *Tornado Spinner* (see Figure 4-8) the moment you try one. In fact, when I first received the Tornado Spinner I wondered if SlikStik had found a way to defy the laws of physics! Other spinners have spin times (how long the spinner will spin with one good twist) measured in seconds. The Tornado Spinner's spin time is literally measured in minutes! Of course, a long spin time doesn't add much to gameplay unless you want to fire the spinner off while you step out for a quick break. However, it is a clear indication of the workmanship and attention to detail that SlikStik has put into their product.

FIGURE **4-8:** The SlikStik Tornado Spinner with contoured knob.
Used by permission of SlikStik.

The Tornado Spinner is a compact design with a slightly different approach than most spinners. It uses the industry-standard $1/4$-inch shaft, with a small 2-inch diameter encoder wheel resting above a heavy barrel-shaped steel weight instead of the traditional flywheel design. The heavy weight and dual ball bearings are what give the Tornado Spinner its incredible spin time. The spinner mechanics are surrounded by a small bracket sized to the width of the components, making it a very compact unit. The Tornado Spinner needs only a 2-inch by 2-inch mounting space beneath the control panel, with a $2^1/2$-inch mounting depth. Mounting the Tornado Spinner is as simple as drilling a single hole between $7/16$ inch and $1/2$ inch for the shaft and four smaller holes for screwing the bracket to the control panel.

Game play with the Tornado Spinner is excellent. Control with the Tornado Spinner is good in both fast-paced games and those needing fine control. The *knurled knob* (meaning it has groves around the edge) is easy to grip and to start and stop spinning. The knobs are available in both skirted and nonskirted shapes in six anodized colors (black, green, red, purple, blue, and natural aluminum). The smaller skirted knob has a better feel, though that is certainly a subjective view. The combination of compact mounting requirements, responsive control, and multiple available colors make this an excellent candidate for your arcade cabinet. You can learn more about the Tornado Spinner online at the SlikStick Web site: `www.slikstik.com`.

Picking a spinner

All of the commercial spinners presented in this section are good choices — there are no lemons in the lot. Of the Oscar Controls line of spinners, the best overall choice is the Vortex Spinner. It has the best feel and sensitivity for the majority of spinner-based games. Its counterpart from SlikStik, the Tornado Spinner, is also an outstanding choice for a multipurpose spinner with excellent feel and responsiveness. Choosing between them is a toss-up and comes down to cosmetics and physical mounting constraints. In fact, many people have made their own ideal spinner by choosing the spinner from one vendor and a knob from the other.

The other spinners from Oscar Controls are also superb choices. For versatility, the Push/Pull spinner cannot be beat. If you are planning to play a game that requires such a controller, such as *Discs of Tron* or *Zwackery*, there simply is no substitute. If you're trying to put a spinner into your control panel on a tight budget, the lower-cost Model 3 will fit the bill. Regardless of which of the available commercial spinners you choose, you are likely to be very happy with your choice. For another perspective on spinner choices, there's a good roundup review of spinners on the RetroBlast! Web site at `http://retroblast.com/reviews/roundup.html`.

Trackball Choices

As you look over the many arcade games available for your arcade cabinet project (see Chapter 14, "Choosing and Loading Software"), you'll quickly realize that no control panel is truly complete without a trackball. Trying to play *Centipede* with a joystick just can't compare to the real thing. One of the best reasons to include a trackball in your arcade cabinet is operating system control. Unless you are using an operating system that's not graphical, such as MS-DOS, you'll need some way to move your cursor. Having to pull out a mouse every time you want to select a game or turn off your computer hampers the arcade atmosphere you're trying to recreate. When you connect a trackball to your computer, it is recognized as a mouse. Because of this, you can have the best of both worlds. You can maintain the arcade look and feel while still being able to control your computer.

Although they differ in appearance, trackballs and spinners are distant cousins to one another and operate under the same principals. Where a spinner has a single optical encoder and recognizes movement in one dimension along the X or Y axis, a trackball has two encoders and moves in two dimensions along both axes. With a spinner you typically move left and right across the screen (sometimes up and down). With a trackball you move freely around the screen. Instead of using a knob and shaft to turn along one axis, trackballs typically have a solid ball resting on two rollers attached to encoder wheels oriented 90 degrees to one another. There may be a third roller providing support that is not connected to an encoder wheel. In Figure 4-9, you can see a partially disassembled 3-inch Happ Controls trackball. The ball sits in the center, surrounded on either side by the horizontal (X) and vertical (Y) axis encoder wheels. Moving straight along the X or Y axis turns one roller and encoder wheel, producing movement in one direction. Moving at any angle other than straight horizontal or vertical turns both rollers, producing movement in the appropriate direction. This works exactly like a mouse. In fact, if you turn a mouse on its back, you essentially have a trackball!

FIGURE 4-9: Happ Controls trackball with the cover off.
Used by permission of Happ Controls.

Unfortunately, trackballs have not received quite as much attention in the home arcade cabinet field as spinners and there are fewer trackball options. There are modified computer trackball projects but there are no start-from-scratch designs. Some of the trackballs designed for personal computers are well-suited for arcade cabinets, but be aware that specific models tend to come and go. Commercial arcade trackballs are available that can be interfaced to your arcade cabinet as well. Factors to consider when choosing a trackball include the size of the ball, color/translucency, mounting requirements, and interface.

Trackballs come in a variety of sizes, ranging from small 1-inch models to large 4^1/$_2$-inch models. The size you should consider depends on the amount of space you have available on your control panel and how often you intend to use the trackball. If your space is limited or you intend to play only a small number of trackball games, a small trackball is your best bet. If you have the space, however, or if you are a fan of trackball games such as *Golden Tee* for the PC, then a big trackball is a must. The sweet spot for trackball size seems to be 3 inches, providing a good compromise in feel versus space required.

You can typically find trackballs in red, white, blue, yellow, green, black, and colorless varieties. A few are also available with an underlying light source to illuminate the trackball. A glowing trackball can really boost the *wow* factor!

Your final consideration in trackball selection is the interface choice. You have four options:

- Arcade trackball to custom arcade interface
- PC trackball to PC interface
- Arcade trackball to PC interface
- PC trackball to custom arcade interface

I'll discuss these options in depth in Chapter 9, "Arcade Controls Using the Mouse Connector," but in general the first two interfaces are the easiest options. Those are simply a matter of obtaining the trackball and the appropriate interface (if it is not already built-in) and connecting them. The third and fourth options require some electronics work or hacking and aren't recommended unless there is a compelling reason to attempt them, such as making a trackball fit with choices you've already made or finding inexpensive parts to use.

Computer trackballs

There are pros and cons to choosing a PC trackball for your arcade cabinet. The primary benefits are price, availability, and ease of installation. Some of the drawbacks include feel and difficulty of installation. What? Didn't I just say installation was easy? On the one hand, connecting a PC trackball to your computer is very easy because that's precisely what it's designed for. Plug the trackball into the appropriate port on your computer, perhaps install a driver, and it's ready to go. The difficult part of the installation comes when figuring out where to mount the trackball. Unlike an arcade trackball, which is meant to be placed in a control panel, a PC trackball is meant to sit on a desk. Take a look at Figure 4-10. The curved housing on the typical PC trackball shown in the top of the figure would make mounting it in a control panel difficult.

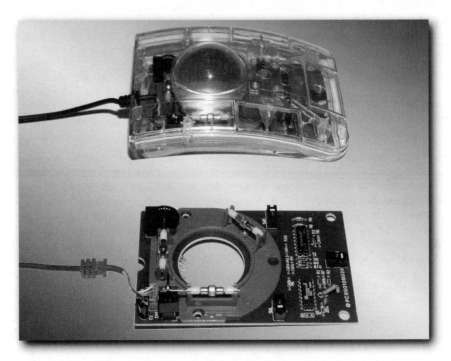

FIGURE 4-10: A typical PC trackball, assembled (top) and disassembled (bottom).

Fortunately, PC trackballs tend to be fairly simple devices and can be taken apart easily. You can see this same trackball removed from its housing in the bottom half of Figure 4-10. The circuit board is flat and has a couple of screw holes for mounting. Designing a wooden enclosure for this and mounting it to the underside of your control panel would not be difficult. Vendors such as Happ Controls sell mounting plates for various sized trackballs that could be used to make the installation look clean and professional.

PC trackballs have the benefit of being relatively cheap and easy to find. Trackballs such as the one pictured in Figure 4-10 can be purchased for as little as $16 from a variety of online and brick-and-mortar stores. It is also possible to find high-quality PC trackballs for as much as $100. You might hesitate to tear apart such an expensive item, however, particularly since an arcade trackball can be purchased for a comparable sum. The most significant drawback to a PC trackball is the feel. The feel of an item is subjective and difficult to describe. However, a PC trackball tends to have a lighter feel that is not well-suited for game play. When you are playing *Centipede*, you want to be able to madly slam the trackball across the screen. Most PC trackballs will stop moving as soon as you let go of them. They're designed for fine mouse control, not game playing.

Arcade trackballs

You'll find that a real arcade trackball complements an arcade cabinet very well. Not only do you get the look and feel of a real arcade trackball, you also retain the benefit of mouse control. Arcade trackballs are available from a variety of arcade parts vendors, and all typically use the same electronic interfaces. This means the technique used to connect a trackball from Happ Controls will work for a Wico or Betson trackball as well. This interchangeability allows you to choose an arcade trackball based on other criteria, such as price and appearance, without worrying about whether or not you can use it.

Arcade trackballs (see Figure 4-11) have a heft and feel that are obviously designed for game play. When you give one a mad spin, it continues to move briefly after you let go while a PC trackball will stop. The first time you play *Centipede* or *Missile Command* with a real arcade trackball instead of a mouse or PC trackball, you'll feel the difference. Arcade trackballs are available in sizes ranging from $1^1/_2$ inch to $4^1/_2$ inches, with the $2^1/_4$-inch and 3-inch sizes being the most popular. The $2^1/_4$-inch trackballs also use the same size ball as a standard pool ball. Several people have given their control panels a distinctive look by using an eight ball as their trackball. The translucent arcade trackballs are also a nice addition to a control panel but are a bit lighter than solid trackballs. This gives them slightly less inertia but does not have a detrimental effect on game play.

FIGURE 4-11: A Happ Controls 3-inch translucent trackball.
Used by permission of Happ Controls.

Connecting an arcade trackball to your PC will involve either some effort in hacking and electrical work or an investment in purchasing a special interface. The inexpensive way involves disassembling a mouse and using its innards. The easier way involves simply purchasing one of several interfaces available for this purpose. As mentioned earlier, the specifics of interfacing trackballs and other components will be covered in Chapter 9, "Arcade Controls Using the Mouse Connector." However, unless you are on a budget, the recommended choice is to purchase one of the dedicated trackball interfaces.

Putting in an arcade trackball will require some thought about space requirements. For instance, the 3-inch arcade trackball from Happ Controls (shown in Figure 4-12) occupies roughly $2^1/_2$ inches above the control pane, and approximately $5^1/_2$ x $5^1/_2$ inches below. As with the Push/Pull spinner described in the previous section, adding a trackball is not something that can easily be done as an afterthought. Even if an arcade trackball is outside your immediate budget, you might consider leaving an adequate amount of space in your control panel to add one later.

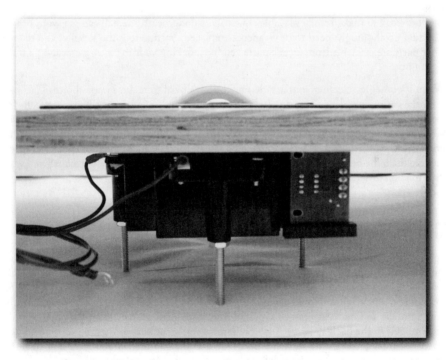

FIGURE 4-12: An assembled 3-inch Happ Controls trackball, showing the 5½ -inch-squared space required.

Used by permission of Happ Controls.

You might think that mounting an arcade trackball involves only cutting the proper sized hole for the ball to extend through. However, trackball mounting is probably one of the more involved jobs when creating a control panel. Different trackball models have different needs, but you will almost always end up cutting a large hole in your panel in the shape of the trackball housing. With a $3/4$-inch panel, if you cut only a circle out then only the tip of the trackball will extend through. You'll want the surface of the trackball housing to be essentially flush with the surface of the control panel. To complete a trackball installation, usually you will add a trackball mounting plate. Happ Controls has two styles of mounting plates available, which fit its company's trackballs as well as those from several other vendors. There is one model in which the mounting hardware is hidden beneath the plate, presenting you with a smooth surface above, and one model in which the mounting bolts are exposed from the top. The smooth surface plate is only a few dollars more and gives the control panel a much nicer look.

You can expect to pay upwards of $100 to $150 for a new arcade trackball from a parts supplier. However, with a bit of patience you can find great deals on them. Either through an after-market source such as eBay or by purchasing refurbished units from the manufacturers, an arcade trackball can be purchased for less than $50. You might need to do some work on a used trackball to make it fully playable. The rollers underneath the ball can get worn or gummed up and might need to be cleaned or replaced. Fortunately, the supplies and replacement parts are available from arcade parts vendors, making your inexpensive deal on a trackball a good one.

When it comes to selecting your arcade trackball, it's hard to make a poor choice. Trackballs from the various vendors all tend to be of high quality and functionality. New trackballs from the arcade parts houses are expensive, while used or refurbished trackballs can be purchased at a substantial discount. Because of the standard interfaces used, your selection can be based on pricing and cosmetic and tactile features. The general rule of thumb is the bigger and heavier the trackball, the better the game play. Your best bet is to pick the size of trackball you want, then to shop different suppliers to find the best deal.

Summary

Spinners and trackballs are almost must-haves for your arcade cabinet project. You can do without them, but you'll be missing out on a large selection of fun games if you do. If you've only got space or resources for one, go with a trackball. Having two axes, a trackball can substitute for a spinner in a pinch, but a spinner cannot substitute for a trackball since it only moves along one axis. Spinners and trackballs can be acquired from a range of sources, from the buy-it-off-the-shelf models to the hack-it-yourself variety. Unless you're looking to exercise your ingenuity or save some money, forego the hacked units in favor of the commercial products. The quality and convenience of the commercial models make them too good of a deal to pass up.

In Chapter 5, "Arcade Controls for Power Gamers," I'll introduce you to a few more arcade controls. You'll see them used less often, but no book on the subject is complete without them!

Arcade Controls for Power Gamers

So, you've judged the joysticks, bought your buttons, selected a spinner, and tried a trackball. What's next? With this assortment of arcade controls, you've covered most of the games available. But, what if you're seriously into racing or flying? What if target practice is more your speed? What if you have fast feet itching for a good dance game? This chapter is for you!

In this chapter, I'll introduce you to the remaining arcade controls covered in this book:

➤ Steering wheels and pedals

➤ Flight yokes

➤ Light guns

➤ Dance pads

All of these make great additions to an arcade cabinet, but few games require them. You'll need to decide if adding them is worthwhile. Each control requires additional effort to install and interface and occupies space on the arcade cabinet. Space, as you probably are beginning to realize, is at a premium on most arcade cabinets. For each control in this chapter, you must weigh the games you want to be able to play against the resources required to install the needed control. I'll take a look at each of the controls in turn.

Steering Wheels and Pedals

Picture yourself driving a classic Porsche convertible. You're cruising along the open road in the Swiss Alps with snow on the ground and sun in the sky. Passing a crystal-clear lake, you come upon a stretch of straight, open road. A catchy tune is playing on the radio that's got your blood pumping, and you decide to open up the speed and see what the car can do. Ready to shift gears and hit the gas, you eagerly reach for. . .a couple of pushbuttons? It doesn't quite work, does it? There are some really awesome driving simulations available for the PC (the one described previously is Need For Speed Porsche Unleashed by Electronic Arts, my all-time favorite), but they just aren't as satisfying without a steering wheel and pedals.

How steering wheels work

Steering wheels — and pedals (assume pedals are included when I mention steering wheels) — usually appear to the computer as a 2-axis joystick. These are devices for which the computer registers how far and in which direction along the X and Y axes the control is pointing. Normally, the wheel part appears as the X axis, and the pedals appear as the Y axis. Figure 5-1 shows the Game Controllers Properties dialog box in Windows XP of a typical steering wheel. The crosshair in the X Axis/Y Axis box shows the position of the wheel and pedals. When the crosshair is in the middle of the box, neither the wheel nor the pedals are being used.

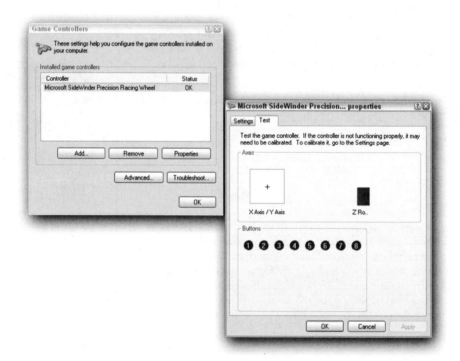

FIGURE 5-1: Game Controllers Properties dialog box, which shows the steering wheel sitting idle.
Screen shot reprinted by permission of Microsoft Corporation.

Steering the wheel left will move the crosshair to the left, and moving the wheel right will shift the crosshair to the right. That's basically intuitive. Slightly less intuitive is what happens with the pedals. Pressing down on the gas will move the crosshair upward along the Y axis whereas pressing the brake will move it downward, as you can see in Figure 5-2. In a game, movement up on the Y axis means accelerate, movement down means decelerate, and movement left or right on the X axis means steer left or right.

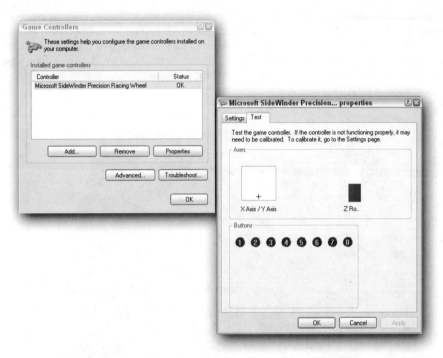

FIGURE 5-2: Game Controllers Properties dialog box, which shows the steering wheel idle while the brake pedal is pressed.
Screen shot reprinted by permission of Microsoft Corporation.

Sharing a single axis for the pedal and brake is referred to as a *single-axis setup*. Some steering wheels use a dual-axis mechanism for the gas and brake pedals. In this configuration, the steering wheel is on an axis, the gas pedal is on a second axis, and the brake pedal is on a third axis. In a single-axis pedal system, you can either brake or accelerate, but, if you try to do both simultaneously, the commands cancel each other out, and the computer does not see either pedal as pressed. In a dual-axis configuration, you can press both the gas and brake pedals together, and the computer will see both inputs. This allows you to do things such as powering through a curve, which uses the gas to accelerate and the brakes to send the rear of the car into a controlled skid. Some games support a single-axis system; some support a dual-axis system. If you are building or hacking your own pedals to the game port, an easy modification can add a switch that will convert your pedals between single- and dual-axis mode. I'll cover this in Chapter 10, "Miscellaneous Bits of Arcade Trickery." Using a switch in your pedals means you can have the best of both worlds.

Because form follows function, almost all steering wheels work under the same principle. Although the design may vary, the core mechanism is likely to be analog in nature, which means potentiometers. In Figure 5-3, you can see the inside of a typical set of pedals with the bottom removed (a lot of warranties were voided in the creation of this book). Two potentiometers sit

in the middle back-to-back, turning when the pedals are pressed. In this case, the two potentiometers are electrically wired in series as one axis, which makes this a single-axis steering
wheel. The steering wheel also has a potentiometer that is connected to the shaft of the wheel
and turns as the wheel turns. Other wheels and pedals have similar mechanisms. This means,
whether you buy, build, or convert a steering wheel, you're likely to be able to get it to work
with your arcade cabinet.

FIGURE 5-3: Inside view of a typical set of pedals.

Buying a wheel

You will find many opinions on what types of steering wheels to purchase. Ultimately, they are
just that—opinions. I cannot recommend one particular wheel—if for no other reason than
the fact that, by the time you read this, the available models are likely to have changed. Today's
hot steering wheel choice may be unavailable or second fiddle to tomorrow's top contender. I
will give you some guidelines to consider when making your choice.

Steering wheels by Act Labs, Logitech, Microsoft, Saitek, and Thrustmaster are among the
popular choices even though many others exist. When it comes to purchasing a steering wheel,
you should spend some time researching your choices. The message forums at the Build Your
Own Arcade Controls (BYOAC) Web site (www.arcadecontrols.com) and various news

groups, such as rec.autos.simulators (`http://groups.google.com/groups?group=rec.autos.simulators`), are excellent places to get opinions on available steering wheels. However, there is no substitute for heading down to your local computer store and trying the feel of the wheels for yourself. As you do, you should take into account the following concerns:

- **How the steering wheel feels.** There is nothing more important than how the steering wheel feels to you. Some things, such as reliability, are *as* important, but, if you're planning to spend any amount of time using the wheel at all, it needs to be comfortable. For instance, a steering wheel that's too small for you will probably cause your arms to cramp with extended play, and a cheap plastic wheel won't feel as good as a deluxe model with a leather grip. Testing the feel may be difficult to do in the store because you're not likely to find steering wheels set up where you can sit and try them. Most displays are at eye level and can be tried only standing up. Give it a good "test drive" anyway. If someone looks at you funny, make a "beep-beep" sound, and wiggle your eyebrows. They'll go away quietly.

- **Don't neglect the pedals.** Pedals should provide some resistance so you don't end up instantly slamming them to the floor but not so much that you get fatigued. Also, the underside should have some mechanism to provide friction on the floor. Having your pedals slip away from you while you're powering through a U-turn at mach-5 is very annoying.

- **The wheel's interface.** Some will connect via the game port; others will connect via the Universal Serial Bus (USB) port (a newer type of connection found on both PC and Macintosh computers). Either is fine. Just make sure it meshes with your game plan. For instance, most computers have only one game port, which supports only one wheel and pedal set, whereas they'll have at least two USB ports supporting literally hundreds of devices.

- **Supported features.** Some steering wheels, such as the Logitech MOMO series, have extra features supported in certain games. However, if you're not planning to play those games, the extra features do not help you and may not be worth the extra cost. Also, make sure the steering wheel indicates it supports the operating system you're planning to use.

- **Consumer beware.** The rest of it is standard consumer shopping sense. Although PC steering wheels will sometimes go on sale, a good one will cost you between $50 and $150. You should probably steer clear of a wheel that sells for $25 or less. (Did I promise not to pun anymore?) Factors such as durability and warranty should obviously be considered as well.

You can also take the steering wheel from a PlayStation (or other game console) and connect it to a PC with a converter. Reported results are mixed, but this can be an inexpensive way to add a steering wheel to a computer. Some extra effort will be involved in connecting the wheel and tweaking software settings to make everything work. Unless you have a compelling reason, I would recommend against purchasing a game console steering wheel for your arcade cabinet. However, one good reason to go this route might be if you were going to have an arcade cabinet housing both a PC and a game console. With a game console steering wheel and a converter, you could use the same controls on both systems.

Building a wheel

For the hard-core do-it-yourselfer, building is the only way to go, and some people like to build their own steering wheels from scratch. These wheels start life as a few pieces of wood and miscellaneous bits of hardware and end up as functional steering wheel masterpieces. There are as many steering wheel designs as there are arcade cabinet designs, but all build upon the common steering wheel principles introduced in the beginning of this section. Normally, a steering wheel includes these four parts:

- The wheel assembly
- The shaft, including a potentiometer
- The mounting platform
- Pedals

The steering wheel is assembled from a few layers of wood in a typical steering wheel shape. This assembly is attached to a shaft composed of various parts from a hardware store, which ends in a potentiometer. Next, this is attached to a platform of some kind, such as a mocked-up dashboard or, in our case, an arcade cabinet. Finally, pedals are made from wood and parts from hardware and automotive stores. The homemade wheels are attached via the game port to the computer and show up as generic driving controllers. Some of the results are very professional with projects running the gamut from desktop steering wheels to fully enclosed racing cockpits.

Covering the details of building a steering wheel and cockpit would take far more than the allotted page limit of this book. However, I will point you in the right direction if you decide to go this route. Several excellent Web sites are available on the subject. The following are some of the best :

- Lew's Wheels at `www.monmouth.com/~lw4750/` is one of the definitive Web sites on steering wheel construction. Lew will walk you through all the steps needed to build a steering wheel and pedals.

- Build Your Own PC Wheel & Pedals at `www.gunpowder.freeserve.co.uk/wheels/` is another excellent how-to Web site. The diagrams are detailed and easy-to-follow. This site is also home to a message forum (`http://members.boardhost.com/wheelforum`) where you can chat with other steering wheel enthusiasts.

- SimRacingWorld has an eight-page article (`www.simracingworld.com/content/36/`) detailing one person's construction of a steering wheel setup.

- Finally, Race Sim Central (`http://forum.racesimcentral.com/`) has a message forum entitled "Building Your Own Cockpit, Wheel, etc." that is an excellent resource.

You'll find other sites and steering wheel projects to look at that are linked from the preceding Web sites. Building steering wheels and cockpits is an entire hobby in itself, which is akin to building an arcade cabinet. Many fans of one hobby end up dabbling in the other as well.

Converting an arcade wheel

Somewhere between the simplicity (and expense) of buying a wheel and the complexity of building a wheel lies the relatively cheap and easy compromise of converting an arcade wheel. Arcade wheels are extremely sturdy and come in a variety of shapes and sizes. They can often be found for as little as $20 at auctions and online. Using an arcade steering wheel has one clear advantage: It's already designed to be installed in an arcade cabinet, so it should be easy to convert. Figure 5-4 shows an example of an upright racing cabinet.

FIGURE 5-4: A three-player upright racing cabinet with wheels and pedals.

You'll run into one interesting issue with arcade steering wheels versus PC steering wheels. Many arcade games use a 360-degree steering wheel, which means it can be turned in a complete circle (for games that require it, such as a demolition derby). Most PC driving games use a 270-degree wheel, which means you can turn sharply left or sharply right but not completely around. A 360-degree wheel uses an optical encoder wheel and appears to the computer as a spinner control. A 270-degree wheel uses potentiometers and appears to the computer as an analog joystick, as discussed in the previous section on buying wheels. If you're planning to play only PC-based driving games, then a 270-degree steering wheel will work fine. If you're planning to play an arcade driving game, either through a PC-remake or emulation (see Chapter 14, "Choosing and Loading Software"), then you might need to consider a 360-degree wheel.

Some arcade steering wheels have used 270-degree wheels. However, most of the older wheels that you're likely to find will be of the 360-degree variety. If you're thinking of choosing a 360-degree wheel, consider the following first. It is possible, albeit unrealistic, to play a 360-degree driving game with your spinner. Add to that consideration the fact that there are a limited number of 360-degree driving games whereas the majority of PC driving games are geared toward 270-degree wheels. Driving a 360-degree game with a 270-degree wheel and vice versa are both fairly unsatisfactory. Ultimately, if you're planning only casual use of a steering wheel, you'll probably be happier buying a PC-based 270-degree wheel than using an arcade-based 360-degree wheel. Some driving enthusiasts have designed steering wheel panels with two wheels — one of each kind — to make sure they always have the right wheel for the game.

Converting an arcade steering wheel to a PC steering wheel is not very difficult. If it's a 360-degree wheel, you'll use a hack similar to that used for spinners and trackballs as covered in the previous chapter, "Taking Your Game Out for a Spin — Spinners and Trackballs." If you'll be converting a 270-degree wheel, you'll need to take into account the potentiometers used. Arcade steering wheels typically use 5K potentiometers (also known as *pots*) whereas PCs typically use 100K pots. You have two options. You can swap the 5K pots with 100k pots and wire the wheel directly into the PC's game port. Doing so is relatively easy. The only difficult part is finding a potentiometer that is physically the right size and mounting it. You can also use an analog-based game pad, such as the Microsoft Sidewinder Dual Strike, which essentially uses 5K pots and connects via the USB port. Because of the similar rating of the potentiometers in the Dual Strike, you can disconnect the Dual Strike's potentiometers from the PCB (Printed Circuit Board) and connect wires from the steering wheel's potentiometers to the PCB instead. This same technique can be used for a variety of analog/potentiometer-based arcade controls such as flight yokes and analog joysticks. I'll cover the details of this hack in Chapter 10, "Miscellaneous Bits of Arcade Trickery." Beyond the interface hacking necessary to use an arcade steering wheel, the rest is just physical mounting, which will vary depending on which wheel you're using and where on your cabinet you wish to mount it.

Shifting gears

You'll need to incorporate a way to shift gears in your steering wheel setup unless you plan to only drive automatic vehicles in games that support them. Most PC-based steering wheels come with a mechanism for shifting gears, either via onboard paddles or an attached gearstick. Standalone arcade shifters are also available in a variety of models. The immediate difficulty you'll run into is that different games incorporate shifters in different ways. There are three main styles:

■ The first is a hi/lo shifter, wherein you're either going fast or slow. The hi/lo shifter usually has one microswitch, which is in low gear when the switch is not pressed, in high gear when it is, or vice versa. Occasionally, you will find a hi/lo arcade shifter that uses a potentiometer that varies from 0K at low to 5K at high. This is actually a throttle, not a shifter, and is not very useful in this instance.

■ The second is a shift-up/shift-down shifter. These are similar to hi/lo shifters in that they are two positional. However, where a hi/lo shifter remains either in high or low gear, these shifters rest in neutral. Pushing into HI tells the computer to up-shift;

pushing into LO tells the computer to down-shift. Once you shift up or down, the shifter returns to neutral. Most PC wheels include paddles with this functionality—one paddle for up-shifting and one for down-shifting.

■ The third style of shifter you'll encounter is a more traditional multispeed shifter with first through fourth (or higher) gears and reverse. The multispeed shifters typically have a series of switches—normally one switch for each gear—although other styles exist.

Which shifter suits your purposes depends on the types of games you wish to play. Most PC-based driving games will use the second style of shifter. Emulated arcade–style driving games might use any of the three styles listed. The drawback to any of these is that, once you've chosen one of them, you have restricted the number of driving games you can play. The following paragraphs describe a few solutions to this dilemma.

Multiple shifters

Declaring that "the right tool for the right job is not just a motto, they're words to live by!" some hard-core driving enthusiasts use multiple shifters on their cabinets. Usually, you'll only have room for these if you're making a dedicated driving cabinet that is free from non-driving controls or are using a swappable control panel scheme. One of the most creative projects I've seen is a sit-down racing cabinet made by Todd Rosen with horizontally rotating control panels (You'll get a look at this cabinet in Chapter 18, "Online Places to Go"). When you're ready to switch from one game to another, you simply rotate the control panel until the appropriate wheel and shifter combination are in place. This is quite a significant undertaking and is not for the casual driving enthusiast.

The Act-Labs GPL USB shifter

You'll appreciate the Act-Labs GPL USB shifter the moment you lay eyes on it (see Figure 5-5). The shifter is an excellent product—simple in design yet well thought out. It is a self-contained shifter apparatus with eight positions that connects via USB and appears to the computer as an eight-button game controller with each gear corresponding to a button. Overlay plates are available, which currently includes five-, six-, and seven-position models. These overlay plates restrict which of the eight positions the gearstick can be moved into, which determines the number of gears available in the game. In the multigear position settings, the shifter locks into each of the gears and stays there until moved. When in gear, the button is pressed; when in neutral, no button is pressed.

The unit I received included two extra overlay plates, one to convert it from an eight-position shifter to a seven-position and a hi/lo model. These plates are not included in the current shipping model. However, creating your own overlay plates out of sheet metal or wood using the original eight-position plate as a template would be easy. With the hi/lo plate I have installed (see Figure 5-6), the shifter registers button 3 for high and button 4 for low. The shifter springs back to center instead of locking into place as the length of the cutouts in the overlay restricts travel, which prevents the gearstick from entering the locked position. You can control the locking versus return-to-neutral behavior in your own custom overlay plate by controlling the amount of travel the gearstick is allowed. With the use of custom overlay plates, you can emulate all three shifter styles listed at the beginning of this section, which provides an all-in-one solution!

FIGURE 5-5: The Act-Labs GPL USB shifter in native eight-position mode.
Courtesy of Act-Labs Ltd.

Software support of the Act-Labs GPL USB shifter is a mixed bag with a limited number of PC games supporting it natively. However, Act-Labs supplies a utility that enables support of the shifter in a wide range of games. Games that do not natively support the shifter generally support up-shifting and down-shifting. In these games, going from fifth gear to second gear requires cycling through fourth and third. Games that natively support the shifter allow you to drop from fifth to second gear without going through the intermediate gears, which allows the appropriate affect of a rapid downshift. The utility provided by Act-Labs mimics native mode support by rapidly cycling through the gears for you. When you physically drop the shifter from fifth to second gear, the utility cycles through fourth and third gears. With this utility, Act-Labs lists 62 games that support the shifter as of the time of this writing. Also, because the shifter appears to Windows as an eight-button game controller, any driving game that allows you to assign the controls should work. MAME falls into this category and works well with the Act-Labs GPL USB shifter.

FIGURE 5-6: The same shifter with the hi/lo overlay plate installed.

Mounting the shifter is easy. It comes with a mounting bracket that screws into the bottom of the shifter, which is adjustable for left-handed or right-handed installation. You can either use a c-clamp to secure it for temporary installation or design a permanent housing. For permanent mounting, cutting a round hole that is just large enough for the shifter plate to be flush with the control panel and then attaching the mounting bracket to a supporting piece of wood works well. The bottom of the shifter is tucked away beneath the control panel, which leaves only the knob, shaft, and overlay plate extended above and provides a realistic look and feel.

Building a shifter

Once more, the cry of "buying is the easy way out!" is heard. Like building a wheel, step-by-step details on building a shifter are beyond the scope of this book. However, also like building a wheel, resources are available online for building your own shifter. Homemade shifters tend to be built along the same lines as the Act-Labs GPL USB shifter described in the previous section. In fact, many of them use the same utility software as the Act-Labs model to provide shifter functionality in racing programs. Building a shifter can be broken down into three parts: mechanical, electrical, and software. The mechanical portion deals with assembling a gearstick and knob, which creates the shifter housing, and physically assembling the parts. The electrical portion deals with connecting the switches and interfacing the assembly to the computer.

Finally, the software portion involves configuring the shifter for use on your PC and supporting the shifter in games, which often uses the Act-Labs utility. Here are a few sites to visit for more details if you would like to build your own shifter:

- The Homemade Racing Controllers site at `www.massey.ac.nz/~jcmarsha/ Wheel/` has a very good write-up on building a shifter, including software drivers to get it to function in Windows.

- The FreeShift site at `http://hem.bredband.net/larlow/how.htm` also has a good write-up with excellent diagrams.

- The Home Built USB H-Shifter site at `http://users.hfx.eastlink.ca/ ~mackaypenny/shifter.html` provides another look at building a shifter and includes several pictures.

- Zooomz Zu Zu Pedals at `http://users.eastlink.ca/~mikegiles/racin/ home.html` provides pictures without accompanying text that are nonetheless worth viewing if you're going this route.

- Finally, How to Build Your Own PC Wheel & Pedals at `www.gunpowder .freeserve.co.uk/wheels/main.htm` has a section on building a gearstick with detailed illustrations.

Final word about steering wheels

Steering wheels turn ordinary driving games from casual diversions to amazing simulations. Many a weekend has been spent at the St.Clair household playing head-to-head *Need For Speed Porsche Unleashed* with our steering wheels. You'll need to consider the games you wish to play before you decide on a particular steering wheel configuration or let the steering wheel you've chosen dictate which games will work properly. If you're planning to stick to PC-based racing games, any PC steering wheel you purchase will essentially work although quality varies. If playing emulated arcade racing games is more your speed, you'll need to consider degrees of motion of the steering wheel and types of shifter. Choosing this route, you'll either need to come up with a compromise solution that handles most of the games you'd like to play or a multiwheel configuration to try to support them all. A good force feedback PC steering wheel with the Act-Labs GPL USB shifter is probably the ideal setup for casual use.

Many classic arcade driving games were upright models. It may then surprise you to learn that I am not a fan of adding a steering wheel and pedals to an upright arcade cabinet. In my opinion, driving games are best played sitting down! You certainly can add a wheel and pedals to an upright arcade cabinet, but you may find it unsatisfying. Does this mean that you should abandon driving simulations altogether? Certainly not. For occasional driving, some people substitute a spinner for a steering wheel. However, you still need to drag out pedals for acceleration and braking or use buttons on the control panel. Either way, it's still not ideal. The best option is to start planning your second project, the sit-down driving cabinet! A driving cabinet with a real bucket seat, large screen, and surround sound speakers makes for one heck of an arcade experience!

Note My recommendation to use steering wheels and pedals with sit-down driving cabinets only is obviously an opinion and not a matter of fact. There are people who use steering wheels quite happily on upright or even cocktail cabinets. If you'll pardon the pun, your mileage may vary.

Flight Yokes

Flight yokes are similar to steering wheels in look and feel. There is usually a set of hand grips that turn like a wheel with optional accompanying pedals (see Figure 5-7). In fact, a good flight yoke can be substituted for a steering wheel for occasional play of driving games. The one significant difference is that steering wheels are designed to control vehicles that stay on a level surface and need to control movement only along the X (horizontal) and Y (forward/backward) axes. Flight adds another dimension of control required along the Z axis (up and down). This is accomplished by allowing the yoke to push in and out or sometimes tilt forward and back, as well as turning left and right. Normally, pushing forward will angle your vehicle down, and pulling backward will angle your vehicle up.

FIGURE 5-7: The CH Products LE Flight Yoke and optional pedals.
Photo courtesy of CH Products.

Buying a flight yoke

The commercial flight yoke field is dominated by the CH Products line of flight simulator controllers (www.chproducts.com/retail/gp_flight_sim.html). Both USB and gameport products are available, which range in price from $100 and go up to $565 depending on model. Yokes from other vendors appear to be in scarce supply with models coming and going quickly. Only CH Products seems to be actively developing, marketing, and supporting quality flight yokes. Reviews of the CH Products flight yokes are overwhelmingly positive.

Building a flight yoke

As with racing enthusiasts, some serious flight simulator fans have built their own flight controls and cockpit simulators. This is another hobby that is akin to arcade cabinet building. With more than 775 projects listed in the database at the Build Your Own Arcade Controls (BYOAC) Web site, you might expect to find at least one project that included a traditional flight controller. However, upon gathering details for this book, I could not find a single arcade cabinet that includes an aircraft flight controller yoke as one of its controls. See the next section for what arcade cabinet fans have been doing instead.

Building a flight yoke follows a similar procedure as building a steering wheel. Projects range from something as simple as a desktop-mounted flight controller to fully enclosed flight cockpits complete with multiple displays and motion simulation. One of these undertakings is not for the casual fan! If you are interested in building your own flight controller or cockpit simulator, you will find many excellent online resources are available to guide you. I have gathered a set of resources to get you started.

- Your first stop should probably be the Cockpits Web ring at http://a.webring .com/hub?ring=cockpits. A Web ring is a collection of Web sites relating to the same topic. As of this writing, the Cockpits Web ring lists 31 sites.

- How to Build a Cockpit at http://home.wanadoo.nl/norbert.bosch/ includes details and pictures on yoke, throttle, and cockpit construction.

- SimPits International at www.simpits.org is a Web site community for flight simulator cockpit designers. It includes articles, links, and forums.

- Finally, Build Your Own Cockpit at http://mypage.direct.ca/b/bsimpson/ byoc~1a.html includes many articles on flight controller construction.

The *Star Wars* yoke

One flight yoke is the Holy Grail to arcade collectors and home arcade cabinet builders alike — the *Star Wars* flight yoke. *Star Wars* was a vector-based arcade game put out by Atari that put you at the controls of a TIE Fighter going up against the Death Star. The game was a runaway hit with both an upright cabinet and an absolutely stunning enclosed cockpit cabinet. The centerpiece of the system was the yoke controller, which is pictured in Figure 5-8. The yoke would turn left and right, and the handles would pivot forward and back. The yoke was analog-based, which means it had potentiometers for the *X* and *Y* axes. Firing buttons at the finger and thumb positions made rapid firing easy.

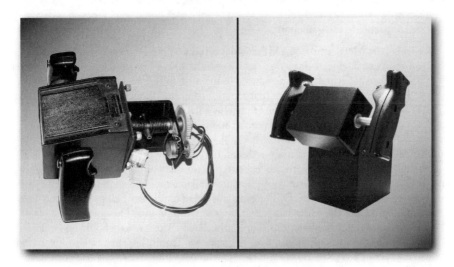

FIGURE 5-8: Left, original *Star Wars* yoke. Right, GameCab.com yoke.
Photo courtesy of GameCab.com.

Like most classic arcade masterpieces, these controllers are no longer made. Collectors covet these yokes for *Star Wars* cabinet restorations while home arcade cabinet builders seek them for their projects. With a limited number of yokes available, this demand has often put collectors and home cabinet builders at odds. See Appendix B, "The Great Debate — Preserving vs. MAME'ing the Past," for more on this topic. Fortunately, as of 2004, this is no longer an issue as commercial replicas of this yoke have become available. GameCab.com (www.gamecab.com) is selling the yoke pictured at right in Figure 5-8, and another vendor has expressed interest in following suit. For updates on the status of *Star Wars*–style flight yokes, be sure to visit the Build Your Own Arcade Controls (BYOAC) Web site at www.arcadecontrols.com.

Building a *Star Wars* yoke

A number of stabs have been taken at building a *Star Wars* yoke controller. The three examples listed here took different routes, and all came out looking great! Not only did they achieve the feel and functionality of the original *Star Wars* yoke, they also managed to re-create the look. Specific details of the construction of these projects are light, and they will probably prove difficult to re-create. However, if you have the skills and determination, these projects will prove inspirational.

- The first of the replica projects is Joey's Arcade Panel Project at `www.arcadecontrols.com/arcade_joey.htm`. Joey's project actually uses optical encoders, so is somewhat different from the original *Star Wars* yoke.

- The second replica belongs to Xiaou2's Matrix Arcade Controls at `www.homestead.com/xiaou2/arcade.html`. Xiaou2's yoke uses potentiometers and is designed to be connected to the gameport.

- Finally, the Metz family MAME cabinet project (`http://members.surfbest.net/jmetz@surfbest.net/mamecab.htm`) is a homemade yoke based partially on the Twisty-Grip design introduced in the next section and partially on an analog USB controller hack similar to that mentioned in the "Converting an Arcade Steering Wheel" section earlier in this chapter. This hack will be explained in detail in Chapter 10, "Miscellaneous Bits of Arcade Trickery."

Another route to a *Star Wars* yoke was a design developed by the folks at Twisty-Grip. They created a plan to build a yoke with the feel and functionality of the original from cheaply available PVC parts. The Twisty-Grip yoke plans are available online for approximately $13 in either downloaded form or via CD. The plans include a checklist of all parts needed, assembly instructions, and more than 120 detailed illustrations and photos. The yoke is made from PVC, which is available at any hardware store, and miscellaneous parts that should be available from local electronics stores or online. Building the yoke will require approximately four to six hours and will cost about $45. Reactions from people who have built a Twisty-Grip yoke have been very good, and this makes an excellent addition to an arcade cabinet.

 On the CD   You can see an animation of the Twisty-Grip yoke in action and a short clip illustrating part of the assembly on the companion CD-ROM.

Converting a *Star Wars* yoke

Most arcade cabinet builders who include a *Star Wars* yoke have opted to convert a real yoke for use with their project. Two pioneers paved the way in this type of conversion — Jude Kelly with his *Star Wars* Controller hack at `www.arcadecontrols.com/arcade_jude.shtml` and Rob Meyers (known as 1UP) with his PacMAMEa at `www.1uparcade.com/index.html`. These hacks take advantage of the fact that the original *Star Wars* yoke used potentiometers. Jude's hack involves swapping the 5K arcade potentiometers with 100K PC gameport-compatible potentiometers whereas 1UP instead wires the existing potentiometers to a compatible USB game controller. Using either of these methods is very easy with the only remaining challenge being physically mounting the yoke to your cabinet. The mounting process will vary depending on the specifics of your cabinet, but the yoke comes with an easy-to-use mounting plate. This makes mounting mostly a matter of finding a good spot and making sure the weight is supported. See Figure 5-9 for a look at a *Star Wars* yoke hack.

On the CD Both Jude Kelly's *Star Wars* Controller hack and the PacMAMEa are included on the companion CD.

Finished!

FIGURE 5-9: *Star Wars* yoke hack.
Photo courtesy of Oscar Controls.

Arcade Guns

Since the dawn of time, humankind has had the urge to go out and hunt dinosaurs, aliens, and undead zombies. Of course, you can't really do that without a good gun. Unfortunately for modern humankind, few guns are available for your arcade cabinet project. The two routes to gun control are light guns and positional guns. Light guns work optically with your screen. They do not keep track of location on the screen until the gun is fired. When the gun is fired, the screen blanks for a moment, and the optics in the gun register where on the screen the gun is aimed. That information is sent to the computer, which registers the shot. Positional guns function much like joysticks, which maintain a known location on screen at all times and register the current location when fired. Figure 5-10 shows examples of both types of guns.

FIGURE 5-10: Fixed positional guns (left); one employing light guns (right).

Light guns

Light guns are the most common for video game systems of any type. When purchasing a light gun for an arcade cabinet, you must first consider the type of monitor that will be used. A gun designed for a VGA CRT monitor cannot be used with an LCD monitor or TV, a TV-based light gun cannot be used with a non-TV monitor, and so on. People have had some success using a VGA light gun with an arcade monitor, which makes sense as both VGA and arcade monitors are CRT-based.

Note When discussing arcade monitors here and elsewhere, assume a raster type of monitor is meant unless specifically stated otherwise. Some arcade monitors are vector-based; most are raster-based. See Chapter 12, "A Picture is Worth a Thousand...Tokens?" for definitions of raster and vector monitors.

Configuration and support

A light gun that supports multiple monitor resolutions will need to be calibrated for use. Calibration is the process in which the light gun and monitor are synchronized so the gun accurately follows your aim. Whenever you change resolution on your monitor, you will need to recalibrate your light gun. Bear in mind that starting a game will often automatically change the screen resolution. If you normally run in 800 × 600 mode (screen resolution), have the gun calibrated accordingly, and then start a game that runs in 640 × 480 mode, you'll need to calibrate again, or your shots will be off.

A limited number of light gun games are available for the PC. In fact, no new gun games were introduced for the PC in 2002. This market is obviously not considered a big one for software developers. The news is a little better if you are planning to use an emulator (described in Chapter 14, "Choosing and Loading Software") with many games supported and active interest in the community in adding more. If you are purchasing a light gun specifically to use with the Multiple Arcade Machine Emulator (MAME), then a visit to www.lightgun.tk is in order. Lightgun.tk is a Web site dedicated to light gun functionality in MAME.

Light gun choices

There are three light guns available for the PC. In the past few years, a couple of gun models have been introduced and then abandoned by their manufacturers, so the choices may vary by the time you read this book. The following are the current three options :

- Virtual Gun by 3rd Party is a realistic-looking black gun that connects via the USB port and retails for around $25. It sports a trigger, autofire, autoreload, and manual reload either by a button on the gun or the (optional included) reload foot pedal. This gun will only support a monitor resolution of 640 × 480. The upside of this is that the gun does not need calibration. The downside is that any games you play must support 640 × 480 resolution. You can find a hands-on review of this gun at www.runriot.pwp .blueyonder.co.uk/arcade/light-gunreview.htm, and discussion about it on this book's BYOAC message forums (www.arcadecontrols.com). Reactions to this gun are mixed. The gun is available from a variety of online sources.

- Act-Labs PC USB Light Gun is a futuristic, sci-fi type of gun that connects via USB and retails for about $35. It features a trigger, reload button, and a switch to put it in calibration mode. This gun supports multiple screen resolutions up to 2048 × 1940 and works with MAME. On its Web site, Act-Labs also lists eight PC retail games and several dozen Web-based games that the gun works with. Currently, MAME developers are working on code to enable dual gun support even though this is still a work in progress. The Act-Labs Web site links to many reviews of these light guns, and discussion can be found on this book's BYOAC message forums. Reactions to this gun are generally positive. The gun is available from the Act-Labs Web site at www.act-labs.com. See Figure 5-11 for a look at this gun.

- Act-Labs PC USB Light Gun — TV Out Version is basically the same as the previous model, but it is designed to function with televisions instead of VGA monitors. To use this gun, your video card must have S-Video output, and your TV will need to be a regular CRT style TV with S-Video or composite inputs. LCD, TFT, and plasma televisions will not work with this light gun. Unlike the VGA monitor version of this gun, the TV version will allow two guns to be connected for multiplayer fun. The gun retails for $39.

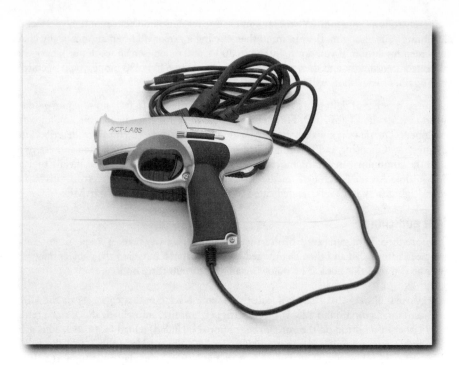

FIGURE 5-11: Act-Labs PC USB Light Gun.
Photo courtesy of Act-Labs.

Light gun support on computers is still in its infancy. This is one area where game consoles such as the PlayStation and Xbox have a serious leg up on PCs. Because the various light guns available are relatively inexpensive, easy-to-connect, and economical in terms of space, it is worth picking one up if you are a fan of such games. However, be prepared for mixed results, and be ready to replace or upgrade your light gun if and when the field matures. The best choice — because of the company's support of the community as well as the quality of their product — is one of the Act-Labs light guns.

Positional guns

A positional gun is a gun that is mounted stationary on the arcade cabinet with the ability to aim left/right and up/down. There are no PC-based positional guns on the market. The only way to go this route is to convert an arcade positional gun for use with your cabinet. Fortunately, if you've read the steering wheel and *Star Wars* yoke conversion sections in this chapter, this is already well-traveled ground. Most positional arcade guns are analog-based (using potentiometers) and function as joysticks. Swiveling the gun left or right is equivalent to moving your joystick left or right, and aiming the gun up or down is the same as pushing the joystick up or down. Taking advantage of this design, these guns can be converted for PC use via either of the analog potentiometer hacks discussed earlier in this chapter. You can replace the gun's potentiometers with PC-compatible 100K potentiometers or connect the existing potentiometers to a suitable PC gamepad. Once again, the details on these hacks will be covered in Chapter 10, "Miscellaneous Bits of Arcade Trickery." The individual who performed the *Star Wars* yoke conversion discussed in the previous section, 1UP, also has done a positional gun conversion that is documented at www.1uparcade.com/projects-t2guns.html.

 On the CD Information on the positional gun conversion performed by 1UP (Rob Meyers) is included on the companion CD.

Dance Pads

If you've stepped into an arcade recently, you've seen them. People of all ages and builds are in front of an arcade cabinet dancing away with a crowd of people behind them cheering or jeering. Welcome to one of the newest crazes to hit the arcade — arcade dancing!

The premise of dancing games is simple. While music plays on the arcade cabinet, instructions on the screen tell you which way to move your feet. Players stand on a dance pad that is divided into squares, which typically are marked by directional arrows. If the machine tells you to move left, you put your foot on the left arrow. If you can do it with some style, so much the better. Think of it as playing Twister to music without the usual contortions and spinal problems although. For such a simple concept, the game is strangely addictive and has acquired quite a following.

Buying a dance pad

The popularity of dancing games in the arcades soon led to the inevitable home versions. The company that arguably started the dancing simulation craze was Konami with its *Dance Dance Revolution*. Konami initially concentrated its efforts on the PlayStation console by selling both games and dance pads. Soon after a version of *DDR* was released for the PC (www.konami hwi.com/DDRPC/index.php), but, unfortunately, no dance pads for the PC were available.

Ah, but that's not a problem for the do-it-yourself crowd, right? Sure enough, a couple of solutions arose. The first took advantage of another trend in the home gaming arena — adapters that convert game controllers from one system to another. PlayStation to PC-USB (PSX-USB) converters are inexpensive, and *DDR* for the PC can be played with a commercially purchased PlayStation dance pad and a PSX-USB adapter. I was able to purchase the game, an adapter, and a dance pad for under $100. Unfortunately, not all PSX-USB adapters will work properly with dance pads. The adapters have to present the PlayStation controller as buttons and not axes. Certain moves in the game require hitting LEFT/RIGHT and UP/DOWN at the same time. You can't do that if the computer thinks you're using a joystick with axes (try hitting left and right with a joystick at the same time). The Boom adapter available from a variety of places including Lik-Sang (www.lik-sang.com) and the EMS USB2 adapter available from Levelsix (www.levelsix.com/) are known to work.

Considering another PSX-USB adapter? Visit the `http://junta.cromas.net/adapters` `.html` page to see if the one you're thinking about is compatible with dance pads.

Building a dance pad

You've probably realized by now that, when I use the phrase "commercially purchased" as I did in the previous paragraph, there is also a home-built solution. Most commercially available dance pads are plastic and hold up reasonably well under casual use. However, for the hard-core dance gamer, nothing short of an arcade-quality dance pad will do. With heavy use, the plastic dance pads have been known to deteriorate and begin to ignore or double-register your steps. Home-built dance pads use wooden frames and metal pads for improved durability and appearance. A growing number of dance game fans are building high-quality dance pads.

The basic concept behind a homemade dance pad is simple. As with most arcade controls, a signal is sent to the computer when two contacts touch. In this case, when you step on one of the squares on the dance pad, the square on top makes contact with a matching square underneath it, which activates the square. To connect it, you disassemble a PlayStation controller and divert the wires that originally went to the controller's buttons to the two parts of each dance-square instead. Building the dance pad is a matter of assembling the base and step spaces from wood (which makes the step squares), covering them in Lucite, and connecting a PlayStation controller. Simple, no? OK, a bit more detail is perhaps called for. Fortunately, several good step-by-step guides are available.

One of the best step-by-step guides to building your own dance pad is included on the companion CD, courtesy of the author, ddrhomepad. The Arcade Style *Dance Dance Revolution* Metal Pad is very detailed and includes links to several other sites that focus on dance pad building.

Dance pads are a great addition to an arcade cabinet. Two other dance programs are available in addition to *Dance Dance Revolution*. *Stepmania* at www.stepmania.com and *Dance With Intensity* (DWI) at http://dwi.ddruk.com are both popular dance programs available for download at no charge. If you're a member of the younger crowd, I'm sure you're already sold on the idea. If you're a member of the classic arcade generation but have kids who'll be playing your cabinet as well, consider adding one of these setups. Not only is it good fun, it's great exercise, too. Trust me, your kids will love it. In Figure 5-12, my daughter tests one of the several PlayStation dance pads playable on a PC-based arcade cabinet.

FIGURE 5-12: A PlayStation dance pad being played on a PC.

Summary

Steering wheels, flight yokes, guns, and dance pads are all special-purpose controls you might want to consider for your cabinet. The majority of games playable on your arcade cabinet will work fine with joysticks, buttons, spinners, and trackballs. However, for games that require one of the specialized controls covered in this chapter, playing without them will offer either a poor experience or will not be possible. The standard set of controls covered in the preceding two chapters will fit nicely on one standard control panel. Adding any of the controls from this chapter will involve an additional degree of complexity—both in physically finding space for them and in interfacing them to your computer. You should consider which of these specialized controls you're likely to play enough to justify the effort and then decide if you're going to incorporate them into your original control panel or come up with an alternative plan, such as a second cabinet.

That's it for looking at the various controls that are available for your arcade cabinet project. Next, I'll begin to address some of the other issues involved in cabinet building, such as building the control panel, in Chapter 6!

Building the Control Panel

A re you ready to dive into the really fun stuff? I hope you've found the book up to this point to be informative and the construction fun! So far, you've learned about the various things you can include in your dream machine and built and painted your cabinet. That's all an excellent start, but now it's time to actually get your hands on some genuine arcade controls! As you continue to follow along, by the end of this chapter you'll have picked exactly the controls you want for your arcade control panel, designed and tested your custom layout, purchased your controls, and installed them into the control panel. I recommend you read this chapter the entire way through once so you can decide on the parts you'll need to order, and then reread the pertinent parts once your supplies are on hand. This is where it starts to get really interesting! What are you waiting for? Jump in!

Laying Out Your Design

Before you pick up a drill, you should plan what you want to create. If you put some time and thought into what your ideal control panel should look like first, you'll be amply rewarded by the appearance and playability when you're finished. There's a world of difference between a well-crafted, multi-player-friendly arcade control layout and a slab of wood with a bunch of controls strewn about. A well-crafted layout will let you enjoy the game play (which is, after all, the point of all this) instead of fighting with the controls, the same way a well-designed car lets you enjoy the drive instead of focusing on where the windshield wipers are. There are several elements to a good design, and I'll cover them in the next few sections.

Choosing your controls

You should first decide on the controls you want to include in your control panel. The rest of the construction and design process will be affected by these choices. Things to consider include the types of games you want to play, availability of the controls, available space, and your budget. I'll take a look at space requirements in the next section. For the rest, I'll start by giving you a quick recap of the controls that have been covered in the preceding chapters (see Table 6-1).

Table 6-1 Control Choices

Controls	Availability	Game Types
Pushbuttons — microswitch	High — multiple sources	All
Pushbuttons — leaf	Rare — aftermarket only	All
Joysticks — microswitch	High — multiple sources	Most general game types
Joysticks — leaf	Rare — aftermarket only	Most general game types
Joysticks — optical	High — limited sources	Most general game types
Spinners	High — limited sources	Specific spinner games such as Breakout, Pong, Warlords
Trackballs	High — limited sources	Specific trackball games such as Centipede, Golden Tee Golf, and a mouse substitute for OS control
Steering wheels	High — multiple sources	Driving games, boat games
Flight yokes	Limited — limited sources	Flying games, driving and boat games
Star Wars yoke	Rare — used market only	Star Wars, flying games, driving and boat games
Guns	High — limited sources	Shooting games
Dance pads	Limited — limited sources	Dancing games

You'll almost certainly want to include pushbuttons and joysticks in your design. It would be virtually impossible to have a functional control panel without pushbuttons, and it's *usually* pointless without joysticks. Most games you'll play will use joysticks. However, you might build a panel without joysticks if you're working on a specific genre of games, such as a cabinet for playing driving games only. I'll assume for this discussion that you're building a multipurpose arcade cabinet. Whether to go with microswitch or leaf, and what types of joysticks to choose, should depend on the factors discussed in Chapter 3, "Pushing Your Buttons and the Joy of Joysticks." Functionally, all will work with your cabinet, so it is the considerations of appearance, feel, and game play that will help you decide what to buy.

Aside from pushbuttons and joysticks, I highly recommend including a spinner and trackball in your panel. Spinners will take up relatively little room and can be tucked away almost anywhere on the panel without impacting the other controls. Trackballs do take up quite a bit of room, but because they perform dual duty as a mouse for desktop control as well as a game controller, I would not build a panel without one. Because of their low profile, trackballs will not interfere with other controls either.

The rest of the controls are not as common on arcade cabinet projects as buttons, joysticks, spinners, and trackballs. Because they all serve specific genres of games, the first question to ask yourself is whether or not you want to be able to play those games on your cabinet. A steering wheel may get used for only one game out of several hundred on your cabinet, but if that game is the one you like to play every day, then by all means plan to include the steering wheel. Also consider your game-playing audience—you may not like dance games, but your kids might be nuts for them. For this second set of controls—namely steering wheels, flight yokes, guns, and dance pads—I would advise against including them unless you have a specific desire for them. If you *do* have a favorite game type that needs these controls, I would not hesitate to include them!

Tip

Take a moment now to jot down the controls you want to include in your arcade cabinet. Don't forget that you can always add or remodel later.

Designing a template

Now that you've decided which controls you are going to include, it's time to start sketching out a design. Visualizing what you're trying to create is invaluable, and few designs survive unaltered after this step. You may find when putting a concept down on paper that you do not have enough room for all your controls, or conversely that you do in fact have enough space to include that one extra item you originally left out. In the following sections I provide some tools and tips for laying out a design. There's a bit of material and things to consider, but I'll give you a sneak preview of the conclusion: After reading all about it, if you're not sure what you'd like to do, I provide a control panel design you can use.

Control templates

A control template is simply a layout of your control panel with the controls placed on it. You can create one digitally on a computer, moving parts around in a paint program and experimenting with design. You can also print out images of individual arcade controls and then place them on a mockup full-sized template and experiment with design by moving them around.

On the CD

On the companion CD, I have included JPEG (a picture format your computer likely understands) templates of many common arcade controls. When printed at 100 percent scaling, these templates are the exact size necessary for mounting the control in your control panel.

You'll need to make sure that whatever program you're using to print them isn't altering the size when printing. Most of the templates have a sizing ruler. You can use the ruled template to verify proper size by comparing with a real ruler. If you don't have a graphics program on your computer, take a look at the "Design Tools" section in this chapter to read about the one included on the CD. If nothing else, most operating systems come with a basic paint program that will work with JPEG images.

Caution

These templates are meant for layout planning and hole drilling. Although they are exactly sized, they are not exact replicas. Most controls use rounded corners on their mounting plates, although some templates have squared corners. This makes no difference for layout planning and drilling. However, do not use these templates to plan flush mounting of the mounting plates, as your corners will be different.

If there's a control that you're planning to use for which I have not provided a specific template, then you can easily create your own. Almost every control you might add can be planned for with a circular, square, or rectangular template. Even the oddly shaped trackball housing (see Figure 6-1) can be planned for with a square template. Creating your own in a good paint program is not terribly difficult.

Cross-Reference

Be sure to check online at the Build Your Own Arcade Controls (BYOAC) Web site (`www.arcadecontrols.com/`) to see if any new templates have been added since this book was written.

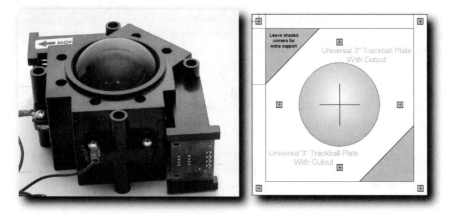

FIGURE 6-1: The Happ Controls 3-inch trackball on the left, and the mounting template on the right.
Used by permission of Happ Controls.

Control spacing and placement

Proper spacing and placement of your control layout is extremely important. Good design with this aspect can make or break the enjoyment you'll get out of your arcade cabinet. The two concerns here are spacing between controls, and placement of controls in relationship to each other and the cabinet.

Note

The information in this chapter applies to ¾-inch wooden control panels. Some control panels in original arcade machines were metal, and a few folks have followed suit in their own cabinets. Metal control panels are about ¼ inch thick, while wooden panels are usually between ⅝ inch and ¾ inch thick. Bear this in mind when you read about spacing.

Spacing

Spacing is primarily a consideration of the physical size of the controls you're going to use, and the size of the hands that are going to be playing them. Take pushbuttons as an example. Physically, the largest part of the pushbutton is the bezel that rests on top of the control panel. In the case of the Happ Controls Pushbutton with Horizontal Microswitch, that bezel is 1.3 inches in diameter (see Figure 6-2).

With this diameter, you could install your pushbuttons to be placed every 1.3 inches as measured from center point to center point. When it came time to play, however, most people would find that too cramped for comfort. Control panels are usually designed with buttons $1^{1}/_{2}$ to $1^{3}/_{4}$ inches apart for buttons that are placed in a group, which is a comfortable distance for game play. Comfort is, of course, a subjective opinion. Someone with smaller hands might want tighter spacing on the buttons, while someone with larger hands might want extra space. Because of this variation, you need to go through the design process before you start installation, to make sure that what looks good as a concept actually feels right in practice.

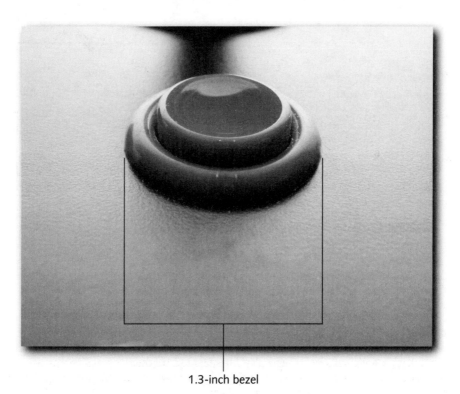

1.3-inch bezel

FIGURE 6-2: A Happ Controls pushbutton installed in a panel.
Used by permission of Happ Controls.

You should also think about the spacing between different groups of controls, such as between player 1's buttons and joysticks. As you play, the part of your hand that's not using the control has to go somewhere. If there are buttons directly next to a joystick, then you'll end up resting your hand on the buttons. Doing so is uncomfortable and will cause button presses you don't want. As another example, be careful of the amount of space between two joysticks. If they are too close together, you'll bump one as you use the other. Don't forget to consider right-handed versus left-handed play also. The spacing may work for your particular style of play, but what about someone else who uses the other hand for the same control?

Even when you've provided for adequate spacing for your controls, an otherwise good attempt can be marred by poor control placement. For instance, you may be able to place a spinner in an empty space behind a joystick. However, using the spinner will mean having to angle your arm uncomfortably to get around the joystick. How much game play will spinner games get in this scenario? While it may be physically possible to cram many controls into a limited amount of space, it is not a good idea to do so. All the controls in the world will do you little good if you can't use them because of poor design. Take a look at Figure 6-3 for an example of poor control placement.

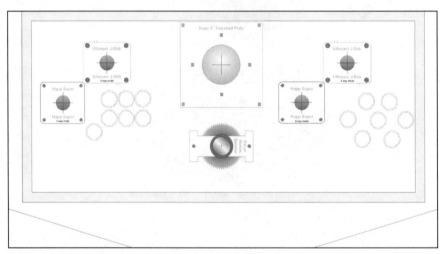

FIGURE 6-3: What's wrong with this control panel design?

Can you spot the several issues with the control panel in Figure 6-3? While the only control panel design that is "right" is the one you're happy with, there are several things in this control panel that are not conducive to game play. I hesitate to label them "wrong" because you may have a deliberate reason to place them in this fashion. However, the following are things in this design that I would not want on my personal panel:

- The trackball is at the back of the control panel. There's enough room for fine control, but some trackball games (like *Golden Tee Golf*) encourage you to slam your hand across the ball, rolling it madly. Try that with this setup and you'll smack your hand into the screen every time.

- The seven buttons grouped on the left are extremely close together. While this technically works, it isn't comfortable and is not necessary because there's plenty of room to space them out.

- The spinner is in front of the trackball. There's plenty of room to play spinner games, but you have to reach across or around the spinner to get to the trackball. Swapping the spinner and trackball and making sure there's a good 6 to 9 inches between them would be a good idea.

- The 4-way joysticks on both sides are very close to the 8-way joysticks. You're likely to bump into one joystick when you use the other.

- The buttons on the right are organized in a confusing fashion. It looks interesting, but probably isn't as useful as the button grouping on the left.

Using all the same controls except for one joystick, a better example of control panel design is shown in Figure 6-4. The issues with the previous design have all been addressed, and the panel is aesthetically pleasing. The trade-off of losing one joystick is well worth the enhanced playability of this new design.

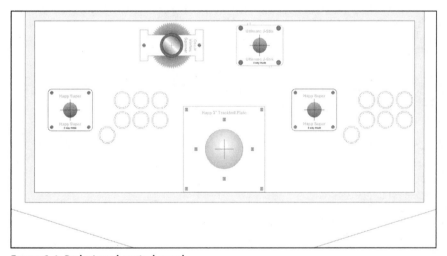

FIGURE 6-4: Redesigned control panel.

One last word on spacing out your controls: Bear in mind the space required below the control panel as well as above. Some controls require much more space below the surface than they do above, such as spinners and trackballs. The templates included on the CD all take space below into consideration.

Design tools

You can use a variety of tools to help you lay out your control panel. From expensive CAD (computer-aided design) programs to simple paper cutouts, any method can be used with good odds of success. I've included a few suggestions for you to consider in the following sections.

CAD and paint programs

Many people with access to them have used CAD programs to design their cabinets and control panels. CAD programs are designed for precisely this kind of work and allow precise design and control. The two drawbacks of these programs are the price and learning curve. CAD software tends to be very expensive, and because of the incredible range of functions, it's often difficult to learn. Mitigating these factors, however, are the resources available online. There are many trial, shareware, and free versions of CAD programs available on the Internet. You can also find excellent tutorials for using CAD software, and you should be able to use the templates included on the CD to give you a head start in the process. Visiting the Internet search engine Google (www.google.com/) and searching for "free cad software" is the place to start if you're interested in this route.

Another tool used in control panel design is a good paint package. Adobe Photoshop, Adobe Illustrator, and (my personal favorite) Paint Shop Pro are some of the many quality paint packages available. A good paint package includes all the tools necessary to design a control panel layout, usually with a much gentler learning curve. All of the image work for this book, including the templates, was done using Paint Shop Pro. This program includes an excellent help system and tutorials. See Figure 6-5 for a sample screenshot.

 On the CD You'll find a 30-day trial version of Paint Shop Pro 8 on the companion CD. A full-featured package is available for about $90, should you choose to purchase it.

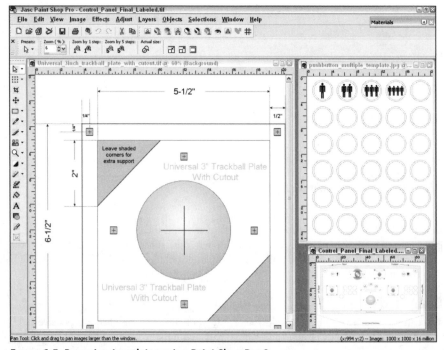

FIGURE 6-5: Preparing templates using Paint Shop Pro 8.
Screen shot courtesy of Jasc Software.

Interactive Control Panel Designer

The creative folks at Move360Media (multimedia Web site designers) put up a tool just for people making arcade cabinets. Called the Interactive Control Panel Designer (or ICPD for short), it is an online tool that runs in your Web browser and lets you experiment with different control panel layouts. You'll find it at www.move360media.com/mame/icpd/ICPD.htm.

The simplicity of cardboard

Don't overlook the simple idea of a cardboard mockup. A very effective way to experiment with control panel layouts is to cut a piece of cardboard into the exact shape and size of your control panel top. Then you can take to-scale template printouts of the controls you're working with and lay them out on the cardboard. Changes are quick and easy with this method. Remember to take into account space available below the control panel top. If your top has a lip that extends beyond the control panel box below it, you'll need to draw that on your cardboard template so that you don't end up putting a control where it simply hangs out into the open. Doing a full-scale mockup this way has several advantages. It's cheap, it's easy, and it's much easier to visualize the final product with a full-sized model in front of you.

Once you've come up with a plan for your panel, seek out some second opinions. Consider posting an image of your design on the message forums at the Build Your Own Arcade Controls (BYOAC) Web site (www.arcadecontrols.com/) for other people to take a look at. The folks there aren't shy; they'll tell you both what they like and what they don't like about your design. It's almost always advice worth listening to, even if in the end you decide you don't agree. Just remember to be a bit thick-skinned; it's hard to hear criticism about something you've spent hours on. Bear in mind that it's meant to be helpful, and if you don't agree, there's nothing lost for having heard their opinions.

Design philosophy

Now that you've got the technical bits under your belt, it's time to talk about design philosophy—the "art" of control panel design. You'll find quite a bit of discussion on this topic on the message forums at the Build Your Own Arcade Controls (BYOAC) Web site (www.arcadecontrols.com/). I've highlighted the main points in the next three sections.

How many game buttons do you need?

How many game buttons you choose to use will depend on the types of games you want to play. Most classic arcade games will work with between two and four buttons per player. If you're into more modern and fighter types of games, then six or seven buttons per player is about right. Four-player games tend to require fewer buttons than two-player games (mainly because there are few four-player fighting games), maxing out at four buttons per player. If you're building a two-player panel, I recommend seven buttons per player. For a four-player panel, I recommend seven buttons for players 1 and 2, and four buttons for players 3 and 4. These configurations will allow you maximum flexibility without appearing cluttered.

Aside from the main player buttons, there are other buttons to think about. You may want to add buttons near the trackball or spinner for games that use these, although many people simply use player 1's buttons for these games as well. Another set of buttons you might not immediately think about are pinball flipper buttons. Several good pinball simulations exist for the

PC, and placing flipper buttons on the sides of your control panels adds a layer of fun to them. Finally, don't forget administrative buttons, as covered in the next section.

Administrative controls

Unlike a real arcade machine, your arcade cabinet may need several *administrative* controls on the control panel, as you may want or need to do certain things on a home arcade machine that you wouldn't or couldn't do in an arcade. Take a look at Table 6-2 for a rundown of administrative buttons you might consider. Note that certain functions may not be applicable to all software. For instance, some games may not allow you to pause the action.

You'll notice that some of the buttons in the table are listed as *not recommended*. My rationale is that these functions are used only during the setting up and updating of your arcade cabinet. Based on the philosophy that you're trying to disguise the computer origins of your project as much as possible to mimic the arcade, you usually won't be doing setup activities during regular game play. Until the cabinet is finished (and during updates), you can drag out a keyboard or mouse for these functions. In normal use, you don't want your guests to accidentally bring up an "assign control keys menu" screen during the middle of a game of *PacMan*!

Table 6-2   Administrative Buttons to Consider

Button	Purpose
Insert coin players 1 through 4	Inserts a virtual credit into the game. Some games require a separate coin-up for each player—hence four separate buttons. Use two buttons for two-player panels. *These buttons are recommended.*
Start game players 1 through 4	Starts the game for players 1 through 4. Use two buttons for two-player panels. *Recommended.*
Pause	Pauses the game during inconvenient phone calls or calls of nature! *Recommended.*
Exit	Quits the game. *Recommended.*
Reset game	Resets the game in play but not the computer. *Recommended, but hidden out of sight.*
Shutdown	Tells the computer to turn off. *Recommended but hidden.*
Mouse buttons 1 through 3	Function as left, middle, and right mouse buttons. Also function as trackball game buttons. *Recommended.*
Configure game	Used to enter game setup options. *Not recommended.*
Enter	Normally needed only during setup. *Not recommended.*
Shift	Used to modify control panel button functions to secondary functions. *Recommendation depends on interface and personal preference.*

The "reset game" button, which is listed as *recommended but hidden*," is one that you will rarely use but might still need during the course of regular game play. For instance, emulator software attempts to faithfully recreate the operation of an original arcade machine, including any original quirks or bugs. Some arcade machines need to be reset the first time they are turned on to switch from startup to play mode. Accordingly, you'll want a reset button somewhere. However, since it will be used rarely and you don't want it accidentally hit during game play, I recommend hiding it somewhere. You might put it on the top or back of your arcade cabinet, in the coin door, or somewhere else easily reachable but unlikely to be accidentally pressed. The same rationale applies to the shutdown button. You'll want it once per game session, but you don't want it accidentally hit during play.

The shift button also needs some elaboration. Some interfaces (see Chapter 8, "Using the Keyboard Connector for Arcade Controls") support the use of a shift button, while others do not. This does not refer to the shift key on the keyboard, but it is similar. Like a shift or control key on a keyboard, a shift button is used to modify the purpose of a button on your control panel. For instance, you might have your player 1 start button function as a pause button when pressed along with the shift button. Some people like this function because it allows administrative controls to be included on the panel without extra space and clutter. Since not all interfaces support a shift button, you'll need to read Chapter 8 first and decide on an interface type if you're considering this.

Smorgasbord or simple?

Before you get too far into the process, you need to consider one more issue. The whole point of building an arcade cabinet is to bring home the experience of the arcade. So, what's the question? The problem is that you face something of a challenge. Machines in the arcade are designed to play only one game or a small set of games that use the same controls. You're trying to design a machine that will be able to play a large number of games, requiring many different controls. Trying to cover every angle leads to the smorgasbord syndrome. Include too many controls and you risk ending up with an unplayable mess. Include too few, and you limit the number of games you can play.

Strangely enough, this is an occasionally heated topic of debate. There are two camps on the issue. On one hand, you have folks who prefer to emphasize the aesthetics of a machine. To them, a control panel with too many controls is just short of an abomination. On the other hand, there are the folks who want to maximize the playability of their cabinet. As long as it works, what's the big deal? The trick is to find that perfect balance between the "mother of all arcade machines" and the "arcade machine wannabe." The control panel design provided for you at the end of this section is a good compromise between the two extremes. Ultimately, however, the only opinion that matters is yours.

Putting what you've learned into practice

Enough talking—time to get busy! Before you move on to the next section, you should put into practice what you've read. Decide on the controls you're going to use and then order them. While you're waiting for your parts to arrive, use whichever method you've chosen to lay out your design. Don't forget to run your design by a few other people for different opinions; this is almost always a useful step. If you're not confident in your design plans, you might want to reverse steps and finalize your layout before you order your controls. This helps to ensure that you get exactly the controls you need, but it does tend to slow the process down a bit. If you've got some downtime while you wait for parts and opinions, you can sneak a peek at the next sections and do some practice work if you have spare wood. Remember, you can always elect to use the Project Arcade control panel design at the end of this chapter as well.

Tip You might notice I haven't covered where to purchase your controls. If you look at Appendix A, you'll find a list of locations to purchase them. Some parts are carried only by specific vendors, others by multiple vendors. As long as they carry the parts you need, which vendor you choose to purchase from is not terribly important.

Installing the Controls

It's almost time to pick up your power tools again! Now that you've picked out your controls and decided on a design, you need to know how to install the controls in the control panel. The techniques listed here will be accurate for almost any arcade control you can find. However, do double-check the vendor's instructions before installing any particular control.

The tools you'll need for installation include a drill and possibly a router and jigsaw. The drill will be used to make holes for the buttons and joysticks. The jigsaw will be used if you need to make large openings, for instance, to mount a trackball. Finally, wood-working veterans sometimes prefer a router for making holes and cuts instead of a drill or jigsaw.

Tip When drilling holes into wood, you might want to clamp a piece of scrap wood underneath and drill through both. This will avoid splintering the wood at the exit point on your control panel.

Before you install the controls, you need to consider briefly if you are going to be adding a Plexiglas cover to the control panel top. If you are, then you'll need to remove the controls to install it and then reinstall the controls. You might want to hold off installing the controls until I cover that in Chapter 15. However, I recommend proceeding as-is. Removing and reinstalling the controls is not that difficult.

Metal versus wooden control panels

Some controls are designed to be installed in metal control panels, some in wooden control panels, and some in either. The difference lies in how far the control will protrude above the control panel. A control designed for a wooden panel that's placed in a metal panel will extend higher than it is meant to, and a control meant for a metal panel that's placed in a wooden panel will end up shorter than intended. There's not much you can do about a control that extends too high other than altering the control (such as cutting a spinner shaft down to size) or using spacers of some kind beneath the panel.

Controls designed for metal panels will work nicely in a wooden panel, however, by having the control recessed into the panel from underneath. This is done with a router, with the recession depth depending on the control used and panel thickness. If you're using a $3/4$-inch panel, then a depth of $1/4$ inch is about right. With a shallower $5/8$-inch panel, you probably will want to recess it only $1/8$ inch deep. If you recess it too much, you run the risk of the wood breaking at that point. Leaving about $1/2$ inch of wood in the panel will provide a sturdy surface. Take a look at Figure 6-6 for an example. In this particular $3/4$-inch thick panel, the joysticks are recessed $1/4$ inch.

FIGURE 6-6: Underneath a HanaHo HotRod control panel.
Used by permission of HanaHo Games.

Buttons

Most buttons, both leaf and microswitch, require a $1^1/8$-inch hole for mounting. The buttons are passed through the hole, and a mounting nut is fastened on the underside. Figure 6-7 shows an example. If you're planning to use leaf-switch buttons in a $3/4$-inch wooden panel, you'll need to rout out a space ($1/4$ inch will do) for them. Even though there are two lengths of leaf-switch buttons, the longer ones are still a bit too short to allow attachment of the mounting nut through a $3/4$-inch panel. If you are using microswitch buttons, a button wrench is a real time and knuckle saver. The mounting nuts on the buttons don't need to be too tight, but getting your hand into tight spaces can be a chore.

FIGURE **6-7:** Microswitch-type button (left) and leaf switch button (right).
Used by permission of HanaHo Games and Happ Controls.

Joysticks

Joysticks will almost all mount in the same $1^{1}/_{8}$-inch hole used for buttons. Although the joystick shaft won't take up the entire hole, you need some room to move the stick around. The mounting plate will attach to the underside of the control panel, usually with carriage bolts from above, although some folks will install them with screws from underneath. Attaching them from underneath leaves you a smooth surface above, while using carriage bolts from above provides more stability. The joysticks will be taking quite a workout and could potentially fall in toward the panel, so if you are concerned, stick to the carriage bolts. Different models of joysticks have different mounting heights, and whether or not to recess them is a matter of functionality and personal preference. Most people will recess the joysticks; having a stick that's a little tall is okay, while a stick that's too short can hamper game play. You can always test-fit the joystick without recessing it first and then make up your mind. Take a look at Figure 6-8.

Some joystick installations are done from above the control panel, with an area for the mounting plate routed on the top so as to flush-mount the joystick. Doing this requires a much bigger hole in the panel to accommodate the base of the joystick, and it isn't recommended. Functionally, however, it is fine. If you go this route, you'll need to install a control panel overlay to cover the mounting plate.

FIGURE 6-8: A joystick recessed into the control panel.
Used by permission of HanaHo Games.

Cross-Reference A control panel overlay is basically a large sticker with some appropriate design that you place over the entire control panel, hiding the installation holes and such. I'll cover that (no pun intended, honest!) in Chapter 15, "Buttoning Up the Odds and Ends."

You might guess that there's not much that can go wrong with a dust cover, but most joystick installations get this part wrong. The dust cover is the washer that sits at the base of the joystick shaft, whose purpose it is to cover the hole in the control panel. It's really not in the least important where it goes, but if you're trying to get that perfect arcade look, then you might consider doing it the proper way. The correct way is to rout an impression in the top of the panel for the washer to rest in so that it's flush with the control panel top. Then you apply your control panel overlay on top of the control panel, sandwiching the washer between the overlay and the wood. It's a bit of effort that's probably not worth the results, and it particularly won't work if you aren't going to use a control panel overlay.

Installing the joystick involves removing the shaft from the base, which requires removing an e-ring from the shaft. An e-ring is a thin, flat semicircle of metal that fits snugly onto a notch in the joystick shaft, holding the entire mechanism securely in place. When you remove the shaft, various parts will come off as well — be sure to note where they go, or have the joystick assembly instructions available. Place the base of the joystick beneath the control panel, and thread the shaft through the control panel and into the joystick base, placing the various components in the same places they were removed from. Replace the e-ring and you're done. Beware! Those e-rings are pure evil and tricky to get on and off. Installing the e-ring requires one hand to hold the shaft, one hand to press down on the actuator on the bottom of the shaft to expose the e-ring groove, and one hand to install the e-ring. Were you counting? Yes, that's three hands! Because the metal e-ring has to be bent open slightly to snap onto the joystick shaft, it's essentially spring loaded. You haven't truly been initiated into the arcade cabinet–building community until you've crawled around on the floor muttering as you look for one of these e-rings after it went flying across the room as you tried to install or remove it! Some specific joystick models vary, so be sure to consult the vendor's instructions.

Tip

Oscar Controls (www.oscarcontrols.com/) sells a joystick mounting plate that fits the mounting holes of several joysticks. This mounting plate can be used to install a joystick meant for a metal control panel into a wooden control panel.

Spinners

Although the specifics of spinner installation will vary depending on which model you're using, all of them are similar. You'll need one hole for the spinner shaft, usually between $3/8$ inch and $3/4$ inch in diameter. You don't want a hole that's too big because there's no dust cover washer and the hole will show under the spinner knob. The spinner will mount to the underside of the control panel in a variety of methods, with none of the commercially available spinners needing to be recessed into the panel.

Above the panel the spinners all work the same. The knob mounts onto the shaft and is fastened with one or two tiny setscrews that are imbedded in the knob. The knob will float above the control panel surface, hiding the shaft hole.

Installing the spinner is a matter of removing the knob, threading the shaft through the control panel hole, and reattaching the knob. It's very important that the shaft be straight and not touch the sides of the hole once installed, or the spinner may bind and not function properly. Fortunately, most of the spinner models currently available have well-designed mounting mechanisms, so this is not difficult to accomplish. Take a look at Figure 6-9 for a shot of the Project Arcade test rig with various spinners installed. The spinners look very similar above, while having very different mounting mechanisms below.

Trackballs

You'll find trackballs to be the most labor-intensive control to install. Most controls install into the control panel with a simple circular hole in the panel. Mounting a trackball requires a hole in the panel several inches in size. It can either be an irregularly shaped hole that matches the shape of the trackball casing, or a larger, square-shaped hole to make it easier. There are three styles of trackballs from different arcade vendors. Functionally and electronically they work the same, but the physical casings that hold the trackballs are slightly different in shape. Either way, accommodating the casing takes a bit more effort than simply drilling a hole.

FIGURE 6-9: Test rig with spinners.
Used by permission of Oscar Controls and SlikStik.

On the CD

The companion CD-ROM includes a one-size-fits-all trackball cutout template that will accommodate all of the trackball styles.

Trackballs are usually mounted with a mounting plate. The mounting plate can either rest on top of the control panel or be recessed into the top of the panel for a flush-mounted surface. There are two styles of mounting plates — one with holes to insert carriage bolts from the top, and one with a smooth surface. The one with the smooth surface has posts underneath that you attach to from beneath the control panel. Both plates have the same mounting pattern — four screws or bolts attach the trackball to the mounting plate, and another four screws or bolts attach the mounting plate to the control panel.

Installing the trackball is not difficult despite the extra effort involved. Begin by cutting the hole for the trackball casing to fit into. I recommend cutting a hole to fit the casing instead of the square hole, as that will leave more wood for the mounting plate to rest on, providing more support. The fitted hole will be six-sided roughly in the shape of a football. Once you've cut the hole, drill four holes in the corners to mount the trackball plate to the control panel. Attach the trackball to the mounting plate, and then insert the trackball assembly into the control panel and fasten it into place. Figure 6-10 shows an example of a trackball mounted using the smooth-surface plate.

Guns

Because there are no standards or conventions for arcade guns, you'll have to determine the best mounting method on your own. I have a couple of points for you to consider while you do so.

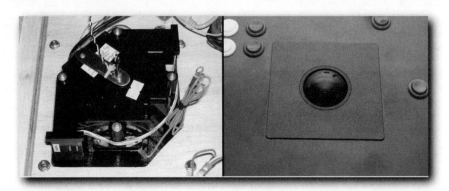

FIGURE 6-10: A 3-inch trackball mounted inside a SlikStik control panel: underside (left) and surface (right).
Used by permission of SlikStik.

For light guns, the only part of the gun you'll be mounting to the cabinet is the end of the cord. The easiest way would be to route the cord through the coin door, and leave the guns in there when not in use. You can also purchase holsters for guns from arcade parts vendors and mount them somewhere on the cabinet — for instance, on the bottom-front beneath the control panel — where they'll be out of the way. However, you then have to have some way for the cords to enter the cabinet to connect to the computer. A grommet hole underneath the control panel box bottom would work nicely, keeping the cord entrance hidden.

If you're mounting positional guns to your cabinet, you'll want them positioned on the control panel far enough back that they won't hit the screen when rotated. Also be sure to leave enough clearance between guns so that players 1 and 2 can both aim inward without interfering with each other.

Steering wheels and yokes

Steering wheels and yokes are another set of controls that are difficult to give specific mounting instructions for — every model is somewhat different. Most steering wheel and flight yokes are meant to be set up on a desk, usually with some kind of clamping mechanism. If your control panel has an extended lip like the Project Arcade panel, then you can mount those wheels and yokes that use clamps to it. This is particularly a good way to do it if you intend to use the control only occasionally, with the ability to easily remove and put it away when not in use. If you're going to use this method, be sure to look at Chapter 13, "Installing the Computer," for an idea on surface-mounting USB ports on the cabinet.

If you're planning to permanently mount a wheel or yoke to your cabinet, you should think carefully about the angle of mounting. Clamping on to the overhang of the control panel is fine for casual use. However, because the control panel angles slightly downward, the wheel or yoke will also be angled slightly downward. This is not ideal for frequent use and will likely cause discomfort. Consider creating a mounting platform that will sit on or attach to the control panel. You'll find an excellent example of how to do this on the 1UPArcade Web site at www.1uparcade.com/projects-yokebase.html.

Instructions on how to create a mounting platform that will sit on or attach to the control panel can be found on the companion CD-ROM.

Dance pads

Unless you're designing a permanent dance machine, you really won't be mounting the dance pad to the arcade cabinet. In that case, you'll just need to make sure you've left enough floor space in front of the cabinet for the dance pad once the cabinet has a permanent home. Once again, if you're going this route, look at the USB port–mounting idea in Chapter 13. If you *are* building a permanent dance machine with a wooden-framed dance pad, then you may want to consider semipermanently fastening the dance pad to the cabinet. You probably don't want a fully permanent assembly, as the cabinet would be difficult if not impossible to move to another location.

Mounting the Control Panel

If you followed the instructions in Chapter 2, "Building Your Arcade Cabinet," then your control panel top already securely mounts to the control panel box with Velcro. If you haven't attached the Velcro yet, now is a good time to do so. With a closed-box design like the Project Arcade control panel, Velcro is pretty much the only way to securely attach the top to the box while maintaining accessibility. In addition to providing access to the innards for maintenance, a removable control panel top also allows for a nice solution to the "smorgasbord or simple?" question raised earlier in this chapter, as explained in the next section.

Multiple control panels

Smorgasbord or simple? Why can't we have the best of both worlds? There's no reason if you're willing to go through a little extra effort and expense. Many people have solved the problem of wanting extra controls without the clutter by using more than one control panel. To make this work, you have to use a modular wiring scheme, which we'll cover in the next chapter, "How it Works — Turning a Computer into the Brains of an Arcade Machine." This will allow you to unplug a control panel from the cabinet and plug in another one. There's usually a main control panel with a couple of standard joysticks, buttons, and probably a trackball and spinner. The bonus panels depend on what you're trying to achieve. One popular choice is to design a panel with a couple of trigger-grip joysticks for a particular set of flying and shooting games. You might create a panel with a limited set of controls to faithfully replicate a favorite game. Whichever panels you decide to create, once you get the wiring worked out it's a fairly simple concept. Each control panel is designed to fit in the control panel box that stays on the cabinet. When it's time to swap panels, you pull the current one off, disconnect the wiring, plug in the replacement panel, and drop it into place. Voila! You have the equivalent of an entirely new arcade machine with about a minute's worth of work. The only trick is figuring out where to store the extra panels when not in use!

You have one other option to consider for multiple control panels. A handful of very clever and dedicated people have come up with schemes for rotating control panels in their arcade cabinets. Like swappable panels, each one has a particular set of controls for a particular subset of games. Instead of removing the existing panel when you want to change, the control panel assembly is simply rotated into the cabinet and another panel rotated into place. This is an ingenious idea and nicely handles dealing with multiple control panels with a minimum of fuss — that is, once you've actually created the rotating panel mechanism!

Specific instructions on how to do this are beyond the scope of this book. There are a few good sites on the Internet you can go to for inspiration if you would like to give this a try. In a nutshell, however, the control panel boxes are designed to allow the panels to rotate down into the cabinet when another panel is rotated up into place. Picture a set of three control panels arranged with the wide edges of each panel touching another panel, so that they form a triangle when looked at from the end. A lazy-susan mechanism of some kind is attached on each short end, and this entire assembly is mounted into the control panel box. Add a mechanism to fasten and release the control panel as needed, and you have the gist of a rotating control panel setup. An excellent example of a cabinet with a rotating control panel is 1UP's PacMAMEa at `www.1uparcade.com/arcade-const-panels.html`.

| On the CD | 1UP's PacMAMEa can also be found on the companion CD-ROM. |

Attaching the control panel box

Now that you have the control panel designed, built, and attached to the control panel box, it's time to attach the box to the cabinet. Recall that we deliberately did not attach it to the cabinet earlier to allow for ease of construction and the ability to fit the cabinet through doorways. If you haven't done so yet, now is the time to move the cabinet from the construction area to its permanent home.

| Caution | Warning! Up until now it's been possible (though not advised) to do things by yourself. Now, however, you should find a friend to help before trying to move the cabinet. With most of three sheets of wood assembled together, the cabinet is going to be bulky and heavy. Don't risk injury to the cabinet or yourself by trying to solo it, even with a moving dolly. Trust me on this one; Project Arcade almost took a tumble down a flight of stairs before I was wise enough to ask for a hand (making this the book that almost wasn't!). Get someone to help; you'll be happy you did. |

Once you've done that, you have a choice to make. If you're convinced that you'll never need to move the cabinet back out the doorway, or if you have a doorway wide enough to accommodate it, you can elect to permanently attach the control panel box to the cabinet. There's nothing particularly complicated about doing it this way. Make sure the box is centered on the base of the cabinet, and use any of the construction methods from the beginning of this book (such as L-brackets or mounting strips) to attach it.

However, if you want to be able to fit the cabinet through standard-sized doorways and to be able to get into the cabinet for maintenance from the control panel area, you'll want to use a detachable mounting method for the control panel box. The best way to do that is with panel clamps available from various arcade parts vendors (see Figure 6-11).

FIGURE 6-11: Two sets of control panel mounting clamps.
Used by permission of Happ Controls.

Panel clamps come in two pieces. One piece has a lip on it and attaches to the control panel box. The other piece attaches to the cabinet and has a spring-loaded lever that clamps to to the lip of the other piece. Close the lever and the clamp pulls down tight on the other piece, securing the control panel box into place. Raise the lever and the control panel box easily releases. With a panel clamp on the left and right sides, your control panel box will not be going anywhere! For added stability, you can attach a couple of 2 × 2 mounting strips to the control panel box underside to make sure the fit into the cabinet is snug. When the box is properly positioned on the cabinet, attach the mounting strips in the corners made by the box underside and the cabinet sides. Make sure you don't fasten the mounting strips to the cabinet as well!

Standalone Control Panels

It's time for a quick segue. Earlier on in the book, I mentioned building a standalone desktop set of arcade controls. You may not realize it, but if you've been building as you follow along in the book, then you've done just that! Rather than dedicating the time and space to a complete arcade cabinet, many people will build a control panel box and control panel and stop there. With a desktop arcade unit, you don't have to purchase all the materials for the cabinet, and you don't have to dedicate a computer and monitor. These make excellent portable arcade units at a third or less of the cost of a dedicated arcade cabinet. They fit well on the top of a desk for casual game play and can be put away when not in use. They're also great responses to the inevitable requests you'll receive when people see your custom arcade cabinet. Build your family and friends desktop arcade units and they'll love you forever! OK, that may be pushing it. However, roughly a third of the projects submitted to the Build Your Own Arcade Controls (BYOAC) Web site are desktop arcade units. Building one is certainly something to consider.

Project Arcade Control Panel Design

Not sure yet what you'd like to do? If in doubt, try the Project Arcade control panel as shown in Figure 6-12. This panel is fairly complete, designed to cover a wide range of game possibilities in a two-player configuration. It includes a spinner and trackball, two 8-way joysticks, and one 4-way stick. It uses 27 buttons, including 7 per player, 3 mouse buttons, 2 pinball flippers, and a handful of administrative buttons.

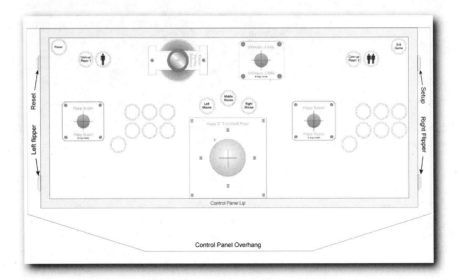

FIGURE 6-12: The Project Arcade control panel layout.

You'll need the following controls (from any vendor unless otherwise specified) to build the Project Arcade control panel:

- One 3-inch trackball
- One Happ Controls 3-inch trackball mounting plate
- 25 horizontal microswitch pushbuttons
- One player 1 horizontal microswitch pushbutton

- One player 2 horizontal microswitch pushbutton

- One pushbutton wrench

- Two 8-way joysticks

- One 4-way joystick

- One spinner

- Assorted screws, nuts, and bolts depending on joystick, spinner, and trackball models (see specific vendor information for parts necessary)

Summary

In this chapter you were introduced to the concepts of good control panel design. If you've been building as you read, then by this point you've decided what controls are going to be a part of your arcade project. You've planned, purchased, and installed your controls into your control panel and attached it to the cabinet. If you're using the Project Arcade design, then you've got a good two-player cabinet almost ready for friends to come play. If you're striking out on your own with your own custom design, then so much the better — your panel fits your unique style! This is the end of Part II, "Designing and Building Your Dream Arcade Control Panel." Take a moment and look back at what you've done so far.

Wow, you've come a long way in only a few chapters! From a pile of wood, hardware, and a few ideas, you've been able to create a full-sized arcade cabinet with a smoking control panel! But . . . it doesn't *do* anything yet, right? It's a bit like Dr. Frankenstein's monster in the movie, lying on the table covered by a sheet. Putting it together was almost certainly a fun and interesting process, but it won't impress your friends yet. In the opening chapters of Part III, "Hooking Things Up Under the Hood — Time to Trick the Computer," I'll show you how to get your controls to talk to the computer in a language it can understand. Ready to give your creation a jolt of lightning and bring it to life? Put on your lab coat, practice your mad scientist laugh, and read on!

Hooking Things Up Under the Hood — Time to Trick the Computer

part

III

How It Works—
Turning a Computer
into the Brains of
an Arcade Machine

Congratulations! So far you have two steps down the road toward arcade Nirvana behind you. It's time for the next step! Think of this book as a fun college-level science course. There's some lab work, some theory, and one whopping final exam. The first part of the book was the introduction to the course, and the second part was the hands-on lab work. That means you still have some theory and the final exam to go!

The theory portion starts in this chapter. Don't worry; you'll find it anything but boring! There are a lot of options available to you, and the next four chapters cover them all. You're going to get into how keyboards and mice work, perhaps take a few things apart (always fun), and generally play with ways to make a computer do things no one thought of a few years ago. I'll start things off with some behind-the-scenes information on the techniques that make this whole thing work. Oh, and the final exam? That's the look on your friends' faces when they come over and get to play with the results of your hard work! Ready to go? Then grab your wires and test tubes—it's time to bring your creation to life!

Digital and Analog

Let's start with a look at how computers talk to their various bits and parts. All the arcade controls that you connect to the computer need to talk to the computer somehow. That means the computer and the arcade controls will have to be able to speak the same language. Fortunately, the computer knows how to speak all the languages used by the arcade parts. Your task is to match the right language from the computer to the right arcade part. It's easy, when you get down to it, because there's really only two languages to worry about—digital and analog.

Digital data

What is *digital data*? There are entire books and courses dedicated to that question. You could take years of study to master the subject. The following explanation is just a brief overview. It's really all you need to know for the purposes of this book and for building your arcade cabinet.

Simply put, digital data is a way of representing information by breaking it down into individual bits of 1s and 0s, or more appropriately for our purposes, the state of the bits being *on* or *off*. Consider a pushbutton, for instance. When the button is sitting in the control panel and no one is touching it, it's off (0). When someone presses the button, it's on (1). To the computer, there is no in-between state. What about when the button is pressed half-way down? The computer doesn't care, and in fact doesn't even know. The button is off until it is on. There's no other state for the pushbutton to be in.

Usually, the individual bits of 1s and 0s are grouped into bunches of 1s and 0s for easier sending and storing of the digital data. These *groupings* are still digital as far as we are concerned. However, as you will see in a moment, groups of 1s and 0s can also be used to represent analog data.

Analog data

Analog data is a more traditional way of representing information. In the real physical world, almost everything is represented in analog terms. It allows for a range of values of information about the state of an item, such as the temperature outside. The temperature can vary over a range of values, some more specific than others (10 degrees, 32.5 degrees, warm, warmer, hot, and so on). In terms of a computer, instead of data about an item being represented in bits, it's represented in a way that presents the data as something more than simply being on or off. Consider a steering wheel as an example. A steering wheel is not simply turned or not turned. It can be turned a few degrees to the left, and the computer recognizes that as a gradual turn. The wheel can be turned many degrees to the right, and the computer recognizes that as a sharp turn to the right. You might think of analog as a way to qualify information about an item. *How* hot or cold is it? *How far* to the left is the wheel turned?

Mixing them together

Fortunately for those of us who are arcade cabinet builders, computers speak both digital and analog. In strict terms, computers of today are digital devices. At the core of the computer, the *central processing unit* (CPU) speaks only digital. However, part of the electronics that makes up a computer includes devices that convert between digital and analog. The game port is the only input connection on the computer that speaks analog natively. All the other input connectors on the computer are digital in nature. There are a couple of analog outputs, such as the sound and video outputs, but only the one analog input. That isn't to say that the other input connectors can't have analog devices hooked up to them. In fact it is quite common to do so. It just means that such devices have to perform an analog-to-digital conversion before they send the data to the computer. As noted in the "Digital data" section, groups of digital bits can carry analog data, at least as far as our arcade machine and computer are concerned. A full understanding of how that works really would take a dedicated book or class. Suffice to say that it works, which opens up many possibilities to us.

Can you identify which arcade controls are digital, and which are analog? A pushbutton is easy; it's either pushed or not pushed (digital). Steering wheels have been discussed — they're analog. What about spinners and trackballs? They might seem analog at first thought, but they speak digitally. They might send a data saying "move 1 left" and the computer will move one left. They might also send "move 20 right and 3 up" to which the computer will respond as well.

Now consider a slightly more complicated question. Are there any controls that can be either digital or analog? What about a joystick? As it turns out, the answer is "yes." Not that there are joysticks that are both digital and analog at the same time, but joysticks come in both digital and analog models. A digital joystick is a simple device. It's basically a stick attached to four buttons underneath, one each for up/down/left/right. Press the joystick up and the up button is on (often referred to as *closed*). Release the joystick and the up button is now off (or *open*). That means the joystick is either pointing up or it's not — a digital situation. Analog joysticks, on the other hand, use *potentiometers* to send positioning information to the computer. With an analog joystick, it's possible to be *degrees of distance* in one direction, for instance 50 percent of the way to the left. It's not a simple matter of pointing left or not pointing left; it's a matter of *how far* you are pointing to the left.

Note

You may have noticed that several terms mean the same thing when it comes to digital terminology. A digital switch that has been pressed can equally be referred to as 1, on, or closed. Likewise, a switch that has not been pressed can be expressed as 0, off, or open. Any one of the phrasings is okay.

Different joysticks lend themselves to different situations. A digital joystick is good for games that don't require positional information to be sent to the computer. Take, for instance, the game of *Donkey Kong* and our poor friend Mario. Recall that when last we left him, brave Mario had narrowly escaped flaming death from a barrel. Once again, Mario needs to run right to avoid another barrel. You press your joystick to the right, telling the computer to send Mario scampering in that direction. You're not telling the computer to run right a certain distance; you're telling it to run right until you tell it to stop. You keep the joystick held right until you run out of the barrel's reach, and then release it. Mario stops running and lives to see another day. Huzzah, well done Mario!

Now picture a flight game that uses a joystick instead of a yoke, such as a jet-fighter simulation. You need to bank left 20 degrees, so you tilt your joystick part-way to the left. Oops, too much and you're banking 30 degrees. You ease the joystick slightly back toward the center until your plane is angled at 20 degrees. When you finish your turn, you bring the joystick back to the center and the plane levels off. This is an example of an analog joystick. This wouldn't work with a digital joystick. You would only be able to tell the computer to bank left, but not by how many degrees. If it worked at all, it would simply send you into a leftward barrel-roll until you let go of the joystick.

This has been touched on earlier in the book but is worth one more look. For the purpose of arcade controls and computers, analog values are generated by potentiometers. The potentiometer sends a *relative* position, such as 30 degrees to the right. Technically, what the potentiometer sends is a *resistance* value. A potentiometer works by varying the resistance as you turn its shaft (see Figure 7-1). Turned completely to one direction, the resistance is essentially zero. Turned completely to the other direction, and the resistance is maximized (the value depending upon the rating of the potentiometer). Normally, the maximum value is 5K ohms (usually referred to as 5K) for arcade controls, and 100K for PC-based controls. The computer decides what the resistance value means. For instance, if there are 256 different positions along the *X* axis, a value of 0K would mean position 0 (far left), a value of 50K would mean position 127 (middle), and a value of 100K would mean position 255 (far right). It's also possible for the device to do its own conversion of the resistance to a digital value and send that to the computer. This lets you use an analog joystick, for instance, that has a *USB connector* (a digital input port).

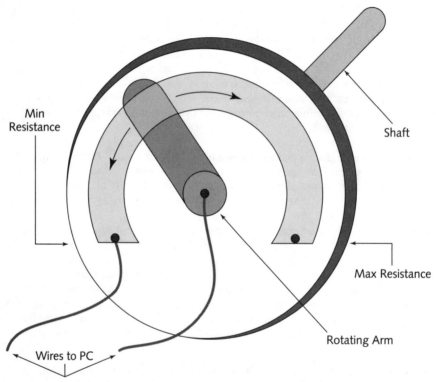

FIGURE 7-1: The resistance increases as the shaft is turned clockwise.

Digital values are generated by switches. The switches can take a variety of forms, but all generate a signal that is on or off, closed or open. In the case of joysticks and buttons, that is usually either a *microswitch* or a *leaf switch*. When the tiny button on the microswitch is pressed down or the two leafs of the leaf switch are pressed together, the switch is closed and sends the appropriate signal. When they are not pressed, the switches are open and send no signal — normally. There is one exception to this, although technically it's really not an exception at all. Microswitches, as discussed earlier, have three contacts — *common* (COM), *normally open* (NO), and *normally closed* (NC). When you connect to the COM and NO contacts, you're using the switch in a situation where it's normally open (that is, not pressed). Only when it's pressed should the button send a signal to the computer. If you connect to the COM and NC contacts, then you're using the switch where it's normally closed (that is, constantly pressed). You want a signal sent only when the button is released. An example of using a button in this configuration might be a button that's used to monitor the back door of the arcade cabinet.

When the door is shut, the button is pressed (normally closed), and all is well. If someone opens the door, the button is released or opened, and it sends a signal to the computer telling it that it's active. The computer then shuts the game down. This is called a *kill-switch* and is occasionally used. An unknown, defective kill-switch has been the bane of many an arcade repair technician who doesn't know to look for it! At any rate, this is entirely a matter of semantics because whether the button is normally open or normally closed, it still has only two possible states and for all intents and purposes works the same. For the purposes of any discussion in this book, assume microswitches are normally open.

Another way that digital values are created and sent to the computer is by *optical encoders*. Mice, trackballs, and spinners use optical encoders. A round disc rotates between two halves of the optical encoder, as shown in Figure 7-2. The disc has holes punched in it around the outer rim at regular intervals. The optical encoder sends a light beam from one half to the other half. When the disc is spun, the holes alternately block and let through the beam of light, which is translated into digital data. The faster you move the physical mouse, the faster the light-dark-light-dark pattern is generated. This corresponds to increased speed of the cursor on-screen. There are actually two wheels (one for the X axis, one for the Y) and two light beams per wheel, which allow the mouse electronics to determine not only how fast you're moving but also in which direction. Although the method of how they're created is different (physical button presses for switches, light beam patterns for optical encoders), the end results are the same. Digital data is generated and sent to the computer.

FIGURE 7-2: An encoder wheel between two halves of the optical encoders.
Used by permission of Happ Controls.

Arcade Cabinet Wiring 101

So now that you've got a good feel for the difference between digital and analog, it's a good time to talk about wiring your arcade cabinet project. Wiring is the *nerve system* of your cabinet: It allows the various parts to talk to one another. Getting the wiring right is a crucial part of creating your project. Fortunately, it's not a difficult task, and there are several options for wiring your cabinet.

Note   The information in this section applies to wiring arcade controls to your control panel. Wiring up lights and power to the cabinet are covered in Chapter 15, "Buttoning Up the Odds and Ends."

Traveling the arcade circuit

The principle behind how electricity flows through an arcade control is very simple. Every switch attached to a joystick, button, or other arcade control is used to complete a *circuit*. A circuit is basically a path for electricity to flow through. The electrons in the circuit flow from the source's negative side to the positive side, usually through one or more components (such as a button's microswitch). The source in this case is your arcade cabinet's *interface*, which is covered in detail in the next few chapters. If the path the electrons flow through is interrupted, then the circuit is broken and there's no electrical flow. If the path is complete, then the circuit functions and electricity flows.

Caution   Although all the material in this chapter refers to low-voltage wiring in the 5- to 12-volt range, it is still electricity. It is unlikely that you would become injured, but it is possible to do damage to your computer components with improper wiring. Please use reasonable caution as you approach your wiring.

The switches used in your arcade controls complete or break the circuit's path, depending on whether they are pressed or not pressed. Normally the switches are not pressed (normally open) and the circuit is broken. When you press the button or move the joystick, the circuit is complete and electricity flows (see Figure 7-3). This alerts whatever interface you're using that something has happened, and appropriate action is taken (for example, Mario jumps another barrel).

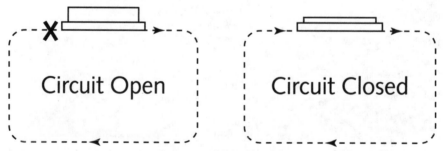

FIGURE 7-3: *Left:* A button not pressed (normally open), breaking the circuit's path.
Right: A button pressed, closing the circuit and allowing the current to flow.

Shopping list

Let's start by looking at the essential components for wiring. You need a few tools, good wire, and miscellaneous consumable supplies. You can find these at any Radio Shack, electronics, or home improvement store.

Tools

You need a handful of tools for the next few steps of your project. You can see a representative sampling in Figure 7-4.

FIGURE 7-4: Most of the tools you're likely to need for wiring. Clockwise from upper left: Soldering iron in soldering station, extra hands, soldering gun, screwdrivers, multimeter, solder-removal tool, and crimping tool.

Tip

A word on tool quality: It's possible to get tools cheaply, and it's possible to get cheap tools. Those are not the same thing. A good tool is almost always worth the price paid for it, whereas a cheap tool may not be a bargain no matter what the discount. If you're going to do a project such as this again (and the fact that you're reading this book means it's quite possible), then consider investing in good quality tools. The amount of effort and frustration they'll save you will more than justify the extra cost in the long run.

- **Soldering iron.** A soldering iron is used to melt solder onto electrical components to make permanent wiring connections. Soldering irons come in different shapes and power ratings. Cheap soldering irons typically have lower temperatures and will take longer to melt the solder, causing no end of frustration. I was once convinced that mastering soldering was beyond me, which was infuriating, as I knew the skill was not complicated. Obtaining a good soldering iron and solder made all the difference.

- **Soldering station.** A soldering station comes in handy when working. A soldering iron gets very hot, and you need a safe place to store it while soldering. The damp sponge is used to clean the iron between soldering jobs.

- **Extra hands.** A solid base with alligator clips to help hold items while soldering solves the problem of needing three hands.

- **Soldering gun.** A soldering gun serves a similar purpose as a soldering iron with a different shape. Soldering guns heat up quicker than soldering irons but can be more difficult to use for precise work.

- **Screwdrivers.** Screwdrivers are needed to attach wiring to screw-on connectors.

- **Multimeter.** Multimeters are used to test electrical components. They have multiple settings to test various electrical properties. They are extremely useful in testing for breaks in wiring.

- **Solder removal tool.** Some of the techniques involve de-soldering a component so you can modify it. A solder removal tool is invaluable for these efforts.

- **Crimping tool.** A crimping tool is used to crimp wire onto wiring connectors, as well as other functions such as stripping and cutting wire.

Supplies

Likewise, you will need various consumable supplies to wire things up. A good rule of thumb for supplies is to buy more than you think you need. Sooner or later you almost always find out that you underestimated your needs. It's better to have some left over than to come up short and have to wait till you can get more before you can proceed. Figure 7-5 shows some of the supplies you're likely to need.

- **Solder.** The soft metal substance is melted onto two electrical components or wires to bond them together and allow for electrical connectivity.

- **Soldering braid.** Soldering braid is a spool of material used to absorb solder when de-soldering. It can be used instead of a solder removal tool.

- **Wiring blocks.** Wiring blocks are long blocks of plastic with screws used for connecting wires together. It can be used instead of soldering or other types of connectors.

- **Electrical tape.** Used for temporary (and sometimes not-so-temporary) connecting of wire, electrical tape is insulative and will not conduct electricity.

- **Wiring disconnects.** Wiring disconnects are male and female spade-type connectors used to connect wiring. Connectors allow for quick removal and reattachment.

- **Connector plugs.** Connector plugs, such as the Molex style in the upper left of Figure 7-5 or the DB-25 style in the upper right (both unassembled), together with their opposite partners allow for quick connecting and disconnecting of multiple wires at once instead of one at a time.

- **Wire.** Obviously, to wire components together you need wire. See the following section for a discussion on wire.

- **Cable ties.** Cable ties are used to neatly bundle cable together, which will help to avoid *spaghetti* wiring.

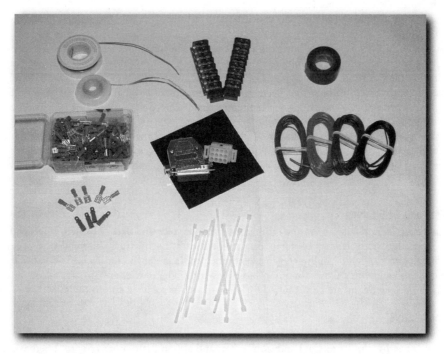

FIGURE 7-5: A well-rounded stock of supplies. *Top row:* Solder and soldering braid, wiring blocks, and electrical tape. *Middle row:* Wiring disconnects, DB-25 and Molex connector plugs, and wire. *Bottom row:* Cable ties.

Some vendors, such as Ultimate Arcade (www.ultimarc.com) and The Real Bob Roberts (www.therealbobroberts.com), sell wiring kits that have assembled some of the supplies and tools for you.

Wire

You have two goals when it comes to wiring your arcade cabinet project. You want it to work, and you want it to be safe. Neither goal is difficult to achieve as long as you put a little bit of thought into it beforehand. There are many different wire choices available to you. I'll discuss several options and make a recommendation in the following paragraphs.

Solid core versus stranded wire

Two different kinds of wire are used in electronic applications. *Solid core wire* is wire that's composed of one single metal strand of wire wrapped in a single run of insulating material.

Stranded wire consists of multiple strands of wire run together in a single wrap of insulating material, effectively forming a single wire. Solid core wire is stiff and holds its shape when bent. It can break with repeated flexing; therefore, it is used in applications that are not likely to see a lot of movement, such as in-wall wiring. Stranded core wire is flexible and not likely to break with flexing. It is used in applications that are likely to see a lot of movement, such as extension cords. Stranded core wire is easier to work with and is usually preferred over solid core by arcade cabinet builders.

18 to 22 gauge wire

Typically, *18 to 22 gauge wire* is used in arcade cabinet construction. It's available in many solid colors, which is useful for keeping track of which wire goes to what control. Wire gauge is a measurement of the size of the wire. The higher the number, the smaller the wire — for example, 22 gauge wire is thinner than 18 gauge wire. Wire of 18 to 22 gauge is roughly a millimeter and a half in size. This wire is well suited for any connection method.

 Using a wire gauge that is incorrectly sized can lead to problems such as the wire heating up, which can be a dangerous fire hazard. For the low voltages used in the control panels, overheating is not likely to occur. However, be aware of the possibility of overheating and take care when wiring.

Cat3 and Cat5 cable

Cat3 and Cat5 cable is used in the cabling industry for voice and data networks. It has eight individually-wrapped wires contained in a single sheath. Each wire is color coded with a different color and is about 1 millimeter in size. Some people prefer to use this cable because the bundle of eight wires allows for quick and easy wiring. These wires are difficult to use quick disconnects with and are better suited for screw-down or soldered connections.

Phone cable

Phone cable comes in a variety of shapes and wire counts. You can obtain rolls of phone cable in round sheaths (similar to Cat3 and Cat5 cable) and also in flat ribbons of wire. There will usually be four, six, or eight wires per cable. Other than the shape and wire count, the properties of phone cable are essentially the same as Cat3 and Cat5 cable.

Ribbon cable

You've probably seen *ribbon cable* inside a computer connected to a CD-ROM or hard drive. It's a flat ribbon of cable with a varying number of small wires inside, usually a high count like 40 or so. The wires are approximately a millimeter or less in size. Some people like the high wire count for cabling purposes. However, all the wires look the same, so you have to identify them by their position in the ribbon and not by color. Doing so can be difficult. Wiring blocks or soldering will be necessary with this cable.

Recommendation

When in doubt, do what the professionals do. Those who know use good-quality stranded 18 to 22 gauge wire to wire arcade cabinets. Bob Roberts of The Real Bob Roberts Web site (www.therealbobroberts.com) recommends 18 gauge wire for power conductors, and 20 gauge for all the rest (22 gauge if you don't have 20). Wire of these sizes is big enough to be able to work with easily, yet still small enough to be neatly bundled for a professional appearance. A big spool of black wire for all the grounding (see the "Grounding" section in this chapter) and several smaller spools of different color for each control are ideal. It's difficult to advise on how much wire to purchase, as that amount will be determined by the number of controls and distance between the controls and the interface used. A good rule-of-thumb estimate is 3 feet of black wire and 3 feet of colored wire per switch. Remember that each button has a single switch, and that joysticks usually have four . Also, don't forget to leave enough slack in your wiring path to be able to lift up the control panel for maintenance. Wire is cheap (you can find it for 5 cents per foot), so stock up.

Wiring techniques

Wire is a way for electrical signals to travel from point A to point B. The method used to attach the wire to the end points depends on what their mounting requirements are. In arcade cabinet projects, the methods used fall into three broad categories: crimp-on connections, soldered connections, and straight connections.

Crimp-on connections

Crimp-on connections involve attaching a terminal connector of some kind to the end of the wire. The top half of Figure 7-6 shows several different crimp-on connectors.

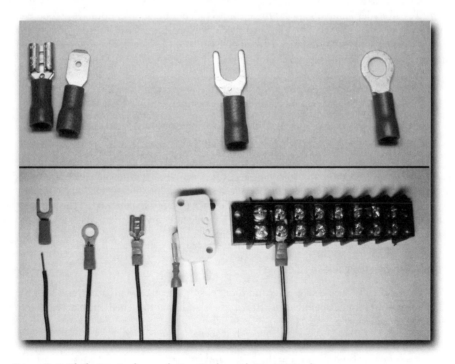

FIGURE 7-6: Blade terminals, spade terminals, and ring terminals.

Using your multipurpose crimping tool, strip off approximately ¼ inch of the insulation from the wire. Insert the exposed copper into the terminal up to the point where the insulation begins, and then crimp the terminal down onto the wire (see Figure 7-6). Give it the tug-test to make sure the wire is properly seated in the terminal—it should not have any give to it. Make sure the terminals you use are of the proper type and size for the wire and component you're connecting. The terminal will have a rating for the wire gauge it supports and a size rating for the connector. For instance, most microswitches use a .187-inch male-blade connector, so your terminal would need to be a .187-inch female-blade connector with whatever gauge rating your wire is. Crimp-on connectors are often used in conjunction with wiring blocks.

Soldered connections

Soldering a wire to a component or two components together is used when a permanent connection is wanted. It is possible to de-solder such a connection, but that is not quickly done; and so for our purposes, consider this a permanent connection. You're most likely to want to solder connections when hacking arcade controls, such as replacing potentiometers in a yoke or steering wheel to make them compatible with a computer game port.

Good soldering technique is not difficult to learn. The core concept is simple: When you use a very hot soldering iron, the solder is heated to the point of melting, at which point it flows onto the components you're connecting. Remove the soldering iron and the solder quickly cools, attaching the two components together and forming a good electrical bond. However, there are some nuances to soldering that, if not grasped, will lead to frustration and bad solder joints. A bad solder joint will appear to be connected, but in fact will not have a good electrical bond and can intermittently fail. I'll start by pointing you toward a couple of good soldering tutorials available on the Internet, and then give you a few pointers. The following Web sites include good introductions to soldering:

- Steve's MacMAME Arcade Experiment at www.starbase74.com/mame/ solderframe.htm (also included on the companion CD-ROM)

- EPE Online's Basic Soldering Guide at www.epemag.com/solderfaq/ default.htm

Caution   Be careful when soldering! The soldering iron can reach temperatures between 500 and 800 degrees or more. You don't want to burn yourself or cause a fire through inattentiveness. Never leave a hot soldering iron unattended! Also, solder isn't pleasant to inhale (read the warnings on the package, as it's nasty stuff). Make sure to have adequate ventilation when soldering. Use reasonable care, and you'll be fine.

A quick step-by-step guide to soldering

1. Assemble all your needed parts and tools, ensure adequate ventilation, and heat the iron for several minutes before using it. An iron that has not reached optimal temperature will not work well.

2. Tin the iron's tip by melting a bit of solder to it. The layer of solder will help promote heat transfer from the iron to the solder and components to be soldered. An un-tinned iron will not work as well.

3. Make sure the surfaces to be soldered are clean. This step is very important. Surfaces dirty with oxidation, oil, or grime will reject the solder, causing it to bead up instead of bond. Flux can be used to clean the surfaces if your solder doesn't have a flux core. If your solder does have a flux core, then you can clean the surface with an abrasive eraser, file, or similar tool. A final wipe with rubbing alcohol will clean the surface.

Warning! Alcohol and a hot iron do not mix! Keep one well away from the other, and make sure the surface has dried off before getting the iron near it.

4. Heat the components, not the solder. Solder flows toward the heat. To properly solder, apply the iron to both components to be soldered at the same time. Touch the solder to the components, not the iron. The heat will transfer from the components to the solder, causing the solder to flow onto the components. Resist the urge to directly heat the solder! See Figure 7-7.

FIGURE 7-7: Properly applying heat to the components to be soldered.

5. Use the flat part of the iron's tip, and not the very point (see Figure 7-8). The more surface area of the iron you apply, the greater the heat transference.

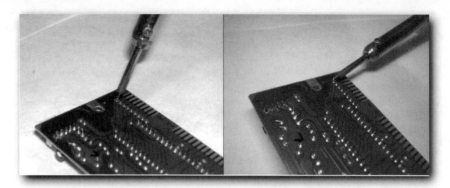

Figure 7-8: *Left:* **Incorrect way to use the iron's tip.** *Right:* **The correct way.**

6. Soldering should occur quickly. It should not take more than a few seconds for the solder to reach melting point and flow onto the components. Leaving heat on circuit boards for too long can damage the components; and if the solder hasn't melted after a few seconds then something is wrong. Check for cleanliness of the components and the iron.

7. Pre-tin wires by applying solder to them and then letting them cool, as shown in Figure 7-9. When it's time to attach the wire to the component, the pre-tinned wire will make it easier.

Figure 7-9: A pre-tinned wire.

8. When you remove the iron from the solder joint, hold the components that have been soldered still for a couple of seconds until the solder has cooled completely. Allowing the components to move before the solder has fully set can cause *cold solder joints* that will not work properly.

9. Clean your iron between soldering tasks by wiping it on a cold damp sponge.

10. Practice soldering on scrap material a few times until you're comfortable with the technique before you work on the real components.

De-soldering is the process of removing solder from a previously joined connection. The process is similar to soldering up to the point where you have the solder melted. If you are using a solder-sucker such as a bulb or vacuum tube, then you simply use that to lift the solder off when it is melted. Alternatively, many professionals prefer the use of a de-soldering braid. This is a flexible wire mesh that you put between the solder and the iron, and then heat the braid. The solder melts and is absorbed into the braid. Either way will work, just be careful once again not to overheat the component you are de-soldering.

Straight connections

A quick and easy way to attach wiring is with a *straight connection*. That means a connection where the wire is attached directly to the component without any extra parts required. For instance, many of the commercial interfaces have screw terminals for the wiring to attach to (see Figure 7-10). Simply strip about ¼ inch of the wire and insert it into the screw terminal. Tighten the screw down onto the wire until snug and make sure it passes the tug-test. Another way to directly connect wire is to a wire block with screw terminals. Unlike the first kind, you actually wrap the wire around the screw and then tighten the screw down onto the wire. This kind of connection tends to get sloppy and is not recommended, if you can avoid it. The one disadvantage of both of these straight connects is that changing or removing things around involves unscrewing each wire, which takes longer than quick disconnects.

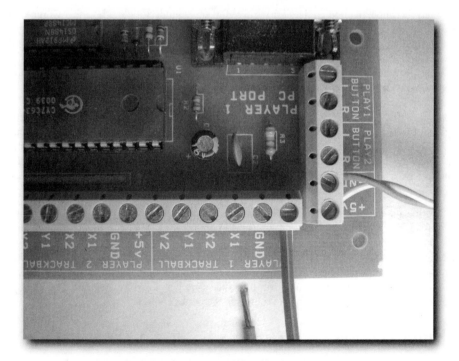

FIGURE 7-10: Attaching wires to the screw terminal block on an interface.

Wiring blocks

Wiring blocks, sometimes referred to as *barrier strips*, are good ways to connect two components together when you don't want to simply wire directly between them. Neatness and ease of wiring are two reasons you might want to use wiring blocks.

Wiring blocks come in strips of varying sizes, with two columns of screw terminals. Each screw terminals is connected to its counterpart in the pair and will conduct electricity to the other side. Each pair is isolated from other pairs and will not conduct electricity to the other pairs. Wiring blocks can be attached to with spade or ring terminals, or directly to the wire.

Grounding

Every switch in your arcade cabinet will have two wires coming from it. One will go to the positive side of the interface you've chosen, and one will go to the ground side. Each switch's positive connection will go to a unique terminal on your interface. The ground side however does not have to go to a unique terminal on the interface. In fact, most interfaces come with only one or two ground terminals, so you need a method to connect all the grounds to those few ground terminals. Bringing all the grounds to the same place is referred to as a *common ground*; you often hear people refer to a ground as a *common* instead. Recall that the microswitches discussed earlier in the book were labeled NO, NC, and COM (for common ground).

You have a couple of good choices for wiring all your grounds. One method that works well is to *daisy chain* the grounds together. Start by attaching a wire from the interface's ground terminal to the first switch's ground. Then attach a second wire from the switch's ground to the next switch. Repeat until each switch's ground is connected to another switch. Attach the last switch's ground back to the ground on the interface, creating a giant loop of linked grounds. Every switch except for the two at each end of the chain will be connected to two other switches. The two switches at the end will be attached back to the interface ground. The advantage of doing it this way is that you use much less wire than you would running a separate ground to the interface per switch, which results in a much neater wiring job. The fact that both ends of the chain are connected to the interface's ground means that even if one of the daisy-chained wires breaks or comes loose, all the controls will continue to function because they'll have a path back to ground. Only if there are two breaks in the ground chain will some of the controls stop working.

The other method to ground multiple devices is to use a wiring block. Recall that every pair in a wiring block is isolated. The way to use a wiring block for common grounding is to connect the screw terminals in one column together, effectively making every screw terminal connect to all the others. You can do this by wiring between them or by using a strip made for this purpose (see Figure 7-11). Then attach one terminal to the ground terminal on the interface, and the rest of the terminals can be used for individual switches. There's a lot more wire involved doing it this way; daisy chaining the grounds is the better choice.

Sharing controls

Sometimes, you may wish to have two separate controls appear to the arcade cabinet as one. For instance, you may have an eight-way joystick and a four-way joystick for player 1's side. Your game will recognize only one set of controls for player 1. What can you do? Fortunately, the solution is easy to accomplish. Simply connect the inputs from one joystick to the same place as the second joystick. That is, the positive side of the up switch on joystick 1 will connect to the same place as the positive side of the up switch on joystick 2, and so on. You can either do that by running wire from each switch to the same terminal on your interface or by daisy chaining the switch from one joystick to the switch on the other and running a single wire from there to the interface. Both solutions work equally as well. The only thing to be aware of is that both joysticks are active at the same time. If you're trying to run the by-now tired Mario to the left on one joystick, and someone moves the other joystick to the right, Mario will stop running and have a nervous breakdown!

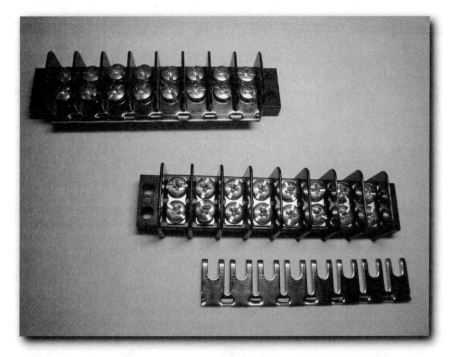

FIGURE 7-11: A wiring block with every terminal interconnected by a metal strip.

Tapping into power

Some of the things you want to have in an arcade cabinet may need power sources. Most of them do not, being simple passive devices. Most buttons and joysticks, for instance, simply open and close circuits when pressed and don't need any power by themselves. Some buttons and joysticks, however, do need a source of power that is a separate circuit from the open/close circuit that detects a button press. For example, the control may be illuminated and so the light or LED will need power. Other devices that use optics instead of physical switches will need a power source to run the optical encoders, such as spinners, trackballs, and the Happ Controls Perfect 360 joystick.

You can get power to these controls from a variety of sources. Some of the commercial interfaces you can purchase include +5v (5-volt) connections you can use. If you don't have +5v available from your interface, you can pick it up from a variety of locations. People have used +5v from the keyboard and mouse ports, USB ports, game ports, and directly from the PC power supply. Of all these, the only one I recommend is directly from the PC power supply.

If something goes wrong in your wiring and there is a short, you can burn out whichever port you're pulling power from and possibly the motherboard. This is usually fatal to the computer, though you might get lucky if there's a replaceable fuse that blows. Unfortunately, that is usually not the case. If something goes wrong and you're using power directly from the power supply, then you might blow out the power supply but the motherboard should be safe. Getting the power supply repaired or replacing it is almost always easier and cheaper than a fried motherboard.

The power cables that come from the PC power supply contain 4 pins: +5v, +12v, ground, and ground. The +5v is usually red and the +12v is usually yellow, but measure with a multimeter to be sure. Tying into these is a simple matter of purchasing an extension or splitter cable, cutting off one end, and wiring that appropriately (see Figure 7-12). Be sure that you seal off any stray wires that you aren't using with electrical tape or wire nuts, or preferably remove them from the plug altogether. Then you can simply plug into the power cable from the power supply. You *could* cut the end off the power cable from the power supply directly, but that's a permanent alteration. Doing it with an extension cable allows you to change things around later.

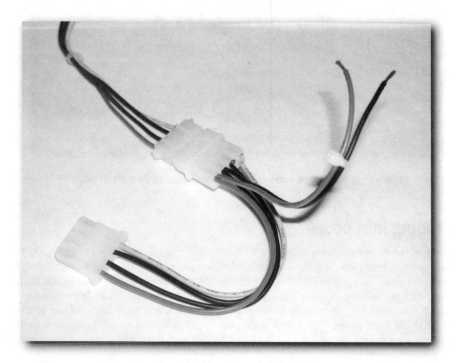

FIGURE 7-12: Tapping into a PC power supply.

Wiring the Happ Controls Perfect 360 joystick

The Happ Controls Perfect 360 joystick is a tad confusing to wire and deserves a bit of additional explanation. Recall that the joystick uses optical sensors instead of physical switches and so needs a power source. The 360 has six contacts underneath it: one each for up/down/left/right, a +5v, and a ground (see Figure 7-13). If you are able to get +5v from the same interface that you're attaching the directional contacts to, then it's easy. Wire each direction to the appropriate connector on the interface, the +5v to the interface's +5v connector, and ground to ground.

FIGURE 7-13: The labeled underside of a Happ Controls Perfect 360 joystick.
Used by permission of Happ Controls.

What if you need to get power from a different source? Say you are getting power directly from the power supply. The four directional contacts will go to the interface as usual. The +5v contact on the 360 will go to the power cable from the power supply. Where does the ground go? Electricity flows only if you have a complete circuit, right? If you wire the ground to the power supply, then the optical encoders have a complete circuit, but what about the directional contacts? If you wire the ground to the interface, then haven't you created an incomplete circuit for the optical encoders? Fortunately, the answer is no. The interfaces all get their power from the same place you're tapping into. All the powered components that attach to the computer ultimately get their power, both positive and ground, from the same source — the PC power supply. By attaching the ground to either the interface or the power supply, you've created a complete circuit for all parts of the joystick. It's easiest to connect the ground to your interface or ground wiring block instead of to the power supply.

Tip

When you wire your joysticks, remember that up is down and left is right. Perfectly clear, right? When you press a joystick to the right, the bottom of the joystick under the control panel is pushing left. Therefore, the left-hand microswitch is the one that activates right, and vice versa. Keep this in mind. A lot of folks get this wrong. Happy wiring!

How It All Works

The entire chapter to this point has been to give you the background for the magic that makes it possible to turn an ordinary personal computer into a laser-blasting, noise-making arcade machine. The core concept is that all the interaction between you and the computer takes place in an analog or digital fashion through the use of devices wired to the machine. It's a deceptively simple concept, but the fact that a circuit's a circuit no matter what hardware components are used is what makes everything work. Whether the circuit is a keyboard button being pressed or an arcade button, a mouse being moved or a trackball being spun, to the computer *it all looks the same.* We can connect to the keyboard interface on the computer and generate an F keystroke by pressing a shiny red arcade button! A spin of a lit-up blue trackball can move the mouse on the screen! I recall the first time I found this was possible that my jaw dropped as I realized the possibilities. All you need to complete the puzzle is an interface that sits between your arcade controls and the computer so that they can talk to each other. I cover that in the next few chapters.

Summary

Your computer is a digital device that interacts with the outside world through other digital and analog devices. Arcade controls are digital and analog devices. The two seemingly separate worlds can be induced to talk to one another, starting with wiring the arcade controls to your control panel in preparation for the next step. Good wiring is a core ingredient for a successful arcade cabinet project. Using the proper tools, materials, and wiring techniques will help you achieve this. It also happens to be a lot of fun!

The rest of the chapters in this section are devoted to making the computer think your arcade controls are in fact regular keyboard, mouse, game-port, and USB devices. First up in the next chapter is using the keyboard interface. Arcade Nirvana, here you come!

Using the Keyboard Connector for Arcade Controls

Y ou are more likely to connect your arcade controls to your computer through the keyboard port than any other way. Everyone who has a computer has a keyboard, but not everyone has a joystick or gamepad. Software developers know this so almost every game made for the computer includes the ability to control it with a keyboard. Even my favorite driving game, *Need For Speed — Porsche Unleashed*, can be played with a keyboard, though I don't recommend it.

Taking advantage of what you learned in the previous chapter, this chapter will show you how to use the keyboard port to interface your arcade controls. I'll start by introducing you to the various methods and products available. At that point, you'll know everything you need to know to be able to select an interface method and start connecting wires! If you're following along and building the Project Arcade machine instead of your own design, I'll fill you in on the method chosen for the machine at the end of the chapter. You've come a long way, but, so far, all you've got is something to look at. After this chapter, your mad-scientist creation will actually be able to *do* something!

Hacking a Real Keyboard

Remember I said you might get to take something apart? I'm sure I heard someone laughing with glee when I mentioned that. Well, now's the time! Probably the least expensive way to connect arcade controls to your computer is by hacking apart a keyboard. (Several keyboards were harmed during the creation of this book.) I'll start by taking a look at how keyboards work and then proceed into turning one into an arcade interface.

How keyboards work

What do keyboards do? In simple terms, a keyboard allows you to press a key, which closes a circuit associated with a particular keystroke. That closed circuit is detected by a mini-computer inside the keyboard called a *keyboard encoder*, which recognizes which key has been pressed. The keyboard encoder takes that information, encodes it in a digital form the main computer can understand, and passes it to the computer via the keyboard port.

The actual physical makeup of a keyboard can vary quite a bit. A typical design includes either a circuit board or a flimsy material (simply flimsy hereafter) that lies underneath the buttons on the keyboard. Laid out on the flimsy is a maze of circuits. Directly beneath each keyboard button on the flimsy are two halves of a circuit. The underside of the button has a conductive material of some kind. When the button is pressed, the conductive material comes into contact with the two halves of the circuit below, which completes the circuit. Variations on this design exist, but almost all are similar. Take a look at Figure 8-1 for an example.

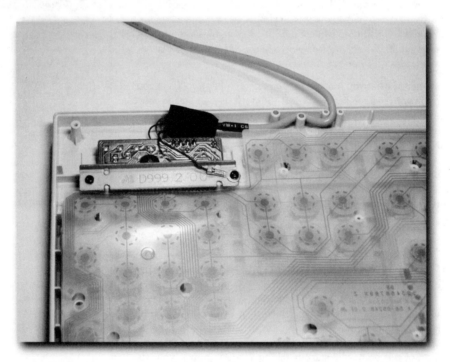

FIGURE **8-1: The circuit traces on the flimsy all come back to the keyboard encoder shown in the top left.**

How the keyboard operates should sound very familiar. It's just like the arcade pushbutton coming down to press the microswitch button, which completes that circuit. The only piece that the keyboard has that is missing in the arcade pushbutton circuit is the keyboard encoder. Could we use the encoder from a real keyboard for our purposes? Take a look at the keyboard encoders shown in Figure 8-2.

Figure 8-2: Some keyboard encoders removed from their keyboards.

Notice the connectors at the edge of the keyboard encoder boards. Those stripes are the contacts that the circuits on the flimsy come back to. If you start counting, you'll realize that there aren't nearly enough contacts to account for all the keys on the keyboard. Even if every key's circuit used a shared common ground, there are still not enough contacts to account for the 100 or so keys found on a typical keyboard. What's going on?

If a keyboard was configured to use *discrete contacts* (one contact per key), there would be over 100 contacts required and a keyboard encoder chip with the same number of pins on it! That would be big and expensive — something manufacturers always try to avoid. Instead, keyboard makers take advantage of a design technique called a *matrix*. No, Keanu Reeves is not going to show up suddenly in your arcade cabinet. A matrix is a method of using a small number of contacts to account for a larger number of inputs by arranging them into a grid. Take a closer look at the keyboard encoder in Figure 8-3. Notice the contacts separated into two groups. There are 14 contacts on the left and 8 on the right.

If the keyboard was set up in discrete mode, there would only be 22 buttons possible on the encoder shown in Figure 8-3 because there are only 22 contacts. However, this encoder is configured in a grid of 14 × 8. This gives a total of 112 possible buttons (14 × 8 = 112) — more than enough for a standard 104-button keyboard. The way it works is that the keyboard encoder has a map of this matrix programmed in its memory. Take a look at the matrix in Figure 8-4. I'll refer to the 14-contact side of the matrix as the *x* side and the 8-contact side as the *y* side.

FIGURE 8-3: A close-up look at the contacts of a typical keyboard encoder.

	X1	X2	X3	X4	X5	X6	X7	X8	X9	X10	X11	X12	X13	X14
Y1	A	I	Q	Y	·	·	·	·	·	·	·	·	·	·
Y2	B	J	R	Z										
Y3	C	K	S	1										
Y4	D	L	T	2										
Y5	E	M												
Y6	F	·												
Y7	G	·												
Y8	H	·												

FIGURE 8-4: An example of a possible matrix using the keyboard encoder from Figure 8-3.

The A button is in the first spot on the matrix (X1-Y1). When the A button is pressed, the encoder sees the circuit that connects the first contact on the 14-contact side (X1) and the first contact on the 8-contact side (Y1) (see Figure 8-5). The encoder looks this up in its map and generates an A keystroke.

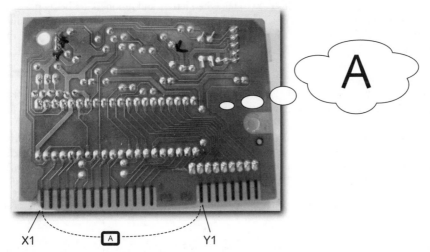

X1 --------- A --------- Y1

FIGURE 8-5: The A button pressed.

Determining which keyboard button has been pressed is a simple matter of the encoder doing a lookup in its table for the X and Y value that is generated by the key press. There is no set standard for how a matrix is designed and laid out. Another keyboard manufacturer might configure its matrix to be 13 × 9, which allows for 117 buttons, with the keystrokes occupying different spots on the grid.

How to hack a keyboard

You may be thinking—based on the previous section's information about how keyboards work—that it should be possible to substitute arcade controls in place of keyboard buttons. In fact, it is, and many people have done just that. With the low cost of keyboards (sometimes with rebates you can even get them for free) and the high number of inputs available, a keyboard hack sounds ideal. It *is* possible to successfully use a keyboard hack, but there are several obstacles to overcome first. Because of the potential drawbacks, I strongly recommend reading this section completely before beginning work. There are alternatives available if you decide a keyboard hack is not for you.

Warning! The rest of the discussion on keyboard hacking can prove hazardous to the health of your computer! There is a +5v (five volt) presence on the encoder board while connected to the computer. If something goes wrong, it is possible to fry the keyboard port on the computer or the motherboard itself. With care, this can be avoided. However, if you are concerned, you may wish to skip ahead to the last section in this chapter covering commercial encoders.

Mapping the matrix

Your first hurdle will be a time-consuming one. Because every keyboard is different, you will have to manually determine the matrix your keyboard uses. I'm assuming you've taken apart your sacrificial keyboard and disconnected the keyboard encoder board from the rest of it. The procedure is simple. First, you need a program on your computer that will tell you what keystrokes are being generated. It's easy to tell when letters and numbers are being pressed with any word processor or notepad application. However, those won't tell you if you're pressing the left shift key, right control key, and so forth. On the *download* section of the Build Your Own Arcade Controls Web site (www.arcadecontrols.com), there are several utilities that will do just that. Download one of them, and fire it up.

On the CD

Ghostkeys 1.1 (by John Dickson) is one of the programs that will tell you which keystroke is being generated, and it is included on the companion CD-ROM.

Start by laying out a grid on a piece of paper matching the X and Y contacts on your keyboard encoder. Next, take a length of wire, and strip off ¼ inch from both ends. Hold (or attach with an alligator clamp) one end of the wire to the first X contact. Then, hold the other end of the wire to the first Y contact, and observe the keystroke that is generated on the computer. Record it on your grid, and move on to the second Y contact. When you're done with all the X1 combinations, move on to X2, and repeat. Continue until you have the entire matrix laid out. This can be quite time-consuming!

After mapping the matrix out, you need to decide which keystrokes you're going to use for your control panel. You need to consider two factors. First, you need to determine which keystrokes are required by the software you decide to use. Many games are programmable, that is, they allow you to choose which keystrokes perform the in-game functions. However, some have hard-coded keystrokes for game control and do not allow changing them. For instance, the fire key in a particular game may be the F key. Even though all your other games use the left control key to fire, you have to use the F in this one. Second, you need to look at how your keyboard encoder's matrix is laid out. Certain keystroke combinations will be precluded from use simply due to where they are on the matrix. The next section, "Difficulties with keyboard hacks," will cover this.

After you map out your keyboard matrix and choose the keystrokes you need, you can begin to wire things up. Take another look at the keyboard encoder from our example in Figure 8-3. The contacts on the edge of the encoder cannot be soldered to, and there's no easy other way to attach your wiring to them.

Follow the path of the circuits back a bit to see where they connect up to solder points. *That* is where you can solder your own wiring to. The best way to proceed is to strip a small amount off both ends of the wire, pre-tin one tip with solder, and solder it to the contact point. Next, take the other end of the wire, crimp a connector on it, and attach it to a wiring block a few inches away, as shown in Figure 8-6. Repeat with the rest of the contacts. It is easiest to solder all the wires first and then attach them to the wiring block. The advantage of doing it this way is that any modifications are done to the wiring block and not to the wiring between the keyboard encoder and the block. This helps to ensure the wiring to the encoder is not damaged. You don't want to have to re-solder it!

FIGURE 8-6: The first of 22 wires connected from the keyboard encoder to the wiring block.

Difficulties with keyboard hacks

I find the physical work of soldering the wiring to the keyboard encoder challenging, which is mostly due to the tight quarters. However, physical challenges aside, there are other issues with keyboard hacks. I'll cover each one of them briefly.

Ghosts in the machine

Keyboard hacks can suffer from *ghosting* problems. Keyboards can be haunted? In this case, I am not referring to any nether-worldly spirits. Ghosting is a potential side affect of having a matrix design. What can occur in older keyboards is when three keys are pressed, a phantom fourth keypress is detected by the encoder even though no physical key was pressed. Figure 8-7 shows why this can happen. Recall that a keyboard encoder works by detecting completed circuits. When you press the A button, circuit X1-Y1 is completed. While pressing the A button, also press the B button to complete circuits X1-Y1 and X1-Y2. If you add the O button, something interesting happens. Not only have you added circuit X2-Y1, but, because the three keys — A, B, and O — involve all four terminal points, there are complete circuits between all combinations including X2-Y2 *even though no key was physically pressed at X2-Y2*. The encoder cannot tell that circuit X2-Y2 wasn't intended to be completed. So, it generates a phantom P keystroke.

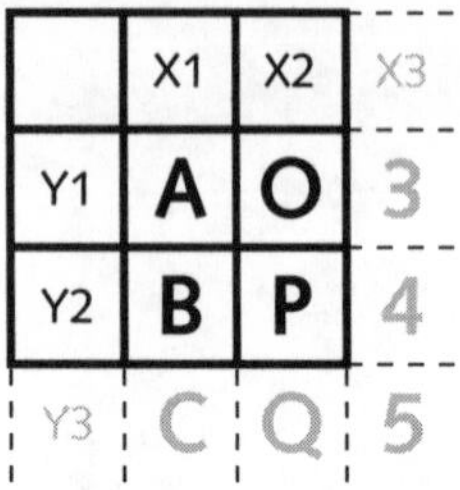

	X1	X2	X3
Y1	**A**	**O**	3
Y2	**B**	**P**	4
Y3	C	Q	5

FIGURE 8-7: A portion of
the keyboard encoder matrix.

This only occurs when three keys in the corners of a rectangular area of a matrix are pressed
simultaneously. Typically, this does not occur when a keyboard is used for typing. However, this
can occur very easily when used for arcade controls. Ghosting could be a problem if, for example, your "up-right" (diagonal movement involving two microswitches) and "jump" keys generated a ghost "quit" key. Picture poor Mario running his heart out, about to jump over one last
barrel to save the damsel in distress, only to have the whole game suddenly exit — leaving
Mario and his lady in lover's limbo forever. That would be enough to make any pixelated per-
sona pack up his bags and go into a less stressful line of work, such as shark dentistry.

Ghostbusting with blocks, design, and diodes

Three solutions present themselves to the ghosting problem. The first is to simply purchase a
new keyboard. Ghosting is a trait of old keyboards from a few years back. Newer keyboards
usually have logic designed into the encoders to block ghost keys from appearing. Recognizing
when two corner keystrokes of a rectangle in the matrix have been generated, the encoder will
simply block the third corner keystroke from appearing. This is known as *keyboard blocking*, and
it has its own drawbacks. There may be times when you *want* those three keystrokes to be able
to function simultaneously. I'd recommend against it, but you may not have a choice depending
on the encoder matrix and requirements of your software. No ready solution is available for
keyboard blocking other than to try a different keystroke combination or different keyboard
encoder.

The second solution is to select the keystrokes that you are going to use from the matrix such
that three corner keystrokes from a rectangle in the matrix cannot be generated. Examine your
matrix map, and make sure that no three keystrokes form a rectangle with a fourth keystroke
that will cause you problems. This prevents both ghosting and blocking. This can be a problem
if your software requires the use of three keystrokes that violates the above rule. However, software that does not allow changing its controls is fairly rare. Another possibility is to choose
keystrokes that are impossible to have occur simultaneously. For instance, the keystrokes you
choose for up, left, and right could safely be chosen even if they would normally be candidates
for causing ghosting because it's impossible to move a joystick in all three directions at the
same time. With careful planning, ghosting and blocking issues are a moot point.

The final solution brings up another electrical component — the *diode*. A diode is a device that,
in simplest terms, only allows electricity to flow in one direction. A diode has two ends: a cathode (-) and an anode (+). Current can only flow from the anode to the cathode but not the
other direction (see Figure 8-8).

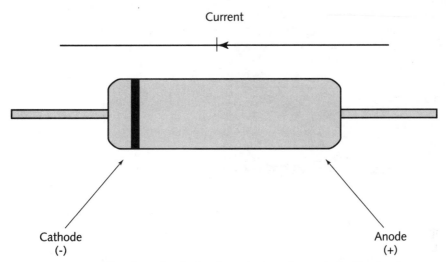

Current

Cathode
(-)

Anode
(+)

FIGURE 8-8: Current flow through a diode. The cathode end is marked with a band.

Ghosting is an electrical issue. With proper diode placement, you can prevent electricity from flowing the wrong way on the matrix, which prevents a ghosting situation. The following is paraphrased from information provided by the folks at Hagstrom Electronics (www. hagstromelectronics.com), a keyboard encoder vendor whose products are introduced later in this chapter.

While scanning the keyboard matrix for activity, a keyboard encoder will normally check columns in the matrix one at a time. When it activates a column, it will check each row to see if any circuits are completed for the current active column. It then moves on to the next column. When three or more switches are pressed that share two columns and one row (or two rows and one column) then electrical ghosting occurs. In many early PC keyboards, you will find a diode in series with each button of the keyboard. On these keyboards, you may press every key on the keyboard at the same time, and the keyboard sends all that information to the PC. By placing a diode in series with each switch, ghosting is prevented. The cathode of the diode is connected to the column side of your matrix, the anode is connected to your switch, and the other contact on your switch connects to the row (see Figure 8-9). Using isolation diodes in a matrix to prevent ghosting is a technique that has been used in keyboards for many years — even preceding the personal computer. Cherry Corporation, a popular manufacturer of keyboard switches, even offers an option of built-in diodes on its switches.

Is your head spinning a bit? Don't worry about the theory. If you're suffering from ghosting problems, pick up some 1N4148 or equivalent diodes (a good electronics store will know what to substitute), and connect them up to the switches having problems. One of two things will happen. Your ghosting problem will go away, or the switch will stop working entirely. If it has stopped working altogether, your diode is in backwards. Reverse it, and all is well.

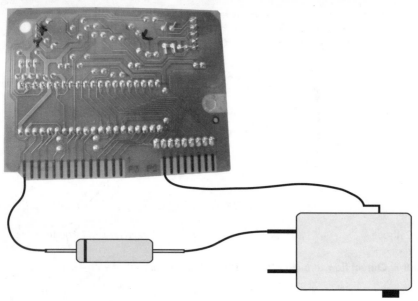

FIGURE 8-9: An example of a diode used to prevent ghosting.

USB keyboard limitations

Be careful about choosing a USB-based keyboard to hack. The USB keyboard interface is designed to limit the number of simultaneous possible keystrokes to six. This isn't a problem when used for games such as *PacMan* or *Donkey Kong*, which are unlikely to need more than two or three keystrokes at the same time. However, modern games such as fighting games can easily require many more than six simultaneous keystrokes, particularly if you are building a four-player control panel. PS/2 keyboard encoders often have a maximum simultaneous key-press limit as well, but it's typically between 10 to 20 or so and is unlikely to cause you issues unless you are building a four-player panel. One final drawback of USB keyboards is that DOS support for them is limited. Newer computers will probably work with USB keyboards in DOS, but older computers probably will not without finding and installing special drivers that are not guaranteed to work.

Keyboard hack recommendations

A keyboard hack is not terribly difficult, but it is fairly time-consuming. You should ask yourself what your time is worth to you. There is some sense of satisfaction for having accomplished a keyboard hack and having spent very little money on it, but, with solderless commercial alternatives available starting at $34, a keyboard hack is probably not worth the effort. I do not recommend spending the time on one unless you are on an extremely tight budget. If you are going to pursue a keyboard hack, there is a good article on the Internet that I suggest consulting as an addendum to the material presented here. Marshall Brooks has created an excellent document (www.mameworld.net/emuadvice/keyhack2.html) expanding on the issues presented here as well as providing matrix maps for several keyboard models. Keyboard hacks are recommended only for those on a tight budget building two-player panels.

Cross-Reference The keyboard hacking guide by Marshall Brooks (Tiger-Heli) is also included on the companion CD-ROM.

Multiple Keyboard Connections

You may find there are times when you will want more than one keyboard device functional at the same time. Why would you want that? Take as an example a situation in which you've created a keyboard hack for your arcade controls, but you still need to be able to operate your computer for non-gaming functions. You *could* simply swap plugs, but you should not do that while the computer is on, and rebooting every time you want to change programs would grow tiresome quickly. Wouldn't it be better to have two keyboard devices plugged in at the same time? Your keyboard hack-based arcade controls would be ready to use whenever you wanted, and your un-hacked keyboard could sit inside the cabinet — ready to be used as needed.

You have a few options if you want to use more than one keyboard device at the same time. All of the solutions are good ones and use different approaches to the problem.

Tip When I refer to using more than one keyboard device at a time, I mean two keyboard encoders with whatever is connected to them. Presumably, it would be a keyboard-based set of arcade controls as one device and a keyboard as the second. It could just as easily mean two sets of keyboard-based arcade controls. Just remember that the phrase "keyboard device" doesn't necessarily mean a keyboard.

Keyboard splitters

A keyboard splitter is not someone who has broken apart their keyboard in order to hack it. A keyboard splitter is a device that converts a single PS/2 keyboard port into two ports. You can find a circuit diagram to build your own on the Internet at `http://home.t-online.de/home/stephan.hans/tricks.htm`, if you are so inclined. If you are not electronically inclined, purchasing a splitter is a better choice. P.I. Engineering sells the Y-key key Dual Keyboard Adapter (`www.ymouse.com/ymouse/whym04.htm`) shown in Figure 8-10. This retails for around $50 and is plug-and-play. Simply plug in the adapter, plug in both keyboard devices, and turn on the computer. Both keyboard devices are fully functional, and the Y-key key is daisy-chainable, that is, it allows three or four keyboard devices to be connected simultaneously.

USB keyboards

A very easy way to have a second keyboard available on your arcade cabinet is to use a USB keyboard. Of course, your computer has to have a USB port, but almost every computer made in the last few years has them. Some of the first computers with USB ports had problems running a USB keyboard until the operating system loaded, which makes configuring the BIOS settings in your computer a problem. However, this is also an unlikely scenario today. Just make sure if you use a USB keyboard that it is your actual keyboard and not used for a hack, because of the six keystroke and operating system limitations discussed in the "USB keyboard limitations" section.

FIGURE 8-10: The Y-key key from P.I. Engineering.
Courtesy of P.I. Engineering.

Keyboard pass-thru

Probably the most elegant solution to the multiple keyboard question is available with many of the commercial keyboard encoders in the next section. They include a keyboard pass-thru connector that allows a keyboard to be plugged into the back of the keyboard encoder device. Not every commercial encoder comes with a pass-thru so you need to read the details on the ones you might be considering.

Customized Keyboard Encoders

You have many excellent alternatives to a keyboard hack available to you today. When I first became interested in this hobby five years ago, keyboard hacks were the only way I knew of to use the keyboard port for arcade controls. In fact, there *were* other possible solutions, but no one had put them and arcade controls together at that time. Since then, not only have vendors with suitable products been discovered, but several cottage industries have sprung up solely to serve the home arcade cabinet industry! In the rest of this chapter, there are many keyboard port-based interfaces you can choose from. There's even one you can build yourself!

All of the following interfaces are custom keyboard encoders suitable for interfacing arcade controls via the keyboard port. Each has a set of features addressing some or all of the problems associated with keyboard hacks. They appear to the computer to be a regular keyboard and are available in prices ranging from $27 up to $140 with the higher-priced models supporting extra features. The next few sections cover the highlights of each model.

Pouring over the next several sections covering 13 different keyboard encoders may prove a bit daunting. I suggest reviewing the comparison chart in Table 8-1 first and then reading the full details on those encoders that catch your eye. However, it's difficult to put all the important details into a single chart so I encourage you to at least skim the introduction to each encoder.

Tip The chart and encoder descriptions that follow refer to *matrix mode* and *direct mode* inputs. Matrix mode refers to a keyboard matrix as described in previous sections. Direct mode indicates the encoder is using a single pin for each input with no matrix involved and hence no ghosting possibilities.

Table 8-1   Keyboard Encoder Comparison Chart

Name	Cost	No. of Inputs	Programmable	Extra Features
ButtonBox	$35–$50	Direct: 27 Matrix: 128	Yes	No
Hagstrom KE18 / KE18 MAME	$45	Direct: 18 Matrix: 81	No	No
Hagstrom LP24	$80	Direct: 23 Matrix: 144	Yes	No
Hagstrom KE24	$100	Direct: 24 Matrix: 144	Yes	Mixing direct and matrix modes
Hagstrom KE72 / KE72T	$120–$140	Direct: 72	Yes	Trackball interface add-on
KeyWiz Eco / Max	$27–$35	Direct: 32	Yes	Shazaaam! key (shift key)
MAMI 24 / 48	$53–$90	Direct: 24 / 48	No	No
MK64	$63–$108	Direct: 64	Yes	Rotary joystick support; shift key
Ultimarc I-PAC[2] / I-PAC[4] / Mini-PAC	$39–$69	Direct: 28 / 56 / 28–36	Yes	Built-in programming; shift key

The ButtonBox

The ButtonBox (www.surf.to/buttonbox) is a build-it-yourself keyboard encoder project designed specifically for interfacing arcade controls. It was designed and made available online by an arcade cabinet enthusiast. It supports both direct mode and matrix mode configurations. It handles up to 27 inputs in direct mode and 128 inputs in matrix mode. Assuming you have the tools and depending on how you build it, building the ButtonBox will cost you between $35 and $50. It consists of two separate components: the main CPU card and the direct or matrix-mode daughter card.

You will have to determine in advance how you want to configure the matrix or direct mode because you will physically construct the daughter card to match your needs. There is no one-size-fits-all daughter card in the design specifications. For instance, if you create an 8×8 matrix for 64 inputs and later decide you want an 8×16 matrix for 128 inputs, you will have to build a new daughter card. However, the design is a well thought out one. As far as wiring goes, follow the plans for the boards in order to end up with screw-down terminals that are easy to connect to.

Programming the ButtonBox requires constructing a special parallel cable to connect to it and then running the programming software. Programming cannot be loaded or saved from disk, and it must be done interactively with the encoder. The programming software can be run within DOS or Windows.

The ButtonBox is an interesting home-brew device and has appeal to those who are building an arcade cabinet for the challenge of it. It is included here for those of you who fall into that category. However, the complexity of construction and the costs involved in gathering all the needed components make this impractical for most people.

Hagstrom Electronics

Hagstrom Electronics (www.hagstromelectronics.com) has an entire suite of keyboard encoders suitable for use in arcade cabinet projects. Prices start at $45 for their entry-level model and range up to $140 for their top-of-the-line models. Hagstrom was in the keyboard encoder business when the home arcade cabinet hobby started taking off and was quick to embrace the community with both product customizations and excellent user support. As an example, with a majority of the arcade cabinet community using MAME (see Chapter 14), Hagstrom modified one of their encoders to better support MAME at no extra cost. All of the Hagstrom encoders referred to in this book have been used by the arcade cabinet community with good results reported. I'll introduce you to the four models they offer for keyboard port connection in this section (Hagstrom appears in the next two chapters as well).

KE18/KE18 MAME
Starting at $45, the KE18 is Hagstrom's entry-level keyboard encoder product (see Figure 8-11).

FIGURE 8-11: The Hagstrom KE18 keyboard encoder.
Copyright © 2003 Hagstrom Electronics, Inc., KE18 MAME .

It supports 18 direct inputs or a 9 × 9 matrix mode of 81 inputs. This unit is not programmable, which means that your software will have to be configurable to work with the keystrokes available to the encoder. However, Hagstrom sells an arcade cabinet-friendly, customized version of the KE18 dubbed the KE18 MAME. The key mappings are the same in matrix mode, but they are different in direct mode. Both sets of keystroke mappings are shown in Figure 8-12.

The KE18 can suffer from ghosting problems in matrix mode so you need to plan your keystroke combinations carefully if you decide to use it in that mode. Obviously, there is no such problem in direct mode. The encoder includes a keyboard pass-thru port, which is a nice feature on an entry-level model. It also includes the ability to enable/disable keyboard repeat (that is, a button held down can generate just one keystroke or repeat keystrokes). The wiring connector on the KE18 is of the standard IDE flat ribbon cable variety. You can either use your own IDE ribbon cable or add the optional screw-terminal board and cable header similar to that pictured in Figure 8-13. With that board, you connect the encoder to the terminal board with the cable and then connect your wiring to the screw terminals.

KE18 Keycode Tables

The following tables list the keycodes that are sent to the
computer by the KE18 in response to activation of an input.

KE18 Lookup Table (9 x 9 Matrix Mode)*

Header Row Pins

	J	K	L	M	N	O	P	Q	R
A	A	B	C	D	E	F	G	H	I
B	J	K	L	M	N	O	P	Q	R
C	S	T	U	V	W	X	Y	Z	Esc
D	: ;	" '	> .	< ,	?	Space	Back-Space	{ [	}]
E	Ctrl	Alt	Shift	Insert	Delete	Home	End	Page Up	Page Down
F	/	*	–	+	F1	F2	F3	F4	F5
G	8 ↑ Pg Up	9 Pg Up	. Del	Enter	F6	F7	F8	F9	F10
H	4 ←	5	6	7 Home	–	\	Caps Lock	Num Lock	Print Screen
I	0 Ins	1 End	2 ↓ Pg Dn	3 Pg Dn	+ =	~	Tab	Pause	Scroll Lock

Header Column Pins

KE18 Lookup Table (18 Input Mode)**

KE18 Header Input Pins

	A	B	C	D	E	F	G	H	I	J	K	L	M	N	O	P	Q	R
Default	A	C	D	E	G	I	L	O	Q	R	S	X	?	{	F1	Space	Esc	Enter
MAME	5	6	1	2	Right	Left	Up	Down	CTRL	Alt	Space	Shift	G	D	R	F	A	S

** - In this mode, keycodes to the computer are initiated by shorting one
Input pin to the provided Ground Connection. Example: Pin **J** to Ground
would produce on "R" on the computer.

* - Keycodes to the computer are initiated in this mode by
shorting one Row pin to one Column pin. Example: Row
J to Column **C** would produce an "S" on the computer.

FIGURE 8-12: Default matrix key mappings along with default and MAME version direct key
mappings.

Copyright © 2003 Hagstrom Electronics, Inc., KE18 MAME documentation.

FIGURE 8-13: Hagstrom provides an optional screw-terminal board for the KE18 similar to
this model.

The KE18 is an entry-level keyboard encoder that is suitable for one- or two-player control panels. Its lack of programmability may limit its appeal to some users, but its cost and support of the native MAME command set make it a good alternative for someone considering a keyboard hack.

LP24

Selling for $80, the LP24 is Hagstrom's next step up in the keyboard encoder field (see Figure 8-14). It is a 24-pin, programmable encoder module that is capable of up to 144 inputs in matrix mode or 23 inputs in pseudo-direct mode (see the following paragraph). Because it is programmable, you can determine exactly which keystroke is generated by any spot on the matrix. Technically, the encoder has 50 pins total in two rows of 25 pins each. Each pair of 25 pins is connected and functions like a single pin. The 25th pair is a ground pin used to erase the LP24's programming if programming errors render it unusable. Therefore, if you take into account the paired pins and discount the mostly unused 25th pair, you end up with 24 usable input pins. Hence, the name of the unit being LP24 and my reference to it having 24 pins instead of 50.

FIGURE 8-14: The Hagstrom LP24 programmable keyboard encoder.
Copyright © 2003 Hagstrom Electronics, Inc., LP24.

Programming the LP24 requires an operating system capable of booting into true DOS mode. A DOS window will not work. This means you cannot program this encoder on a Windows XP machine, for instance, but Windows 98 will work. If you're interested in this encoder but have Windows XP, you could use another computer to program it and then bring it to your XP machine to use. Programming is accomplished via an interactive program through the keyboard cable. Once you've booted up in DOS mode and run the programming application, you're presented with a basic menu. First, you select the size of your matrix. To use it in direct mode, simply assign it to use a 1×23 sized matrix, which effectively makes it a 23-input direct mode encoder. The size of the matrix cannot exceed the number of pins available on the LP24 so the maximum matrix size is 12×12, or 144 possible inputs. Then, you fill in the keystrokes desired in the on-screen matrix grid, save the configuration to the encoder (and a backup to disk), and exit the program. Although you can save and load the configurations from disk, the programming application does not support a *batch mode* of operation so you cannot automate the process. Like the KE18, the LP24 can suffer from ghosting so you need to design your matrix carefully to avoid that.

Wiring the LP24 is similar to the KE18. However, because the LP24 has a total of 50 pins versus the KE18's 40, it will not work with an off-the-shelf IDE ribbon cable. Although the IDE ribbon cable is smaller and the pin spacing matches, the edges of the IDE ribbon cable connector will bend some of the unused pins on the LP24 if you try to use it. You can purchase a 12-inch wiring harness connector from Hagstrom to use with the LP24 or make your own with parts available at electronics stores. The encoder includes a keyboard pass-thru and supports enabling/disabling keyboard repeat.

The added ability of the LP24 to program key configurations make this well suited for a two-player control panel. It will also work for a four-player control panel, but it will need to be in matrix mode with proper attention paid to the matrix configuration to avoid ghosting issues.

KE24

Retailing for $100, the KE24 is Hagstrom's distant cousin to the LP24 (see Figure 8-15). It has a 52-pin header on it with 24 pairs of input pins and 2 pairs of ground pins. Programmable like the LP24, the KE24 distinguishes itself by allowing any combination of matrix and direct mode configuration of the 24 available input pins, including true direct mode functionality. This means you could configure the encoder to have 24 direct inputs or up to a 12×12 matrix for 144 inputs. You could also elect to have a combination, such as a 10×10 matrix with four pins in direct mode. This would present you with 100 keystrokes possibly susceptible to ghosting and four keystrokes guaranteed not to have ghosting issues. This gives you a tremendous amount of flexibility as you design your keystroke inputs.

You may have noticed the extra serial port connecter on the KE24. This has two functions. The KE24 is a multifunction device capable of sending input and output through the serial port as well as the keyboard ports. You could use a custom keyboard device to control a serial port-based robot, for instance, without having a PC involved at all. This is very flexible, but it is not particularly useful for our purposes. For arcade cabinet builders, the serial port on the KE24 will be used to program the encoder. Programming the encoder is similar to the LP24 except the KE24 can be programmed both in DOS and Windows. Once you load the programming application, you assign the various pins to be in matrix or direct mode and fill out the matrix map according to your preferences. The KE24 also supports the programming of macros (up to 16 key sequences) in the matrix so you could generate a series of moves with one button push. Save the configuration to the encoder (and a backup to disk), and you're ready to go. Like the LP24, you can save and load configurations for the KE24 from disk, but it cannot be automated.

Wiring the KE24 will require a homemade wiring harness because Hagstrom does not list one as an available accessory. These are not difficult to make with parts from an electronics store. A standard IDE flat ribbon cable will fit over some of the pins but will bend others at the ends unless modified. The KE24 includes a keyboard pass-thru and the ability to not only enable/disable keyboard repeat, but it also includes the ability to configure the delay and speed of the repeat.

The unique flexibility of the programmable KE24 to have both matrix and direct mode configurations make this an intriguing candidate for an arcade cabinet. It is well-suited for either a two- or four-player control panel.

FIGURE 8-15: The Hagstrom KE24 programmable keyboard encoder.
Copyright © 2003 Hagstrom Electronics, Inc., KE24.

KE72/KE72T

The KE72/KE72T (see Figure 8-16) is the flagship of the Hagstrom keyboard encoder line. This model was designed specifically to be suitable for arcade cabinet builders after consultation with many members of the gaming community. Depending on configuration, the unit retails between $120 and $140. By adding support for industry-standard trackballs or spinners (KE72T model) as well, it is more than a keyboard encoder.

FIGURE **8-16:** The Hagstrom KE72 programmable keyboard encoder with optional trackball interface chip installed.

The KE72 supports the highest number of direct inputs of any encoder currently available at 72 programmable inputs. It does not support a matrix mode. Programming the KE72 can be done through the keyboard cable or serial cable for Windows 98/95, and serial cable only for Windows 2000/XP. Hagstrom truly listened to the needs of the gaming community as the encoder can be programmed automatically through batch files. Programming is accomplished by running a command line programming utility that reads a configuration file and applies it to the encoder. If you need multiple configurations for different games, simply create a unique configuration file for each game and load it before running the game. Through the use of batch files, you can automate the entire process to load the proper configuration and run the game with a single click!

Because the encoder runs in direct mode only, ghosting is not an issue, and all 72 keystrokes can be generated simultaneously without key blocking occurring. The keystrokes generated can include any found on a standard keyboard, and also can include macros of up to 32 keystrokes with a single button press. Other features tailored to the gaming community include the trackball interface, which not only supports trackballs and spinners, but also has three mouse buttons as well. This requires using the PS/2 mouse port as well as the keyboard port. The KE72 includes a keyboard port pass-thru. It also has soldering points for attaching Num-Lock, Caps-Lock, and Scroll-Lock LEDs to your control panel. Some games, mostly a few emulated by MAME, will light up the LEDs to correspond to coin inserts or in-game action. Upon request, Hagstrom will solder in a connector and include an appropriate cable for the LEDs so that you only need to purchase the LEDs themselves. They will charge a nominal fee for this service.

Wiring the KE72 can be done with two IDE flat ribbon cables, as the two wiring headers were designed specifically to fit the IDE standard. Combine this with the optional wiring break-out board shown earlier in Figure 8-13 for an easy wiring job. Although the KE72 physically looks like a PCI card, it is designed that way solely for mounting purposes. There are no electrical connections on the PCI-style mounting. You can either elect to mount the KE72 in a PCI slot or screw it to a spot on your control panel as with any other encoder.

Of all the encoders available from Hagstrom, the KE72T is the most ideal candidate to run a four-player control panel. The added ability to run a trackball or two spinners (but not both) along with 72 direct inputs, make it almost a one-size-fits-all solution!

KeyWiz Eco/Max

The KeyWiz line of products (www.groovygamegear.com) is a recent arrival to the arcade controls community that has come on strong with an aggressive feature set. Two models are available (see Figure 8-17) sporting the same core features. Pricing starts at $27 for the economy model (Eco), and $35 for the maximized model (max).

The KeyWiz supports 32 direct inputs and does not have a matrix mode. It includes a shift key dubbed the Shazaaam! key that allows 24 inputs to have a secondary function, for a total of 56 possible inputs. The KeyWiz has a few unique features that help it stand out. Normally the purpose of a shift key is to provide for specific functions that you don't want available during normal play. However, you have to press two buttons to activate that function. The folks at KeyWiz offer a simple but elegant alternative to this, providing an adapter cable that will let any single button generate a shifted keystroke. It's a simple concept, but KeyWiz thought of it and makes it available to you.

The KeyWiz shines when it comes to programming, with a full-featured programming utility. One unique feature is the ability to associate configuration profiles with certain games. You can create and store up to 15 different configurations in the programming software. When you press the button corresponding to a particular configuration, it not only loads the configuration, it can also optionally launch the application! You can also assign a profile to a Windows icon and run it all with a single click. The KeyWiz is programmable in both DOS and Windows.

FIGURE 8-17: The KeyWiz Max model with screw-terminals and keyboard switched pass-thru.
Copyright © 2003 IDVT, Inc.

Another unique feature is to have two configurations resident in the KeyWiz while in use. One is the default MAME-compatible key set, and the other is your customized configuration. Change back and forth on the fly by activating the Shazaaam! key and pressing left on your joystick for MAME, right for the custom configuration. The KeyWiz ships with the MAME-compatible configuration as a default. Custom configurations are not stored when powered off and must be loaded at boot-up (which can be automated easily).

Wiring the KeyWiz ranges from difficult to easy depending on which model you purchase. The economy model comes with solder points for the inputs. If you are skilled at soldering, this may be a good consideration to save a few dollars. The max model comes with standard screw-terminals that make wiring easy. The max model also adds a switchable keyboard pass-thru port. Either the KeyWiz or the keyboard is active at one time, but not both.

The KeyWiz is a full-featured line of products and represents serious competition to the other encoder manufacturers. Because of the relative newness of the product line, they do not have as big of an installed user base as some of the other encoder lines. Their feature set, pricing, and user support are all excellent, so expect that to have changed by the time the first update to this book comes out.

MAMI 24/48

The Multiple Arcade Machine Interface (MAMI) line of products is the creation of 3Tronics Technical Services (www.3tronics.com/index.html), another relative newcomer to the arcade cabinet community. They have two products available with 24 and 48 direct input models available, respectively. The 24-input model ranges in price from $53 to $60, and the 48-input model ranges from $86 to $90, both depending on which variation of the model you purchase. You can purchase three different variations of each model: one with solder points to connect to, one with ribbon-cable connectors similar to traditional IDE ribbon cables (but of a different size), or standard screw-terminals. With the small price difference between the low end and high end of each model, it is probably worth purchasing the screw-terminal variations.

The MAMI products are not programmable, but can be ordered with customized key mappings. By default, they ship with a fairly standard MAME-compatible configuration. They are designed to support one joystick and up to eight buttons per player, with the MAMI 24 geared for two players and the MAMI 48 meant for four-player panels.

Wiring the MAMI encoder will depend on which variation you purchase. Either the ribbon cable or screw-terminal models will be easy to wire with material available from any electronics store. Wiring to the entry-level models will require some skill with soldering. All versions of the MAMI come with a keyboard pass-thru standard.

The MAMI is a relatively recent line of products in the arcade cabinet community, and their impact on the community remains to be seen. The developer behind the MAMI has 15 years of experience developing miniature electronics devices. You may wish to visit their Web site to determine the latest pricing and feature sets of their products, as these may have changed from the time this book was written.

MK64

The MK64 (www.mk64.com/ron) is another vendor who came from the arcade cabinet-building community. The encoder (see Figure 8-18) is priced between $63 and $108, depending on the accessories (various cable kits) purchased with it. As you may gather from the name, it supports 64 direct mode inputs.

The MK64 has a couple of interesting features. Similar to a few of the other encoder options, it includes a shift key function that allows seven keystrokes to serve dual purposes. It also supports assigning up to 16 macros to different keystrokes, with up to 63 steps per macro. Perhaps its most unique feature is built-in support for rotary joysticks. You may recall that rotary joysticks have handles that rotate to 12 different positions, designed for aiming in certain games. The MK64 is the only keyboard encoder product with native support for the rotary joysticks, although a separate stand-alone device is available as an after-market add-on for other encoders. The MK64 also supports enabling/disabling keyboard repeat.

Programming the MK64 is a manual process involving script files. Although they are a bit involved to create initially, doing so is not difficult, and sample scripts are included with the encoder to get you started. Because the programming is performed via command line reading of the script files, the MK64 can be reprogrammed on the fly with batch files. Thus, while more involved to configure initially, it allows for automatic reprogramming based on the needs of any particular game you might play. The MK64 can be programmed in both DOS and Windows.

FIGURE 8-18: The MK64 programmable keyboard encoder.
Used by permission of Ronald Michallick.

One very unique feature is the ability of the MK64 to identify which control panel is connected if you have swappable control panels. You accomplish this by dedicating one or more of the input pins as ID pins. Each panel you build gets a unique ID. Through use of a batch file, by recognizing that a new panel has been installed, you can configure the encoder to take any number of actions, such as reprogramming the encoder to match the panel or listing only games that work with that particular panel.

Wiring the MK64 is straight forward. The ribbon cable connectors can be used with cabling kits available from the vendor, or with standard IDE and floppy cables or parts available from electronics stores. The encoder includes pins for hooking up LEDs, but you will have to add the required resistors (see Chapter 15, "Buttoning Up the Odds and Ends," for details) yourself.

The MK64 is a solid encoder for the price. By adding support for rotary joysticks, the MK64 has distinguished itself in the market. The high number of inputs makes the unit suitable for both two-and four-player panels, and the extra features of the encoder are an added bonus.

Ultimate Arcade Controls

Ultimate Arcade Controls (hereafter Ultimarc, www.ultimarc.com) is probably the first of the cottage industries to spring up over the past few years in response to the needs of the arcade cabinet building community. Ultimarc is extremely well regarded, providing top-notch customer support, and has probably sold more encoders to the community than any other vendor. Following are two of their keyboard encoder products. A few of their other products appear in the next few chapters.

I-PAC²

The I-PAC² (see Figure 8-19) is Ultimarc's entry-level product, offering 28 programmable direct mode inputs with shift-key functionality. This allows one of the keys to double as a shift key similar to a shift key on a keyboard. When pressed by itself, the key simply generates what it has been programmed for. When pressed in conjunction with one of the other 27 buttons, it generates an alternate keystroke for that button, affectively doubling your total inputs to 55. The I-PAC² is available for $39 for the PS/2 keyboard-port model, and $43 for the USB model. Through some sophisticated programming, Ultimarc has designed their product not to suffer from the six-simultaneous-keystroke limit that native USB keyboards have.

FIGURE 8-19: The Ultimarc I-PAC² programmable keyboard encoder.
Used by permission of Ultimarc.

You'll be pleasantly surprised by some of the sophisticated features available with the I-PAC² for the low costs involved. The encoder includes a keyboard pass-thru, a jumper to toggle between a pre-programmed MAME configuration and your own configuration, and several programming options. With the pre-programmed MAME configuration, most users will be able to plug the encoder in and use it without having to program it at all.

Ultimarc has provided four different methods to program the I-PAC[2]. First you need to set the jumper on the encoder to allow for programming (as compared to using the default MAME configuration). This needs to be done only once and can be left in that mode to allow reprogramming whenever needed. The first two methods involve running the I-PAC configuration application. Both a DOS mode and Windows mode are included on the encoder's CD. The Windows version is pictured in Figure 8-20.

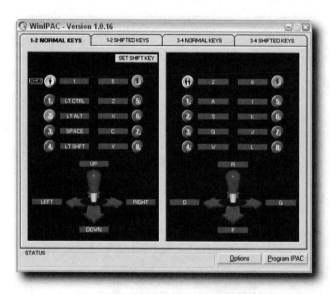

FIGURE 8-20: Programming the I-PAC[2] with the Windows application.
Used by permission of Ultimarc.

Programming is straightforward. Click on the control you want to change, and then press the button you want assigned to it. The labels on the programming menu correspond to the labels on the wiring blocks on the I-PAC[2]. Save the configuration to the encoder (and a backup to disk) and you're done. You can also program the unit on-the-fly by pressing a special keystroke combination (requires a second keyboard plugged into the pass-thru) that brings up a built-in configuration menu. It has all the functionality of the two programming applications except for loading and saving to disk. Finally, demonstrating an understanding of the needs of arcade cabinet builders, the programming applications can be used in command line mode to read in a configuration file, allowing for automated programming of the encoder. Also, at least one front-end application (Chapter 13, "Installing the Computer") has built-in support for the I-PAC, enabling programming to be changed within the game environment.

Some of the other features include the ability to be used with a Macintosh computer along with a native Macintosh programming application, a third-party developed Linux programming application, and the ability to daisy chain the encoders for even more inputs. Also, there is an optional 32-inch LED harness that attaches to the encoder's board, emulating a keyboard's Num-Lock, Scroll-Lock, and Caps-Lock LEDs. The long harness and design of the LED mounting allow you to mount them to your control panel, adding colorful red, yellow, and green lights that will correspond to certain MAME functions.

Wiring the I-PAC^2 is straightforward. The inputs are attached to by screw-down terminal blocks and include two ground terminals. By daisy chaining your grounds on your controls, all your wiring can come directly to the encoder board without requiring extra wiring blocks.

The I-PAC^2 is tailor-made by Ultimarc to suit a two-player control panel. The impressive list of features and high quality of design have made it a favorite of arcade cabinet builders. The low cost of the encoder makes it an attractive alternative to a keyboard hack.

I-PAC^4

The I-PAC^4 is Ultimarc's follow-up to the successful I-PAC^2. It is the big brother to its predecessor, having double the number of inputs. Essentially, it is two I-PAC^2 units installed on one board. The I-PAC^4 retails for $65 in the PS/2 keyboard configuration, and $69 in the USB port configuration. See Figure 8-21.

FIGURE 8-21: The Ultimarc I-PAC^4 four-player model.
Used by permission of Ultimarc.

Everything written about the I-PAC^2 holds true for the I-PAC^4 as well, except for the number of inputs. The I-PAC^4 has 56 inputs broken into two groups, each with a separate shift key. This allows for a total of 110 inputs. The rest of the feature set is the same, including the programmability, LED harness, and multi-operating system support.

The I-PAC[4] is effectively the same as purchasing two I-PAC[2] units, with a slight cost savings and the convenience of programming all inputs with one interface. Custom designed by Ultimarc for people building four-player control panels, it has quickly become a favorite among the arcade cabinet building community.

Mini-PAC

Ultimarc's Mini-PAC is the latest encoder to join their line-up. This unit works identically to the I-PAC[2] and supports 28 inputs using either a PS/2 or USB connection. The $2^1/_4$-inch Mini-PAC can be seen in Figure 8-22.

FIGURE 8-22: The Ultimarc Mini-PAC with optional wiring harness.
Used by permission of Ultimarc.

The Mini-PAC adds trackball and spinner support to the I-PAC[2] functionality, requiring that the encoder be used in USB mode. The Mini-PAC is primarily targeted at OEM and frequent cabinet builders, with the available wiring harness, 28 encoder inputs, and trackball/spinner functionality designed to allow for quick hookup. Prices for the Mini-PAC range from $29 for the encoder and PS/2 cable only up to $69 for the encoder, USB cable, trackball cable and full wiring harness.

Encoder wrap-up

You are likely to be satisfied with any of the encoder choices presented in the previous sections. The economy models make excellent alternatives to keyboard hacks, providing the functionality of a keyboard hack with less effort involved. The higher priced encoder models justify their increased costs with extra features such as programmability, keyboard pass-thrus, and other miscellaneous features. Most of the vendors have been supportive of the arcade cabinet building community for quite some time, and will be happy to answer any questions about their products that you might have. My best advice to you when determining which model to choose is to analyze your current needs and thoughts for the future. Purchasing a budget model might help the bottom line now, but will limit your expansion possibilities. If you're constructing a limited purpose system, such as a PacMan clone for instance, a low-end encoder will work fine. I would recommend looking at the high-end models if you're planning a multi-purpose arcade cabinet, however. With the difference between the bottom and top of the lines being approximately $100, you're better off buying the encoder with the best feature set to match your needs and not to economize on this point.

The Project Arcade control panel design uses 32 keyboard port based inputs. That includes all controls except the trackball, spinner, and three mouse buttons. With their excellent customer support, feature set, and number of supported inputs, I decided to use the Ultimarc I-Pac[4] for the Project Arcade cabinet. The 56 inputs will give me ample room to grow in the simplest manner possible should I decide to remodel. I could just as easily have chosen one of the other high-end encoders with 32 or more direct inputs. With the prices being so close, I did not feel it was worth the extra work involved to use a matrix.

Summary

The keyboard port is your best choice for interfacing arcade controls to your computer. Almost every game playable on a personal computer allows for keyboard control. Keyboard hacks can be an extremely low-cost way to go, and can either be fun or infuriating to build depending on your temperament and soldering skill. Personally, if the luckless Mario depends on my soldering skills, then he'll never escape the barrels and rescue the princess! Most people will be happier with a commercial keyboard encoder.

Keyboard ports are a great way to connect your arcade controls, but they're not the only way. Put your mad-scientist coat back on, because in the next chapter you'll be dissecting some mice!

Arcade Controls Using the Mouse Connector

Ready to experiment with some mice and their cousins? Don't worry, no actual mice were harmed in the creation of this book, though their computer-based brethren were not as lucky. Using mouse-based technology to interface arcade controls is quite popular and follows similar principles to using keyboard technology. What can you do with mouse-based connections? Quite a bit as it turns out. You can play trackball and spinner games, hack a 360-degree arcade steering wheel, hook up the Happ Controls optical rotary joystick, or control your desktop with arcade controls!

Throughout this chapter, I will refer heavily to trackballs and spinners. However, the discussions apply equally well to other optical arcade controls. It's just easier to say "trackballs and spinners" than it is to say "trackballs, spinners, rotary joysticks, 720-degree joysticks, 360-degree steering wheels, and so forth . . ." every time I want to refer to optical-based controls. Bear that in mind as you read.

How Mice Work

First, a promise: I will forgo any attempt at mouse humor in this section. The jokes are too easy and won't make it past my editors, who have threatened me with the bargain bin rack if I do not keep my pun-to-information ratio low. If at any point while reading this chapter an obvious joke occurs to you, please feel free to laugh out loud and assume I hid it there deliberately.

Mechanical versus optical

You can pick up two different kinds of mice at any computer store. The first is a mechanical mouse that contains a ball underneath the mouse that spins optical wheels inside the mouse body. These interact with optical encoders to generate mouse movement. The second is a purely optical mouse with no physical moving parts. A mini-camera in the mouse takes snapshots of the surface beneath the mouse at a rate of over 1,000 images per second. Any change in the surface beneath the mouse is detected by the mouse electronics and digital processor, which thereby determines speed and movement. To date, no hacks of optical mice have been used for arcade controls. They do not lend themselves to this purpose due to their lack of optical encoders. For the purposes of this chapter, any discussion that does not explicitly state otherwise refers to a traditional mechanical mouse. Figure 9-1 shows a mechanical mouse.

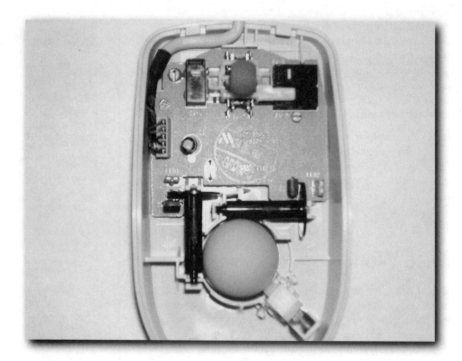

FIGURE 9-1: The inside of a mechanical mouse.

Optical encoders

Because you will find an optical encoder in every device mentioned in this chapter, it would be a good idea to take a closer look at how they work. Examine Figure 9-2.

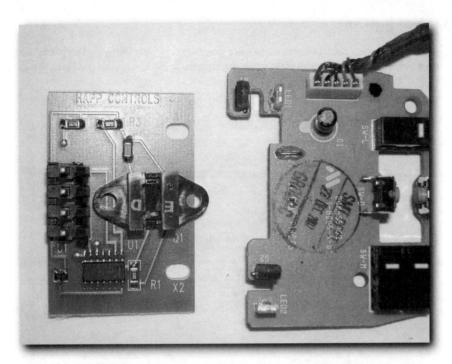

FIGURE 9-2: A close-up look at a couple of different optical encoders. A Happ Controls arcade version is on the left, and a disassembled mouse is on the right.
Used by permission of Happ Controls.

Recall from earlier in the book how these work. Optical encoders consist of three parts. There's an infrared LED and an infrared sensor facing each other, and a spoked wheel that spins between them. The LED is sometimes referred to as the emitter, and the sensor is referred to as the detector. When the ball of the mouse moves, it rotates the spoked wheels. As the spoked wheel spins, it breaks up the light from the emitter to the detector, which creates a light-dark-light pattern. The detector sends this pattern to the mouse electronics, which encodes it in a digital form for the computer.

Technically, the infrared sensor-and-detector combinations come in pairs. Sometimes, the pairs of detectors will be plainly seen as two separate components, but the two detectors will often be encased in one physical component. Both are equivalent. The pair of detectors let the mouse determine not only the speed of movement — based on the pace of the light-dark-light pattern — but also the direction of movement. There is one pair for the X axis and one pair for the Y axis. However, for the sake of discussion, I'll refer to each pair simply as a single unit, such as a detector instead of a pair of detectors.

Notice it is the detector that does the work of communicating to the electronics of the mouse. You'll use this to your advantage in the "Hacking a Mouse" section later in this chapter.

Mouse buttons

Mouse buttons work and look similar to microswitches in arcade buttons. The plastic button part of the mouse housing pushes down on the tiny button in the mouse microswitch. Take a look at Figure 9-3.

FIGURE 9-3: A close look at three microswitches on the mouse circuit board.

Though the actual physical plastic housing that presses on the microswitch will vary from mouse to mouse, the microswitches all look basically the same. Three pins connect the microswitch to the circuit board. Although they will probably not be labeled, they are NO, NC, and COM, just like an arcade microswitch. Because the button should do something only when pressed, the circuits are wired only to the NO and COM pins. In fact, some mouse boards won't even bother to solder the third pin, or, if it is soldered, the pin won't actually have any trace circuits connecting to the rest of the circuitry (see Figure 9-4).

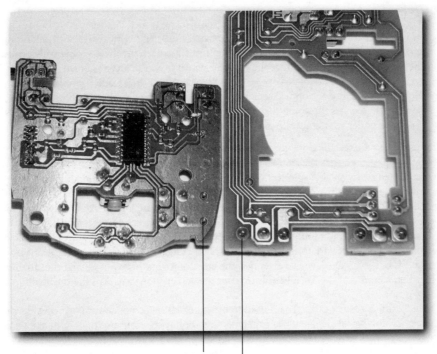

Third button pin, not soldered

Third button pin, soldered,
no circuit trace connection

FIGURE 9-4: The mouse board on the left shows the third pin on the buttons, unsoldered.
The board on the right shows that the traces do not connect.

Hacking a Mouse

Using what you learned in the previous sections, you can hack a mouse to use as an interface for your optical arcade controls. I'll be discussing trackballs and spinners, but the information applies equally as well to steering wheels, optical rotary joysticks, and other optical devices. You have two options for hacking a mouse device, as described in the following sections.

The same concern that exists for keyboard hacks exists for mouse hacks. If something goes wrong, it is possible to damage your mouse port or motherboard. When using a mouse hack, test only on a spare computer if possible and certainly never on a computer with irreplaceable data. Do not attempt any of the hacks described while the mouse is plugged into the computer!

Physical hacks

Physical hacks involve connecting the circuit board (PCB) and optical sensors from a mouse to the encoder wheels of an arcade control device. The only hack involved is physically positioning the two separate devices so that the encoder wheel from the arcade control fits properly between the emitter and detector of the mouse PCB. When the arcade controls spins its encoder wheel, the mouse's optical sensors detect the motion and respond accordingly. No standard method exists for doing this because it depends on the devices you're using and spatial requirements under your control panel.

Physical hacks are usually done for spinners only. It's relatively easy to mount a mouse PCB beneath a spinner so that the spinner's encoder wheel bisects the optical encoder. In fact, the first commercially available spinners used this method. Zip ties and hot glue guns are two favorites for fastening the mouse PCB in the proper position. Because trackballs use two sets of optical encoders set several inches apart, it's not possible to use a physical hack without modifying the mouse PCB. One possibility is to desolder the emitter and detector sets from the mouse circuit board and mount them, appropriately spaced, onto two separate electronic breadboards. Next, connect wire from the parts on the breadboard to their former locations on the mouse PCB. By doing so, you've extended the electronics but have not altered the circuitry. Then, you can mount the breadboards in place at each encoder wheel of the trackball.

Note A breadboard is a blank circuit board used to mount electrical components. Engineers use them to make prototypes of circuits while experimenting; hobbyists often use them to make permanent circuits. They're available at any electronics store.

Depending on the mouse and software driver used, you may run into a problem. Because the arcade encoder wheel and the mouse optical encoders were not designed with each other in mind, the sensitivity may be off. Two remedies present themselves. You can adjust the sensitivity in the operating system and the game you're playing to see whether that fixes it. If not, replacing the encoder wheel with a bigger, spaced-out wheel may improve matters. Oscar Controls sells a couple of encoder wheels, as seen in Figure 9-5. One is a $3^1/_2$-inch, 66-tooth wheel, and the other is a smaller $1^1/_2$-inch, 36-tooth wheel.

Finally, if you'd like to design a physical hack without using a mouse, such as building your own spinner from scratch, Oscar Controls sells an optical board (Figure 9-6). This is the same board used in their spinner products, and it is simply a pair of emitters and detectors with pins to connect your wiring to. Because there is no extra circuitry or encoder chip, you'll also need an encoder board such as one of the ones listed in the "Purchasing Optical Encoders" section later in this chapter. Being able to mix the optics, the encoder, and the physical components gives you a great deal of flexibility in designing a custom optical arcade control.

Note You will occasionally notice two different things referred to as optical encoder boards. There is one part that contains the actual optical parts (the emitter and the detector) and another part that contains the circuitry and the chip that encodes the signals digitally for the computer. On a mouse, this is all combined in one PCB. Arcade controls, on the other hand, often have the two parts separated. Oscar Controls gives a nod to that by referring to their board as an optical board and not an optical encoder board. In other places, the usage may not be as precise.

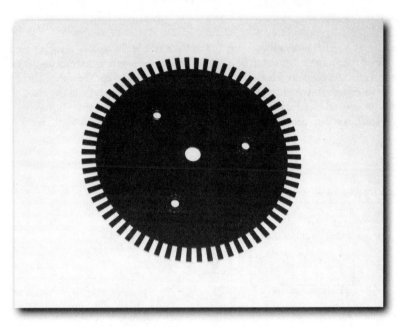

FIGURE 9-5: The Oscar Controls 3½-inch encoder wheel.

Used by permission of Oscar Controls.

FIGURE 9-6: The Oscar Controls optical board.

Used by permission of Oscar Controls.

Electrical hacks

Electrical hacks are a much more elegant way to interface arcade controls to mice. These hacks take advantage of the fact that the detector halves of the mouse's optical sensors do the talking with the optical encoder chip on the mouse PCB. If you could intercept the point where the detector sends its signals to the encoder chip, could you send the signals from the arcade control's detector instead (see Figure 9-7)? As it turns out, the answer is yes — usually! Occasionally, you'll run into problems, as explained in the "When it doesn't work" section a bit later on.

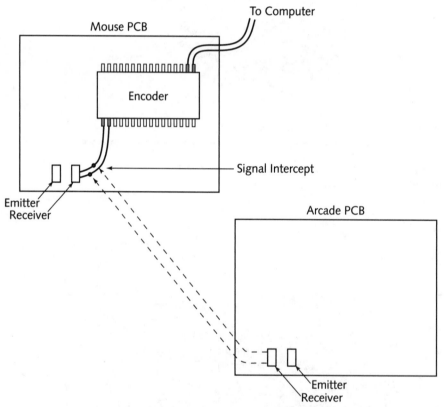

FIGURE 9-7: **Replacing the mouse detector's signals with those from the arcade control.**

How to make it work

You'll need to know a bit more about how optical sensors are wired to understand how an electrical hack works. The detector portion of the sensor sends two signals to the encoder chip, which requires two pins. The emitter and detector also need and share a power source so each side has one pin for power. Remember that the detector side of the optical sensor is actually a pair of infrared receivers. If the detector side is split into two physical components, then each half of the detector will have one pin for signal and one pin for power. The power pin on one will be electrically tied to the power pin on the second half of the detector. Because the power pins are tied together, they effectively function as one pin. On a detector that is housed in one physical casing, the shared power is actually just one pin. This means that, whether you have a split or combined detector component, there are three pins to consider (see Figure 9-8).

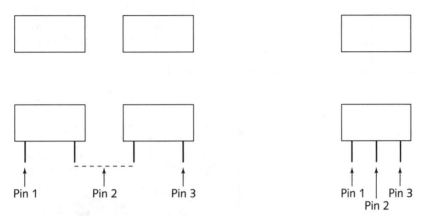

Pin 1   Pin 2   Pin 3   Pin 1 | Pin 3
                                                          Pin 2

FIGURE 9-8: Separate components on the left; a combined unit on the right, all with three effective pins.

Identifying the pins

You'll need to identify which pin on the detector side is the power pin. *Usually*, this is the middle pin, but, because manufacturing methods differ, you should not take that for granted. You will not be using the power pin so it's important to find it. You can determine this by following the traces on the circuit board. This pin should trace back to the emitter opposite and to the other detector as well. You can also determine the power pin with a multimeter.

Caution

This next piece involves disassembling the mouse, connecting the PCB of the mouse to the computer, and turning it on. I have one more warning. If something goes wrong here, it is possible — although unlikely — to cause damage to the mouse port or motherboard. If in doubt, don't do this. Alternatives are available in the "Purchasing Optical Encoders" section later in this chapter.

There will usually be four pins in the mouse cable from the PC to the mouse PCB. One will be +5v, and one will be ground. If you're lucky, the pins will be labeled where they connect with the PCB. The +5v may be a red wire, and the ground may be black or sometimes white. Set your multimeter to DC voltage, plug the removed mouse PCB into the computer, and turn the computer on. Be very careful not to short out any pins. You should put something nonconductive, such as a static bag, underneath the mouse PCB.

Touch the positive lead of your multimeter to the likely +5v pin (the underside at the solder points is your best bet), and touch the negative lead to the likely ground pin. Your multimeter should read a positive five volts. If it reads negative five volts, you have the pins reversed. If it reads something else more than a tenth or so off, you have at least one wrong pin altogether.

Once you know where the ground pin is on the PCB, touch the negative lead to that, and touch the positive lead to one of the pins underneath the detector. The power pin will read +5v when you've found it. Verify that touching the other pins underneath the detector does not produce +5v. If it does, something is wrong. If it does not, you're in business. Repeat for the other detector. You have now isolated the power pins attached to the detectors.

Replacing the detectors

Now that you know which pins are which, it's time to remove the detectors. This is where you get to exercise your soldering and desoldering skills. I found a desoldering braid easiest to use in this circumstance (see Figure 9-9). Using appropriate caution, desolder the detectors from the mouse PCB. You can desolder the emitters if you'd like as well, but it is not necessary. Some people like to remove them to save a small amount of power.

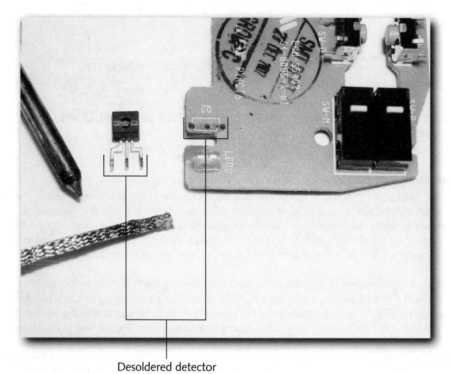

Desoldered detector

FIGURE 9-9: Showing the desoldered and removed detectors.

You now have a couple of options for replacing the detectors. You *could* solder wires directly into the holes left by the detectors and then run them back to your arcade control. I do not recommend it because that limits your flexibility. One suggestion is to connect short runs (two inches or so) of wire to the holes and crimp quick-disconnects on the other ends. Another possibility is to attach wiring headers or wiring blocks to the mouse PCB. In Figure 9-10, you can see a few examples. From the left, there are wiring headers on the Oscar Controls interface, wires with quick disconnects on one side of a mouse hack, and (unfortunately) a wiring block whose pins were too big to fit in the holes on the other side of the mouse hack. Any of these methods will allow you to easily connect and disconnect your mouse hack while working on the system. Make sure at this point that you do not permanently wire anything so you can troubleshoot if necessary.

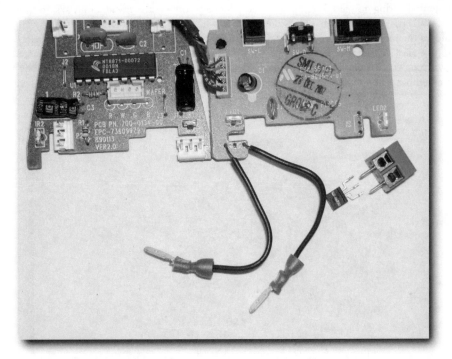

FIGURE 9-10: Different methods of wiring detector replacements.
Used by permission of Oscar Controls.

Connecting your arcade control

Here's where the really amazing part happens when, after all the theory and wiring, you get to plug something in and see it work! Read this section through before you begin. You should now have some method to connect up to the two signal circuit traces on the mouse PCB formerly occupied by the detectors for both the horizontal (X) and vertical (Y) axes. Examine your arcade control now. If you are connecting a trackball, there are two optical boards — one for each axis. If you are connecting a spinner, there will be only one optical board. I will describe a trackball hack for the rest of this section. However, if you are attempting a spinner hack, the details are exactly the same except you will be connecting only one optical board instead of two. Instead of matching the X axis from the trackball to the X axis of the mouse PCB, you'll need to decide whether you want your spinner to control the X or Y axis on the mouse PCB. If in doubt or only using one spinner, connect to the X axis.

There are four pins coming off of each encoder interface board from the trackball. Two of them are signal pins, one is +5v power, and one is ground (see Figure 9-11). This should sound awfully familiar. Both the mouse detectors and the optic boards have two pins for signaling. By connecting the two signal pins from the trackball optic board to the matching two signal pins (now your wiring connectors instead of detector pins), you will be able to send the trackball's signals to the mouse encoder! Once again, I find this to be simply amazing! There are two potential wiring gotchas. First, you may accidentally connect the trackball's X axis to the mouse PCB's Y axis, or vice-versa. This will be evident when scrolling the trackball left and right moves the mouse cursor up and down. The second possibility is reversing the two signal pins on the axis, such that scrolling up moves you down, or vice versa. Both are easily corrected by swapping your wiring around until the proper pins are connected to the proper locations. Remember that you were strongly encouraged to use quick-disconnect wiring!

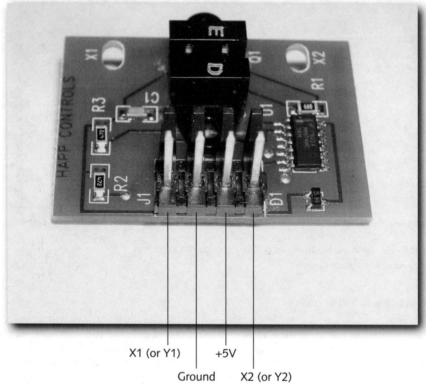

X1 (or Y1)   +5V

Ground   X2 (or Y2)

FIGURE 9-11: A standard arcade optical board with labeled pins.
Used by permission of Happ Controls.

However, you're not quite finished yet. None of the wiring will work without power to the optical boards. But, I didn't tell you to wire anything to the power pin on the mouse PCB so how do you get power? Recall that, as long as the ultimate source is the PC's power supply, all power and ground is equivalent. My recommendation is to tap into one of the leads coming from the PC's power supply, although grabbing +5v and ground from another source in the computer will also work. If you are doing more than one hack, you should consider attaching two wiring blocks to your control panel, which dedicates one to +5v from the power supply and one to ground from the power supply. This will let you connect multiple devices to the power easily.

Now that you know where the wires go conceptually, it's time to actually connect things up. You can either use the trackball's original wiring harness and devise an adapter wiring harness to connect to it, which modifies the trackball's wiring harness directly, or create a new wiring harness altogether. If you have the trackball's wiring harness, I recommend using it intact by creating an adapter. The harness will have six pins — one +5v power, one ground, two X-axis signals, and two Y-axis signals. The pins are labeled — pin one is ground, pin two is +5v, pins three and four are the Y axis, and pins five and six are the X axis. It's possible that your wire scheme will differ from these so you may need to do some detective work to be sure. The inner two pins on the optical boards should be +5v and ground with the outer two pins being signaling.

The connector block on the wiring harness is a standard, six-pin male Molex connector. The matching female Molex connector is available at any electronics store. Connect six wires to the female connector, preferably using red and black only for the +5v and ground pins. Then, connect pin one to ground and pin two to +5v (presumably on the appropriate wiring blocks in your control panel unless you are obtaining power elsewhere). Connect pins three and four to the mouse PCB's Y axis, and connect pins five and six to the PCB's X axis. If you are not using the trackball's wiring harness, you'll need to create your own wiring harness using the techniques discussed previously in this book and parts available from any electronics store. So long as the wires ultimately connect to the same places as described here, the specific method used is unimportant.

Congratulations! If all has gone well, you have successfully connected your arcade control to the computer by using a mouse hack. Now is the time to plug everything in, turn it on, and see whether it worked! Spin your trackball or spinner, and the cursor should move on-screen. If it worked, great! If not, read on to the next section.

When it doesn't work

Argh! All of this effort, and it doesn't work! Now what? Think you should have bought the "Project Basket Weaving" book instead? Don't panic. Probably up to a third of the hacks attempted don't work on the first try. There are a few things you can look at to try to figure it out.

Wiring

First, go over your wiring one more time. Step back through your hack. Are all the wires connected to the right spots? Are all your solder joints good? One common problem is a solder joint that is too big and spills over to another circuit trace. The circuit traces on a mouse PCB are very small and close together. You can fix a problem like this with some judicious desoldering and resoldering.

The highs and lows

You may also be running afoul of the difference between a device that's considered active high versus one that's active low. Let me explain that briefly. (Strap on the seatbelt because this one gets a bit techie.) The optical sensor that the encoder wheel spins between is also referred to as a phototransistor, and you can think of that as a switch. Instead of physically pressing it off and on, the light-dark-light pattern turns the switch off and on. Remember that a switch sits in the middle of a circuit, which completes the circuit when the switch is closed and breaks the circuit when the switch is open. One end of the phototransistor switch is continuously connected to the circuit. The other end of the phototransistor switch is open (i.e., circuit is broken) when the encoder wheel is blocking the infrared light (dark) and the switch is closed (i.e., circuit is complete) when the wheel is allowing light through. You can therefore think of the light-dark-light pattern as closed-open-closed or "circuit-complete - circuit-broken - circuit-complete."

The side of the phototransistor switch that is continuously connected to the circuit is what determines whether it is considered active high or active low. Whether this side is attached to the +5v or ground side of the circuit determines whether the unit is labeled active high or active low. For instance, when a trackball is connected to an interface, the dark signal (i.e., the circuit is open) must be pulled either high or low electronically by a resistor. Whether the trackball's signal needs to be pulled high or low depends on the requirements of the interface. To confuse the matter a bit more, different vendors have not always used the terms "active high" and "active low" to mean precisely the same thing. Don't panic yet because the next paragraph brings this to a happier conclusion.

I did not mention this earlier because most devices are active high and compatible with most mouse hacks. However, Wico trackballs are known to be active-low devices. It doesn't really matter whether you use active-high or active-low devices, *as long as you're consistent*. Your mouse and your arcade control both need to use the same method. Confused? Don't worry, here's the important part. It may be possible to connect an active-low device to an active-high interface (like a mouse hack) by adding a 1K resistor between the power pin of the optical board and the +5v or ground (depending on what it's connected to in the first place) of the circuit. Several folks who have run into this problem have resolved it by adding the resistors as described. If you are running into this problem and need more assistance, hop on to the message forums at www.arcadecontrols.com, and describe your situation. Odds are that someone there will be able to assist.

Not all mice are the same

Finally, if all else fails, you might need to try another mouse. It's possible that the mouse was damaged in the hack attempt or simply has electronics that are different enough that they won't work for this particular hack. Logitech mice, for instance, are generally known not to work. Cheap, hackable mice can be had for less than $10, so it's probably worth it to you to try another mouse.

Another look

Several people have created and documented electrical hacks of this nature. If you're feeling a bit fuzzy about this, you may wish to look at their efforts to gain another perspective. This will also let you see the specific brands used in their hacks that you might want to consider. A few good examples include:

- Bob Akaye's Betson Imperial (Wico) 3-inch Trackball Mouse Hack at www.members .shaw.ca/bakaye/tballhack.htm.

- MAMEWAH's Hacking a Mouse to a Happ Trackball page at http://mamewah .mameworld.net/mousehack.html.

- 720 Circular Spinner Joystick mouse hack at `http://link.mywwwserver.com/~jstookey/arcade/720/720-arcadejoy.php`.

- The Massive MAME Project's Trackball Hack at `www.mameworld.net/massive/How-to/Trackball_Hack/trackball_hack.html`.

- ZeitGeist's Mouse to Trackball Hack page at `www.arcadecontrols.com/files/Miscellaneous/Mouse_to_Trackball_Instructions.pdf`.

Hacking buttons

Hacking arcade pushbuttons to a mouse to enable left, middle, and right mouse click buttons is very easy. Recall from the "Mouse buttons" section earlier in the chapter that mouse buttons are almost exactly the same as microswitches in arcade controls. Using the same techniques described earlier for an electronic mouse hack, desolder, and remove the mouse button switches. Extend wiring from the vacated button spots on the mouse PCB to your microswitches for your pushbuttons (hopefully using some modular, quick-disconnect wiring method). Make sure you're using the NO and COM leads to wire to. Connect everything up, and you should have working mouse buttons using arcade pushbuttons. It's really as simple as that.

Purchasing Optical Encoders

If you're thinking that a mouse hack is too much effort without a guarantee of results, then you're in luck. You can find a few commercial optical encoders with a range of prices and features that will accomplish the same thing with predictable results. All come from vendors you've already met in previous chapters. Start by looking at Table 9-1 for a side-by-side comparison. Note that, when it states one trackball is supported, you can also read that as saying two optical boards because a trackball has two boards, which means you could also use it for two spinners.

Table 9-1   Optical Encoder Comparison Chart

Name	Cost	Number of devices supported	Interface type
Happ Controls USB Trackball Interface Kit	$40	1 trackball, 3 mouse buttons	USB
Hagstrom Electronics KE72T	$140	1 trackball, 3 mouse buttons, and keyboard encoder functions	PS/2 mouse port

Continued

Table 9-1 *(continued)*

Name	Cost	Number of devices supported	Interface type
Hagstrom Electronics KE-USB36	$80	1 trackball, 3 mouse buttons, and keyboard encoder functions	USB
Hagstrom Electronics ME4	$35 ($50 with full cabling)	1 trackball, 1 spinner, 3 mouse buttons	PS/2 mouse port
Oscar Controls USB Mouse Interface	$9 — spinner harness $12.50 — spinner and button harness $17 — trackball harness	1 trackball, 2 mouse buttons	USB
Ultimarc Opti-Pac	$39 — serial interface $44 — USB interface	2 trackballs, 4 spinners, 2 buttons per player for players 1 and 2	Serial or USB

Note Unless specifically stated otherwise, the interfaces presented here are designed to work with active-high optical arcade controls, such as the Happ Controls trackball. It is possible that an active-low device, such as the Wico trackball, will work with the addition of 1K pull-up resistors, as explained earlier in this chapter.

Happ Controls USB trackball interface kit

Happ Controls (www.happcontrols.com) offers a USB model trackball interface kit for $40. The kit supports one trackball and up to three mouse buttons. Alternatively, you could connect two spinners, steering wheels, or other optical devices instead of one trackball; though, you would have to modify a wiring harness to fit. Being a USB device, the trackball will automatically install as a plug-and-play mouse in all modern operating systems. DOS-based systems will need a USB driver with no guaranteed results. The interface has a small footprint (2.5" × 1.7") and comes with appropriate wiring harnesses for the pushbuttons.

Because the interface comes with the wiring harness, connecting it is easy enough. Connect the pushbuttons and trackball, connect the USB cable, and then turn on the computer. There is no need to worry about power and ground connections because they are supplied by the USB cable.

The Happ Controls USB interface has received good reviews from the people who have used it. Trouble-free installation, reliable function, and relatively low cost make it a good candidate for a dedicated trackball (or other optical device) interface.

Hagstrom Electronics

Hagstrom Electronics (www.hagstromelectronics.com) has three interface models that provide optical device support. One is a dedicated unit, and two are multi-purpose units that range in price from $35 to $140. Like their keyboard encoder line, these interfaces have all been well received by the arcade cabinet community. Hagstrom has a strong reputation for customer support and service.

Hagstrom KE72T

The Hagstrom KE72T (www.hagstromelectronics.com/ke72det.html) was covered in the previous chapter so I'll provide only a brief summary here. The unit costs $140 with the trackball chip installed and will support 72 programmable keyboard inputs along with a trackball and three mouse buttons. The interface will connect through the keyboard and PS/2 mouse ports. You will need either to create your own wiring harness or to purchase the trackball wiring harness for an additional $10 (see Figure 9-12).

FIGURE 9-12: A Happ Controls trackball connected to the KE72T with the Hagstrom-supplied interface cable.

Used by permission of Happ Controls and Hagstrom Electronics.

As previously mentioned, the KE72T is the flagship of the Hagstrom line and has received excellent reviews from those who have used one. The combination of 72 keyboard inputs along with the trackball interface provides an extra layer of functionality and makes it an excellent candidate for a single-interface control panel.

Hagstrom KE-USB36

Hagstrom's follow-up to the KE72T, the KE-USB36 (www.hagstromelectronics.com/keusb36.html) is also an amazingly flexible device (see Figure 9-13). At $80, the unit provides all the functionality of the KE72T and more even though it has a maximum of 36 programmable keyboard inputs. The interface connects via a single USB connection.

FIGURE 9-13: The Hagstrom KE-USB36 encoder.
Used by permission of Hagstrom Electronics.

The KE-USB36's programmable inputs can be designated as either keyboard inputs or as one of the three mouse buttons. The programmable inputs are direct mode so there are no concerns about the ghosting that matrix solutions can suffer from. Fully populated with a trackball and three mouse buttons, you are left with 33 available keyboard inputs. This is enough for two players with a joystick and seven buttons apiece with room left over for several administrative buttons. You could also configure it to support four players with a joystick and four buttons apiece with only one input left over.

Programming the KE-USB36 is done via a GUI interface in Windows through the USB cable. Each keystroke can be as-is or can be set as a combination keystroke with the Shift, Control, or Alt keystrokes.

Wiring the interface is similar to the KE72T with a standard IDE cable header on the board. You can either use an IDE cable or purchase the IOX36 breakout board ($16) mentioned in the previous chapter and attach your wiring to the screw-down blocks. The interface uses the same wiring connection for the trackball as the KE72T with the option to build your own wiring harness or purchase the one from Hagstrom for $10 (see Figure 9-14). One additional feature that MAME fans will appreciate is the connections for Caps Lock, Num Lock, and Scroll Lock LEDs. The board already has the necessary resistors built in so all that is required is to attach the LEDs via standard wiring. Because the unit gets its power through the USB interface, no additional power wiring is required.

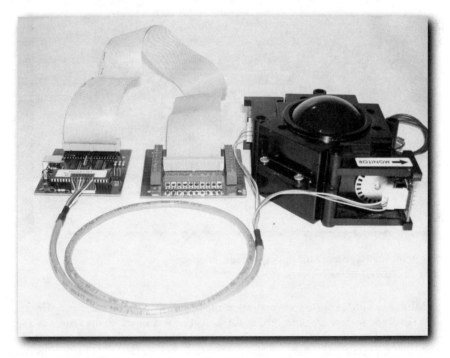

FIGURE 9-14: The KE-USB36 interface on the left attached to the IOX36 breakout board in the middle and a Happ Controls trackball on the right.
Used by permission of Hagstrom Electronics.

Hagstrom's KE-USB36 comes with an incredible range of features at an affordable price. Its USB interface means DOS users may wish to look elsewhere, but, for all other operating systems, purchasing this interface is a wise choice. The combination of keyboard and trackball inputs, along with the bonus LED connections, makes this one hard to beat.

Hagstrom ME4

Already have a keyboard encoder solution and just need a trackball or spinner interface? The Hagstrom ME4 (www.hagstromelectronics.com/ME4.html; see Figure 9-15) is a good candidate to consider. The ME4 supports one trackball, one spinner, and three mouse buttons for $35 ($50 with all required cables).

FIGURE 9-15: The Hagstrom ME4 optical encoder interface.
Used by permission of Hagstrom Electronics.

The ME4 uses a PS/2 mouse port connection and operates with standard mouse drivers. Both the trackball and spinner are functional at the same time and appear to the system as a single mouse device. There are two jumpers on the interface, which allows you to define the axis and direction of the spinner. If the spinner spins left when you think it should be spinning right, you can switch the jumper to correct it.

Wiring the interface can be done with your own custom-made harness with parts available from any electronics store. However, with all the interface cables necessary available from Hagstrom for $15, you'll probably be happier just purchasing them instead of making your own. The unit takes its power from the PS/2 interface so no external power hookups are necessary.

By the time you read this, Hagstrom may have updated the interface to work with both active-high and active-low devices. Visit its Web site at www.hagstromelectronics.com for updated information. You can also use the 1K pull-up resistor method to connect an active-low device. Remember that most optical arcade controls are active high-based.

Supporting both a trackball and spinner along with three buttons in a single interface, the ME4 makes an excellent optical interface for those of you who already have a keyboard solution.

Oscar Controls USB mouse interface

The arguably dominating force in the commercial spinner business, Oscar Controls (www.oscarcontrols.com), also makes available its interface (see Figure 9-16) that starts for as little as $9 with a spinner wiring harness. The interface is a pre-made USB mouse hack that will support one trackball or two spinners and two mouse buttons.

FIGURE 9-16: The Oscar Controls USB mouse interface.
Used by permission of Oscar Controls.

The Oscar Controls mouse interface supports all the features of a regular mouse, including plug-and-play functionality with standard mouse drivers. It is a USB interface so use with DOS-based machines may be problematic. The interface can also be purchased with left and right mouse button wiring headers and harness for $12.50, and a Happ Controls trackball wiring harness is available for an additional $8. The trackball harness plugs straight into the standard, six-pin Molex connector so no modification of the arcade harness is necessary. All power to the interface is supplied through the USB connection. Also, this interface specifically has been proven to work with active-low controls by the addition of 1K pull-up resistors.

The Oscar Controls USB mouse interface offers the advantages of a low-cost mouse hack without the effort involved. Supporting one trackball or two spinners, you could purchase two of these interfaces with cabling for the cost of one of the other commercially available interfaces. This is an excellent choice for those who already have keyboard encoder solutions. Oscar Controls is a frequent contributor to the arcade cabinet building community and has an excellent reputation for support and service.

Ultimarc Opti-Pac

Wrapping up the lineup of optical encoders is the Ultimarc Opti-Pac (www.ultimarc.com/ optipac1.html; see Figure 9-17), which is available for $39 with a serial cable and $44 for USB. The Opti-Pac is Ultimarc's counterpart to their highly successful I-PAC keyboard encoder. It supports a whopping two trackballs and four spinners (one trackball and two spinners per player) with up to two mouse buttons per player. No other interface supports as many simultaneous optical controls.

FIGURE 9-17: The Ultimarc Opti-Pac.
Used by permission of Ultimarc.

The Opti-Pac is full of features designed for the home arcade cabinet builder. It supports both USB and serial port connections and has onboard jumpers to switch between active-high and active-low support. One very nice feature is the automatic selection of either the trackball or spinner for each player. When both controls are idle, whichever control is moved first becomes the active functioning control. The other control is disabled while the first is in use. If both controls are idle for ten seconds, the active status is reset, and both controls are available. This allows the benefit of having both a trackball and spinner for a player without the problem of accidentally bumping one and interfering with the other.

Power is supplied to the interface in USB mode even though an external +5v power source is necessary in serial mode. A cable is supplied to draw the +5v power from an I-PAC if one is available. Otherwise, any power source in the computer will work. The Opti-Pac comes with screw-down wiring block terminals that are clearly labeled for easy wiring. Connecting the Opti-Pac in USB mode is simply a matter of plugging it in. Connecting in serial mode requires one serial port to activate player one's controls and a second serial port to activate player two's controls.

Of all the optical encoders available, the Opti-Pac is the most versatile. The ability to support both active-high and active-low controls, the serial and USB interfaces, and the total number of controls supported make this the clear contender for control panels with multiple, optical-based arcade controls. Ultimarc is another vendor with a strong presence in the arcade cabinet building community that is known for excellent support and customer service.

Note Don't forget that the Ultimarc Mini-PAC in the previous chapter also supports a single trackball and spinner.

Optical encoder wrap-up

All of the commercial optical encoders in this chapter are good candidates for interfacing optical arcade controls. They come from vendors with a proven track record in creating devices of this type, and there is not a lemon in the bunch. You should match the feature set and pricing to your needs and choose accordingly with confidence. For those of you who are new to the hobby, the range of choices available is a marked departure from a few years ago when few options existed. From the $9 Oscar Controls spinner interface to the $140 full-featured Hagstrom KE72T, a solution is available for every budget. Some extra attention will need to be paid to the interface chosen if you are planning to use an active-low arcade control, such as the Wico trackball.

Multiple Mice

As a rule of thumb, you can have one trackball or two spinners per mouse device. No matter how you interface your controls, the computer ultimately thinks your arcade controls are a two-axis mouse. Depending on your needs, you may want to have more than one mouse device available on the computer at a time. In one scenario, you might need two physical mouse devices that appear to the computer as a single mouse. In another scenario, you may prefer the computer to recognize that you have two distinctive mouse devices. The first situation allows you to have different mouse-based devices all controlling the same cursor, such as a trackball and spinner both controlling player 1's action. The second situation allows separate arcade control, such as two players competing against one another in a trackball-based game.

Whether a second mouse device is treated by the computer as being the same device as the first or as a separate device depends on the connection method and the software involved. By itself, Windows does not support the concept of separate mouse control. Windows will recognize two mice, but both will be configured to control the same cursor. From an operating system point of view that makes sense, why would you want to control two separate cursors on the screen? However, from a game-playing point of view, that's obviously a different story.

If two mouse devices (hereafter, I will refer to them as "mice" even though I mean trackballs, spinners, and other optical arcade controls) are physically or electronically connected to the same port, then they will appear to the computer as a single mouse no matter what software is used. If two or more mice are connected through separate ports, with the right software, the computer can be convinced that they control two separate mouse cursors. In the case of USB, two USB mice are considered to be in separate ports even though both are USB due to the way USB is designed.

Multiple distinct mice are supported primarily in certain emulators (see Chapter 14). Multiple mice that appear as a single mouse are supported essentially in every application. This is usually done with a trackball and spinner combination that both control a single player's cursor or perhaps two spinners that each control one axis of a single mouse. In the case of two spinners on one mouse, the game software will know that the X axis represents one player and the Y axis represents the second player. The operating system will simply consider it one mouse.

Multiple ports

The easiest way to have multiple mice is simply to use multiple ports. From Windows 95 and up, Windows has supported the use of dual-pointing devices controlling the same cursor. Mice can be connected via the PS/2 mouse port, serial port, and USB ports. It is possible to have PS/2 and serial port mice living side-by-side, two USB port mice working together, or any other combination thereof. By being connected to multiple ports, this configuration allows the possibility of distinct mice, which depends on the capabilities of the game software.

Mice splitters

Splitters are also available for both the PS/2 mouse port and serial port. The splitter is a physical Y device that combines two individual mice into a single port. They are available from a variety of sources. By far, the most popular is the Y-mouse dual mouse adapter (see Figure 9-18) from PI-Engineering (www.ymouse.com). These retail for $50, and various versions, including a serial port model, are available. You can also find schematics for building your own splitter on the Internet, but success is problematic so they are not included here.

Because splitters combine multiple units into a single electrical signal, it is not possible to control separate cursors this way. All mice connected via a splitter appear as a single mouse to the computer.

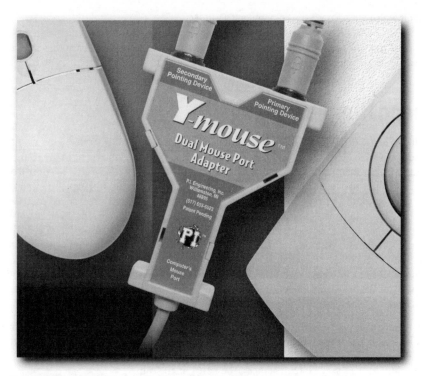

FIGURE 9-18: The PS/2 mouse port Y-Mouse splitter from PI-Engineering.
Courtesy of P.I. Engineering.

Switchable mice

You may encounter a drawback with having more than one mouse-type arcade control connected at a single time. (That is, both devices are connected at the same time!) The possible drawback is having one control accidentally move the mouse cursor in one direction while you're trying to move another in another direction. This wasn't so much a concern with joysticks because they don't have any drift to them. However, spinners and trackballs can easily drift a bit if accidentally (or, in the case of a nefarious opponent, deliberately) brushed against.

That's probably not a major concern, but, if you'd like to prevent the possibility, there's an easy circuit you can make that will switch between your trackball and spinner, which deactivates one when activating the other. Essentially, you place a single switch between the mouse and trackball on the axis the spinner uses. If your spinner is on the X axis, the switch toggles between the trackball and mouse having the X axis functional. The circuit was designed by Oscar Controls (www.oscarcontrols.com) and was meant to be used with their USB mouse interface, but it is easily adaptable to other mice interfaces as well. The circuit is available online at www.oscarcontrols.com/DPDTswitch.shtml.

On the CD The circuit is also included on the companion CD-ROM.

Don't forget that the Opti-Pac from Ultimarc, which was mentioned earlier in this chapter, has a built-in timer to prevent this problem from occurring.

Recommendation

You have so many excellent choices for interfacing optical arcade controls that you may be feeling hard-pressed to choose the right one. Only you can determine what is right for your particular situation, but I can make some general recommendations. If you're trying to control a single trackball or spinner, or even a couple of them, a mouse hack is an inexpensive way to go. Rather than build one, save yourself some aggravation, and purchase a pre-hacked mouse interface from Oscar Controls. If you'd like extra functionality, give some consideration to any of the other commercial optical encoders. For a DOS-based system, the Hagstrom KE72T, ME4, or Ultimarc Opti-Pac are your only choices. For Windows and other USB aware systems, any of the commercial encoders will work. If you're planning a panel with many optical arcade controls, the Ultimarc Opti-Pac is your hands-down best bet. If you're looking for a one-size-fits-all encoder for keyboard and mouse inputs, the KE72T or KE-USB36 from Hagstrom are your best bets, which depends on the number of inputs you need.

So what went into the Project Arcade cabinet? I elected to go with the Hagstrom ME4 this time. The simplicity of the plug-and-play and the optional wiring harnesses made it the quickest and easiest choice. I could just as easily have gone with any of the other commercial encoders, but, for this set of circumstances, the ME4 fit the bill.

Summary

In this chapter, you have been introduced to the many ways you can connect optical arcade controls, such as trackballs, spinners, and rotary joysticks, to your computer. Whether you choose to build or buy a solution at this point, you have enough information and options at your fingertips to connect things up. You can have a simple, single trackball connected or multiple devices such as a trackball and spinner. Now that all the decisions have been made, if you haven't yet, it's time to wire things up and see what happens. Got your lab coat on? Lighting storm going on outside? Have Igor stand by, attach the electrodes, and bring your creation to life! Congratulations! It's an arcade control panel!

You are a long way, if not all the way, to a completely functional Project Arcade system! If you are following the Project Arcade design specifications, your control panel is essentially finished. If you're just building a control panel without a cabinet, you can jump straight to Chapter 14 to start playing games! If you're building a full-sized Project Arcade cabinet or want to explore some of the other creative things you can add to your project, you'll want to move on to Chapter 10. Either way, you're on the home stretch where things just continue to get more interesting and more fun. Keep going!

Miscellaneous Bits of Arcade Trickery

I n this chapter, you'll learn some of the more advanced tricks you can use to hack arcade controls to your arcade cabinet. Interested in attaching a genuine *Star Wars*-style Atari flight yoke to your arcade cabinet? Maybe you'd like to include a couple of stationary machine guns for defending the Earth from tyrannical cyborgs? These are some of the things you can do with the information in this chapter. Read on!

Gaming with the Gameport

I'll start by introducing you to the PC gameport. When IBM first came out with their version of a personal computer, they adopted a typical no-nonsense, IBM, business-oriented approach. Monochrome monitors, sound limited to beeps, and a limited number of connection ports designed for printers and modems made up the IBM-PC. People who purchase personal computers aren't interested in playing games, right? Well, the purchasing public quickly set them straight on that score, demanding color screens and ways to make their computers fun. The PC gameport was IBM's first nod to the fact that personal computers could be used for more than just business activities. It has evolved little since its initial design and has since been replaced by USB ports as the gaming interface of choice. Still, there are some things that can be done quite easily with the gameport, and so I'll spend a bit of time talking about it here.

Note This section obviously applies primarily to IBM-PC-compatible computers. Macintosh computers use the ADB port for joysticks, and other computers may have different ports as well. If you have a non-IBM-compatible computer, the immediately following technical information probably will not apply to you. However, the Game pad hacks section and the rest of the chapter likely will.

How the gameport works

The gameport is a 15-pin port you'll usually find as part of your sound card. It is often on the motherboard as well (see Figure 10-1).

FIGURE 10-1: A close-up look at a dedicated gameport card with two ports.

You can connect up to two joysticks to a single PC gameport as originally designed. The interface supports four digital and four analog connections. The four digital connections come in the form of buttons with switches, and the four analog connections come in the form of 100K potentiometers. In the early days of the personal computer, this allowed you one joystick with two potentiometers (X and Y axes) and four buttons, or two joysticks with two potentiometers and two buttons each. Using two joysticks requires the use of a Y-cable because the pins for all the inputs are contained in one single port. Later development produced gameport-based steering wheels, yokes, and pedals, but these are still potentiometer-based analog devices and appear to the computer as simple joysticks.

Gameport pinouts

You will find the design of the gameport straightforward, based on what you've read so far. Throwing a curve into the mix, however, a second standard for the PC gameport called the *gameport+MIDI* was introduced. This standard replaced two pins from the original gameport design and supported the use of MIDI (musical instrument digital interface) devices as well as joysticks. It is extremely rare to find an original PC gameport these days because almost all manufacturers ship their products with the latter gameport+MIDI standard. The pinouts are labeled in Figure 10-2.

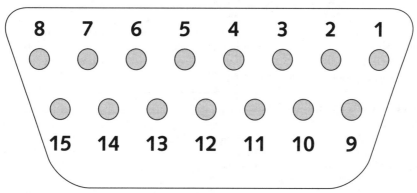

FIGURE 10-2: Looking into the gameport connector.

Table 10-1 shows the pinout specifications. Notice the differences in pins 12 and 15.

Table 10-1	PC Gameport and Gameport+MIDI Pinouts	
Pin	*Gameport*	*Gameport+MIDI*
1	+5v	+5v
2	Button 1	Button 1
3	Joystick 1 — X axis	Joystick 1 — X axis
4	Ground	Ground
5	Ground	Ground
6	Joystick 1 — Y axis	Joystick 1 — Y axis
7	Button 2	Button 2
8	+5v	+5v
9	+5v	+5v
10	Button 4	Button 4
11	Joystick 2 — X axis	Joystick 2 — X axis
12	Ground	MIDI transmit
13	Joystick 2 — Y axis	Joystick 2 — Y axis
14	Button 3	Button 3
15	+5v	MIDI receive

The gameport was designed to be cheap and simple because even though IBM was wrong in their assumptions about playing games on the PC, still surely no one was going to spend a lot of money on it, right? This decision in hindsight was a poor choice, and it has plagued the PC game industry since it progressed beyond the days of the original IBM-PC. Problems with timing and interface speed are among the challenges presented by gameports, which has led to the growth of USB- and keyboard-based controllers. Still, advancements in programming and design have led to improvements in the use of the gameport, and it continues to be useful to this day. You can use the pinouts listed in Table 10-1 combined with what you've learned about connecting arcade controls to do some pretty interesting things.

Connecting buttons and joysticks

First I'll look at connecting pushbuttons to the gameport. You probably can guess how it will work. All you need to do to activate any of the four pushbuttons is to connect its pin to ground. Put an arcade pushbutton with its microswitch wired in between the button's pin and ground, and you've created a pushbutton circuit that will turn that button on and off. Not terribly complicated.

Connecting an analog joystick (remember this section applies to joysticks that use potentiometers, not digital joysticks) is also straightforward. A 100K potentiometer is connected between one axis pin and +5v pin for every axis you want to connect. For instance, you'll connect the center leg of the X and Y potentiometers of joystick 1 to +5v pins on the gameport. One of the outer legs of each axis' potentiometer is then connected to the appropriate axis pin of the gameport, as described in Table 10-1. You may be wondering why you need to connect only two legs of the potentiometer instead of three. Whether you use two or three legs depends on how the interface is designed. In this case, the gameport is measuring the resistance only between the center leg and one outer leg. Which leg you connect depends on the orientation of the potentiometer, toward or away from you. Once connected, if the joystick moves in the opposite direction than expected, move the wiring to the other outer leg to correct it. For the rest of this section, I'll assume you're looking at the top of the potentiometer and will be wiring to the center and left legs from that perspective. Take a look at Figure 10-3 for an example.

Compare the pinouts in Table 10-1 with the diagram shown in Figure 10-3. Pins 2 and 4 are tied together through the microswitch to generate button 1. Pins 7 and 4 make the circuit for button 2. The two potentiometers connect pins 1 and 3 for the X axis of joystick 1, and pins 6 and 9 for the Y axis of joystick 1. Using the information in Table 10-1, you could easily expand upon this wiring diagram to add buttons 3 and 4, as well as the axes for joystick 2.

Note You'll find more than one type of potentiometer in electronics stores. You want linear potentiometers. Audio type potentiometers will not work properly for these kinds of connections.

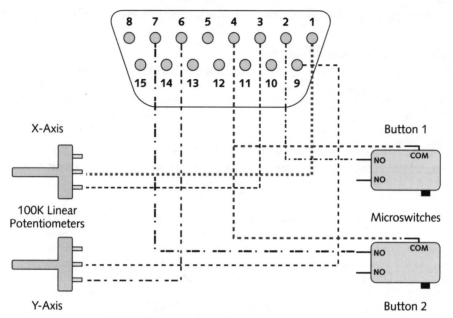

FIGURE 10-3: Wiring diagram for a simple two-button joystick.

Because the PC gameport supports up to four axes, just about any potentiometer-based analog arcade controller can be connected to this port. There are a couple of things to think about when converting an arcade controller to a PC. First, verify the rating of the potentiometers. With most arcade controls using 5K potentiometers, you'll need to remove them and replace them with PC-friendly 100K potentiometers. Second, if you are connecting something that uses an odd number of axes, you may run into problems. The PC normally expects to see both an X and Y axis under most drivers, although Windows XP does provide support for three-axis controllers. To be sure your controller will work if it has an odd number of axes, you should direct connect the final unused axis on the gameport. You can do this simply by connecting two pins. For instance, if you're using only the X axis of joystick 2, connect a wire from pin 13 to pin 1 or 9. Remember that for the X and Y axis pins, you connect to +5v and not to ground!

You can branch out from here to connecting wheels, flight yokes, and other devices to your computer through the gameport. The default drivers built into Microsoft Windows (particularly Windows XP, though earlier versions also have some built-in drivers) support a wide range of possible combinations of gameport buttons and axes.

Just about every combination you might encounter, from flight yokes and steering wheels to joysticks and other devices, will be supported with default drivers in Windows. Other operating systems may need to install specific drivers, such as the Linux joystick driver available at `ftp://atrey.karlin.mff.cuni.cz/pub/linux/joystick`.

On the CD The Linux joystick driver is also included on the companion CD-ROM.

Connecting wheels and flight yokes

I talked quite a bit in Chapter 5, "Arcade Controls for Power Gamers," about connecting arcade steering wheels, pedals, flight yokes, and positional guns to your computer. Bear in mind that the one thing these all have in common is that they have potentiometers inside controlling their movement. Details on how to hack them to the computer should begin to fall into place now. I'll discuss wheels in the rest of this section, but the principles apply to the other controls as well.

Wiring a steering wheel is easy enough. Connect the center leg of the wheel's potentiometer to +5v on pin 1 of the gameport, and connect the left leg to pin 3 (joystick 1, X axis). So far this isn't any different from connecting a joystick, except that instead of a joystick moving left and right you have a wheel turning left and right. It gets a bit trickier when it comes to the pedals.

Warning: It's getting technical again! You might want to brace yourself with a cup of coffee before you proceed. Ready? OK, here goes. In Chapter 5, I referred to the difference between a single-axis and dual-axis mechanism for steering wheel pedals. On a single-axis pedal system, the gas and brake use two potentiometers connected in series that appear to the computer as a single axis. On a dual-axis pedal system, the brake and gas use two separate potentiometers that appear to the computer as separate axes. Wiring for both types is shown in Figure 10-4. Note that any buttons, such as those for shifting up and shifting down, are wired the same as in Figure 10-3 and are not shown.

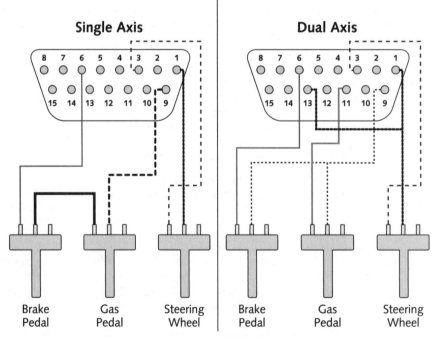

FIGURE 10-4: Wiring for a single-axis system (left) and a dual-axis system (right).

As shown in Figure 10-4, the center leg of the gas pedal in a single-axis system connects to pin 9 (+5v), and the left leg of the brake pedal connects to pin 6 (joystick 1's Y axis). The left leg of the gas pedal connects to the center leg of the brake pedal, which puts the two potentiometers in series, making them appear as one unit to the computer. In a dual-axis system, both center legs connect to pin 9 (+5v). The left leg of the gas pedal connects to pin 11, and the left leg of the brake goes to pin 6. Also note that because there are a total of three axes configured, pin 13 is jumpered to pin 1 to ensure the computer sees four axes total (otherwise it might see only two of them).

Is your head spinning yet? Don't worry about the specific details; they're important only when you're actually wiring. The general concept to take away from this is that with one method of wiring you have the gas and brake pedal acting as a single unit, and with another method of wiring, the pedals act as separate units. Some games work with single-axis pedals only; some allow the flexibility of dual-axis. Wouldn't it be great if you could use one set of wheel and pedals for both game types instead of having to have two sets of wheels? You can! Notice that pins 6 and 9 are used in both situations, with pin 11 added in the dual-axis circuit. Using a *double-pole, dual-throw* (DPDT) switch available from any electronics store, you can convert between single-axis and dual-axis as needed.

Credit for the switch design circuit goes to Lew's Wheels at www.monmouth.com/~lw4750 and to Build Your Own PC Wheel and Pedals at www.gunpowder.freeserve.co.uk/wheels. I won't attempt to describe the full details in text here; visit the two Web sites for pictures and more info. Essentially, however, when you switch between settings, the connections between the potentiometer legs and the gameport pinouts are rearranged as required to convert between single- and dual-axis pedals.

Other analog controls

You'll find wiring other analog devices to the gameport fairly easy after reading about steering wheels and pedals. Pretty much the only other analog controls of importance not yet discussed are positional guns. Other analog controls probably exist, but they do not have a significant enough presence in the arcade world to merit a specific mention. The discussion of positional guns here applies to those devices as well.

Positional guns are really nothing more than oddly shaped joysticks. They mount to the top of the control panel and allow you to pan left and right and up and down. Sound familiar? Joysticks move left and right and up and down. Other than the fact that they have built-in firing buttons and a different physical construction, inside they're all the same. One potentiometer controls movement along the X axis, and another controls movement along the Y axis. As long as you make sure the potentiometers are 100K rated, you can connect these devices to a gameport just like a joystick.

Game pad hacks

Directly wiring your arcade controls to the gameport is pretty fascinating and can give you a big sense of accomplishment. How many other people can take a handful of electronic components, mix them together, and make a joystick or steering wheel? It's a pretty small group to say the least! However, übergeek status aside, it's a lot of work that isn't necessarily required to get the results you want. So many inexpensive game pads and joysticks exist that it's easier to pick one up and hack your arcade controls to it rather than wiring directly to the gameport.

Hacking a computer gamepad (or joystick, steering wheel, etc. — hereafter I'll just refer to all computer game controllers as gamepads) has a couple of advantages. The costs can be low with the use of used or generic gamepads. Even broken gamepads can often be salvaged for a project like this. Also, because just about every computer has a gameport of some kind, game developers usually included support for gamepads (although not as often as keyboard support) in their games. Finally, gamepad hacks are usually much easier than keyboard hacks and do not suffer from the ghosting and blocking problems that keyboards do. Your biggest hurdle in hacking a gameport gamepad will be in finding one! Due to the huge success and deployment of USB, most gamepads are now USB based. eBay (www.ebay.com) or large consumer electronics stores are your best bet for finding a good cheap gameport gamepad.

Hacking an arcade control to a gamepad is a lot like hacking a keyboard. Button presses or potentiometers sit in the middle of a circuit that sends a particular signal to the computer. Removing the physical mechanism of the gamepad and substituting your own button press or potentiometer to the gamepad's circuit board should sound familiar to you. Gamepad circuit boards typically have soldering points that you can connect wiring to, and they sometimes will even have wiring headers that you can use instead of soldering!

Digital hacks

Digital hacks refer to hacking gamepads that use switches. This applies not only to the pushbuttons but also to the directional controls. Many gameport-based gamepads use a little 4-way direction pad (see Figure 10-5) for movement, similar to Nintendo controllers. Wait! Haven't I been saying that gameports use analog controls for movement? Four axes and four pushbuttons, right? Yes, but like many things in the PC world, programmers have worked around initial limitations to stretch the capabilities beyond the original design. Using a combination of hardware and software techniques, gamepad designers have been able to move beyond the original specifications of gameport joysticks. Gameport gamepads with a directional pad and six or more buttons are now common designs, although they are still using the original gameport specifications.

When you peel apart a gamepad, you'll find that the design is fairly simple. Any particular digital (pushbutton) control is usually a three-layer affair. There's a hard plastic button or pad that you directly press. Below that is a plastic membrane with conductive material on the underside. Directly beneath that lies the circuit board, with two halves of a circuit that the membrane makes contact with when pressed (see Figure 10-6). It's starting to sound an awful lot like a keyboard, isn't it?

You should not solder directly to the button contacts on the gamepad. You may have success doing so, but the connection will probably be weak and likely to fail. If you'll look at Figure 10-7, you can see what happened after a test solder to the contacts on my gamepad. The contacts lifted right off the PCB! Presumably this is due to the heat applied during the soldering. However, do you notice the tiny holes on the circuit traces coming from the contacts? Soldering a wire there is much easier! Even though this particular contact is ruined, I can still use this board by wiring to the soldering points on the circuit traces. Most gamepads will have soldering points you can attach your wiring to. You should look for the circuit traces that the various contacts have in common; that will be your ground. Solder a wire to the nonground side of the contact (at the soldering point), and attach the other end to your pushbutton or joystick microswitch. Solder a single wire from the gamepad's ground to a wiring block and run the ground from your microswitches to this wiring block. There's no need to solder both sides of every contact. You can also daisy chain the grounds, as described in previous chapters.

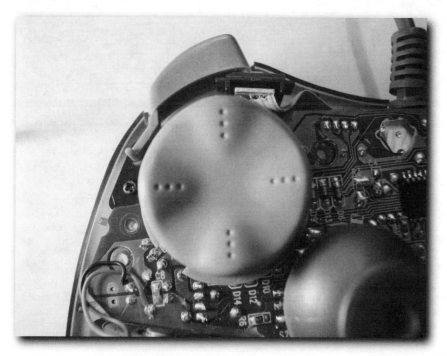

FIGURE 10-5: A partially disassembled gamepad showing the directional pad.

FIGURE 10-6: Peeling away all the layers reveals the circuit board. Two different styles of contacts are shown: Solid (left) and interweaved (right).

FIGURE 10-7: Showing the ruined contact. The solder point is to the bottom right, beneath the ruined contact, and has a wire soldered to it.

Analog hacks

Analog hacks deal with hacking gamepads that use potentiometers for directional control. You may find it easier to use a true PC joystick to hack rather than a gamepad because the potentiometers are likely to be bigger and easier to get to. Once again, you have two possible ways to perform an analog hack. If the gamepad or joystick you're using as your interface uses the same rating of potentiometer as your arcade control, then all you need to do is to wire the outputs of the arcade control to the gamepad's circuitry. If they do not match, you'll need to replace the potentiometers in the arcade control with potentiometers rated the same as the gamepad and then wire the outputs of the arcade control to the gamepad's circuitry.

Recall that analog arcade controls typically use 5K potentiometers, whereas PCs normally use 100K. This means you are probably going to have to swap out the potentiometers. Before you do, however, be sure to read the *Microsoft SideWinder Dual Strike* hack in the *USB gamepad hacks* section in this chapter. Replacing potentiometers can be tedious, and finding one the right size isn't always easy.

Figure 10-8 shows a look at the inside of a driving-yoke controller. On the right hand side, you can see a potentiometer with three wires coming out of it. Make sure you are orienting the potentiometers in the same direction, and the hack is as simple as wiring the output legs of the arcade control's potentiometer to the same place that the PC gamepad's potentiometers are wired to. Obviously, you'll need to make sure the gamepad's potentiometers are disconnected first!

Potentiometer

FIGURE 10-8: Inside the yoke, with the potentiometer controlling the *Y* axis exposed and pointing to the right.

Replacing this yoke's potentiometer would not be terribly difficult. The security bolt holding it in place would need to be removed and the wires clipped. (You won't be using them, so there's little point in desoldering them.) Vendors tend to use off-the-shelf parts when they can, so finding a 5K potentiometer the right size should be possible, though you may have to resort to ordering online. Happ Controls sells a 100K potentiometer that should be a perfect fit for many arcade controls (part number 50-2032-00 at www.happcontrols.com). Remember that you want a linear potentiometer!

Wrapping up the gameport

Many excellent online resources were visited during research for this section. Two good places to read and learn more about the PC gameport are Tomi Engdal's joystick documents at www.epanorama.net/documents/joystick/index.html and the Control Center's joystick history essay at www.joy-stick.net/articles/essay.htm. More details about steering wheel connections specifically can be found at Lew's Wheels at www.monmouth.com/ ~lw4750, and Build Your Own PC Wheel and Pedals at www.gunpowder.freeserve .co.uk/wheels.

Using the USB Port

USB ports are a lot like the Borg from *Star Trek*. "We are USB. You will be assimilated. Resistance is futile!" Just about everything you can connect to a computer also has a USB version, if it hasn't done away with its original version altogether. Keyboards, mice, sound systems, networks, and yes, gamepads can all be found with USB connections today. There are many advantages to using USB. Plug-and-play almost always works properly with USB, devices can be plugged in and removed at will, and USB support can be found in several operating systems and computers. This means that a gamepad, for instance, can be manufactured that works with Windows, Linux, and Macintosh computers with little to no extra effort on the manufacturer's part. Add to this the fact that you can have well over 100 USB devices on a computer, and the possibilities of USB for an arcade cabinet become obvious!

USB Features

USB stands for *Universal Serial Bus*. It was developed as an answer to the limitations suffered by other ports and protocols used to connect devices to a computer. If you'd like to really dive into how the USB protocol and hardware works, visit the USB homepage at www.usb.org. Some of the features particularly of concern to arcade builders include:

- **Power** — USB cables have four wires. Two wires are used for data, one wire is for +5v power, and one is for ground. USB supplies up to 500 milliamps of +5v power to peripherals that need it. You can tap into this power for arcade hacks, but I do not recommend it. (Use the computer's power-supply cables instead.)

- **Expandability** — The USB standard allows for up to 127 devices to be connected. Part of the standard includes USB hubs, which will expand a single port into many ports. Hubs can be powered or unpowered. If you have many devices that draw power through the USB cable, you should use a powered hub so that you don't try to draw more power than the computer is supplying. You won't hurt anything by doing so, but your USB devices may not work.

- **Hot-swapping** — USB was designed to allow for quick insertion and removal of peripherals into a computer. Being able to remove a peripheral without powering off the computer is referred to as *hot-swapping*. You can use this on your arcade cabinet, for example, to plug in a steering wheel for occasional use, removing it when done without turning off your cabinet.

There's more to USB, of course, but these are the main points of interest to us. You can use USB connections in some interesting ways in an arcade cabinet project. One I've already touched on, using an arcade control in a temporary situation when you don't want it permanently mounted on your cabinet. Because USB supports hot-swapping, you can plug in the control, play a game, and then unplug it without causing problems.

Another interesting way to take advantage of USB expandability and hot-swapping is to use it for extra players. Say that you've built a two-player arcade cabinet, and that's how it gets used most of the time. Occasionally, however, the gang comes over for a rousing arcade session. Take turns? Bah! Connect two more game controllers to the USB ports, and turn your two-player cabinet into a four-or-more-player cabinet. Arguments are avoided and a good time is had by all!

USB ports are usually found on the back of the PC, though vendors have begun to place them at the front and sides as well. However, your computer is going to be buried inside the cabinet. How can you get to it for controls you want to have removable? One excellent suggestion for an arcade cabinet came from the message forums of the Arcade Controls Web site (www. arcadecontrols.com). The USB standard allows for cable lengths of up to 5 meters (about 16 feet). Take a USB extension cable, plug one end into the computer, and mount the other end somewhere accessible in the cabinet. Consider a hidden connection underneath the lip of the control panel, or perhaps two connections — one on each side of the cabinet for additional players on the left and right. Voila! You have a well concealed but easily accessible expansion port available for use!

Connecting to the USB port

You really have only a couple of options for connecting to the USB port. You can purchase an arcade control or interface that uses USB, such as the Act-Labs USB light gun (www.act-labs.com/), or you can hack a USB gamepad.

USB interfaces

You've already seen many USB interfaces in previous chapters, such as the Ultimarc Opti-Pac and the Hagstrom Electronics KE-USB36. Happ Controls also has a line of USB interfaces for connecting arcade controls to your computer. Unfortunately, pictures were not available in time for this book, but they can be seen online at the Happ Controls Web site (www.happ controls.com). There are four models available:

- **Driving USB UGCI** — Supports a steering wheel, brake, throttle, shifter, eight buttons, two coin-ups, and a trackball with three mouse buttons.

- **Flying USB UGCI** — Supports an analog joystick with POV hat, rudder pedal, throttle, two buttons, two coin-ups, and a trackball with three mouse buttons.

- **Fighting USB UGCI** — Supports two eight-position digital joysticks, six buttons per joystick, six buttons, two coin-ups, and a trackball with three mouse buttons.

- **USB Trackball Interface Kit** — Supports a trackball or steering wheel with up to three mouse buttons.

Prices on the Happ Controls USB interfaces range from $40 for the trackball kit to $182 for the other kits. However, prices occasionally vary so you should check their Web site for up-to-date pricing. A software development kit is available for the three UGCI models to allow keyboard mapping for the various attached controls. The USB kits from Happ Controls have received good reviews from those who have used them.

USB gamepad hacks

Hacking a USB gamepad is virtually identical to hacking gameport gamepads. In fact, were it not for one particular item, I would not have anything to tell you here at all. However, this one item more than merits space in the book. Enough suspense? Okay. Recall that though it's possible to wire a potentiometer directly to the PC's gameport, a USB port has only two wires for data. These two data signals are digital in nature and cannot directly communicate with potentiometers in any meaningful fashion. Therefore, any USB analog gamepad has to include electronics onboard to convert to a signal the computer can understand. Because the conversion is done on the gamepad and not by the computer, the gamepad is not constrained by the 100K requirement of the gameport. This is significant.

How does that help? The Microsoft SideWinder Dual Strike is a USB gamepad with analog controls that use 5K potentiometers! Technically, it uses 20K potentiometers that have a restricted range of motion, limiting them from 0K to 5K, but it amounts to the same thing. Remember analog arcade controls also use 5K potentiometers. With six programmable buttons, a shift button for a second round of programmable functions, and two 5K potentiometers, the Dual Strike is an arcade-control hacker's dream! Unfortunately, the Dual Strike (along with the entire SideWinder line) is no longer being made. However, you can still find them on eBay relatively inexpensively.

1UP, the creative talent behind PacMAMEa, at www.1uparcade.com, used Dual-Strike hacks extensively in connecting an Atari Star Wars flight yoke and positional guns to his incredible arcade cabinet. His instructions for performing the Dual-Strike hack are available online at www.1uparcade.com/projects-dualstrike.html. Other USB gamepads may also use 5K potentiometers, but the Dual Strike is the only one documented to date.

 The instructions for the Dual-Strike hack are also included on the book's companion CD-ROM.

Other Miscellaneous Tricks

Are there any other ways to connect arcade controls to a computer? Well, there are a couple more that haven't been brought up yet. As a sneak preview, you can use the parallel port (and sometimes USB) to connect Nintendo, PlayStation, and other gaming-console controllers to your PC. It's also possible to connect arcade controls to the PC via the parallel port, but there is little compelling reason to do so. Any connections via the parallel port require special drivers and/or software support, and with much easier solutions available, it's not worth the effort.

 On the companion CD-ROM, you'll find some information about using your favorite gaming console's controller on your computer.

One last bit of interface wizardry to pass on to you is Druin's Rotary Interface (Figure 10-9), available at http://connect.to/rotary. It allows you to connect one or two 12-position rotary joysticks to an arcade cabinet for games that use them. These joysticks use a mechanical interface, not an optical one. The rotary interface is designed primarily for use with MAME (Multiple Arcade Machine Emulator; see Chapter 14, "Choosing and Loading Software"). Each time the joystick is rotated, the interface sends a clockwise or counterclockwise signal to MAME. The interface is designed to be used as a companion to a direct mode (nonmatrix) keyboard interface and cannot connect to a computer directly. They start at $50 with shipping, and a scaled-down, single-joystick model is available upon special request for a lower cost. The rotary interface is also available as an upgrade to the SlikStik commercial arcade control panels and cabinets (Chapter 17, "Buying Your Way to Gaming Nirvana").

FIGURE 10-9: Druin's Rotary Interface.
Used by permission of Jason Penney.

Summary

In this chapter you learned about the PC gameport and how it can be used to interface arcade controls. Though the gameport is an old and simple interface, it is uniquely suited for easy analog-arcade-control connections. You also took another look at the USB interface and learned how the Microsoft SideWinder Dual Strike is particularly useful to arcade cabinet builders. Things are wrapped up with the introduction of Druin's Rotary Interface for rotary joysticks. Between these subjects and the past few chapters, you've picked up many different options for connecting arcade controls to your arcade cabinet.

In fact, you've now finished all the arcade control and interface selection information this book has to offer! You've successfully peeled back the veil of mystery surrounding how arcade controls work, and mastered the techniques necessary to design your own dream arcade-control system. Think back on how much you've learned! In the end, it's all pretty simple and boils down to one concept: An arcade control is simply a way of completing a circuit. It may be a discrete digital circuit that's either on or off (such as a pushbutton), or it may be an analog circuit that generates a varying degree of resistance (such as a steering wheel). Either way, the different designs and pretty colors all do the same thing in the end. Connecting an arcade control is a matter of choosing one of several possible interfaces and connecting your control circuits through them. This concludes Part III, "Hooking Things Up Under the Hood."

Coming up next is Part IV, "Putting Together the Final Pieces," in which I'll cover the remaining steps necessary to put an arcade cabinet together. Start with Chapter 11, "Audio — Silence Isn't Golden," where you'll learn about the various audio-related choices you have. There's more than you might think! Keep going, and in a few more chapters you'll be completely finished and the envy of all your friends!

Putting Together the Final Pieces

part

IV

Audio — Silence Isn't Golden

Y ou and your pal Mario have dodged flaming barrels, risked life and limb climbing rickety ladders, and finally rescued the damsel in distress from a gorilla who's seen too many King Kong movies — only to have her and the gorilla run off together. Alas, poor Mario, left in a lurch! Bravely carrying on, Mario discovers a secret passage into the Land of Video Game Clichés. Successfully dodging countless crazed turtles and unspeakably vile villains (thanks to your masterful guidance with *real arcade controls*), Mario comes to a pivotal moment. Perched on a crumbling ledge with seconds to spare, a mob of flaming barrels building a pyramid to reach him from below, Mario must quickly choose between running left or right. In one direction lies certain painful death and video game obscurity (the bargain bin!). In the other lies video game-superstar Valhalla, where the gorillas serve cold drinks, the damsels in distress do their own rescuing, and barrels are used only as planters. Which way is which? Which way to go? Suddenly, Lara Croft swings down guns a-blazing and urgently whispers "Mario, you have only one chance at this! The path to safety lies *KAPOW!* *KAPOW!* . . . got it?" "Wait!" yells Mario as Lara does a swan dive into the pile of barrels, sending them scattering before running off into the darkness, "I couldn't hear you over the shooting! Which way, which way!?" If only your arcade cabinet had a good sound system, perhaps Mario might have been able to hear her!

OK, sound is probably not that important, but you (and Mario) still want a quality sound system in your arcade cabinet. Good sound can make the difference between a fun gaming session and one that leaves you in a heart-thumping adrenaline rush. There's a whole science (art?) dedicated to creating perfect sound. Enthusiasts build their own speakers, fine-tune each speaker's audio levels, and use meters to determine perfect placement in the room. I'm not going to subject you to any of that! That's appropriate for designing a home theater, but, for an arcade cabinet, the job isn't quite as hard. With some careful thought and planning, you'll have a sound system that will make Mario proud without breaking the budget!

Speaking of Speakers . . .

If you're planning only to play games on your arcade cabinet, speaker selection isn't quite as critical as if you're planning to use it as a multipurpose, multimedia station. Most arcade games had fairly basic speakers in them. After all, the players are right in front of the machine. Do you really want or need the sound to drown out the machine next to it? On the other hand, if you really dig the sound of thumping gorilla feet and laser beams, or if you're planning to use your machine for more than just games, then consider investing in a quality set of speakers. What else can you do with your arcade cabinet besides games? I'll cover that later in this chapter, but imagine your cabinet doubling as the household jukebox!

Unlike a lot of other choices in your cabinet, you should try to select a set of speakers you know you'll be happy with in the long run because replacing them later will be difficult. You'll be cutting a hole or holes in the speaker panel to match the shape of the speakers and fastening them into place. Replacing them later will limit you to using something that fits the already existing holes or finding some way to disguise the difference. You can avoid that with some extra consideration before you start.

A lot of folks toy with the idea of surround sound on their monster arcade cabinet. At first blush, that might seem like a good idea, but it may be overkill in this case. It depends quite a bit on what kind of gaming you intend for the cabinet. If you're planning to stick to emulated arcade classics, you should remember that almost all of them used only mono or stereo speakers. If you're thinking of playing a wider mix, including modern PC games, then surround sound makes more sense. Hearing the sounds of footsteps behind you while running around in a deadly maze adds an element of gaming not to be missed!

Choosing PC speakers

You have a couple of options when it comes to choosing speakers for your cabinet. You can choose a set of PC speakers, or you can choose something else. How's that for vague? I should probably have said you can choose the simple way or the more involved way. PC speakers are obviously the simple way. (Note that PC speakers refer to external stereo speakers designed to work with a computer and not the tiny speaker built into the computer case.) Aside from physically mounting them, connecting PC speakers is simply a matter of plugging in the cables in to your sound card. Depending on quality, They can be had for as little as a few dollars up to a few hundred dollars. My personal favorites are the Klipsch ProMedia 2.1 computer speakers (www.klipsch.com; see Figure 11-1). The sound quality is amazing, and they have a relocatable volume control pod that I'll discuss a bit later in this section.

Other speaker choices

Other speakers can be used in an arcade cabinet as well. Car stereo speakers, home audio bookshelf speakers, or projects speakers from electronics stores have all been used successfully in arcade cabinet projects. If you're planning to use non-PC speakers, there are a couple of things you'll need to consider.

FIGURE 11-1: Klipsch ProMedia 2.1 stereo computer speakers.
Photo courtesy of Klipsch Audio Technologies.

Power

Like anything electronic, speakers need power (in the form of amplifiers, in this case). Most computer speakers have built-in amplifiers. Most other speakers, such as car stereo or arcade speakers, do not so you'll need to supply one. Without an amplifier supplying power to the speakers, you will barely be able to hear anything, if they work at all. You can either purchase an external amplifier or kit (try Radio Shack or Parts Express at www.partsexpress.com) or hack an existing amplifier. Many people have successfully hacked a cheap PC speaker that has an amplifier and wired it to their non-PC speakers. Inside the PC speaker is a circuit board with the amplifier and associated electronics (Figure 11-2).

Using these amplifiers is quite easy. Disconnect the PC-speaker wires from the amplifier, and connect the wires from your speaker in their place. Repeat this for the other speaker. You can either clip the wires and use quick-disconnects, or you can solder them directly to the amplifier board. Quick-disconnects are much easier and are recommended. The second speaker is likely to plug into the amplifier through a $\frac{1}{8}$-inch stereo plug so you may need to hack or build an appropriate cable. Voila! You have an instant, amplified, stereo-speaker set using higher quality arcade or car stereo speakers!

Note If you're thinking of using a PC-speaker amplifier hack, take a look at Oscar Controls' tutorial. For another method, visit M.A.F.I.A. (Mr. Arcade's Fast Inexpensive Amplifier) page at http://home.woh.rr.com/ultimatearcade/mafia/mafia.htm.

FIGURE 11-2: Amplifier from generic PC stereo speakers.

On the CD The Oscar Control's tutorial is included on the companion CD-ROM, courtesy of Oscar Controls.

An audiophile would mention matching the impedance of the new speakers to those originally attached to the PC speaker's amp (speakers are usually rated at either 4 Ohms or 8 Ohms). Practically, mixing them up does not matter much for an arcade cabinet. You may slightly degrade the sound quality or shorten the lifespan of the speakers/amp—depending on whether your impedance is higher or lower than originally rated—but the odds are against this causing you a problem for the life of the cabinet.

As an alternative to hacking an amplifier, some older sound cards have an amplified speaker-out connection as well as a line-out connection. Self-powered/amplified speakers use the line-out jack whereas cheaper unpowered/unamplified speakers are connected to the speaker-out jack. If you have a sound card with stereo-out, you can wire unamplified speakers directly to the sound card's plug. One drawback is that volume control can be more difficult this way. Sound cards available today typically include only line-out connections, so this isn't an option for most people.

For those who want to truly shake the house, a PC speaker amplifier won't do it. If you're going to use car stereo speakers, why not use a car stereo amplifier to truly crank out the sound? It works, and people who have done it are quite happy with it. However, using a car stereo amplifier to power the speakers in your arcade cabinet is probably overkill. There's nothing wrong with it, but your time and effort are probably better spent elsewhere. Serious audio enthusiasts would argue with me on this point so you may wish to experiment before you make a final choice. I have one word of caution. Car amplifiers require a lot of power and can easily overload a PC power supply that's also powering other components. Use a dedicated power supply if you plan to use a car stereo amplifier.

Magnetic interference

Car stereo speakers and those from electronic project stores can work very well in a cabinet. However, be careful if you chose to pursue this route. These speakers usually aren't magnetically shielded. Have you ever held a magnet up to a video monitor? *Don't try it now!* You'll get a wavy picture with distorted colors straight out of the '70s. Distortion caused by strong or long-term exposure to magnets can be difficult — if not impossible — to fix. If you mount car stereo speakers to the speaker panel over your monitor, you may end up with unwanted (but sometimes pretty) distortions in your picture. It's unlikely to cause a permanent problem with brief exposure so you can see whether magnetic interference is going to be an issue before you attempt to solve it.

You can combat this problem by attaching a set of bucking magnets to your speakers. A bucking magnet is a magnet between $1/2$ to $3/4$ the size of your speaker's magnet, which you attach to the speaker magnet in reverse polarity so that they try to repel each other (see Figure 11-3). Because they will repel each other, you'll need to use a good industrial-strength adhesive to permanently attach them. The sound quality is not affected, but the magnetic fields are muted, which allows you to place the speakers close to your monitor without adverse affect. You can find these at Parts Express (www.partsexpress.com) for less than $1.

You can also deal with magnetic interference by installing shielding. Thin sheets of metal designed for this purpose are available from a variety of online locations. However, shielding is harder to work with and more expensive than using bucking magnets, and I would not recommend it.

Car stereo and hobby speakers do have one advantage over PC speakers. They're designed to be mounted flat into a panel like the one in your arcade cabinet. Their low-profile design and mounting holes make them an easy addition to a cabinet. If you can counteract any magnetic interference to the monitor, these speakers can work out very well.

FIGURE 11-3: A bucking magnet attached to a car stereo speaker.
Photo courtesy of Oscar Controls.

Speaker recommendations

If you have cheap or easy access to non-PC speakers, they can produce excellent sound quality and volume. Even a cheap pair of PC speakers can give you sound as good as or better than a 20-year-old arcade cabinet mono-speaker. They probably won't sound as good as car stereo or hobby speakers. However, for quality of sound and ease of installation, the best speaker choice for an arcade cabinet project is a set of moderately priced 2.1 or surround-sound PC speakers.

With non-PC or cheap PC speakers, you may not get a dedicated subwoofer. Good speakers are great for an arcade cabinet, but there's nothing quite like well-tuned, booming bass thumping in time to the firing of a laser beam to make you appreciate the desirability of a subwoofer. A 2.1 or surround-sound system with subwoofer is *highly recommended!*

Mounting speakers

For the purposes of this section, I'm going to assume you're using a set of 2.1 PC speakers with a subwoofer, such as the Klipsch ProMedia 2.1 speakers recommended earlier, and that you're following the Project Arcade plans. If you are using another solution, the specifics of mounting will vary, but the principles will remain the same.

Start by determining where you will mount the speakers. Most people will want to mount their speakers behind the marquee, facing down toward the monitor. Some may choose to mount them elsewhere, such as side mounts on the cabinet. Following the Project Arcade plans, you'll be mounting them behind the marquee.

Speaker covers

The next step is determining exact placement on the speaker panel. You'll want them as far as possible to the left and right and close to the front edge while still allowing enough room for wiring and speaker-cover placement. Start by considering what kind of covers you'll place over the speakers. Will you be cutting out slots in the panel for the sound to come through, as shown in Figure 11-4? This can be done with a router.

FIGURE 11-4: Routed speaker cutouts on a cocktail cabinet.
Photo courtesy of Oscar Controls.

Easier and more popular is the use of speaker grills to cover the speaker holes in the cabinet. However, you'll be amazed at how difficult it can be to find properly sized speaker grills for your cabinet. The ones available at local retailers are usually the wrong shape or entirely too big. Fortunately, I've tracked down a few online resources for likely candidates. The speaker grills used in Project Arcade are available from Mike's Arcade (www.mikesarcade.com) as well as Arcadeshop Amusements (www.arcadeshop.com). Round speaker grills are available from Wico (www.wicothesource.com) and from Happ Controls (www.happcontrols .com). You also might consider using the speaker covers that come with the Klipsch speakers, as was done on the VectoRaster cabinet (www.pcreliability.com/vectoraster/ index.htm).

If you'll be using speaker grills, you want to plan your measurements around them and not the speakers. The speakers should be a bit smaller than the grill and will be centered in the grill's space. If you're planning to use just routed speaker cutouts or some other method that doesn't use a grill, then you'll want to base your measurements around the speakers themselves.

Positioning your speakers

Whether you use grills or some other method, you'll need to position your speakers between the marquee retainer and the monitor-area glass. I'll be covering both a bit later on, but the marquee retainer is an L-shaped strip that attaches to the edge of the speaker panel and holds the marquee in place. The monitor-area glass is a glass or Plexiglas sheet that covers and protects the monitor area. The speakers will be placed so that they rest between the marquee retainer and the monitor cover. You should allow between $1/2$ inch to 1 inch from the edge of the speaker shelf for the marquee retainer. You'll have about $6^1/2$ inches from the edge of the shelf to the point where the monitor Plexiglas rests, which means your speaker grill can occupy about $5^1/2$ inches or less between the marquee retainer and the Plexiglas.

Caution

You are about to drill and cut holes into your speaker shelf—a step that will be hard to fix if something goes wrong. Before you touch the shelf, I highly recommend you follow the steps below on a piece of scrap wood. Make sure you're comfortable with how it's done before cutting into the cabinet itself. Remember that it never hurts to have a second set of eyes look at something before you begin. Don't forget your breathing mask and goggles!

The rest of the steps below assume you'll be working on the bottom of the speaker shelf. You can also remove your top- and back-angled panels and work from above the speaker shelf. I chose to work from below to make it easier even though that did mean I had to apply a coat of paint after I was done to cover up marks made during the work. Either method works; choose the one that suits you best.

Using a pencil, draw a line parallel to the edge of the speaker shelf about $1/2$ inch from the edge. Draw another line about $1^1/2$ inches from the left and right sides of the cabinet, which makes a 90-degree angle with the first line. This is the corner that you'll place your grill cover against.

Cutting holes for your speakers

Next, you'll need to determine the size and placement of the cutout for your speakers. You'll want to cut out enough wood to expose the actual sound-generating portions of the speaker while leaving enough wood to provide a mounting surface. I've included a mounting template for the Klipsch ProMedia 2.1 speakers, as shown in Figure 11-5.

On the CD

The mounting template for the Klipsch ProMedia 2.1 speakers is also found on the companion CD-ROM.

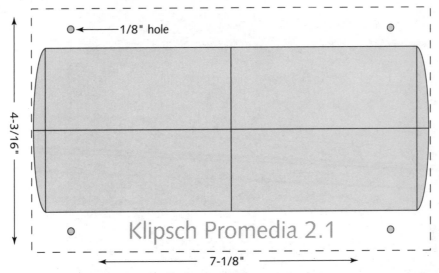

FIGURE **11-5: Klipsch ProMedia 2.1 mounting template, not to scale.**

Calculate the difference in the height and width between the speaker grills and the speakers, and divide those numbers by two. That will give you the offset you'll use when placing your template on the speaker shelf for cutting. For instance, the speaker grills used in Project Arcade from Mike's Arcade (www.mikesarcade.com) are $5^{1}/_{2}$ inches by 9 inches. The Klipsch ProMedia 2.1 speakers are $4^{3}/_{16}$ inches by $7^{1}/_{8}$ inches. A bit of quick math will show that the speaker template will need to be mounted $1^{1}/_{4}$ inches below the line you drew parallel to the edge ($5^{1}/_{2}$ minus $4^{3}/_{16} = 1^{5}/_{16}$; rounded to $1^{1}/_{4}$ for easy measuring) and $1^{7}/_{8}$ inches in from the line you drew on the side. If the math starts to make your head hurt, don't worry about it too much. The speakers will be hidden behind the speaker grill so, as long as they are mounted securely and there's a hole for the sound to come through, exactly where they get placed isn't critical. You're probably safe just eyeballing the measurements. Print out a couple of copies of the templates, measure them to make sure they are scaled at 100%, and then tape them in place as shown in Figure 11-6.

Drill the holes for the speaker-mounting screws. and Then, using a router or jigsaw, cut out the gray area on the template. Don't worry too much about how it looks because it will be covered by your speaker grill. Repeat this for the other speaker. After a coat of touch-up paint, you should end up with something that looks like Figure 11-7. Notice the unevenness of the cut-out on the right. I had a moment of distraction while operating the jig-saw. All I can say is never sneeze while operating power tools. However, it will be covered by the grill—no worries!

FIGURE 11-6: Underside of speaker shelf with templates in place.

FIGURE 11-7: Speaker shelf underside with cut-out speaker holes.

Attaching the speakers

Mounting the Klipsch speakers onto the speaker shelf is easy enough once you've got the holes cut and the paint touched up. Start by removing the speaker stands and the volume control pod. The speaker stands unscrew from the bottom, and the volume control pod will slide forward with a bit of effort. Next remove the speaker grill in order to expose the speaker hardware and screw holes. The screws holding the speaker together are $3/4$ inch long. You're going to remove those and use $1^1/2$-inch screws to mount through the speaker shelf into the speaker, which holds it firmly into place. The screws are just a bit too short to really hold well so you'll want to counter-sink them about $1/4$ inch. You could also try to find $1^3/4$-inch screws instead. Take a look at Figure 11-8.

FIGURE 11-8: Klipsch ProMedia 2.1 speaker with cover and screws removed. Replacement screws are on the left; original screws are on the right.
Used by permission of Klipsch Audio Technologies.

You'll want to mount the speakers with the wiring jack toward the outside walls. This will let you neatly route the speaker cable down the sides instead of dangling it down the middle. Be sure the screws are tight through the wood and into the speakers. If they're loose, the back of the speaker enclosure will fall off, which will probably break the speaker as it goes. Give the speaker a tug test to make sure it's secure. You want to make sure that the speaker won't fall when the cabinet is moved around. When the speakers are securely in place, cover them with the speaker grills, and you're done! Figure 11-9 shows what the installation will look like.

FIGURE 11-9: Left: securely mounted speaker. Right: grill-covered speaker.
Used by permission of Klipsch Audio Technologies and MikesArcade.com.

The subwoofer

Your last task is to mount the subwoofer somewhere. There are mixed camps on this. Some people contend you should mount the subwoofer outside the cabinet because they are designed to be placed in the open air and enclosing them can alter the acoustics. Other people think that there's enough open space inside the cabinet that it won't make a difference and, if anything, will magnify the bass effects. As usual, it comes down to your personal preference. I suggest placing the subwoofer inside the cabinet and fine-tuning the output with a relatively "boomy" song or game playing. If you don't like it, just move the subwoofer outside the cabinet. Because you're likely to be working in the cabinet for some time yet, I recommend staking out a suitable spot for the subwoofer and then placing it aside until you're ready to unveil your creation.

The final word on speaker mounting

If you're planning on using surround-sound speakers, you have some additional challenges. The front and middle speakers are not terribly difficult to place. The middle speaker would fit ideally behind the marquee with the front speakers either behind the marquee also or possibly mounted directly on the sides of the cabinet. The surround rear speakers are where you'll need to do some creative thinking. In my study, I have in-wall wiring with my surround-sound speakers mounted in the ceiling. I have an outlet in the wall behind my computer that the wiring is connected to. My rear-speaker outputs plug into this and give me surround-sound audio in my room. A similar concept can be used in your arcade cabinet project if you have the opportunity to run wiring in the walls. You can also follow the steps of a few audiophile cabinet builders who have used telescoping arms to mount the rear speakers to their cabinet. The arms mount to the back top of the cabinet and extend out past the player, which positions the rear speakers behind you.

Note   You might be considering dismantling the speaker or subwoofer enclosure to make it easier to mount. *Don't!* Speaker design consists of more than the electronics and physical parts. The enclosures are an important part of the overall sound quality. Removing the speaker/subwoofer enclosure changes the pressure and airflow and will have an adverse affect on the sound.

Volume control

Your last point of consideration with speakers is volume control. Sometimes, you may want your cabinet **loud**; sometimes, you may want it *quiet*. If you're using the Klipsch ProMedia 2.1 speakers or a similar set, you're in luck! The volume control pod connects to the subwoofer and has a long cable (Figure 11-10), which allows you to place it just about anywhere that's convenient for you.

FIGURE 11-10: Klipsch ProMedia 2.1 volume control pod.
Photo courtesy of Klipsch Audio Technologies.

I recommend placing the control pod somewhere easily reachable but out of sight, such as on the inside-front panel, which is accessible through the coin door. For the Project Arcade cabinet, the pod is mounted to the left of the coin door on the side of the panel that's hinged so that, when the front panel is opened, the control pod cabling is not in the way. If you have a similar speaker set or are using a hacked amplifier, you should be able to do something very similar.

If you don't have an easily relocatable volume control knob, it's possible to make one. In a nutshell, what you do is split the speaker cable and wire an audio taper potentiometer in between. Note the difference in this potentiometer and the linear taper potentiometers used in analog controls! If you use a long enough run of cable, you will be able to install the volume control anywhere you wish. One nice perk of doing it this way is that you can drill a small hole in an appropriate spot on the cabinet, thread the potentiometer shaft through the hole, and mount a knob just like a real stereo volume control. Building a volume control will cost you somewhere between $15 and $20.

On the CD — If you'd like to do this, I've included a step-by-step tutorial on the companion CD-ROM courtesy, once again, of Oscar Controls.

Volume controls that go between the amp and speakers are called "L-pads." If you'd like to use one but aren't interested in building it yourself, you can purchase an Arcade Cabinet Volume Control from 3Tronics (`www.3tronics.com/arcade_volume.htm`), makers of the MAMI keyboard encoders, for $35 plus shipping. L-pads are also available from Radio Shack and Parts Express (`www.partsexpress.com`).

Now that you've looked at all the considerations for speaker selection and installation, it's time to take a look at what you can do with your sound system. I'll take game playing for granted, but what else can you do with your creation?

Arcade Jukeboxes

How about an arcade jukebox! What's an arcade jukebox? Recognizing that their arcade cabinet project was going to be a centerpiece of their home game room, many people started thinking about other purposes for their arcade cabinets. When you think back to days spent in an arcade, what comes to mind besides playing games? Noise and music — arcades are loud! There's almost always someone playing music on a jukebox competing with the sounds of the arcade machines. Now, with compressed audio files and software, you can re-create that atmosphere at home!

Note — The rest of this section talks about playing compressed music files on your computer — usually in MP3 format — although others are possible. Like many things, it's possible to obtain MP3 music files both legally and illegally. Regardless of your opinion of the music industry and how it operates, the law is the law, and significant consequences are possible for copyright violations. Please, keep it legal!

Building an arcade jukebox

First, I'll bring up a quick diversion. Instead of using your arcade cabinet as a jukebox (won't you be playing games on it?), why not have a dedicated jukebox? Aside from actually going out and purchasing a real jukebox, you have a couple of resources available if you'd like to have your own jukebox at home.

MAMERoom.com (www.mameroom.com), makers of a variety of commercial-quality arcade cabinet plans, has just released a wall-mounted jukebox plan for $35 — $60 with full-sized cutout templates. The jukebox measures roughly 1½ feet wide by 3 feet tall with a maximum depth of about a foot. It's designed to work with a 15-inch flat-panel LCD monitor. Alternatively, you can pick up a real jukebox that's seen better days and convert it into a PC-controlled arcade jukebox. JukeboxControls.com (www.jukeboxcontrols.com) is a Web site dedicated to building or converting a jukebox into an MP3-, video-, and Karaoke-playing home entertainment center. If you'd like to add a computerized jukebox to your game room, give them a visit!

Jukebox software

If a fully dedicated jukebox isn't for you but you'd still like to be able to play music on your cabinet, consider one of the many jukebox software programs designed to work with your arcade cabinet. They run the range from simple overlays for Winamp (software for playing MP3 format music files on your computer at www.winamp.com) to full music- and video-playing software packages designed to be controlled with an arcade joystick. There are many available; I'll highlight a few and point you to the rest. Unless otherwise stated, all programs run under Windows.

Arcade Jukebox

Arcade Jukebox (http://home.att.net/~mark.schwartz) is a simple MP3-playing jukebox application intended for use on arcade cabinets. All controls can be enabled with a joystick and four buttons, or a mouse/trackball can be used, which makes it very cabinet-friendly. Arcade Jukebox reads MP3 ID3 tags (part of the MP3 music format that identifies a song's artist, album, and other information) and can sort your music by title, artist, album, year, and genre. The database-driven program will automatically search for all your music tracks in the directory you specify, including subdirectories. The jukebox comes with a set of backgrounds, or you can add your own.

After a few moments configuring the software, I quickly grew to appreciate Arcade Jukebox. I configured it for random play (after 10 seconds, it will randomly play tracks from your collection) with a colorful background and let it play while I did other things. It is not excessively feature-laden, but software bloat isn't always desirable. Arcade Jukebox does what it's designed to do and looks good.

On the CD   Version 8 of Arcade Jukebox is included on the companion CD-ROM.

Digital Jukebox

Digital Jukebox (`www.rastaworld.com`) is another jukebox application specifically designed to work with arcade-emulation cabinets. It has built-in support for several commercial control consoles (I'll look at those in Chapter 17, "Buying Your Way to Gaming Nirvana") as well as the standard MAME layout, and it includes a configuration wizard for customizing the software to your needs. It supports a radio mode with a customized time interval before automatic play starts. It quite startled me when it started playing unexpectedly while I was studying the screen!

Some of the features include subdirectory searching with play lists broken down by subdirectory, which allows you to customize song categories, album cover support, and ID3 tag support. Songs can be selected with the keyboard or joystick/buttons, a mouse/trackball, or randomly in radio mode. Digital Jukebox can be downloaded in a 15-day trial version and can be purchased for $16 with lifetime upgrades. With screensavers and slideshows built in among other features, this software is one to keep an eye on.

Virtual Music Jukebox

Virtual Music Jukebox (`www.virtualmusicjukebox.com`) is a full-featured jukebox program with support for arcade cabinets. It features random (radio) play mode, play by album, and other song-selection modes. It can play Windows video files (WMV format) as well as MP3 and Windows music files (WMA). Your music can be grouped into libraries so you can choose, for instance, a classical library for quiet times, a rock library for parties, and so on. Virtual Music Jukebox supports album cover, lyric display, and windowed and full-screen modes (see Figure 11-11).

Virtual Music Jukebox includes touchscreen and dual-monitor support, skins for changing the appearance, and a variety of other features. The program is available in a demo version with a limited number of albums supported and with the full version costing $19.95.

 The demo version of Virtual Music Jukebox is included on the companion CD-ROM.

Other jukeboxes

There are many other music-playing programs and jukeboxes you might want to consider for your arcade cabinet or jukebox cabinet. Some of them, such as DosCab/WinCab, JukeboxFX, and Dragonator Jukebox, are designed to work on arcade cabinets. Others, such as eJukebox and Winamp are just designed to be good MP3-playing programs.

The arcade jukebox field is still in its early stages, and there's no clear winner in the field yet. If you're looking to include a jukebox in your game room, you might be happiest dedicating a PC and full surround-sound speaker system to it. Otherwise, an arcade cabinet-friendly jukebox program makes a good compromise!

 The list of links for this chapter on the companion CD-ROM includes a full listing of jukeboxes you can try.

FIGURE 11-11: Virtual Music Jukebox in default mode, no album covers.

Summary

The sound system is often an overlooked part of an arcade cabinet project, but it is clearly as important as anything else. You obviously want to hear what you're playing with the option to control the volume to suit the environment you're playing in. A really good sound system with a subwoofer will add an element of gaming that can surpass that of the original arcade! If you add an optional jukebox program, you can really have a whole arcade in one cabinet.

So, you've paid attention to what you hear, but what about what you see? Coming up next, I'll take a look at the options you have for video!

A Picture Is Worth a Thousand . . . Tokens?

chapter

12

in this chapter

☑ Electrical Warning

☑ A Basic Understanding of Monitors

☑ Monitor Types

☑ Mounting Monitors

You've put together a styling arcade cabinet, concocted a perfect blend of authentic arcade controls, and added in a Mario-saving sound system that lets you hear every zap and explosion. What about the monitor? All the rest may seem pretty silly if you don't have a great video system to go with it. A nice bright, big and bold, in-your-face monitor is the perfect complement to the attention to detail you've put into the rest of the cabinet so far. Fear not. I've shown you the way thus far, haven't I? You may be surprised to find out how many choices you have when selecting a monitor for your arcade cabinet. Computer monitors, arcade monitors, and televisions are possible paths to your dream arcade machine — each with their own strengths and weaknesses. Read on to see what's right for you!

Electrical Warning

Warning! Danger! The information in this section can help you avoid hurting yourself—potentially fatally. Don't skip it! A few minutes here might save your life. If you do not read this section, then you should not proceed any further in building your cabinet.

Wonder what I'm going on about? Throughout the book, I hope my sense of humor has come through. However, there's nothing funny about what I need to tell you here. Monitors can be dangerous. What you don't know can hurt you; what you know but don't respect can also hurt you. What can hurt you can also prove fatal. There's no joking here. This subject is serious.

 You may notice I'm really trying to get your attention on this one. Take the warnings in this chapter seriously. Improper handling of a monitor can hurt you!

A monitor acts as a big capacitor or battery. When powered on, a monitor has a huge electrical charge in it. Here's the important part. Monitors can carry a huge electrical charge *even when turned off and unplugged!* They may have between 20,000 and 30,000 volts without a connected power source! Like a battery, that electrical charge is looking for somewhere to go. Complete a circuit between the two terminals of a battery with a light bulb, and the bulb glows. What do you think might happen if you touch the wrong part of the inside of a monitor? You may end up completing a circuit between the monitor and the ground, which places you in the role of the light bulb. Unfortunately, *you don't glow — you just get hurt!* If you're unlucky, in rare occasions, it can even prove fatal.

Now, any electrician reading this may be frowning right now. They'll tell you it's not voltage that does you in, it's current. You'll barely notice one milliamp of current. Current greater than 16 milliamps can force your muscles to contract, which makes you unable to let go of the electrical object that's hurting you. Twenty milliamps of current can cause paralysis to your respiratory muscles so you cannot breathe, and 100 milliamps of current running across your heart can make it stop pumping blood properly and simply quiver (fibrillation). As little as two amps can stop your heart outright and cause internal organ damage (Source: www.cdc.gov/niosh/elecovrv.html). As a frame of reference, a standard household outlet normally provides at least 15 amps of current.

How much current will you expose yourself to if you touch the wrong part inside the monitor? It depends on the circumstances. Remember, the formula is voltage = current × resistance. Rephrased, current = voltage ÷ resistance. That means the current varies as the resistance varies. If you accidentally touch the wrong part inside a monitor, which creates a circuit with you in the middle, your body provides the resistence. If your skin was very dry, the resistance would be high, and the current would be lower. If your skin was damp, for instance, if you were in a humid environment or were perspiring, the current would be higher — possibly high enough to do you harm. So, what is the answer to how much current you might be exposed to? The answer is, I don't know. It depends on your monitor's electronics, what you might be touching, and skin moisture. Are the odds in your favor that the current will be low enough not to hurt you? Frankly, the odds are against you getting seriously hurt or killed. However, do you want to play the odds when your life is at stake? Is it worth taking a chance with careless behavior? The answer is clearly an emphatic *no.*

What could happen if you are accidentally shocked by a monitor? As you've just read, you could have problems with your breathing, your heart beating, and internal organ damage. However, even if you only get a "mild" shock and don't suffer any of these immediate physical injuries, related injuries can occur. Involuntary muscle spasms can cause your limbs to jerk, causing them to slam into sharp metal objects inside the monitor frame or possibly encounter other electrical components. If you are carrying your monitor and drop it from the shock (or accidentally knock it off onto the floor), it can break. A monitor is a vacuum-filled container of thick glass. If it breaks suddenly, the force of the air rushing in to fill the vacuum can cause shards of glass to go flying, with you at ground zero!

I'm not trying to scare you, but I am trying to make you pause and consider before you get near the inside of a monitor. I probably don't need to elaborate on the danger any further. It can be summed up as follows. The inside of a monitor is potentially dangerous to you. Touching the wrong part inside a monitor can cause you immediate physical harm or death. Even a mild shock can cause you to react involuntarily, possibly causing you second-hand harm. Please, take this seriously, and treat your monitors with extra care. Wiley Publishing and I want you safe and healthy for our next book! Thanks!

Does this mean you shouldn't handle a monitor? Of course not. With proper care and handling, you can safely choose, mount, and operate a monitor for your arcade cabinet. Which parts of the monitor should be safe to handle, and which parts are dangerous? The answer is simple. Never touch any part of a monitor other than the frame, interface cables, or screen. Other parts of the monitor should only be touched by trained professionals.

A Basic Understanding of Monitors

Let's move on to a lighter topic — the parts of a monitor. From here on out, when I use the term "monitor," I mean the whole category of monitors, including computer monitors, arcade monitors, and televisions, unless specifically stated otherwise. For instance, the phrase "computer monitor" refers specifically to an ordinary monitor like you'd see on an average office desk.

Note Look out — it gets techie for a bit here! You should at least skim the next few sections and then read the last paragraph where I sum it up. Mastering the full details isn't necessary, but the gist will be important when it comes time to choose a monitor.

The rest of this section deals with monitors of the cathode ray tube (CRT) variety. Those are monitors that have rectangular screens facing the viewer with a large body behind that tapers to a small neck as shown in Figure 12-1 (the labels in the figure will be discussed in the "Anatomy of a Monitor" section that follows). Relatively recent technology advances have led to monitors that do not follow this model, such as flat-panel LCD displays. You *can* use one of these in your arcade cabinet if you'd like, but I won't be covering the details of how they work.

Monitor technology is 60 to 100 years old. Of course, there have been many improvements in that time. However, the basic principle has stayed the same in CRT-based monitors. In the neck of the monitor tube is an electron gun that fires a beam of electrons at the screen. The inside of the screen is coated with a layer of phosphor dots that glow briefly when struck by the electron beam. Monochrome monitors have only a single color of phosphor, whereas color monitors have three different-colored phosphor spots arranged in groups coating the entire screen. These colors are red, green, and blue, and this is where the term "RGB monitor" comes from. Combining different combinations and intensity levels of red, green, and blue produces the different colors we see on the screen (see the extreme close-up in Figure 12-2). You'll have to look at the picture on the companion CD-ROM to appreciate the full effect. However, do you notice the pattern of three spots in every grid? Those are the red, green, and blue spots of phosphor. You wouldn't know it by looking at it, but that is an extreme close-up of a bright white screen on a television!

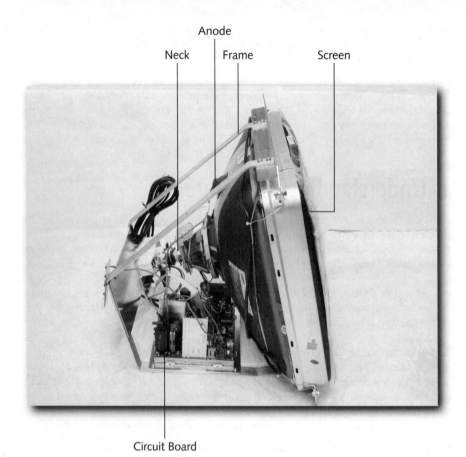

FIGURE 12-1: A cathode ray tube exposed.
Used by permission of Happ Controls.

Color monitors actually have three electron guns — one for each color. If you look closely at a CRT, you can see the three different-colored dots covering the screen. Electronics in the monitor modify the direction and intensity of each electron beam so that it strikes the appropriate red, green, or blue phosphor dots, which combine to make the colors and images you see on the screen. This is accomplished by the deflection yoke, which applies a magnetic field that alters the path of the electron beam as required. Each electron gun has a corresponding deflection yoke. In practice, people often refer to the electron guns and the deflection yokes as single entities ("the electron gun" and "the deflection yoke").

After it is struck and glows, the phosphor begins to immediately fade and has to be hit with the electron beam again to refresh the glow. The rate at which the electron beam refreshes the phosphors is known, plainly enough, as the refresh rate. A higher refresh rate makes a smoother picture. A lower refresh rate can cause flicker. Different types of monitors are designed to work at different refresh rates. This is important because the input video signal (from the video card for a computer monitor, from the TV tuner in a television) has to send a signal at a refresh rate the monitor is capable of. A mismatch between the video signal's expected refresh rate and the monitor's capability can cause problems, including a loss of picture to actual damage to the monitor itself!

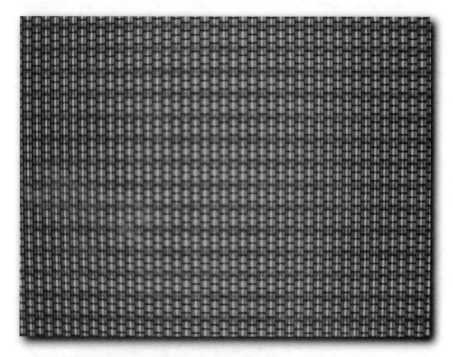

FIGURE 12-2: Close-up of a color television screen.

This is a very simple description of exactly what makes a monitor work, but it covers the highlights of what you need to know when building an arcade cabinet. There's much more to what makes a monitor tick. If you're interested in learning about it, read the "How Television Works" guide at http://entertainment.howstuffworks.com/tv.htm, the "TV and Monitor CRT (Picture Tube) Information FAQ" at www.repairfaq.org/sam/crtfaq.htm, and the PC Technology Guide at www.pctechguide.com/06crtmon.htm.

To quickly sum up how a monitor works, beams of electrons are fired from guns in the neck of the monitor tube. Magnetic fields from components called *deflection yokes* help steer the path of the electron beams. The electrons hit phosphors on the inside of the screen, which causes them to glow. The speed at which this happens is referred to as the refresh rate. There you have it — an entire course in monitor technology in only five lines. You should hear me explain economics!

Anatomy of a monitor

Before you handle a monitor, you need to be able to identify some of the important parts.

 This section in particular attempts to give you an overview of how a monitor works. It—in no fashion—should be considered a complete course in monitor theory and will not make you an expert in monitor safety! Always respect the hazards of a monitor, and do not touch the electronics.

Anode and cathode

You can think of anodes and cathodes as the positive and negative ends of a circuit. The anode is the positive side of the circuit; the cathode is the negative side. It's a common misconception that electricity flows from the positive to the negative side. Actually, the opposite is true. Electrons flow from the negative to the positive or from the cathode to the anode. The cathode portion of the CRT is part of the electron gun in the neck of the tube (Figure 12-3). Even though you shouldn't be touching any part of the inside of a monitor, be particularly careful of the neck of the tube. It is the most fragile part of the tube. If it breaks (for instance, by something falling on it), then the monitor is worthless.

Electron Gun and Cathode

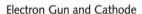

FIGURE **12-3**: Electron gun and cathode in the neck of the tube.
Used by permission of Happ Controls.

Once an electron has struck the phosphor, which causes it to glow, it needs somewhere to return to. At the top of the tube is the anode (technically referred to as the "second anode"), a suction cup covering an electrode that enters an opening in the tube. It's really an indentation into the tube — not a hole — with the vacuum sealed beneath it. The suction cup has nothing to do with sealing the vacuum. The electrode is connected to a large wire that attaches to the flyback transformer on the circuit board. The flyback transformer generates the high voltages you'll find in a monitor. The electrons in the tube are attracted to the anode's positive charge and return through the wire back to the circuit board. This anode is where the extremely high (20,000–30,000) voltage is! You cannot tell in the gray-scale picture (Figure 12-4), but the wire is usually a bright red to catch your attention.

Anode   Flyback

FIGURE 12-4: The anode and flyback transformer.
Used by permission of Happ Controls.

Notice the prominent warning tag on the anode wire — don't count on the insulation of the wire protecting you. Take extra care to stay away from the suction cup, wire, and anode component on the circuit board! It's important enough to repeat once more. The monitor can retain a charge even when it has been unplugged for a long period of time. Unless you know the monitor has been discharged, assume high voltage is present. See "Discharging a Monitor" later in this chapter for more information.

Circuit boards

The circuit boards take the incoming video signal and convert it into information needed to control the electron guns and deflection yokes. Two circuit boards are usually in a monitor (see Figure 12-5).

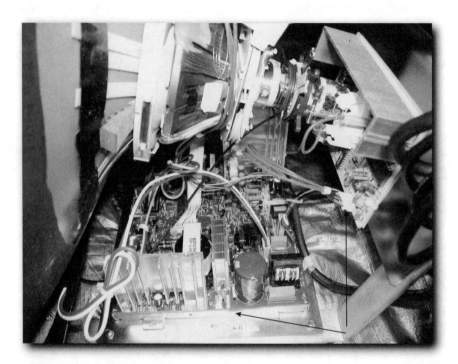

FIGURE 12-5: A typical arrangement of two circuit boards.
Used by permission of Happ Controls.

The first is the "main" board where the power and video signals are connected, which is shown underneath the deflection yoke in the figure. Attached to the base of the tube's neck is the second circuit board, which is often referred to as the neck board. This is the board that directly controls the electron guns and is connected to the main circuit board. The circuit boards are not any safer to touch than the rest of the monitor's insides and should be left alone. The only user-serviceable parts on most monitor circuit boards are fuses and monitor controls such as horizontal hold, vertical hold, and so on.

Note Even though the fuse on the circuit board can be easily replaced, you should be asking why the fuse blew. It could have been a power surge in the household current, or it could be a symptom of something wrong with the monitor. You are probably safe replacing the fuse once, but, if it blows again, you certainly should consult an expert for repair. Remember the cardinal rule. Treat the inside of a monitor extremely carefully!

Deflection yoke

The deflection yokes sit at the base of the tube in front of the electron guns. As the electron beams pass through the yokes, the yokes generate the magnetic fields that alter the path of the beams. The yokes are electromagnets, which generate a magnetic field when current flows through them and generate no field when there is no current. Electromagnets are basically tightly wound coils of copper wire, as you can see in Figure 12-6. Remember the magnetic fields. They'll be important a bit later on in the chapter.

FIGURE 12-6: A close-up of a deflection yoke.
Used by permission of Happ Controls.

Isolation transformers

An isolation transformer is a component that sits between the household electrical outlet and the monitor's electrical connection (see Figure 12-7). It takes the household electricity in and sends electricity right back out to the monitor. Does it seem kind of redundant? It performs a very important job by keeping both the monitor and *you* safe. Allow me to segue briefly. In a household electrical outlet, you will find three prongs: hot, neutral, and ground. The circuit in whatever electrical appliance you use is between the hot and neutral prongs (I'll refer to them as wires from now on). The ground exists as a safety that ultimately should be connected to a metal rod buried in the earth (hence, the term "ground" or "grounded"). If you measure with a multimeter between the hot wire and neutral wire in a standard outlet, you'll find it reads about 110 volts. You'll find the same reading between the hot wire and the ground wire. The neutral wire is designed to be the return path for the current whereas the ground is designed to be a fail-safe in case something goes wrong. You might find an electrical outlet where the ground and neutral wire have been reversed. The outlet still supplies electricity, and you may not know anything's wrong, but your ground wire is no longer a safety measure. In fact, it's now the default return path for the current!

FIGURE 12-7: One of many different possible isolation transformers.

Assume for this discussion that the household electrical wiring is properly connected. (If in doubt, don't assume. Have it tested by an electrician!) If something goes wrong inside the appliance, the hot wire can come into contact with parts of the appliance that you might be able to touch. A principle of Ohm's law is that current will follow the path of least resistance. Because human bodies contain lots of water, we don't offer much electrical resistance. If the appliance frame becomes electrically hot (that is, becomes connected directly to the hot wire) because of a problem, and you touch it, you will probably make the easiest return path for the current. That means 110 volts at an unknown current (remember, your body's resistance will vary) will flow through you to ground. Ouch! This is where the ground wire comes to your rescue. The ground wire is deliberately tied into the frame of the appliance. If something goes wrong, and the frame becomes electrically hot, the ground wiring normally has less resistance than the human body, and the current returns through the ground wire instead of through you!

The way many monitors are designed, the metal monitor frame is often (deliberately) tied into the neutral wire of the electrical system. The monitor frame is not tied directly to the household ground at all. I'm not sure why it's still done this way, but it's a throwback to the way televisions were made when the monitor chassis was "live" (electrically connected). Without an isolation transformer, everything has a common ground. The AC electrical system in your house and the wiring in the monitor both ultimately connect to the same ground. Touching the monitor frame would make you the easiest path back to ground for the current, which puts you in the middle of a high-voltage circuit. You're the easiest path back to ground because the monitor frame isn't tied into the third ground wire of the household electrical system. Once again, ouch!

This is where an isolation transformer comes into play. An isolation transformer electrically isolates the electrical flow into the transformer from the electrical output of the transformer that feeds the monitor. There's only a hot and neutral wire feeding the monitor. There is no third ground wire. If you touch the frame at that point, the household ground you're touching with your feet or other part of your body (such as a hand touching an electrical outlet while plugging in a cord) isn't part of the circuit feeding the monitor. By isolating the monitor's power from the building's power, you won't complete a circuit to ground by simply touching the monitor frame. No ouch this time!

Warning! An isolation transformer does not make the inside of a monitor safe to poke around in! The inside of the monitor still has hot and neutral electrical points. If you accidentally touch both a hot and neutral inside the monitor, then once again your low resistance makes you an easy circuit for the current to flow across, which gives you a nasty shock. What an isolation transformer *does* do for you is make the frame safe to touch, assuming everything is working properly.

I have a sound piece of advice. Never assume anything when working with an exposed monitor! A problem with the monitor's wiring or the isolation transformer can mean that the safety measures designed into the monitor are not functioning.

Some monitors require an isolation transformer for proper (safe) use, and some do not. Monitors that are enclosed, such as televisions or computer monitors, do not require an isolation transformer. The functionality of the isolation transformer is built into the internal workings of the monitor. Monitors whose inner workings are exposed, such as arcade monitors, often will require an isolation transformer. Newer arcade monitors most likely incorporate the workings of an isolation transformer and will not need a separate isolation transformer. How can you tell? The monitor will be explicitly labeled as not requiring an isolation transformer. I have heard of at least one example when a monitor was incorrectly labeled, so your safest bet is to consult the manual that comes with the monitor or contact the manufacturer. One school of thought says it is safer to use an isolation transformer even if it's not necessary than it is to not use one that's needed. There is one rule of thumb. If the monitor is an enclosed unit such as a television or computer monitor, you do not need to be concerned about it. If the monitor is exposed, such as an arcade monitor or a monitor that was designed to be enclosed but has been opened, then you should be very concerned about whether an isolation transformer is required!

How to safely handle a monitor

Having done my best to impress upon you the dangers of monitors, I want to assure you now it *is* possible to safely handle and install a monitor in your arcade cabinet. Observe the following safety guidelines as you do so, and you shouldn't have any problems.

General guidelines

The first rule for handling monitors safely is that you should always have someone near you (but not right next to you) when you are handling your monitor. That person's job is to help you if you get in trouble. If you get shocked or injured, he or she should be able to provide first aid and/or call for medical help. If for some reason you *must* handle the monitor when it is still plugged in, then the person should be ready to help if you get hurt and cannot get away from the electrical current. You will need to make sure the person understands that he or she should never touch you in those circumstances! If electricity is flowing through your body, and the person touches you, he or she will also get shocked and will be unable to help himself or herself— much less you. Your helper should instead be prepared to unplug the power source from the wall and have a nonconductive long-reach object, such as a plastic broom handle, to separate you from the monitor. Other guidelines you should follow:

- Make sure the monitor is unplugged. The only reason for a nonprofessional to be tinkering with a monitor while it's plugged in is to adjust the user-adjustable settings, such as horizontal hold. At all other times, if you're going to move or handle the monitor for some reason, make sure it's been unplugged for at least a half hour to allow the various capacitors to discharge, and, even then, don't assume they have in fact done so.

- Do not attempt to discharge the charge inside the monitor unless you are professionally trained to do so. Unless the inside electronics of the monitor are being worked on (which you should not do if not professionally trained), the monitor does not need discharging for basic mounting procedures. *Do* take extra care that you do not touch the electronics inside the monitor at all times.

- Wear safety gear. You might consider wearing insulated gloves and safety goggles. You should certainly wear rubber-soled shoes or sneakers. This will insulate you from the ground. Remove any loose jewelry so it doesn't accidentally come into contact with something in the monitor.

- Watch your back. Monitors are heavy! A healthy adult can probably lift a 19-inch monitor without issue. If you have any kind of back issues or need to lift a monitor bigger than 19 inches, you should use the buddy system.

- Hold the monitor only by the frame. This keeps your hands away from the sharp or electronic components inside the monitor, which keeps you safe and avoids damage to the monitor as well. It bears repeating. *Do not touch the inside electronics of the monitor at any time!*

- Use two people or a mirror to adjust the picture. Some monitors have adjustments in front so you can see the results while you make adjustments. However, many have the controls in back so it is impossible to see what you're doing while you make adjustments. Resist the urge to try to reach around the back and make adjustments while you're in front. That's a good way to grab the wrong thing and get zapped. Have a friend assist you, or use a mirror to observe the screen while you make adjustments.

Discharging a monitor

I'll start by stating that I will not attempt to tell you how to discharge a monitor. If you have been professionally trained in the field, then you know what to do to safely discharge a monitor. If you have not been trained professionally, then it would be irresponsible to try to show you how in this book. To attempt to do so would put you at an unnecessary risk of getting hurt. Instead, have the monitor professionally discharged by an arcade or television technician. Fortunately, a monitor rarely needs to be discharged. Once it's safely installed in your cabinet, there should be little reason to move or work on the monitor.

Discharging a monitor is the process of removing the built-up 20,000–30,000-volt electrical charge inside the tube. Most modern monitors have a circuit built into them that automatically discharges the tube when powered off. Older monitors are not likely to have this discharge circuit, and any monitor with the discharge circuit may have a malfunction such that the automatic discharge does not work. Never assume that a monitor has been discharged unless you know it has been directly discharged and has not left your sight since then. Monitors can build up a secondary charge after being discharged once, so even after a discharge, treat it with caution. Professionals will discharge a monitor once, wait a few minutes, and then discharge again.

You can find instructions on the Internet on how to discharge a monitor. Some of them are good. Some of them are bad. You shouldn't attempt to follow any of them unless you have been professionally trained. Some of the instructions will give you information that may lead to damage to the electronics in your cabinet, and some may prompt you to take actions that just are not safe and may cause you harm. Even the good and valid instructions may assume knowledge you do not have and skip mentioning an important step or concept. Please, if you don't already know what you're doing, do not attempt to discharge a monitor by yourself. Your safety is worth much more than the cost of a $75 service call by a trained technician.

Cross-Reference If you're really interested in becoming trained on the subject, be sure to read Chapter 18 for information on an arcade training school.

Proper care and feeding of a monitor

You won't need to do very much to keep your monitor in good operating condition. New monitors should last a good five years or so before needing any electrical maintenance. Used monitors, or any monitor that's having various display issues, will probably benefit from a "cap-kit." Applying a cap-kit to a monitor means replacing the capacitors on the main circuit board with new capacitors. Over time, capacitors can dry out and lose their original electrical properties. For just about any monitor problem other than a totally dead monitor, the first solution is always to apply a cap-kit. The cost of a cap-kit is normally less than $10. However, applying a cap-kit involves discharging the monitor, removing the circuit board, desoldering, and soldering. Once again, unless you have been trained, leave that to a professional.

Other than a cap-kit, the only other electrical maintenance required might be an occasional degaussing or replacement fuse. Remember that, if you have to replace a fuse more than once, something is probably wrong, and the monitor should be inspected by a technician.

Degaussing is the process of demagnetizing the monitor. Keep in mind that the electron beams are guided by magnetic fields. That means they are sensitive to external magnetic fields as well. If an external magnetic force is strong enough, it can alter the path of the electron beam and distort the colors and picture on your monitor. You will commonly see this when unshielded speakers are placed too close to the monitor. However, even the earth's natural magnetic field can cause monitor distortion. Monitors are adjusted at the factory for the specific hemisphere the monitor is sold in and the orientation of the monitor. Modifying either factor, such as moving to the other hemisphere or taking an upright arcade machine's monitor and laying it on its back in a cocktail cabinet, can cause the monitor to interact differently with the earth's magnetic field, which causes distortion. Fortunately, it's easy enough to fix. Monitors have a built-in degaussing circuit that activates when you first turn the monitor on. That's the two clicks and brief wobbling you see when you press the power button.

Some monitors may not have a degaussing circuit or may have a defective circuit. In that case, you can use an external degaussing coil to correct magnetic problems. Degaussing coils are available from arcade parts supply houses. Some people will substitute an appliance that generates its own magnetic field, such as a soldering gun that has a built-in transformer. To degauss, hold the coil in the center of the monitor and then turn on the coil. Wave the coil around the monitor using an increasing spiral motion to cover the whole screen, and, when you've extended your spiral beyond the sides of the monitor, turn it off. It's important to note that degaussing coils will burn out if you leave them on too long. Monitor degaussing circuits typically should be activated only after being off for 20 minutes or more.

You may think this last bit of maintenance advice goes without saying, but it is amazing how often it's overlooked. A clean monitor is a clear monitor so clean your monitor! Only clean the front of the screen; don't clean the back of the tube or the monitor electronics. Also, don't use a regular spray cleaner on a monitor screen because it can eat away at the anti-glare coating many monitors have. Use a cleaning solution advertised for monitor screens or simply use a water-dampened rag. If you are cleaning a used monitor for the first time, you will be very surprised at how grimy it really is!

Monitor Types

Now that you've taken a look at how monitors work and basic safety, it's time to get into the fun stuff! You have essentially three choices for a monitor — arcade monitors, televisions, and computer monitors. Degree of difficulty, cost, and arcade authenticity are all factors to consider when making a monitor choice. Different monitor types require different interface methods and levels of complexity. Arcade monitors and televisions are generally cheaper than the same-sized PC monitor. Finally, arcade monitors and televisions will give you a more arcade-authentic picture whereas PC monitors will give you a clearer picture with more flexibility. I'll touch on these subjects as I describe each monitor choice in the next few sections.

Monitor resolution and refresh rates

You'll need to understand the different monitor resolutions and refresh rates before you can pick the monitor type that's right for you. You're probably familiar with standard computer resolutions of 640 × 480, 800 × 600, and 1024 × 768. That means 640 pixels horizontally by 480 lines vertically, and so on. You may not know that some games, particularly emulated arcade games, can use resolutions as low as 320 × 200. As a rule, almost every monitor is capable of resolutions of 640 × 480. However, it gets murky from there. Not every monitor is capable of

800 × 600 or higher resolutions or the unique resolutions such as 320 × 200 used in arcade games. Computer monitors certainly can handle the full range of higher-standard resolutions, but they cannot run at the unique resolutions used by arcade games. Televisions and arcade monitors generally can handle the lower resolutions, but they often cannot support 800 × 600 and higher resolutions.

Fortunately, the software and hardware takes care of many of these issues for you. If you choose a computer VGA monitor, the lower-resolution arcade games can still run even though the monitor doesn't support the lower resolution. This works because the software and hardware in the computer adjust the picture to match the capabilities of the VGA monitor. However, even though you can get a lower-resolution picture to fit on a higher-resolution monitor, it doesn't work the other way around. Remember that televisions and arcade monitors can't usually support higher resolutions. That's fine for most arcade games that don't need higher resolutions. However, if you're also planning to run modern, high-end arcade games, you probably won't be happy at lower resolutions. That high-end video card capable of 60 frames per second at 1024 × 768 resolution is a waste if your monitor cannot handle more than 640 × 480.

Note   Strap in your seatbelt. It's getting techie once more! It's important to have a basic understanding of this so grit your teeth and plow through it. You might skim through it once, read the rest of the chapter, and then come back to this section to fill in the gaps.

Understanding refresh rates is a bit more complicated. The picture on your screen starts by creating a single horizontal line at the top from left to right. The signal is briefly turned off while the electron guns are refocused to the left again and drop one or more lines down. The time during which the electron beams are off and moving back to the left is called the horizontal retrace or blanking period. Then, the next horizontal line is drawn from left to right. This repeats until the entire screen is drawn at a speed so fast that it appears as a single picture to you. You should be aware of two refresh rates. The horizontal scan rate (or horizontal refresh rate) is the speed at which the monitor draws a single line on the screen from left to right. The vertical scan rate (or vertical refresh rate) is the speed at which the electron beams move from the top of the screen to the bottom. The horizontal scan rate is much higher than the vertical scan rate because the monitor has to draw an entire horizontal line before the vertical scan can move to the next line. Vertical refresh rates are measured in Hz (hertz, or cycles per second) whereas horizontal refresh rates are measured in kHz (kilohertz, or thousands of cycles per second).

If the horizontal scan rate is very fast, then the corresponding horizontal retrace period is also fast. This means there is less vertical progression before the guns turn back on and the next horizontal line is drawn. If the horizontal scan rate is slower, then there is more vertical progression during the horizontal retrace period. This means that, at slower horizontal scan rates, horizontal lines are skipped such that you have a line on, then a line off, then a line on, and so on. These skipped lines in between drawn lines are sometimes referred to as scan lines. On older arcade games or televisions, you can actually see the skipped lines. Your brain will normally tune these out, but, if you deliberately look for them, you can see them. Figure 12-8 shows a close-up of a television screen with a white area on top and a blue area beneath. Once again, you'll need to view the image on the CD-ROM to get the full color effect. However, even in gray-scale, you can see the dark horizontal lines. These are the lines that were skipped during the horizontal retrace.

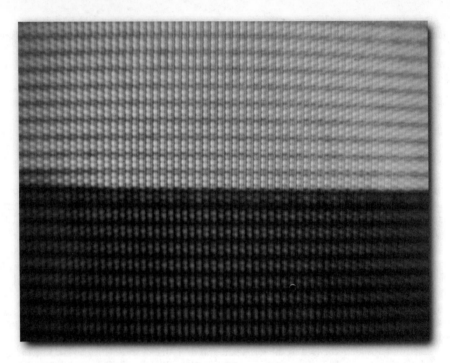

FIGURE 12-8: Extreme close-up of a television screen showing scan lines.

The combination of the vertical and horizontal scan rates dictates how many horizontal lines are drawn on the screen in one "frame." If you increase the horizontal scan rate, then more horizontal lines can be drawn on the screen in the same amount of vertical scan time, which produces a better picture. You could also achieve a similar increase in horizontal scan lines by reducing the vertical scan rate so that there is more time to draw horizontal lines before the vertical scan progresses. However, decreasing the vertical scan rate will produce flicker on the screen, which you will notice. Even vertical scan rates you can't consciously notice may still bother you. For instance, many people report eye fatigue or headaches after prolonged periods in front of a computer screen. Most arcade monitors and televisions use a 60 Hz vertical refresh rate. Most computer monitors support varying vertical refresh rates from 60 Hz to 100 Hz or higher.

When shopping for a computer monitor, you will often see the vertical refresh rate mentioned. However, when discussing resolutions for arcade games, it is the horizontal refresh rate that is of interest. There are three standard monitor resolutions used in arcade machines:

- Standard — Horizontal refresh rate of 15.75 kHz
- Medium — Horizontal refresh rate of 25 kHz
- High — Horizontal refresh rate of 31.5 kHz

Here is where monitor resolution becomes important to you. Most video cards for computers are designed to work only with computer monitors, which are high resolution. That means most video cards are incapable of running at a refresh rate low enough to operate a medium- or standard-resolution monitor. I'll show you ways around this as I discuss each monitor type in the next few sections.

I've only given you a mid-level overview of monitor refresh rates and resolutions so far. There's more to understanding the subject that isn't necessary for the scope of this book. If you'd like to learn more about monitor refresh rates and resolutions, you can visit a couple of good Web sites: Arcade Monitors on the PC2Jamma Web site at www.mameworld.net/pc2jamma/monitors.html and the Arcade Monitor FAQ on the Ultimarc Web site at www.ultimarc.com/monfaq.html. The Randy Fromm arcade school also has excellent material for learning more (see Chapter 18 for more information about Randy Fromm's arcade school).

Arcade monitors

The original arcade monitors were simply modified televisions, which operate at standard resolution. Later on, monitors tailored to the arcade market were developed with medium and high resolutions. Most classic arcade games use standard-resolution monitors (15 kHz). Whatever the resolution, these monitors all fit into a category called *raster* monitors. In simplest terms, the screen is drawn as a series of dots. Another type of monitor was occasionally used that drew pictures on screen as a series of lines, known as a *vector* monitors. Initially using raster monitors was more expensive than using vector monitors, but that quickly changed. Vector monitors were more difficult to maintain and more prone to failure. Once raster monitor prices dropped, vector monitors fell out of favor. Few vector games were ever produced.

Raster monitors

Raster arcade monitors can be one of the most economical choices you will find. Often, older, used monitors can be found anywhere at prices from free to $100. New arcade monitors start in the $200 to $250 range for 19-inch models and up from there for bigger models. See Appendix A, "Where to Find Arcade Parts for Your Project," for details on where to find a monitor.

Some people prefer to use an arcade monitor because of the authentic appearance. Graphics on these monitors will show scan lines and have that familiar pixely appearance you will remember from the arcade. Take a look at Figure 12-9 for an example. It shows a close-up of an image on my original Atari *Crystal Castles* game. The effect is exaggerated because of the viewing distance, but it shows what you can expect from an arcade monitor.

Mounting an arcade monitor is not difficult. They are designed with open frames meant to be fastened to an arcade cabinet in some fashion. All you will need to do is to mimic the mechanism used, such as mounting brackets or bolting it to a shelf.

Interfacing to an arcade monitor is a challenge. Arcade monitors will only work at their specified horizontal refresh frequency, which is normally 15.75 kHz for standard-resolution monitors. Attempting to drive them at a higher frequency will not work, and it may damage the monitor. How do you get around this problem? You have three possibilities.

FIGURE 12-9: Close-up of an arcade monitor.

VGA hack

The first attempts at using arcade monitors involved directly connecting the VGA card to the monitor. That meant three challenges to overcome. First, arcade monitors do not have VGA-style connectors. Second, some method had to be used to get around the incompatible refresh rates. Finally, output voltages usually differ between arcade games and VGA cards.

Connecting the VGA card to the monitor is not terribly difficult. VGA connectors have 15 pins, as shown in Table 12-1:

Table 12-1 Standard VGA Pinouts

Pin	Description
1	Red video
2	Green video
3	Blue video
4	
5	Ground

Pin	Description
6	Red ground
7	Green ground
8	Blue ground
9	(Optional: +5 volts)
10	Sync ground
11	
12	
13	Horizontal sync
14	Vertical sync
15	

The pins that are important in a VGA to arcade hack are 1, 2, 3, 5, 13, and 14. These will correspond to the same connections on the monitor. The monitor should have a Molex-style connector attached to the circuit board with the connections for red, blue, green, ground, and sync. You'll need a VGA extension cable to connect between the VGA card and the arcade monitor. Clip one end of the VGA cable, and expose the wires you need. Connect the six wires corresponding to the pins listed previously from the VGA cable to the corresponding pinouts on the arcade monitor's cable. You can either purchase a matching Molex connector for the wires from your VGA extension cable or clip the connector from the arcade monitor and use quick-disconnects to cable everything together. I do not recommend clipping the monitor's cable, if you can avoid it. The horizontal and vertical sync from the VGA cable should be twisted together and connected to the single sync pin on the arcade monitor. Some arcade monitors may have separate horizontal and vertical sync pins, and they can be connected directly instead of twisting the syncs together. *Do not turn anything on yet!*

Remember your safety precautions! Handling the input connector to the monitor is safe. Touching the inside electronics of the monitor is not.

A couple of good tutorials on the Web will walk you through this hack. If you'd like to see another perspective on it, visit the PC2Jamma page at www.mameworld.net/pc2jamma, *Dragon's Den's* VGA to RGB Cable Hack at http://dragonsden.emuunlim.com/ddvgatutl.htm, and Rockman's tutorial at www.arcadecontrols.com/arcade_pc2arcade.html.

Now that you've physically connected the cabling, you need to tackle the incompatible refresh rates. Doing so requires installing software on your computer that will program the VGA card to output the proper refresh rate signals. ArcadeOS, which is available at the PC2Jamma page, is a DOS-based menu system that includes the ability to program a VGA card for arcade monitor use. Most people who do a VGA hack use ArcadeOS. ArcadeOS has two drawbacks. The first is that it works in DOS only. The second is that it obviously can protect your arcade monitor from receiving an incompatible signal only when it is running. That means that, from the time you turn your computer on until ArcadeOS is running, your VGA card is sending out an unmodified signal that can hurt the monitor. ArcadeOS is programmed to beep when it's loaded so leave the arcade monitor turned off until the beep and then turn it on.

Another driver that works with arcade monitors is Mon-ARC PLUS (also called Mon-ARC) that is available at `http://homepage.ntlworld.com/andrew.lewis5/arcade/monarc.htm`. Mon-ARC supports both DOS and Windows 98 and is a terminate-and-stay-resident driver you load in the `autoexec.bat` file. If that didn't make sense, don't worry. Instructions come with the driver at the above Web site. However, in simple terms, what it does is sit in memory and convert the VGA card's signal to one the arcade monitor can use. Like ArcadeOS, you have to wait for the driver to be loaded before turning on your monitor.

Both drivers work with a limited set of video cards. The good news is that those cards are fairly easy to track down, but, as time goes on, they may become rare. Their individual Web sites keep a list of compatible video cards.

The final issue is adjusting for different voltages. Arcade circuit boards usually send a 5-volt signal to the arcade monitor. VGA cards send out a 1-volt signal. A low-voltage signal from a VGA card will produce a darker picture on the arcade monitor if not corrected. Fortunately, it's easy to correct. Ultimarc (`www.ultimarc.com/vidamp.html`) sells a video amplifier for $15 that will adjust the voltages for you. Also, some arcade monitors have adjustments on them to switch between 1-volt and 5-volt input levels.

VGA hacks are relatively inexpensive because, with the possible exception of an inexpensive video amplifier, you don't have to purchase additional hardware to go between the video card and the monitor. Their limitations take away from the seamless recreation of the arcade feeling, but those who use them feel the use of a real arcade monitor more than makes up for the minor inconveniences. Keep reading for alternatives.

Scan converters

Scan converters have been around for some time and are primarily used to convert from a VGA card's output to a television's composite or S-Video input. Output quality varies with a correspondence between the quality and the cost of the converter. As of this writing, although a few people have tried, I know of no one who is actively using a scan converter in his or her arcade cabinet. I'm including scan converters here for completeness and to advise you that they probably aren't worth your time.

Ultimarc's ArcadeVGA

Ultimarc (whom you've encountered in previous chapters) recently came out with the ideal solution to the arcade monitor challenge. They market a VGA video card called the ArcadeVGA (`www.ultimarc.com/avgainf.html`) that is designed to work with arcade monitors. It offers all the benefits of a VGA hack and overcomes all the drawbacks. You will still need a cable to connect from the VGA card to the arcade monitor. You can hack your own as described in the previous section or purchase a pre-hacked cable from Ultimarc. The video card is available for $89, and the pre-hacked cable is available for an additional $6. Both are shown in Figure 12-10.

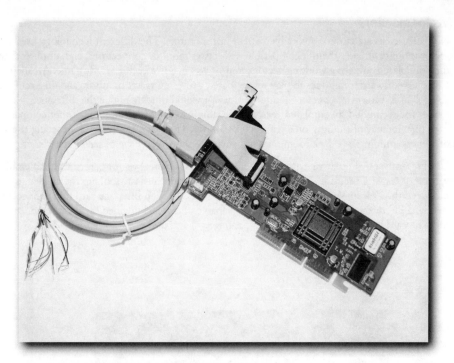

FIGURE **12-10: The ArcadeVGA and pre-hacked cable.**
Used by permission of Ultimarc.

Some of the many features of the ArcadeVGA include:

- Designed to work with 15 kHz and 31 kHz arcade monitors.

- Will display in boot up, DOS, and Windows (98, 2000, and XP). No need to wait before turning on your monitor.

- Special display modes designed to emulate various arcade games, such as 300×256 resolution.

- Support for rotating desktop in Windows to allow for vertical monitor mounting.

- Displays Windows resolutions of 640×480 and 800×600, including support for 3D-enabled games.

The ArcadeVGA uses modern video card chipsets (currently based on the ATI Radeon 7000 chipset with 64 megs of RAM, but likely to be upgraded as newer chipsets comes out), which makes it a powerful card for standard Windows games as well as emulated arcade games. Because the card natively outputs at 15 kHz, no extra drivers (beyond the video card's Windows drivers) are required. Like all Ultimarc products, the ArcadeVGA has received positive reviews from the arcade cabinet building community. If you intend to use an arcade monitor, I recommend this method.

Vector monitors

No VGA hacks are currently possible with vector monitors. The different technology used in vector monitors makes them incompatible with raster monitor connections, and, until recently, the only place you'd see a working vector monitor was inside a vector arcade game. Arcade emulators use software techniques to play vector-based games on raster monitors and do a remarkable job at it. However, a vector monitor enthusiast would quickly notice the difference. No matter the technique, an emulated vector game running on a raster monitor cannot compare with the vibrancy of running on a real vector monitor. There is something about seeing the glow of *Tempest* running in a dark room on a real vector monitor you have to see to experience.

Until recently, no alternative existed. You either purchased a real vector game or ran an emulated version on a raster monitor. A group of hard-core vector enthusiasts took up the challenge and produced the Zektor Vector Generator (ZVG). The ZVG is an interface card that connects to a standard PC through the parallel port and is capable of displaying video on a real vector monitor! The card costs $239 (www.zektor.com/zvg/) and is shown in Figure 12-11.

FIGURE 12-11: The Zektor Vector Generator.
Used by permission of Zektor, LLC.

Game makers created approximately 30 vector games. Two emulators are available from the Zektor Web site that are designed to work with the ZVG and emulate the 30 vector games. Unfortunately, new vector monitors have not been made for more than 20 years. This makes vector monitors difficult and expensive to obtain, and they are not available from the Zektor folks. You can find vector games and monitors at arcade auctions and on eBay (www.ebay.com).

Because of the limited number of games supported by the ZVG, it should be considered a niche product. However, it is one heck of a niche to fill, and it does it very well. Unlike raster monitors, various vector monitors were used for the 30 different games, and different vector monitors were not compatible with each other. Producing a card capable of running on any vector monitor was quite a feat of engineering. After building a general-purpose arcade cabinet, you might consider a dedicated vector game cabinet. Imagine how impressed your friends will be when they discover that not only do you have a monster arcade cabinet, but you also have a genuine vector monitor-based cabinet as well! OK, you may need to educate them on the difference. However, seeing is believing. Once they compare a vector game running on a raster monitor to the same game running on a real vector monitor, they'll be standing in line for their turn at the vector.

Televisions

Using a television for your arcade machine will give you similar results as using an arcade monitor. The picture quality may not be quite as good, but the interface techniques are easier. The main advantages of using a television are that they are readily available and relatively inexpensive compared to other monitor choices. You can find 24-inch televisions in the $150 range and 27-inch televisions between $200 and $250. Figure 12-12 shows the same screen shot on a television that was taken from an arcade monitor in Figure 12-10.

The picture does not appear to the eye as blurry as it shows up on the camera, but it certainly is not as crisp as the original arcade monitor picture. However, it does produce the scan line effect you would find on a real arcade monitor. The quality of a television picture will vary depending on which method you use to connect to it and what video card is being used. NTSC televisions (the kind used in America) typically will accept composite video and S-Video inputs as well as the traditional coax cable. Many video cards on the market include a video-out option with either S-Video or composite video outputs. The ATI All-In-Wonder cards have produced acceptable results. If you are choosing this method and have the option, use the S-Video connection instead of composite video. The picture quality will be better with S-Video than it will be with composite.

One final limited option is to use an SCART connection. Connecting to a television via the SCART connector is very close to connecting to an arcade monitor via a VGA hack. SCART connectors are typically seen in European televisions and are not an option in American televisions. If you have a television with an SCART connector, visit the MAME SCART page at www.jayma.org/mamescart/. Using the SCART connector with the ArcadeVGA video card from Ultimarc essentially turns your television into an arcade monitor with a very nice arcade-quality picture.

FIGURE 12-12: Close-up television screen shot.

Mounting a television can be a bit trickier than an arcade monitor. Because televisions come in enclosed cases, there's no mounting frame for you to use. You will need to place the television on the monitor shelf in the cabinet and use some method to fasten it into place. The shelf will hold the weight so you only need to find a way to prevent the television from shifting when the cabinet is moved. L-brackets might be a good choice, but you will only want to use them to wedge the television into place. Do not screw them into the case of the television and by no means should you remove the television's case! Some people have done just that to fit a bigger television into the available space, but doing so involves quite a bit of risk. Televisions are not meant to be exposed, and the metal frame may shock you even if you do not touch the anode or other electrical components!

Using a television will give you a bit more flexibility than using an arcade monitor. Because video cards that support video/television output handle all the necessary conversion, you can run Windows on a television. Depending on the capabilities of the video card, resolutions of 640×480 up to 1024×768 are possible. This makes a television an option to consider for those who want a near arcade-quality picture without giving up the ability to run Windows.

Computer monitors

A computer monitor is by far the simplest solution for an arcade cabinet. Unfortunately, it's also fairly expensive. Monitor prices vary considerably as technology advances and various sales occur, but you will essentially find a 19-inch computer monitor costs about the same as a 27-inch arcade monitor or television. The picture quality is excellent, as you are probably familiar with, but it is obviously not as authentic as an arcade monitor with visible scan lines. Take a look at the by-now familiar *Crystal Castles* screen shot (Figure 12-13). This time, it was taken from a computer monitor.

FIGURE **12-13: Close-up of a screen shot from a computer monitor.**

Notice that the picture quality is crystal clear. Although you can see the scan lines in this close-up photo, you don't see them with the naked eye. Computer monitors are capable of multiple resolutions with very high vertical refresh rates, which provide a picture that is easy on the eye. Obviously, with the multi-resolution capabilities of a computer monitor, you will be able to play any computer game you choose. Interfacing to a computer monitor is simply a matter of plugging in the VGA cable. Many people prefer to use computer monitors for the simplicity and flexibility. Mounting a computer monitor has the same considerations and warnings as a television. Please, do not open the case of a computer monitor. Use it as-is with the case. Because computer monitors usually do not have built-in speakers like a television, you do not lose a significant amount of space to the case.

However, you do lose that authentic arcade look and feel with a computer monitor. Enter the hybrid monitor. In recent years, manufacturers have come out with arcade-style monitors with VGA connections. The Happ Controls Vision Pro 27-inch SVGA monitor (www.happ controls.com/monitors/49615700.htm) is one such model. It is a high-resolution monitor capable of 640 × 480 and 800 × 600 resolutions. It is made in the same open-frame manner as regular arcade monitors with similar picture quality. Take a look at the same screen shot on this monitor (Figure 12-14). Notice you can see some of the arcade monitor pixelization, but the overall quality is extremely clear.

FIGURE 12-14: Close-up of the Happ Controls SVGA arcade monitor.
Used by permission of Happ Controls.

Similar models are available from Wells Gardner (the D9200, which is available from Happ Controls at www.happcontrols.com/monitors/49520320.htm among other places), and a new line coming from Neotec (www.neotecgraphic.com/trisync.htm) that will be available in 19-inch and 27-inch models. The Vision Pro and Wells Gardner models have a variety of sizes available as well; see the Happ Controls Web site for more information.

Because these monitors are designed with open frames like other arcade monitors, mounting them is easy enough. All of them come with universal mounting frames with holes in the frame you can use to bolt them to the cabinet. An easy way to do that in the Project Arcade cabinet is to test-fit the monitor on the shelf and draw a pencil line where the monitor frame rests when you have the monitor positioned to your personal taste. Pull the monitor back out, and mount a small strip of wood about ⅛ inch behind the line. Make sure the strip is securely fastened to the shelf and then remount the monitor. You can then fasten the monitor to the mounting strip. Remember, the mounting strip is not meant to be weight bearing. Its job is to prevent the monitor from sliding around when you move the cabinet. The monitor is probably heavy enough that this will not be a problem, but the extra security is peace of mind.

These monitors can be expensive (list price of $500 for the 27-inch Vision Pro from Happ Controls), but they offer the best of all worlds. You get authentic arcade look and feel, VGA compatibility, and the option of running in DOS or Windows with the ability to handle any game your computer can play. Next to the arcade controls, the monitor is the most important part of the cabinet. The enjoyment you will get out of a good-quality monitor will more than offset the price over the lifespan of the arcade cabinet.

Choosing a monitor

As with everything else, choosing a monitor comes down to a personal choice. You will need to balance your budget against your ultimate goal. Do you want an arcade-quality picture at a relatively low cost? Consider an arcade monitor with the Ultimarc ArcadeVGA card. Do you need to run Windows on your cabinet inexpensively? A television is your best bet if you want an arcade-like picture. If your budget is a bit more flexible, and you aren't concerned about an arcade-authentic picture, then a computer monitor is probably your best bet. Finally, if you have the budget for it, an arcade-style VGA monitor will give you the best of all choices. Take a look at Figure 12-15 for a comparison of all four choices. Clockwise from the upper left, you have an original arcade monitor, a television, a computer monitor, and an arcade-VGA hybrid monitor.

FIGURE 12-15: Four different monitors showing the same screen.

For the Project Arcade cabinet, I elected to go with the 27-inch Vision Pro arcade-VGA hybrid monitor from Happ Controls. The excellent picture quality combined with the flexibility of a VGA monitor made this an obvious choice.

Monitor Mounting

Mounting a monitor in your arcade cabinet will vary depending on the specific model of monitor you have chosen. I've touched on mounting a bit in the previous sections, but here are a few more items to consider.

Bezels

No matter how you mount your monitor, you will probably want to hide the mounting mechanism. You'll never see mounting brackets or a monitor shelf in a real arcade cabinet, and you don't want to see one in yours either. Arcade manufacturers use bezels to hide the inner depths of the arcade machines. A bezel is a rectangular-shaped piece of material that surrounds the monitor and covers the gaps. You can make a bezel from foam board available at any good hobby store or purchase a pre-made bezel from arcade shops such as Happ Controls (www.happcontrols.com/monitors/monitors.htm).

I used a 27-inch plastic bezel from Happ Controls for Project Arcade. These fit the Vision Pro monitor perfectly, and they are oversized so that they can be tailor fit to your cabinet. Trimming the excess is easy with a sharp knife and a straight-edge. Start by measuring the amount of trim needed on all four sides and then marking appropriately on the bezel. Lay the straight-edge down on the bezel's backside against the marks you made, clamp them together, and then score the bezel three or four times (Figure 12-16). You may end up cutting through it altogether or have a fine score on the backside. Fold the bezel trim away from the score, and it should snap cleanly off. I suggest erring on the side of being too big for your first cuts and then test fitting to see if it needs trimming. Better to cut twice to perfection than to cut once and discover it's too small.

Monitor orientation

One thing you might not have considered is the orientation of your monitor. Most people think of a monitor oriented in a horizontal position when they think of an arcade cabinet. Figure 12-17 shows an example of a monitor mounted horizontally.

A majority of modern arcade machines use horizontally mounted monitors. However, many older classics used monitors turned 90 degrees vertically. These were games such as *Donkey Kong* or *Gyruss*. Figure 12-18 shows an example.

FIGURE **12-16:** Trimming the bezel.
Used by permission of Happ Controls.

FIGURE **12-17:** A typically mounted monitor.

FIGURE 12-18: A vertically mounted monitor.

What's the difference, and which method should you use? Emulators can rotate the screen to display any game at either orientation. To play a vertically oriented game on a horizontally oriented monitor, emulators will leave black vertical bars on the left and right sides to keep the aspect ratio of the game correct. This is fine on a 25-inch or larger monitor, but, on a smaller 19-inch monitor, the picture becomes pretty small. Some people handle this by having two arcade cabinets — one with a vertically mounted monitor and one with a horizontally mounted monitor. If you start to collect these beasts, then that's a pretty good idea. If you only want one ultimate arcade cabinet, an innovative solution exists for those of you with some woodworking skill and initiative — rotating monitors.

Most rotating monitors are mounted by attaching a wooden circular frame around the monitor. The monitor frame rests on wheels mounted in the cabinet and is rotated either through a slit on the side or through access behind the cabinet. Some people have even gone so far as to use a motorized mount that rotates their monitor at the touch of a button! If you're interested in following any of these plans, visit these Web sites for more details:

- Mr. Salty's Arcade — www.mrsalty.net
- The Sturcade — http://users.adelphia.net/~bsturk/mame.html
- JelloSlug's Arcade — www.jelloslug.mamehost.com
- Carlos' Centipede Extended — www.retrospieler.de
- Boon's Plain MAME Cabinet — http://plainmame.emugaming.com

- Mike's MAME Machine — `www.geocities.com/SiliconValley/Garage/9000/arcade/index.htm`

- The Lillypad — `http://lillypad.4mg.com`

You need to consider the effects of magnetism with a rotating monitor. As a monitor is rotated from one orientation to another, the different orientation to Earth's magnetic field may produce minor color distortion. You'll need to include some means of degaussing the monitor in your plans, whether with a built-in degaussing circuit or an external coil.

Rotating monitors are certainly very innovative. If you're going to use a smaller monitor, it's something to consider. However, if you're using a larger monitor, a rotating monitor is probably more trouble than it's worth. A vertical picture on a horizontally oriented 25-inch monitor will be the equivalent of a vertical 19-inch monitor, which is more than acceptable.

The angle at which you mount your monitor is your last consideration for monitor mounting. Most of the pictures shown so far are of monitors essentially parallel to the slope of the cabinet. If you're going to mount your monitor in an upright fashion like this, it should at least slope parallel to the cabinet. It will look better this way and will allow players to look down slightly. If the monitor was mounted with no angle, players would have to crook their neck to play, which would rapidly grow uncomfortable.

However, some games mounted their monitors at a steep angle — almost laying it down. Players look down as they play their games (see Figure 12-19).

FIGURE **12-19: A sharply angled monitor.**

Games that used a monitor in this orientation include some of the *Pac-Man* titles and the Nintendo VS series of arcade machines. Looking down at a monitor at this angle is comfortable and unlikely to cause neck aches during prolonged play. Mounting a monitor at this angle is more of a challenge. When a monitor is mounted on a shelf parallel to the cabinet's slope, the monitor shelf holds the weight. If the monitor is mounted at a steeper angle, then the force of gravity pulls the monitor down the slope. You'll need to use an appropriately strong method of mounting to accommodate a monitor at this angle.

The Project Arcade monitor

The Project Arcade cabinet uses a 27-inch arcade-computer monitor hybrid from Happ Controls. The monitor is mounted horizontally and is angled parallel to the arcade cabinet's slope, as can be seen in Figure 12-20.

FIGURE 12-20: Project Arcade with mounted monitor.

Summary

Wow, there is certainly a lot more to monitors than you might think at first! Above all, you should always have a healthy respect for the hazards inside a monitor. A bit of carelessness when working with an exposed monitor can have serious health consequences. Once you've gotten past the basic theory and safety information surrounding monitors, you have four main choices. You can choose an arcade monitor, a television, a computer monitor, or a hybrid arcade-computer monitor. Each type will dictate different interface and mounting requirements as well as provide different levels of arcade authenticity. Once you've chosen a monitor, your last decision will be the orientation and angle at which to mount the monitor.

You're so close to having a fully functional home arcade cabinet that you can probably see it in front of you now! In the next two chapters, I'll talk about installing and configuring your computer as well as finding and loading the game software that makes the cabinet work. Look out — Arcade Nirvana awaits!

Installing the Computer

"**I**gor! Igor, where are you? Ah, good. There you are. What are you doing? Stop playing *Pac-Man* with that keyboard and come over here. It's time!"

"Now, doctor? Are you sure? Is your creation really ready? I'm afraid, doctor. I'm afraid!"

"Be still, Igor! There is nothing to fear and nothing to lose but the keyboard itself! We have worked long and hard for this moment, and it is time. We have long since assembled the cabinet body, and it is ready. Have we not installed the monitor for the eyes, the speakers for the ears? Did we not select an interface for the nervous system, and provide it genuine arcade controls to play with? No, Igor, be not afraid. It is time — time for the most essential part of all!"

"Doctor! You can't mean your creation's ready for . . . for . . . ."

Note　At this point, maniacal laughter interrupts Igor, and thunder and lightning flashes in the background. Everyone in the audience gasps in horror and waits in breathless anticipation as the mad scientist (you) prepares for what comes next! Unfortunately, this is only a printed medium. You will need to supply the special effects and audience yourself. Please do so before continuing. Thanks! — Author.

"Yes! Yes, Igor, bring me what is to be my creation's brain! It is time to bring my creation to life! Bring me . . . *the computer!*"

"But doctor — you haven't talked about the computer yet. The audience may get confused. You may get confused!"

"What? Oh yes, you're right. I forgot! Very well then, let us proceed. Bring me the first circuit board, my *Building Computers for Dummies* book, and a cup of hot cocoa! Oh, and bring my fuzzy bunny slippers, too — I have a long night of research ahead of me!"

"Yes doctor . . ."

chapter 13

In this chapter, I'll talk about installing the computer into your arcade cabinet, and configuring it to minimize the *computerness* of it while maximizing the arcade atmosphere. You can set up your computer so that from the moment it boots up to the time you're playing your first game, it looks as much as possible like a real arcade machine. There's some interesting stuff ahead. Read on!

Configuring Your Computer for Total Arcade Immersion

I'm assuming for this section that you have a working knowledge of computer terminology and how a computer works. If you do not, then some of this section may seem a bit foreign to you. I'll attempt to make it so you can follow along even if the terms and concepts aren't familiar to you. However, if you find that you'd like to know more, consider picking up a copy of *PCs For Dummies* by Dan Gookin and Wiley Publishing. I'll be concentrating on Windows-based computers, but similar concepts will apply to Linux and Macintosh users.

Picking a computer

Just about any computer you pick for your cabinet will work, as long as you have an idea of what kind of games you will be able to play. The nice thing about re-creating a classic arcade cabinet is that many classic arcade games and emulators do not require high-end computers. Even an old 486 or low-end Pentium computer will work for a large number of great arcade classics. These games are also not terribly demanding in terms of memory and video requirements. Lower-end machines like these, however, will limit your ability to play more recent titles and emulators.

A good mid-level machine, such as a low-end Pentium III or Celeron-based computer, will do an excellent job of running almost all of the arcade emulators available on the Internet today. It will also run a good majority of the non-emulator games in the market as well. Video and memory demands will be higher at this level. You'll want a decent 3D video card and at least 64 megs of RAM in the computer (though I recommend 128–256 megs) to be able to play modern video games on your cabinet.

To be able to play cutting-edge video games as well as to future-proof your cabinet for tomorrow's emulators, you should consider a relatively new computer. A Pentium IV or high-end Celeron CPU with 256 or more megs of RAM, along with a top-end 3D video card, will let you play anything out there now and in the near future. Of course, this is always a losing game. In a year, the high-end computer you have now will be yesterday's news, and the newest video games will benefit from yet again higher amounts of RAM and newer video cards. This is one game you can keep up with, but won't ever win!

Along with the essentials such as a video card and RAM, you'll want to think about a few other things for your computer:

- **Sound card.** Any sound card that is SoundBlaster compatible will work. Older computers that have sound cards that are not SoundBlaster compatible will probably work in most games, but will give you problems in some of them.

- **CD-ROM drive.** Essentially a given, but all video games sold these days come on CDs.

- **USB ports.** Many arcade controls can be made to interface through a USB port, and more are likely to be developed in the future. Even if you aren't using one now, you may want to in the future.

- **Network card.** A network card in the computer has two benefits. The first is that you can use it to provide maintenance access to your computer remotely via an in-house network, without having to open the cabinet. The second is that a network card will allow you to hook up your arcade cabinet for high-speed online or local network multi-player gaming action.

- **Modem.** You might want to consider a modem for your computer if you do not have high-speed broadband Internet access. However, modem access to the Internet is slow, and you will probably be at a disadvantage against players who have high-speed access.

The good news is that it does not have to be that expensive to have a computer near the cutting edge of technology. I was able to purchase a 2.6 GHz Pentium IV computer with Windows XP, 256 megs of RAM, and a 3D video card for $200 after rebates during the post-Thanksgiving holiday sales in 2003. Granted, those kinds of deals are not the norm, but you should be able to pick up a decent computer system for your cabinet at prices ranging from $300 to $600 year round. Also, don't forget that the computer is the one part of your arcade cabinet that's easy to upgrade as time goes on. Don't bust your budget here — put in the most you can afford, even if that means using an old computer you have gathering dust, and upgrade it as your gaming demands and budget afford.

Setting up your computer

I recommend performing the initial setup of your computer outside the cabinet. This lets you make sure everything works while it is easy to get to. Once you've got the operating system installed and the environment configured the way you like, you can install the computer into the cabinet. You're likely to be continually tweaking and updating the computer throughout the lifespan of your cabinet, so don't worry about having it 100% complete before you put it in.

Choosing an operating system

You have several options when it comes to operating systems for your computer. Your easiest and most flexible choice is to use one of the Microsoft Windows operating systems. Almost every emulator and video game comes in a version that runs under Windows. If you have a licensed copy of Windows 98, then you may want to consider using it for your arcade cabinet. Up until Windows XP, Windows 98 was hands-down the best operating system for game playing that Microsoft made. Full details on why this is so would take many pages, but in short Windows 98 provided the most stable home-consumer (game)-oriented version of Windows available at the time. Windows XP continued this emphasis, providing the best of modern-day operating systems while maintaining the attention to the home-consumer market. Some older games do not run under Windows XP, though most will with a bit of configuration. To date I am unaware of any games that will run on Windows XP that won't run on Windows 98, but that day will come.

Other operating systems you might consider include DOS, Macintosh, and Linux. You will limit the number of commercial video games you can play by using one of these choices, but most of the arcade emulators have versions for these operating systems. You can run DOS by booting Windows 98 into DOS mode, using a version of MS-DOS if you have a license for it, or by obtaining a freeware version such as FreeDOS (www.freedos.org). You will need to go online for more information on Macintosh and Linux choices. Two good places to start are MacMAME.net (www.macmame.net) for information on running MAME on Macintoshes, and Xmame (http://x.mame.net) for MAME on Linux.

My recommendation is that you either choose Windows 98 (second edition) or Windows XP for your arcade cabinet, with my preference being Windows XP. Either makes a fine choice and will provide a maximum level of flexibility for your cabinet with a minimum amount of configuration issues.

Basic operating system installation

Installing your operating system (OS) should be fairly straightforward using the instructions included with the OS. There isn't much I need to tell you about the basics of operating system installation, but I do have some guidelines for you to consider. Keep in mind the purpose of your computer when you're installing the operating system and applications. Unless you have other plans, the whole point of this computer is going to be to play games. Any options in the operating system that don't help with that point should be eliminated, if possible. When you're running the operating system installation, choose the custom install instead of default. Examine each option and decide if it's absolutely necessary. Something like a paint program probably isn't necessary for your gaming system. However, it doesn't normally run until you manually select it, so is probably safe to leave. On the other hand, the Microsoft Messenger service does run constantly by default and probably doesn't add anything you want in a gaming system — take it out.

Be aware of things installed by software applications that sometimes sneak in by default. For instance, Microsoft Office and some other applications have a *quick-start* feature that loads part of the program in memory when the computer starts up, so that the application loads faster when you click it. That's great in a work computer, but once again takes up resources unnecessarily in a gaming computer. Either don't install the application at all (do you need to do word processing on your arcade cabinet?) or make sure they don't install extra things you don't want, such as quick-start. Look out for things installed by hardware installation drivers as well. Does your video card include a taskbar icon that lets you quickly change resolutions, record video, or watch TV? That's great, but it runs continuously and takes up memory and resources. Unless you're planning to use any of those features in your cabinet, take them out. Here's a hint: Look on the bottom right of your taskbar (see Figure 13-1). Any icon you see there is something running and taking up resources on your computer.

If your computer came with the operating system and application pre-installed, which is likely for most commercially purchased computers, then it is probably full of resource-stealing extras. Try this on a machine running Windows 98 or XP: Click the Start button, then Run, and type **msconfig** in the dialog box. Click the "Startup" tab, and look at all the things that are set to run when you turn your computer on (see Figure 13-2). You may be surprised at all the things that are loaded before you ever start to use your computer!

Running Applications

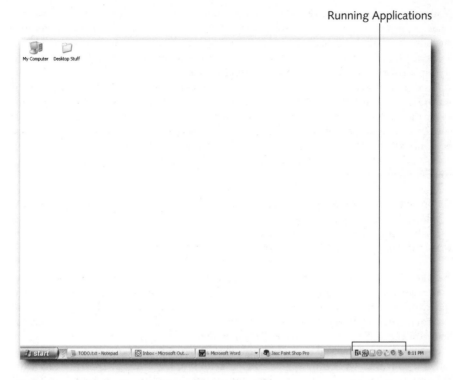

FIGURE 13-1: Seven applications running on the taskbar.
Screen shot reprinted by permission from Microsoft Corporation.

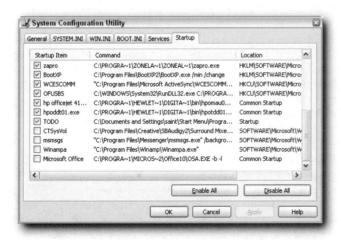

FIGURE 13-2: A look at msconfig on a typical Windows XP computer.
Screen shot reprinted by permission from Microsoft Corporation.

Notice the checkbox next to each item. It's possible to turn an item off so it no longer starts when the computer starts. Some of the things that run are necessary for the computer to operate, however! You can examine each one to see if it is clear what its purpose is, and whether it looks safe to turn off or not. For instance, notice that I've turned off the Microsoft Office startup assistant (osa.exe) and Messenger service (msmsgs.exe). Deciding what to turn off and what to leave on can be a tricky affair. Some choices are obvious, some are obscure (what does regsvr32.exe do anyway?). You can turn off items one at a time, and then reboot your computer to see the effect. If something stops working that needs to work, you can re-run msconfig to correct it. If the computer stops working so badly that you can't run msconfig, then you can boot into safe mode. Do so by pressing the F8 key immediately after the computer starts to boot, and choose safe mode from the startup menu. Once Windows is running in safe mode, you can undo your changes.

Performing the steps in the previous paragraph should be perfectly safe. However, the unlikely possibility that something may go wrong and corrupt your operating system or data always exists. Do not do these steps on a computer that has the only copy of the family finances on it! Make sure you have a backup of anything important on the computer before you start tinkering.

Another thing I highly recommend on a computer that came pre-installed or that has been in use for a while is scanning for spyware programs. Spyware refers to programs that install themselves on your computer for the purpose of gathering information (usually marketing information) and reporting it back to someplace on the Internet. Some may have been installed with your consent, while others may have snuck in without making it obvious to you. Either way, even if you're not connected to the Internet, these programs will take up system resources you'd rather use for gaming. A good spy-busting program is *Spybot Search & Destroy* available free from www.safer-networking.org. This program scans your computer for such programs, notifies you about what it finds, and gives you the option to remove them. Another excellent spy-buster is *Ad-aware* available from www.lavasoftusa.com.

Spybot Search & Destroy is included on the companion CD-ROM.

Once you have your operating system installed and/or cleaned up, you should consider preventative security measures. No computer should be without a good measure of security to prevent problems and spy programs from occurring in the first place. Make sure you have a good anti-virus program (such as *Symantec Anti-virus,* among other good choices) installed on your computer. If you are going to have the machine connected to the Internet, you should also have a personal firewall installed. My favorite is *Zone Alarm* (www.zonelabs.com), which has a free basic version, or a full-featured version (recommended) for $50.

Tweaking the operating system

You can do a few more things to the basic operating system configuration to minimize the appearance of running a computer and make maintenance easier. For instance, both Windows 98 and Windows XP require you to log on to the computer by default. You certainly don't want your arcade cabinet to boot up to a logon screen! Fortunately, getting rid of the logon screen is easy. Start by downloading a copy of *Tweak UI* from Microsoft. *Tweak UI* is a user interface tweaking tool that Microsoft released in response to public demand, but does not support. It allows you to tweak and configure many different parts of your operating system safely. *Tweak UI* comes in one version for Windows 95 through Windows 2000, and another version for

Windows XP. You can find it by visiting the Microsoft Web site (`www.microsoft.com/`) and searching for either "*Tweak UI* Windows 98" or "*Tweak UI* Windows XP" depending on your need. Microsoft frequently changes the locations of files, so I can't guarantee exactly where the utility will be. As of the time of this writing, the XP version was located at www `.microsoft.com/windowsxp/pro/downloads/powertoys.asp`, and the 98 version could be found at `www.microsoft.com/ntworkstation/downloads/PowerToys/Networking/NTTweakUI.asp`.

Tweaking the logon

Once you've installed the *Tweak UI* program, run it and browse through the various options. You'll see there are many things you can do with this handy utility. The Windows 98 version uses tabs; the Windows XP version uses a tree-like menu structure. I will refer to the XP version, but the same steps can essentially be taken on the 98 version. Click the logon-autologon menu (in Windows 98, just click the logon tab). Here you can check a box to tell Windows to automatically log you on to the computer when it starts, and you can tell it what username and password to use (see Figure 13-3). Enter the username and password you are using on the computer, click OK, and you will no longer have to log on to the computer when it starts.

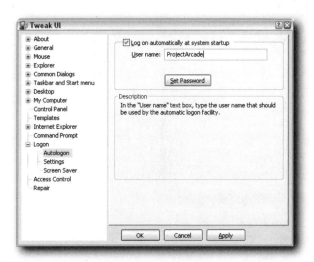

FIGURE 13-3: Setting the logon under Windows XP *Tweak UI*.
Screen shot reprinted by permission from Microsoft Corporation.

Note   Windows 98 and Windows XP use user profiles to maintain separate settings from user to user. This lets one user select a background screen, for instance, and another user a totally different background screen. Each gets his or her own background screen when logging on without having to change it each time. This is handy for a computer that has multiple users with unique needs. For your gaming cabinet, however, you'll probably want everyone to use a single username so they always get the same environment you've set up for the arcade cabinet. From here on out, make sure any changes you make occur while you're logged in using the same username you selected in the autologon section of *Tweak UI*.

Clean your desk!

Another thing both versions of Windows suffer from is a messy desktop. Icons for this, icons for that; icons here, icons there; icons, icons everywhere! On an arcade cabinet, all you want to see are games and perhaps jukebox programs. You certainly don't need to see a trash can! This is another area where some ingenuity and *Tweak UI* can help with. First, run *Tweak UI* and choose the "desktop" menu (see Figure 13-4; Windows 98 version will vary slightly). Notice you can turn off several of the standard Windows desktop icons. That's a good start!

Turning off the network neighborhood icon in Windows 98 disables networking. In Windows XP you can turn off the network icon without that problem. If you want your arcade cabinet networked and you're running Windows 98, the best you can do is to change the default network neighborhood icon and title to something else to disguise it, or investigate different user interfaces in the *Shell games* section later in this chapter.

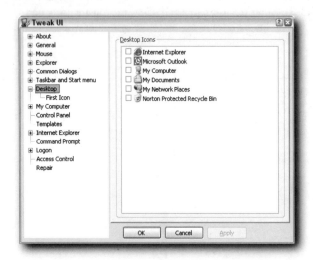

FIGURE 13-4: Desktop settings in *Tweak UI* for Windows XP.
Screen shot reprinted by permission from Microsoft Corporation.

Next, make a new folder on the desktop called "Desktop Stuff" by right-clicking an empty spot on the desktop and choosing new folder. Select every remaining icon on the desktop that you do not want shown, and move them into the folder you just created. Make sure that your taskbar has the quick-launch toolbar showing on it (small icons you can activate with a single click). If it's not there, right-click the taskbar, choose properties, and turn the quick-launch toolbar on. Now, right-click the folder and drag it to the quick-launch toolbar on the taskbar. Let go, and make sure you choose to move it instead of copying it. Voila! The desktop is now cleared of everything but what you want on it. You can gain access to the desktop icons by choosing the folder on the quick-launch toolbar, so you haven't lost access to anything.

The last thing you'll want to do is to go to the properties for the taskbar, and make sure "autohide" is turned off. This will stop the taskbar from popping up and down whenever the mouse is near it. Finally, grab the top of the taskbar (the cursor will turn into a double-headed arrow when you're in the right spot) and drag it down until it disappears. You'll still be able to get to the taskbar by dragging it back up when you need it later, but otherwise the only sign of anything computer oriented on your screen will be a small line at the very bottom of the screen. Figure 13-5 shows my Windows XP desktop with all the icons removed and the taskbar hidden. You can just barely see the double-headed mouse cursor sitting on top of the taskbar line. The desktop may look a bit plain right now, but you'll be jazzing it up in the *Sights, Sounds, and Themes* section later in the chapter. Still, notice that there's nothing *computerish* left. Your desktop cleanup is complete!

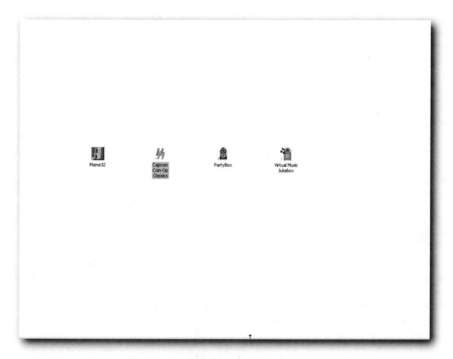

FIGURE 13-5: A fully functional but cleaned up Windows XP desktop.
Screen shot reprinted by permission from Microsoft Corporation.

Remote control

You should think about one more thing before considering the basic operating system installation finished. How are you going to access and update the computer after it's in the cabinet? Getting to the computer in the cabinet won't be too difficult, but do you really want to have to do that every time you want to update or add a game? There is a better way. Remember the network card I recommended earlier in the chapter? If your computer is available on your household network, accessing it for updates and maintenance is easy. Walking you through installing a home network is beyond the scope of this book, but it really is not difficult. You probably guessed it, but Wiley Publishing has a book that will help you. The book is called *Home Networking For Dummies* and is written by Kathy Ivens.

If you have your arcade cabinet's computer on a network, you can use basic Windows networking to share files and copy updates to your arcade cabinet. The really neat part comes in when you remotely control your arcade cabinet from another computer in the house (or even across the Internet, though I don't recommend it for security reasons). Using some method to remotely control your arcade cabinet's computer, you can update or maintain it without ever having to open up your cabinet or crawl around in back!

Windows XP includes a built-in application called *remote access* for this purpose. It works very well, but I do not recommend it because running it on the arcade cabinet's computer will involve setting it up and a bit of typing each time. Since the goal of the arcade cabinet is to be keyboardless, this presents a problem. There is an excellent freeware alternative called VNC (www.realvnc.com). VNC is a remote-control program available for many operating systems, including Windows 98 and Windows XP. It can be installed on your arcade cabinet's computer and either configured to always be running, or to run with a simple double-click using your trackball and arcade buttons. Once it's running on the arcade cabinet's computer, you can run the viewer program on another computer on the network, and remotely take control of the arcade cabinet's computer. It's fast, takes up few resources on the host computer, and works great!

On the CD

VNC is distributed under the GNU General Public License. This is a distribution license that maintains the original owner's copyright while allowing free distribution of the software. As required by the GNU license, both the VNC software (Windows version) and the source code are included on the companion CD-ROM.

Sights, sounds, and themes

Now I'm going to talk to you about something that can be really fun — dressing up your computer with arcade sights and sounds to complete the illusion that you're playing a real arcade machine! This is often referred to as eye candy (and ear candy). Normally, it doesn't do anything for your computer in practical terms; it just looks and sounds pretty. However, because you're trying to recreate the arcade experience, dressing up the sights and sounds of your computer is almost a necessity!

Configurable eye and ear candy

Let's start by taking a look at the parts of the operating system that can be configured with different sights and sounds. Both Windows 98 and Windows XP support these configurations. Table 13-1 shows the items that can be controlled, along with the applet in the control panel (click Start ➪ Settings ➪ Control Panel) used to configure them:

The Internet is full of different bits and pieces of graphics and sounds you can download and apply to the items in Table 13-1. Finding them is easy with a search on Google (www.google.com). Choosing them is an exercise that can easily take days as you stumble on one idea after the next. Imagine turning on your arcade cabinet and having it come up to a picture of the light cycles from Disney's *Tron* movie while the Master Control Program announces, "I'm going to have to put you in the game grid." Your friends will get goosebumps the first time they see and hear that — very cool!

Table 13-1   Configurable Sights and Sounds

Item	Description	Control Panel Applet
Background	The wallpaper (the picture on your computer's desktop) and the background colors (if you have no wallpaper).	Display
Screensaver	The screen saver that runs when your computer has been idle.	Display
Mouse cursors	The various shapes your mouse cursor takes when in use (15 different cursors).	Mouse
Icons	The icons used on the standard desktop, such as for "My Computer."	Display
Appearance	The various sizes, colors, and fonts for different windows and buttons on the desktop and in the Windows environment.	Display
Sounds	The .wav sound files that are played in association with certain events, such as starting or exiting Windows.	Sounds
Startup screens	The screen shown when Windows is starting up and when it's shutting down.	Special (see text following)

Desktop themes

You have two choices for installing all but the startup screens in Table 13-1. I'll get to the startup screens in a moment. For all the rest of the items, you can manually edit each item by replacing the default with the icon, wallpaper, or sound you've downloaded from the Internet. This can be a lot of fun, but can take a lot of time. Once again, there's a better way. Microsoft considers all of these items to be categorized as a theme. Once you've got it configured exactly the way you want, you can save all the customized settings as a theme file and share it with your friends. When your friends install the theme file, they'll get all the same cursors, icons, colors, fonts, wallpaper, sounds, etc., that you have. The nice thing is that many (hundreds, if not thousands) of people have already made themes to share! Try a Google search and you'll be inundated with Web sites to browse. You'll find themes from old arcade classics all the way up to modern-day cutting-edge games.

Installing a theme is done in a slightly different but mostly similar way in Windows 98 and Windows XP. In Windows 98, choose the desktop themes applet in the control panel. In Windows XP, choose the themes tab on the display applet in the control panel (see Figure 13-6). Before you do anything else, you should save the current configuration of your computer under your own personal theme. That way, if you don't like the results from testing different themes, you have your old standby to fall back on. Give it a name such as "mytheme.theme" so you'll always be able to find it when you need it.

FIGURE **13-6: Themes tab on the Display Properties dialog box, Windows XP.**
Screen shot reprinted by permission from Microsoft Corporation.

For the most part, themes are compatible between Windows 98 and Windows XP. When you install a theme, however, they likely will be searching for different directories, depending on whether they were packaged on a 98 machine or an XP machine. On your Windows XP machine, if you create a C:\Program Files\Plus!\Themes\ folder, then themes from Windows 98 machines will install properly. In Windows XP, themes can be saved anywhere and default to the My Documents folder, which is unique to each user.

Installing a theme is as simple as unpacking it (themes are usually downloaded as a .ZIP file or as a self-extracting .EXE file), then using the operating system's theme manager to select the theme. All the cursor, icon, wallpaper, sound, and other changes will be made automatically simply by choosing the theme. It couldn't be easier!

As well as doing a search on Google, you can find video game themes on the Web sites or CDs of your favorite games and game developers. For instance, the Atari *Arcade Hits* CD (which I'll tell you more about in Chapter 14, "Choosing and Loading Software") includes a desktop theme for each of the games on the CD. Some other video game themes, wallpaper, or movies can be found on Namco's Web site at www.namcoarcade.com/downloads.asp, Atari's Web site at www.us.atari.com/freebies, Sega at www.sega.com/vault/home_vault.jhtml, and Digital Leisure at www.digitalleisure.com.

For more desktop themes, try the search words "desktop themes video arcade game" on Google (www.google.com). Finally, stop by ezthemes.com (www.ezthemes.com) and click on the games link for a huge collection. Careful, searching for and playing with themes can be addictive. Have fun!

Startup screens

If you eliminate the logon screen and decorate your computer with a good arcade-oriented theme, you're most of the way to hiding the computer behind your arcade cabinet. You need to tweak one more thing, and then you'll have a computer that's as close to an original arcade cabinet as is possible. That last piece is the Windows startup screen. Both Windows 98 and Windows XP display a Windows logo when booting up. If you know how to do it, changing the startup screen for something more appropriate (for instance a picture of Pac-Man or perhaps a nice logo like "Project Arcade") is easy to do. The procedure is different in Windows 98 and Windows XP, as described in the next two sections.

Windows 98

If you're using Windows 98, you can actually replace three screens. The first is the startup screen, the second is the screen displayed as Windows is shutting down, and the third is the screen displayed when Windows has completed shutting down (if your computer doesn't just power off). Those files are C:\logo.sys, C:\windows\logow.sys, and C:\windows\logos.sys, respectively. These files are 256-color Windows bitmap files with dimensions of 320 × 400. You can use any compatible bitmap file by simply naming them appropriately and copying them over the other logo files. Be sure to make backup copies of your originals first! The C:\logo.sys file may not exist at first on your system — that's fine, just copy your own to the C:\ directory and Windows will pick it up.

It's also possible to have an animated startup logo for Windows 98! The image won't actually move, but the colors will cycle through a range of colors, giving the appearance of animation. Animated (as well as nonanimated) logo screens can be found once again with a good Google search. For more information on creating animated Windows 98 logo screens, as well as a collection of screens to get you started, visit the XrX page at www.nucleus.com/~kmcmurdo/logos.

Windows XP

The only logo screen you can replace on Windows XP is the startup screen. The startup image is a 640 × 480 picture with 16 colors with a small animated bar. Beyond the small bar of moving dots, Windows XP startup screens cannot be animated as they can with Windows 98 startup screens. Also, Microsoft made it a bit more difficult to get to the Windows XP startup screen by imbedding it in a file that's part of the operating system. That file is ntoskrnl.exe, found in the C:\windows\system32 directory as well as other directories (the one in the system32 directory is the important one). Before you make any changes to this file, be sure to back it up. If this file gets corrupted, your operating system will stop working!

You should use a utility to safely replace the startup screen in the ntoskrnl.exe file. There are several good programs you can try. Two are commercial programs, both of which have trial versions you can use to see if you like them before you buy them. The first is BootXP, available at www.bootxp.net. The second is Inno Logo, available from www.milsoft.net/innologo. They support automatic backups of your original ntoskrnl.exe file, previews of the boot screen before you apply it, and restoration of the original if you decide you don't want to use custom bootup screens. The other program you might want to try is LogonUIBootRandomizer (www.belchfire.net/~userxp), a freeware program that will randomize your bootup screen quietly so that it's different every time you start the machine.

Launching your games

Now that you've installed the operating system and configured the look and feel, it's time to consider the games you're going to play. Specifically, how will you select and run a particular game? Booting your computer up with a custom arcade startup screen and arcade sounds makes it look like you're running a real arcade machine, but having to click Start ⇨ Programs ⇨ Mygame ⇨ Rungame, and then opening the cabinet to insert the game CD can sure spoil the effect fast. Isn't there a better way? You're reading *Project Arcade* — of course there is!

One-click game launching

The first thing you'll want to do away with is the concept of double-clicking with a mouse to run a game. Hopefully, you've installed a trackball to use in place of the mouse, and have push-buttons configured as mouse buttons on the control panel. You can use these to move the cursor to a game you want to play, and then use the pushbutton to run it. You don't want to have to press the pushbutton twice to run the game — too computer-like. A single press of a push-button should launch whatever game you're selecting. Fortunately, this is easy enough to do in Windows. In Windows XP, open the control panel, and double-click the "Folder Options" icon. On the general tab, make sure the "Single-click to open an item" option is selected, as shown in Figure 13-7. On a Windows 98 machine, the steps are slightly different. Double-click the "My Computer" icon, drop down the "View" menu, and select "Folder Options." Then click the "Custom" bullet, choose "Settings," and set Windows to use a single click.

Front ends

The single-click setting works great with single video games that launch directly into game play after you click. However, many of the arcade games you may play will be through emulators that run multiple arcade games. You don't run the game directly; you run the emulator. The emulator, in turn, starts the game. Many of these emulators have a common trend — they are not easy to use. Those with a menu system to choose the game are sometimes confusing or have to be configured. Some of them are command-line based even though they run under Windows and don't have a menu system. Running a particular arcade game requires typing the name of the emulator followed by the name of the game you're trying to play. Typing? That's not very arcade-like!

The problem is that programming a computer to emulate an arcade machine's hardware and software can be very difficult. Emulators are almost always in a state of development to perfect game emulation. In fact, I do not believe I have ever seen an emulator that was declared completely finished! Making the game work properly is a significant technical achievement that requires a lot of time and talent on the part of the programmer, and so the rest of the details, such as designing an easy-to-use interface and menu system, do not always get enough attention. This makes many otherwise excellent arcade emulators difficult for novices to use. Once you're playing the game itself, the controls are arcade authentic and game play is intuitive. Getting to that point isn't always. The solution to this problem? Enter the front-end software program!

FIGURE 13-7: Choosing single-click in Windows XP.
Screen shot reprinted by permission from Microsoft Corporation.

A front-end software program does the tedious bits of setting up a game for you. If an emulator requires typing to start, the front end will do that for you. If you have to set up some options such as screen size, the front end will do that, too. Essentially, a good front end turns a process that normally requires a keyboard and mouse into a simple trackball, joystick, and fire-button operation. Very slick! Some do this with a simple text display of available games, while others show you an image of the games. Many of the popular ones now are *skinnable,* meaning that you can design (or download) your own look and feel for the front end, with custom wallpaper, game selection images, background noises, and more. One of my favorite front ends actually lets you walk through a virtual arcade full of cabinets to play, just like you were there in person!

Note One of the best features of a front end is the way it looks, with a picture or screen shot of the game you're about to run. Unfortunately, space and copyright issues prevent showing you those here. You'll need to visit the front-end Web sites or download them to get the full effect!

There are many (*many!*) front-end packages available. I'll start you off by directing you to MAMEWorld (www.mameworld.net), where you'll find a frequently updated listing of front-end programs. As of this writing, there are more than 30 listed! Choosing a front end is kind of like choosing a car — there's no one right answer for everyone. You should at least browse through the various front-end Web sites to see if you like a front end's look and features, and experiment with those that catch your eye. However, I'll highlight a few personal favorites being actively developed and updated here. The front-end arena is constantly in flux, with front ends being updated and new front ends being introduced. Be sure to visit the BYOAC message boards' software forum (www.arcadecontrols.com) to see what's new!

With the kind permission of their authors, several of the front ends listed in the following sections are included on the companion CD-ROM! Look for *"On the CD!"* at the end of each description to see if it's included!

ArcadeOS

Available from www.mameworld.net/pc2jamma/frontend.html, ArcadeOS is a DOS-only front end that lists your games in text on the screen against an arcade background image. Some of the features of note are both horizontal and vertical modes, to best fit on your monitor no matter what orientation you're using. It's controllable by both trackball/mouse and joystick/keyboard, supports multiple emulators as programmed, and allows you to customize it to support even more emulators and games. It's most unique feature is built-in support for arcade monitors that require 15 kHz refresh rates. ArcadeOS is part of the PC2Jamma project (more information in Chapter 17, "Buying Your Way to Gaming Nirvana"). ArcadeOS will run right out of the box, so initial use is easy. Configuring and customizing ArcadeOS for emulators other than MAME is mildly complex, but there is a support forum at the MAMEWorld message forums (www.mameworld.net). It is open-source software, meaning the programming code for the front end is available for you to download, tweak, and possibly even contribute your changes to the next version.

AdvanceMenu

AdvanceMenu (http://advancemame.sourceforge.net) is an emulator front end that runs under DOS, Windows, Linux, and Mac OS. Like ArcadeOS, AdvanceMenu has support for arcade monitors as well as other monitors. It supports both horizontal and vertical orientations with many different display modes for choosing games — full-screen snapshots, text lists with snapshots, tiled snapshots, icons, and more. AdvanceMenu is controlled by a joystick/keyboard. A unique feature of AdvanceMenu is support for customized sounds when navigating the menus, with the ability to assign a unique sound to each game. You can also have a background sound playing while in the front end. Another nice feature is a screensaver mode where it will cycle through arcade game screen shots when idle. AdvanceMenu supports multiple emulators, and is mildly complex to configure. It is also an open-source software program.

For the rest of the front ends, I will only mention mouse and keyboard support. Obviously, if it uses a mouse, then your mouse-hacked trackball will work, and likewise for a keyboard-hacked joystick.

Dragon King

Dragon King (www.oscarcontrols.com/lazarus) is a Windows-based multi-emulator front end with both keyboard and mouse support. It has several nice features that make it a good fit for an arcade cabinet. Dragon King supports customizable skins, screensavers and sounds, and an animated startup video among other features. The front end can be configured to support an arcade monitor as well as other monitors. Startup configuration for MAME support is easy with Dragon King walking you through the process. Configuring advanced features and additional emulators is of mild to medium complexity. Dragon King does not have a dedicated support forum, but the author is a regular member of the BYOAC (www.arcade controls.com/) message forums and chat room. *On the CD!*

Emulaxian/FE-3Darcade

Emulaxian/FE-3Darcade (hereafter simply Emulaxian, www.i-modernist.com/ emulaxian) is the front end that arguably has the *eye candy* category all but won. This is the front end where you can roam around a virtual arcade with real background noises and sounds, virtual players in the arcade, and cabinets that you can walk up to and play. When you select a cabinet, the front end loads the game and you run it full screen, returning to the virtual arcade when done. Many other options are available for the front end aside from the virtual arcade mode, such as a spinning wheel used to select games, a traditional text listing with screen shots, and others. Virtually everything in this front end is skinnable and customizable. You can choose to have the background arcade ambiance continue while you play your game, or to have it silent when you're in the game. Probably the front end's neatest feature is the use of 3D arcade cabinet models, so that instead of generic boxy cabinets in your virtual arcade, you can design or download models that look like the real thing. Another nice feature is that this front end can shut down your computer when you exit, preserving the arcade illusions a little bit more. Very nice! I've only begun to touch on the potential of this amazing front end. This one should be high on your list to try! Emulaxian runs multiple emulators and games as well as MAME. It supports both horizontal and vertical orientation, keyboard and mouse control, and is easy to configure for basic operation through a menu-based configuration procedure. Advanced operation is mildly complex to configure. Support for this front end can be found in its message forums located at http://echo.messageboard.nl/2243.

EmuWizard

EmuWizard (www.whizzoconsulting.com/pages/projects/emuwizard.html) is a good basic emulator front-end program. It runs under Windows, and is controlled by either the keyboard or a joystick via the game port. EmuWizard is skinnable, coming with a default skin and an ArcadeOS look-alike skin. Games can be selected via the traditional text listing with screen shot, or in a screen shot snapshot mode only. Configuring basic entries for the front end is easy via a text-based configuration file, and mildly complex when it comes time for advanced configuration options. Standout features include the ability to send keystrokes to your emulator (for instance, to press OK for you if your emulator has a pause before it lets you into the game), and the ability to shut down Windows with a particular keystroke combination. The simple look and feel of this front end is easy on the eyes. EmuWizard is open-source software.

Game Launcher

Game Launcher (www.dribin.org/dave/game_launcher) is a simple multi-emulator front end that runs on DOS, Windows, and Unix. Games are selected from a text listing displayed against an arcade background screen shot. The front end supports horizontal and vertical monitor orientation, and will play background music from an MP3 list or music CD. Game Launcher is controlled by either a keyboard or game port joystick, and has just enough menu animation to give it some pep without being annoying. Configuring the front end is easy enough via text-based configuration files. Game Launcher is an open-source software package and is supported via an e-mail list.

MAMEWah

MAMEWah (http://mamewah.mameworld.net) is the multi-emulator front end that has taken the arcade cabinet-building community by storm recently. It is inspired by ArcadeOS but runs under Windows. MAMEWah is a textbox and screen shot type of front end that is skinnable and has many different layouts available for download. It also comes with a layout (skinning) design tool to help you make your own skins. The front end uses keyboard controls only, and it has built-in support for reprogramming the IPAC keyboard encoder. You can play MP3 music files in the background while in the front end, and it will also launch an internal slideshow or an external screensaver when idle. Configuring the front end is about on par with the rest of the front ends with the ability to configure it from within the program, but it also has one unique feature. There is a third-party tool available for configuring MAMEWah (http://uk.geocities.com/david.butler4@btinternet.com), making it the only front end I am aware of that has its own front end! MAMEWah has quickly developed a large fan base and is under frequent development. MAMEWah has a dedicated support forum at www.mameworld.net/pc2jamma/frontend.html, but the programmer is also a regular member of the BYOAC (www.arcadecontrols.com) message forums. *On the CD!*

Front-end recommendations

It's really hard to point to a single front end and declare it the one you must try. You're better off taking a good look at all the front ends and choosing the one that suits your particular wants and needs. Consider the operating system you'll be using, support for the games you want to run, degree of difficulty to install and use, and finally the look and feel. The short list of front ends given here are those currently the most popular among the arcade cabinet-building community members, but remember, there are many more out there you might want to try. Bear in mind you don't have to choose just one. You might run Emulaxian/3D-Arcade for when you really want to wow someone, and MAMEWah when you want something more traditional. Experiment. Trying different front ends is part of the fun!

Shell games

For those of you who *really* want to disguise the Windows engine behind your arcade cabinet, consider coming out of your shell — the Windows user interface shell, that is! Explorer (not to be confused with Internet Explorer, a different program) is the user interface that Windows presents you with when it starts up. It's the desktop, the icons, the start menu, etc. One of the nice touches in Windows, however, is that you don't have to use Explorer as your shell. Any executable program can be used as a shell. For instance, you might choose to use a front-end program as your default Windows interface!

Changing the shell in Windows 98 is very easy. Edit the C:\windows\system.ini file (make a backup first!), and find the line that reads "shell=explorer.exe" near the top of the file. Change the explorer.exe to the name of your front end or other shell replacement, including the full path (such as C:\frontend\myfrontend.exe) if it's not in the C:\windows directory. Reboot the computer and you'll be running a brand-new user interface! If things go bad, reboot the computer and start it in command mode. Use the DOS edit command to modify the system.ini file and change it back to Explorer, reboot, and then try again.

Playing shell games in Windows XP is more complex than Windows 98. Changing the shell requires making a few edits in the registry. If it's not done correctly, strange things can occur, like the Explorer shell opening up on top of your custom shell unexpectedly. On the other hand, several really good shell replacements exist to look at, and trying them out is once again a lot of fun. Here's one thing you might consider: Unlike Windows 98, Windows XP can support a different shell for each user. You can keep Explorer as your primary shell on your primary XP user account, and create new user accounts to try different shells. If things go wrong, just reboot the computer, log on as the primary account using Explorer, and fix it.

You can find full details on changing shells in Windows XP online. I recommend spending some time reading about it before deciding to put it into action. An excellent resource on all things shell-like is the Shell-Shocked Web site at http://shell-shocked.org. You can find tutorials on shell replacement, reviews and opinions of different shells, and much more there. Among other things, there's a tutorial on how to manually change your shell using the registry editor. However, if you'd like to try this, I recommend using a shell-swapping utility that will make the changes for you. One of the most popular is Shellon version 2 (www.dx13 .co.uk/programs/index.html, version 3 is in beta at time of writing). Shellon will handle all the details of experimenting with different shells in both Windows 98 and Windows XP.

Aside from using one of the previously discussed front ends for your shell, you might want to use one of the excellent full-fledged shell replacements available. Litestep (www.litestep. net) is very popular and extremely customizable. You can find hundreds of themes for Litestep, and if you can't find one to your liking you can make your own. Would you like nothing but game icons on the desktop? Litestep can do that. Want everything arranged in menu bars against an arcade background? Litestep can do that, too. Another popular shell replacement is Aston (www.astonshell.com). Like Litestep, Aston allows you almost total freedom to design the perfect desktop, with many pre-packaged themes to try if you don't want to make your own. Both Litestep and Aston work with Windows 98 as well as Windows XP. Litestep is free, while Aston is shareware for a very reasonable $30.

Be careful changing your shell; if something goes wrong, it can be difficult making your computer operational again. You should also make sure you have some way to turn off the computer properly if you change your shell, such as the ability to shut down Windows that some front ends have. Not every front end can do that, and if you use one of those as your shell, you'll end up with an arcade cabinet that can be turned on but cannot be properly shut down! The full shell replacements such as Litestep, of course, will not be a problem. Because changing the shell in Windows 98 is so easy, I wouldn't hesitate to try it if you're so inclined. If you're running Windows XP, it depends on how computer adept you're feeling. The minimalist approach would be to just run a front end in the startup folder and not change the shell. If you're feeling adventurous, then I suggest giving a few different shells a try!

Virtual CD-ROM drives

I've got one final bit of advice for hiding the computer behind the scenes. Games and emulators that install themselves completely to the hard drive won't require any intervention when you want to play them. That's good. However, games that require inserting a CD anytime you want to play disrupt the arcade illusion. Finding a way to install those games fully on the hard drive would let you enjoy them without having to insert the CD. Fortunately, programs allow you to do just that. These programs allow you to copy the contents of the CD to the hard drive, and create virtual CD-ROM drives on the hard drive. The computer is fooled into thinking a real CD is inserted and runs the software as if that were the case. Except for the fact that the CD exists as a virtual drive on the computer's hard drive instead of as a real physical medium, everything works the same. For instance, the CD has to be virtually inserted into the virtual CD drive before it can be used (which can be automated with a single click). Also, software that has to be installed off a real physical CD will still have to be installed off the virtual CD. In fact, you'll want to make sure that you install the game off the virtual CD instead of the real CD, in case the program expects to find the CD in the same drive every time it is run.

You'll encounter two possible drawbacks when using virtual CD drives. The first is that some CDs cannot be converted this way due to copy-protection schemes. The virtual CD programs are frequently updated to get around this, but not all CDs can be copied to the hard drive. The second drawback is a huge impact on space requirements. A typical CD holds 640 megs of data. Copying the CD to the hard drive requires that same amount of space, although some virtual CD programs may compress that data on the drive. After you account for the space the virtual CD requires, installing the program off the virtual CD will then occupy still *more* space on the hard drive. One good game can take a gigabyte or more of space on your system! Fortunately, with hard drive prices plummeting, you should be able to find a good-sized drive inexpensively. Still, the extra drive space required is certainly something to balance against the inconvenience of having to swap CDs.

I recommend you take a look at two programs if you'd like to use virtual CD-ROM drives. The first is CD Emulator (www.cdrom-emulator.com), and the second is Virtual CD (www.virtualcdonline.com). Both have received praise from the computing industry for doing what they claim to very well. They are available in a try-before-you-buy model, with CD Emulator running $30 and Virtual CD costing $40 at time of writing. Some of the features you'll find in either program include DVD support, 20 or more virtual CDs active at one time, and the ability to have desktop shortcuts to the CD with auto-run enabled. This last feature means that once you've installed the virtual CD, you can run it with a single click on the desktop without navigating the virtual CD program's menus. Combined with the fact that you don't have to insert a physical CD, this makes running a CD-ROM game as easy and intuitive to the player as any other game on your arcade cabinet!

 Note It's not a secret that a virtual CD program can be used to make illegal copies of a game. In no way, shape, or form should anyone consider this section an endorsement of software piracy. It's illegal and immoral, and there's no legitimate justification for it. Please, use the software only for its intended purposes.

Installing the Computer into the Cabinet

I really struggled when it came time to mount the computer in the cabinet. It wasn't that I had a hard time physically getting it into place. My problem was deciding whether I should place the PC in the cabinet as is, or dismantle the PC and install the separate components in the cabinet like a real arcade machine. PCs are designed to work assembled as a whole, so there's normally no reason not to leave it as is. However, stripping it down to the components and fitting them into place in the cabinet just has that *übergeek* coolness factor to it. Real classic arcade machines have circuit boards exposed when you look inside the cabinet; why not yours? In the end, pragmatism won out over impulsiveness. I simply had no good reason to take the PC apart other than the fact that I wanted to. You might consider it, so I'll go into when and how to do so.

Reasons to take your PC apart

Besides "I want to," there are a couple of good reasons to consider disassembling your computer prior to placing it in the cabinet. The first is possible heat concerns. There's plenty of airflow in the Project Arcade cabinet design, so heat should not be an issue. However, if you have used a different or altered plan, heat may be an issue. The faster computers get, the more they need good airflow for their fans to cycle the hot air out and cool air in. If your cabinet restricts airflow, for instance if it's essentially completely sealed, then you might want to consider uncasing your computer. It's unlikely that this will be a problem, however. In fact, you may be better off leaving the computer assembled because of the design of the airflow inside the case. I recommend leaving it in the case first, and measuring the temperature when it's been on for an hour or two. If you do have a heat problem, you might also consider installing a fan in the back door of the cabinet like the one shown in Figure 13-8.

Probably the most compelling reason to take your PC apart to mount it in the cabinet is a lack of space. If you're building a cocktail, countertop, or other oddly shaped cabinet that your computer won't fit in, then you have no choice. Some people in this situation have elected to have the computer sit next to or behind the arcade cabinet, but I would avoid that if you can — you lose some of the illusion that way. If you're building one of these space-limited cabinets, but haven't picked up your computer yet, search around for compact cases. Computer components have shrunk so much that manufacturers have been able to make extremely small packages for full-featured computers.

If none of the previous constraints apply to you, then I recommend leaving the computer in the case. The components will be protected from accidental damage, and the entire unit will be easier to remove for serious upgrades or replacement as compared to having to unmount multiple components from the cabinet. Still, I can't help thinking about how authentic it would look . . . .

FIGURE 13-8: A heavy-duty cooling fan from Happ Controls.
Used by permission of Happ Controls.

How to mount a disassembled PC

You should consider accessibility and safety when it comes time to mount a disassembled PC into a cabinet. If your cabinet has an opening front panel, then accessibility is a given. If it does not, you need to think about how you're going to access the computer's parts when needed. For instance, sooner or later you'll probably want to insert a CD into the CD-ROM drive. You'll need to do this if you're installing a new game, even if you have a virtual CD program (however, if you have a virtual CD program *and* network access, you can avoid using the cabinet's CD-ROM drive altogether). You could mount the CD-ROM drive near the back of the cabinet where the opening is (if you've followed the Project Arcade plans), or at the front of the cabinet so the CD can be inserted by opening the coin door. Make sure you allow enough room for the CD tray to fully open!

The placement of your motherboard guides the placement of the rest of the computer components. Hard drives, floppy drives, and CD-ROM drives all connect to the motherboard via ribbon cables of a limited length. This means, for instance, that you probably cannot mount the motherboard against the back wall of the cabinet and then expect to mount the CD-ROM drive at the front. I recommend the use of stand-off feet (see Figure 13-9) to mount the motherboard to the cabinet rather than screwing the motherboard directly to the wood. This will allow some airflow beneath the motherboard, and avoid potentially shorting the motherboard out if something metallic (such as a quarter or exposed screw) is underneath. This will also leave enough room for the brackets of the cards in the computer, which descend below the edge of the motherboard and otherwise would have to be bent.

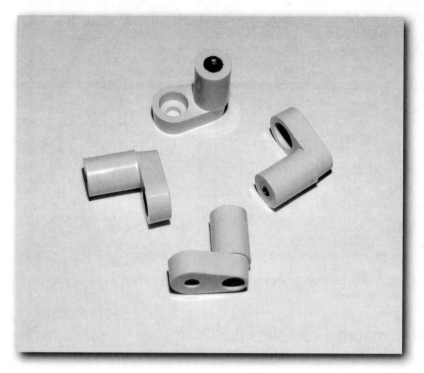

FIGURE 13-9: Circuit board mounting feet from Happ Controls.
Used by permission of Happ Controls.

I recommend mounting the motherboard vertically against the sides of the cabinet if possible instead of on the floor of the cabinet. That way, if something does fall, it's less likely to hit the computer parts and cause damage. The rest of the components can be mounted wherever they make sense, as they do not have exposed parts like the motherboard. All the various drives have mounting holes on the sides, and you can use their original mounting cages from the computer or angle brackets to mount them to the cabinet. Make sure to keep the underside of the drives raised off the wood for the same reasons as for the motherboard. Also, if you have a speaker or subwoofer in the cabinet, make sure to keep your hard drives away from it. Figure 13-10 shows a good example of mounting components in a cabinet.

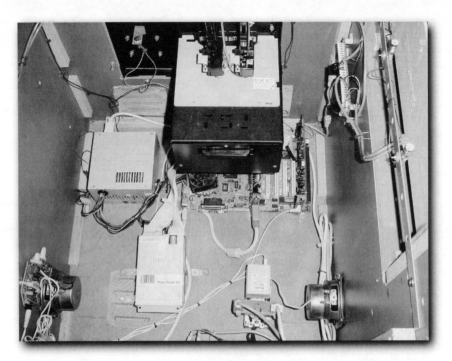

FIGURE **13-10:** Motherboard and components mounted directly inside a cocktail cabinet.
Photo courtesy of Oscar Controls.

How to mount a complete PC

Mounting a complete PC inside a cabinet is easy enough. Put it in place and forget about it, right? Well, almost. You should consider some precautions against the PC falling during rough game play or moving of the cabinet. A couple of shelf brackets will secure the PC nicely. I picked up ornamental shelf brackets from a local hardware store, and then padded them with felt to protect the finish of the computer. After double checking that the computer was far enough forward to reach when needed, but far enough back that the CD-ROM door could open, I positioned my brackets (see Figure 13-11). Note that you only need to screw the brackets into the wood, not into the case of the computer!

Special consideration — mounting USB ports

Remember when I talked about mounting external USB ports for things such as light guns or extra gamepads? This is a good time to tackle that. Now that you've got your PC secured in the cabinet, you can decide the best way to route the cables for your USB ports. The easiest way to do this is to take a pair of USB extension cables (with a type "A" plug and a type "A" receptacle), and route them from the computer to an easily accessible location. Some folks, for instance, run the extension cables to behind the coin door. Plugging in extra devices into the USB ports then requires opening the coin door. If you're only going to use the USB ports rarely, then a simple solution like this is probably best.

FIGURE 13-11: PC secured in cabinet.

However, if you expect to get frequent use out of your USB ports, then a permanently mounted solution is required. This is the route taken with the Project Arcade cabinet. Choose two spots at the front of the control panel box underneath the lip (approximately 10 inches from the corner is about right). Using a Dremel tool or router, cut out two rectangular openings the same size and shape as the receptacle end of the USB extension cables. Next, use a hot glue gun to seal the extension cables into their mounting holes (be careful not to get glue in the receptacle end itself). The USB extension cable from Happ Controls has mounting screw holes, so you don't need to use hot glue for those. The other end of the cables snakes through the grommet hole in the back of the control panel box and down to the computer. You now have easily accessible USB ports available on your arcade cabinet (see Figure 13-12)! When the USB ports are not being used, they are difficult to see because of the overhanging lip and will not detract from the appearance at all. Just be careful when you remove your control panel to disconnect the cables from the computer first!

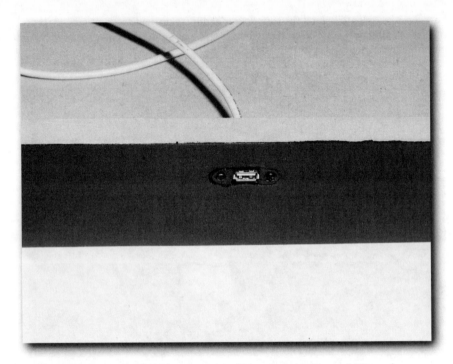

FIGURE **13-12: Happ Controls USB extension cable mounted in the control panel.**
Used by permission of Happ Controls.

Summary

"Igor! Igor, I'm ready now. Bring me the computer!"

"Sorry, doctor, I installed it while you were studying. See how nice a job I did? I'm particularly proud of the electrodes on the sides. I took them from that other project you were working on."

"But I'm the mad scientist. That was my job! I read all these books! I . . . . It does look very good, though. The electrodes are a nice touch. Oh, very well, Igor. How about a nice game of *Pac-Man?*"

Once again you've gone through a lot of material in this chapter. When all is said and done, you're able to almost completely disguise the fact that there's a computer running your arcade machine. Now, from the moment you start up to the moment you shut down, your arcade cabinet can look, sound, and feel like a real classic arcade machine!

Now that the cabinet has a computer in it, isn't it about time to install some games to play? I think so, and I'll tackle that in the next chapter!

Choosing and Loading Software

You've now got all the parts you need to achieve gaming Nirvana, including a personal arcade cabinet, custom arcade controls, an audio and video system, and a computer to run it all. It's time to invite some old friends over — friends like *Pac-Man*, *Frogger*, and *Centipede* — to play a few games and bring back some memories! Your cabinet will also let you make new friends, such as Sonic the Hedgehog and Ryu from *Street Fighter*. Broadly speaking, games for your arcade cabinet can be broken into three categories: emulators, commercial games, and shareware titles. In this chapter you'll discover some of the many wonderful games you can play on your new arcade cabinet and where you can go to find still more. Are you ready to play? It's time to get rewarded for all your hard work!

All About Emulators

For me this is how it all began: A long time ago, in a place far, far away (with apologies to George Lucas). . . I was randomly surfing the Internet when I came across a reference to something called MAME. Here was a program that claimed to allow you to play a real arcade game on your PC! I'd played arcade re-creations on the computer before and had been disappointed. They were okay, but they didn't live up to the original and didn't hold my interest long. A bit skeptically, I decided to give this a try. I downloaded it, installed it, and fired it up.

Wow!

First the screen went black. Then the program made funny images on the screen while the "arcade machine" on my computer booted up. There were flashes of familiar looking arcade characters and strange symbols and letters. Next a promising looking title screen appeared! The program made a familiar noise when I eagerly inserted my virtual quarter, and it beeped at me when I pressed player 1. Then, suddenly, there it was!

It had the same background music I remembered from the arcade original. It made the same sounds when I moved and fired. The tricks and strategies I used to use worked the same way—the game played exactly the same as I remembered. I had no doubts; this was the same game I had poured quarter after quarter into years ago! It was like the feeling a child gets the first time he visits Disney World, and I felt just like a kid again. This was arcade magic, and it was on my very own computer! A whole new yet old world had just opened up to me, and I was hooked!

You are very likely to have gotten involved in this wonderful hobby because at some point you also learned about emulators. Emulators allow you to play your favorite video games on your computer instead of on the arcade machine or video game system the game originally was designed for. For the most part, using an emulator requires more effort than simply buying a game and installing it. There are also some legal considerations of which you should be aware so you don't run afoul of copyright laws. In the next few sections I'll talk about these issues and point you down the path toward emulator happiness.

How does an emulator work?

Just about every video game, except the oldest such as *Pong*, works under similar principles. At the heart of the system is a microchip, a cousin to the CPU at the heart of your computer today. Connected to this microchip are various bits of electronic circuitry and other chips that control the audio, video, and game controllers. All of this together can collectively be referred to as the *game hardware* (see Figure 14-1). Additional chips give instructions to the hardware—draw a maze here, move a ghost there, fire a laser and make a laser beam sound. These sets of instructions, even though they are contained in a physical chip, are considered the game software. The combination of hardware and software is housed in a cabinet and becomes the video game you know as *Pac-Man* or *Asteroids*.

The cheapest computer you can purchase today has hundreds of times the power of the hardware used in classic video games. Is it possible to put the software from those video games into the computer and play them? Without emulation, the answer is no. The hardware in your computer is different from the hardware in those video games. They aren't physically interchangeable and they don't speak the same language. But all microchips are basically the same at the very core, aren't they? Ones and zeros, executing instructions and producing results, right? Well, yes, essentially. That leads to some interesting possibilities. What if you could write a program on a computer that would teach it to speak the language used by the hardware in those video games? Would it be able to play the video game software then? Enter the emulator!

An emulator is a program written to emulate, or imitate, hardware from a different system. The emulator receives instructions from the software designed for the original hardware and translates it into instructions that the current computer's hardware understands. No matter what hardware the original instructions were designed for, once it's translated to the computer's native hardware the results are the same. An image on the screen that looks like the original video game's image, with the same sounds and movement, is just as good as the original, right? Well, an arcade collecting enthusiast might dispute that. Emulation is *hard*. Just because it looks and sounds the same doesn't mean it's exactly the same. For instance, different hardware runs at different speeds. Not only do emulation programmers have to interpret the instructions from the emulated system correctly, they have to get the timing right as well. It might be arcade perfect, but if the ghosts in *Pac-Man* move so fast that they're a blur on the screen then it's not much of a game. Emulation programmers are pretty good at getting it very close to the original, but an arcade collector would probably insist there are minor differences. To the average person, however, if it looks like a duck and sounds like a duck, it must be a real video game!

FIGURE 14-1: Typical hardware from a classic arcade game.

By themselves, emulators will do nothing for you. Remember, an emulator mimics the *hardware* portion of the video game. To actually play a game, you also need to have the *software* that was used in the games. Because the software was actually encoded onto microchips (not a CD or floppy disc), it is commonly referred to as a ROM. ROM stands for Read Only Memory and usually refers to a microchip that has data encoded on it that cannot be altered. Microchips that can have their contents altered do exist, and video game software can be found on all kinds of microchips. Collectively they're all referred to in the community as ROMs. Obtaining ROMs is a subject entirely unto itself, and I'll talk about it at length in the section entitled "Are Emulators Legal? The Ethics and Laws behind Obtaining ROMs." As a rule, no emulators come with ROMs.

Emulation is an old trick in the computing industry, and many different kinds of emulators exist. You can find emulators for just about every classic computer there is, from the venerable Apple II to the obscure X68000. You can also find emulators for game consoles such as those from Atari, Nintendo, and Sega. In this chapter I'll stick to discussing emulators for arcade machines. If you'd like to learn more about other types of emulation, visit some of these Web sites:

- Retrogames at www.retrogames.com/
- Vintage Gaming Network at www.vg-network.com/
- Zophar's Domain at www.zophar.net/

Emulation tends to attract people of all ages and backgrounds. Some of them have an *interesting* sense of humor. Most of what you'll find will be rated PG, but you are also likely to encounter some strong language. Also, like almost every other form of media, sex made its way into the arcades. Without warning, you may stumble into a screenshot of an emulated arcade game featuring nudity. For the most part your Web surfing will be safe, but those who may be offended should take note that it's a wild, wild Internet out there and you may encounter anything.

Emulators you should try

You'll find many, many emulators if you start to poke around the Internet. I'll save you some time and highlight a few you should start with. By no means is this an extensive list, however. You'll find many links at the Web sites listed in the previous section if you want to experiment with others.

MAME

Although it is not the first emulator, the Multiple Arcade Machine Emulator, otherwise known as MAME, is by far the best known and most popular. MAME is the brainchild of Nicola Salmoria, a talented programmer from Italy. Nicola had been working on a variety of standalone emulators that each emulated a single arcade game. Then, in early 1997 he released MAME version 0.1, which supported five games in one package. History was made that day, as MAME continued to grow from its humble origin to become the giant project that it is today. As of the time of this writing, MAME supports 4000+ arcade games and is developed by a team of more than 100 volunteers.

MAME is first and foremost a documentation project. As time goes by, classic arcade games suffer from the ravages of age and begin to disappear. It can be difficult to find older arcade games in working condition, and many can no longer be found in any condition at all! The people who develop MAME share a love and fascination for arcade games and learn all they can about a particular game or aspect of video game design. They then contribute what they know and are able to learn to the MAME program, so that this information is recorded and preserved for the future. This is an important distinction that end users of MAME sometimes lose track of. The point of MAME is not to play games; the point is to preserve the games.

A game that worked in one version of MAME may not work in the next, as the developers discover that something in the game wasn't correctly emulated. It may have worked, but it wasn't faithful to the original and so needed to be fixed, even if fixing it made it unplayable for some reason (for instance, requiring a feature that hasn't been implemented yet). That may be frustrating to someone who simply wants to play the game, but rest assured the MAME developers will keep at it until the emulation is as perfect as they can get it and the game is working.

The obvious but very nice side effect of documenting the many arcade games in a program such as MAME is that it enables the average user to play those games. As mentioned previously, however, there are some very important legal considerations before you do so. I'll talk about that in the "Are Emulators Legal?" section as well. Playing games on MAME is simply amazing. Once a particular game's emulation has been perfected, the sights, sounds, and playability are virtually indistinguishable from the original. Often, the only things lacking are the real arcade controls and arcade cabinet, but since you're reading this book that won't be a problem for you! The list of games you can play in MAME is impossible to include here, but among the 4000+ games in the current version, just about any arcade game you remember can be found. What you won't find are recent games that are presumably still in the arcades making money. The MAME developers are very sensitive to the impact that MAME might have on the arcade manufacturers. MAME's goal is to preserve and document arcade machines, not put arcade machine operators out of business.

Many versions of MAME are available. The official home of MAME is www.mame.net/. There, you'll find the DOS and Windows command line versions of MAME. These are the versions that require you to type the name of the game you're going to play on the command line — for instance "mame centipede" — and are best used with a front-end program on an emulation cabinet. MAME is another open-source program. Ports of the official version of MAME can be found for many different computers and operating systems, even versions that run on digital cameras and on cell phones! Along with ports to different hardware and software platforms, derivatives of MAME exist. These are modified versions of MAME that add extra features, such as versions with built-in graphical user interfaces (GUIs). MAME is updated constantly and is at version 0.77 at the time of this writing. The ports and derivatives are also updated often to reflect new changes in MAME but sometimes lag behind by several versions.

MAME32 (www.classicgaming.com/mame32qa/) is the version of MAME recommended for a quick and easy start. It runs under Windows and includes a GUI. The GUI allows you to display your game choice by title or icon and also displays a screen shot, marquee, flyer, title screen, or cabinet image of the game you're selecting (see Figure 14-2).

On the CD MAME32 is included on the companion CD-ROM! Following the requirements of the MAME license, the source code is also included if you'd like to take a peek at what makes MAME tick.

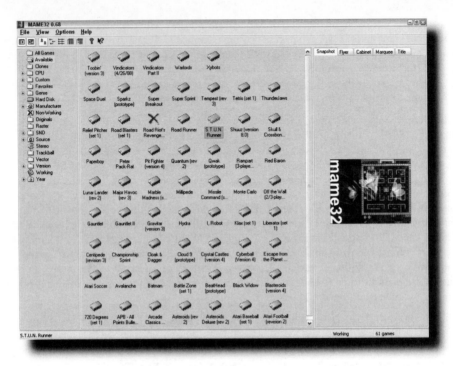

FIGURE 14-2: MAME32 displaying games by icon.

MAME32's GUI is controllable by keyboard, joystick, or mouse/trackball. I recommend using a trackball if you have one on your cabinet, as it will be the easiest. The interface can be configured in a variety of ways, such as turning off the folder list and the screen shot list, leaving you with a simple window showing icons of your available games. You can also change the background to a custom image as well as change the fonts and colors.

MAME32 allows you to categorize your game selection in some interesting ways, such as by genre, manufacturer, or by customized lists of favorite games. It also lets you configure the many options that MAME supports, such as configuring it to mimic the scanlines of an arcade monitor. Figure 14-3 shows you most of the options that can be configured easily with MAME32.

FIGURE 14-3: MAME32 configuration screens.

Some of the other versions of MAME you might be interested in for your arcade cabinet include the following:

- AdvanceMAME, available from `http://advancemame.sourceforge.net/`, is an unofficial version of MAME designed with extra support for television and arcade monitor displays. It is available for DOS, Windows, Linux, and MacOS among other operating systems.

- MAME Analog+, found at `www.urebelscum.speedhost.com/index.html`, is another unofficial version of MAME developed by a member of the arcade cabinet-building community. It specializes in tweaking MAME so it will support analog arcade controls that the original does not. Presently, this version's biggest claim to fame is the ability to have multiple mouse-based controls for different players (for instance, for a competitive game of Marble Madness). No other version of MAME supported this before it was added to Analog+.

- No Name MAME (`https://sourceforge.net/projects/noname/`) is another version of MAME developed by an arcade cabinet-building community member. Its goal is to take the best features of all the various MAME derivatives and to incorporate them into a single version.

If you'd like to learn more about MAME (and I recommend it as I've barely touched the surface here), there are several excellent sites for you to visit. Start, of course, at the home of MAME at www.mame.net/. Once you've explored there, stop off at MAMEWorld (www.mameworld.net/), which is by far the biggest MAME resource on the Internet. If you need help getting MAME set up and running properly, visit the easyEmu site at www.mameworld.net/easyemu/ (hosted by MAMEWorld). Finally, the alt.games.mame Usenet newsgroup (http://groups.google.com/groups?q=group:alt.games.mame) is a resource that should be on your list, but bear in mind my earlier caution about the wild nature of the Internet. The newsgroup can occasionally get a bit *frisky*.

Daphne

"Dragon's Lair—The fantasy adventure where you become a valiant knight . . ." Thus began a new chapter in arcade history and a new era of video gaming magic. *Dragon's Lair* was an *animated* laser disc–based video game in which you played the part of Dirk the Daring—a brave adventurer setting out to rescue princess Daphne from the clutches of the dragon's lair. It was a fully animated cartoon-style game that practically defined the term *eye candy*. Instead of pixelated graphics, you were treated to real animated movie sequences from the studios of Don Bluth, who is responsible for movies such as *Anastasia* and *The Secrets of NIMH*. This was the first of many popular laser disc–based video games that hit the arcades starting in the early 1980s.

Daphne (www.daphne-emu.com/) is an emulator, named after everyone's favorite princess from *Dragon's Lair*, that specializes in emulating laser disc–based video games. No home arcade cabinet is complete without a copy of Daphne running on it. Daphne has some hefty requirements, and you'll need a reasonably fast computer with Windows XP for best results, although Windows 98 will work. Versions are also available for Linux and MacOS.

Daphne will emulate *Dragon's Lair*, *Dragon's Lair II*, *Space Ace*, and a host of some 15 or so other laser-disc games. You will need to supply the laser-disc video files because they are copyrighted material and do not come with the emulator. You can obtain them either from the original laser discs from the video games (which will be difficult—check eBay at www.ebay.com/) or from re-creations of the games sold by Digital Leisure (recommended—www.digitalleisure.com/). Be sure to purchase the PC DVD-ROM version, not the CD-ROM version or the regular DVD version if you're buying them from Digital Leisure. The video files will be copied to your hard disk to run with the emulator. Daphne can also be connected to a laser disc player from an original arcade cabinet and be played straight off the original laser discs!

Note If you can obtain re-creations of the games for your PC, why would you want to run an emulator version instead? Two reasons come to mind. First, running them under the emulator will let you run multiple laser disc–based games under a single game interface. Second, having the video on your hard disk instead of the CD/DVD means you won't have to insert the CD/DVD each time you want to play.

Obtaining the video files and configuring Daphne can be fairly complicated but is well within the abilities of anyone who has built their own arcade cabinet! Be prepared to do a bit of reading at the Daphne homepage before you can get it working. Two utilities are available to help you. The first is dvd2daph, available from www.laserarchive.com/dvd2daph/. This utility will convert the video files from the DVD into the format required by Daphne as well as create the companion files needed. The second utility is Dirk (www.jaegertech.com/index.pl/dirk), a front-end program for configuring and running Daphne. Daphne also comes with its own front-end program to try or can be launched from a command line, making it compatible with other front-end programs such as those introduced in Chapter 13.

Although it can be frustrating to get Daphne running properly, once you've done so the reward is well worth it. Laser disc games represent a unique genre in video game history, ranking up there with *Pac-Man* and *Pong* as defining the lure of the arcade. The first time you see one of those games running on your cabinet will be another of those jaw-dropping moments that occur when you build your own arcade cabinet. To quote *Dragon's Lair*, "Lead on adventurer—your quest awaits!"

HanaHo's Capcom arcade emulators

HanaHo (www.hanaho.com/) is a company that has been involved in the arcade industry for many years, primarily making arcade cabinets, such as the Dragon's Lair cabinet, for video game companies. It also manufactures home-use arcade joysticks and cabinets that I'll introduce you to in Chapter 17, "Buying Your Way to Gaming Nirvana." When emulation started gaining momentum, HanaHo used its ties to the video game industry to embrace the concept and produced several emulation packages. The first of these was the Capcom Coin-Op Classics titles (see Figure 14-4). These packages are actually based on the MAME emulator but also include licensed copies of ROMs from video game manufacturer Capcom. The first package is only available when you purchase a HotRod joystick from HanaHo. It includes 14 Capcom titles including such hits as *1941*, *Street Fighter II*, and *Ghouls'N Ghosts*. A similar but larger collection is also available with their upright arcade cabinet kit.

FIGURE 14-4: Capcom Coin-Op Classics selection screen.
Used with permission of HanaHo Games.

HanaHo also has a series of Capcom emulation game packs that can be purchased without purchasing one of their joysticks or cabinets. The games are published by Selectsoft Publishing and can be found online and in retail stores. They come in packs of two or packs of five games each, available for between $6 for the two packs and $20 for the five packs. As a bonus, each collection includes a single game that will play on a Pocket PC PDA! The collections include the following:

- Capcom Arcade Hits Volume 1 — *Street Fighter* and *Street Fighter II Champion Edition*
- Capcom Arcade Hits Volume 2 — *1942* and *1943 Battle of Midway*
- Capcom Arcade Hits Volume 3 — *Commando* and *Gunsmoke*
- Capcom Coin-Op Collection Volume 1 — *1942*, *Commando*, *Sidearms*, *Vulgus*, and *Ghost'N Goblins*

These emulation packs come with an easy to use front end (see Figure 14-5) and support customizing controls, making them arcade cabinet friendly. HanaHo has plans for more emulation packs down the road. Visit the Build Your Own Arcade Controls (BYOAC) Web site (www.arcadecontrols.com/) for updates.

FIGURE **14-5:** Capcom Coin-Op Collection front end.

Other emulators to try

MAME, Daphne, and the HanaHo Capcom emulators cover most of the arcade games emulated to date. A few years ago there were many more emulators under active development, but most have been abandoned in favor of MAME. However, you might want to give some of the other emulators a try. Some of them may have interfaces that you might prefer over MAME, while others may be optimized for a select set of games that run faster than MAME. Remember that MAME is a documentation project designed to be portable to multiple platforms. Games drivers are programmed to be identical to the original and are programmed in C, which is very portable but not the fastest programming language. Other emulators do not operate under the constraints MAME places upon itself and so can use techniques that improve speed. For instance, they may be programmed in a language that is faster than that used in MAME but sacrifices portability, or they may program shortcuts that are not faithful to the original code but produce similar results. The following emulators are arcade cabinet friendly and support a good number of games:

- Raine (www.rainemu.com/) is an emulator that supports several hundred arcade games made in the late 1980s through the early 1990s. Raine is capable of running these games quite well on modest machines and will even run on old machines such as late-model 486 and early Pentium computers. Versions are available for DOS, Windows (with a graphical user interface), and Linux. Installation is easy—simply uncompress the downloaded package and place the ROMs you've legally obtained into the appropriate folder. If you need assistance, there is a message board at the Raine homepage. The EasyEmu Website (www.mameworld.net/easyemu/) also has a tutorial on installing and running Raine.

- Nebula (nebula.emulatronia.com/) is an emulator that runs Capcom and NeoGeo arcade games. It has a full screen GUI that looks like many standard front ends with screen shots on the right and a game list on the left. The background, colors, and sound are customizable as are the keys used to control the games, making it a good candidate for an arcade cabinet. Nebula runs games that are included in other emulators but has more modest system requirements. If your games are running slowly on your older computer, Nebula is a good emulator to try.

- Zinc (www.emuhype.com/) is another good emulator for arcade cabinets with older PCs. It runs a handful of arcade games from Sony and Namco whose hardware is based somewhat on the Sony Playstation. It is *not* a Sony PlayStation emulator. It is command line only but can be run with any customizable front end. Zinc supports customizing the keys used to control the games, making it easy to fit into your cabinet's controller scheme.

Visit Zophar's Domain (www.zophar.net/), Retrogames (www.retrogames.com/), or the Vintage Gaming Network (www.vg-network.com/) for more resources and information about emulators.

Are emulators legal? The ethics and laws behind obtaining ROMs

You're now entering a very sticky area in the arcade cabinet-building and emulation scene — the question of whether or not this whole thing is legal. What? How could building a personal arcade cabinet be illegal? Obviously it's not, but the emulation scene is not quite so clear. The question hinges on copyright laws. A full treatise on copyright law would be impossible to include here. There are people who spend their entire professional careers in just this area of the law. However, the situation can be summed up as follows: Copyright laws grant the owner of a work, such as a video game, the right to control when, how, and where that work is copied until the copyright expires. Until the copyright expires, no one may reproduce or copy the work unless given explicit permission to do so by the copyright holder. Copyrights expire anywhere from 50 to 100+ years after they are granted, depending on when the work was created and under what circumstances it was created — for video games, the period is typically 95 years. The first arcade game, *Computer Space*, was released more than 30 years ago in 1971, meaning every arcade game out there is clearly covered under a current copyright.

What does that mean to people interested in this hobby? It means you have to be careful about the software you install on your cabinet to make sure you are not in violation of copyright laws. Emulators seem to be okay. Unless they use copied portions of the programming code used in the original arcade machines, creating a program that acts the same as another program appears to be allowed. Notice I've used the words *seem* and *appears*. That's because there are some companies that claim that emulation is a violation of copyright laws. Nintendo, for instance, clearly states their position regarding emulation on their Web site's legal area (www.nintendo.com/corp/faqs/legal.html). In a nutshell, Nintendo's stance is that emulators are vehicles for piracy and are thus illegal. Sony is another company with a dim view of emulation. Two commercial emulators were created that mimicked the Sony PlayStation without Sony's permission. One was called Virtual Game Station by Connectix, and the other was called Bleem!. Sony took both companies to court for copyright and trademark violations. In both cases, Sony ultimately lost with the courts ruling that reverse engineering and emulation were fair and legitimate practices. Ultimately, market forces killed both of these emulators, with Connectix being purchased by Microsoft and the marketer of Bleem! simply shutting down operations.

So, although some manufacturers believe unauthorized emulation is illegal, the courts have so far ruled otherwise. Since the Sony PlayStation cases a few years ago, I am not aware of any further legal action involving emulators. It is possible that this situation might change someday, but I believe the precedent has been firmly set. ROMs, however, are another matter. Unlike emulators, which are original works of programming, ROMs are copied directly from the video games. They are not reverse engineered nor are they original works (usually); they are simply direct copies. That's clearly illegal, right? Not necessarily, and I'll explain the details in the next few sections.

Note

Keep in mind one thing: IANAL. IANAL is Internet-speak for "I am not a lawyer" and means that the information here should not be considered as legal advice. This section should only be taken as my personal understanding of copyright law. My opinion is based on several years of being involved in the retro gaming community and observations of the statements of gaming companies, along with the few legal actions that have occurred such as the Sony versus Bleem! case. I am fairly certain my understanding is accurate, but bear in mind that it is only an opinion, albeit an informed one.

The white area—when you're clearly legal

The only way you can be certain that you are obeying copyright laws is when you have obtained a ROM through a legally authorized source. Until recently, this meant the ability to obtain verifiably legal ROMs was severely limited. Although emulation and reverse engineering seem to have withstood legal challenges in court, most arcade manufacturers view emulators as competitive to their own products at best and illegal at worst. No matter what their viewpoint, it seemed no manufacturer saw any profit in allowing ROMs to be purchased alone.

Arcade manufacturers did see profit in the retro gaming craze, however. Several titles produced by the manufacturers for the PC market were actually based on emulation. You've already read about one, the HanaHo Capcom game packs. These were either sold by the copyright holders or by companies who had obtained licenses from the copyright holders to do so. People purchasing these games were purchasing the right to run those ROMs on their computers, *using the emulator sold by the copyright holder.* The important distinction to note is that although the copyright holders were selling the right to play the game as a whole, they were not selling ROMs to be used however purchasers saw fit, such as with MAME.

Although manufacturers had begun to realize the potential of selling arcade games to the PC market, very few were made available. Thousands of arcade games were made, and only a very small percentage were translated and sold for the PC. Naturally, if there is a demand, a way will be found to fill it, and emulators filled the void left by arcade manufacturers. Unfortunately, although the emulators themselves were legal, for a long time there was almost no way for most people to legally obtain the ROMs to play in them. Two ROMs were made legally available, as the copyright holders announced their support for MAME and granted the public the right to use the ROMs in MAME for noncommercial purposes. These two games were *Gridlee,* © 1983 Videa, and *Robby Roto,* © 1999 Jay Fenton. A third ROM that appears to be free from copyright restrictions is *Poly-Play,* © 1985 VEB Polytechnik Karl-Marx-Stadt. This was an East German company that disappeared when the wall came down. Normally copyrights are passed on to another party when the original copyright holder no longer exists, but in this case, with the entire state and legal system disappearing, the copyright does not appear to exist anymore. These three ROMs can be downloaded from the MAME Web site at www.mame.net/.

Other than those three ROMs, no other legal ROMs were made freely available for a long time. Those running other ROMs on their emulators were most likely doing so without the consent of the copyright holder. The copyright holders were either unaware or did not believe pursuing the copyright violations was a good business practice. After all, these games were many years old (20+ years in some cases) and had stopped making them money long ago. Those who were committing copyright violations by using these old ROMs were the same people who were buying their new PlayStation, Dreamcast, and PC game titles. Alienating them by pursuing legal action against them would not help and might hurt their bottom line. Other manufacturers vigorously protected their copyrights, primarily by sending cease and desist letters to Web sites making ROMs available for download and threatening legal action. Even though *Pac-Man* and *Donkey Kong* came out in the early 1980s, the *Pac-Man* and *Donkey Kong* franchises continue to thrive to this day, with new games in the series coming out every few years. Protecting their copyrights appeared to make good business sense to these manufacturers, and generally a letter was enough to make the copyright violations stop. To my knowledge, no one has been sued or prosecuted for distributing or possessing ROMs, because anyone who did receive such a letter complied with the company's legal right to protect their intellectual property and removed the ROMs in question. So, in general, the ROM situation was a murky mess.

Then in 2003, a company called StarROMs (www.starroms.com/) set up shop. They negotiated the rights with Atari to sell some of Atari's ROMs for use with emulation. Suddenly, there was a legal source to purchase ROMs! Currently StarROMs has 61 titles from Atari available at a price of around $2 each. This was exactly what the emulation community had been demanding for years! At the time of this writing, it's too early to tell if this will prove to be a viable business model for the industry. Hopefully the emulation community will embrace this source of legal ROMs and make it a success. Personally, I purchased every ROM available from StarROMs the day they opened. Those are the ROMs you see in the screen shot of MAME32 earlier in this chapter.

That is the state of legally obtaining ROMs for use with emulators today — a few ROMs available for free and a small but promising handful available for sale. Hopefully, other copyright holders will see the success of this business model and follow suit with their arcade game ROMs as well. Time will tell.

The grey area — ROMs you own in other media

Aside from the white area in which clearly legal ROMs are available, there's a grey area in which ROMs *might* be legal for use on your emulators. The question is one that has not been tested in court and has not been clearly defined as it applies to ROMs and emulation: *If you have purchased the ROMs in some other format, do you then have the legal right to use them on your computer with an emulator?* The answer to this has broad implications for the emulation community. Many ROMs can be purchased in the form of packaged emulation-based games, such as the Capcom titles from HanaHo. Does that give you the right to use those ROMs with MAME? What if you own an original arcade game, including the ROMs inside it. Can you use copies of those ROMs on your computer? What if you own just the circuit board from the game with nonworking ROMs from a cabinet that has been destroyed? Other interesting situations come to question, such as if you purchase an emulation-based program designed to run on a game console like the Sony PlayStation. The PlayStation disc has copies of the original ROMs from the arcade game on it. Does owning that disc allow you to have a copy of those ROMs on your computer even though it's for a totally different system? What about copying the video files off DVD-ROMs that you've purchased to use with the Daphne emulator? Unfortunately I can't give you a definitive answer to all these questions, but I can draw some parallels for you to consider.

I think that a very similar situation presented itself with the debut of cassette tapes and VCRs. Copyright holders objected that these devices would be used for piracy and would lead to the demise of their industries. Legal battles were waged, and the courts ruled otherwise. You are allowed to make a cassette tape copy of a CD you own for your own personal use, for instance to play in the car. You are allowed to record a television show on a VCR and play it back at a time more convenient for you (a concept known as time-shifting). A similar objection arose with the advent of recordable CDs and DVDs. Manufacturers were concerned once again about piracy. Consumers demanded the right to record their own material and make backups of their legally purchased software in case the original was destroyed. Once again it was determined that it was in the public's best interest to allow this use. You are allowed to make a single archival backup of digital material such as a CD-ROM game to keep for your own use in case the original is damaged. Could these court decisions legitimizing these rights to legally copy material be applied to ROMs? If I purchase a CD-ROM of music then I can use it in my car's cassette player. If I purchase a commercial emulation package or a circuit board with ROMs from an arcade game, can I use those ROMs on my computer with MAME? It would seem to me like a similar situation, but there is no court precedent that I'm aware of that answers the question. (In recent years, a law arose that put emulators themselves into some legal question. More on that after we cover copy protection.)

Note Far from bringing about the demise of those industries, cassette tapes and VCRs actually helped the industries profit. For instance, many movies make much more money from sales of VCR tapes and DVDs than from the theater releases.

To be fair to the manufacturers, piracy is a big problem in this and many other countries. How much revenue is lost depends on who you ask, but there is no doubt that there is a significant amount of illegally copied material floating around out there. Some manufacturers came up with techniques to prevent copying of their software, methods that made copies useless. Techniques and products were then developed that circumvented those copy protection schemes. New copy protection schemes were then invented. This went on back and forth for many years. Then a law was passed called the DMCA, the Digital Millennium Copyright Act, that made it illegal to circumvent copy protection schemes built into digital material. This may have a possible impact on emulators. Many arcade game ROMs were encrypted (a form of copy protection) to prevent unscrupulous manufacturers from making bootleg copies of their arcade games. For instance, a bootleg version of *Donkey Kong* (which did not have encrypted ROMs) was created called *Crazy Kong*. Bootleg copies of arcade games became a serious problem in the arcade industry until encryption was used. The problem this made for emulators was that to run encrypted games, the programmers had to break the encryption used in those games! Breaking encryption is a method of circumventing copy protection, which now appeared to be against the law!

So, is it legal for you to use ROMs you've obtained from other media on your computer with an emulator? Obviously I cannot give you a clearcut answer because the matter has not been addressed by the courts. I personally own a *Crystal Castles* arcade game made by Atari, but I also purchased the ROM from StarROMs when it became available.

Also, I must once again remind you that I am not a lawyer and this is not legal advice. It will be very interesting to see if this ever does go to court. I suspect that the market demand will cause manufacturers to realize that there is profit to be made, and more vendors will follow the lead of Atari and Capcom — making the matter moot. It will be up to us to support them if and when they do so!

The black area — ROMs you do not own

This brings up the final matter to consider in regard to ROMs — circumstances under which it is clearly illegal to obtain and use a copy of a ROM. Simply put, if it doesn't fit into either of the previous two scenarios, it's probably illegal. A common myth on the Internet is that you are allowed to download and play a ROM that you do not own, so long as you delete the ROM within 24 hours. This is a fallacy. There is no such provision for a 24-hour grace period within any copyright laws that I'm aware of. If you don't own it and aren't purchasing it, you have no legal right to obtain it (with the obvious exception of ROMs whose copyright holders have given permission to do so).

This leaves the majority of arcade games unobtainable by legal means. There are several thousand arcade games that have been made. Even allowing for use of ROMs that are available in different media and those that can be purchased, the average consumer can hope to have a few hundred legal ROMs at best. What about the rest of the games? A commonly stated opinion goes something like this: *The manufacturers no longer make money off this copyrighted material (the ROM) but are refusing to allow me a legal means to purchase it. Therefore, I am justified in illegally obtaining a copy of it for my own personal use so long as I do not profit from its use. If they gave me an alternative, I would use it, but they have not so it is their own fault.* The point to realize is that that is an entirely moral argument. Should the manufacturers give you a means to use their copyrighted ROMs? Do the copyright laws extend too long? I have an opinion but it really isn't pertinent. The law is clear that copying material under a copyright without the copyright holder's permission is not permitted. Using ROMs you have not legally obtained is a violation of copyright laws and should not be done on those grounds alone.

Commercial Arcade Software

Many people build an arcade cabinet strictly to run emulation software and overlook a wide selection of other great titles that should be considered. Any game that has an arcade theme and does not require typing is a likely candidate. There are some genres that simply won't work well in an arcade cabinet. First-person shooters such as *Doom* and strategy games such as *Myst* probably aren't the best choice. That still leaves many games to consider. Many of these games are older and may be difficult to find on store shelves. However, they are easily (and often cheaply) found online and at used game stores such as Game Stop (www.gamestop.com/).

Microsoft's arcade series

Microsoft produced a series of hit arcade titles in cooperation with Atari and Namco that were among the first to bring an authentic arcade experience to PC users. The first title was *Microsoft Arcade*, which came with five Atari titles: *Centipede, Asteroids, Missile Command, Tempest,* and *Battle Zone.* The next title was *Revenge of Arcade*, which included 5 Namco arcade titles: *Motos, Ms. Pac-Man, Xevious, Rally-X,* and *Mappy.* Finding these two titles at retail stores is difficult, but they are readily available on eBay costing between $10 and $20. The last title, *Return of Arcade Anniversary Edition,* can still be easily found and includes five Namco games: *Pac-Man, Ms. Pac-Man, Dig Dug, Pole Position,* and *Galaxian.*

Games from all of these titles were big hits in the arcades and will make an excellent addition to your arcade cabinet. These titles all have extremely modest system requirements and are designed to run with keyboard controls, meaning they'll work well with keyboard-hacked arcade controls. Sound and game play are authentic, although the windowed mode may be a bit distracting.

On the CD A trial version of Microsoft's *Return of Arcade Anniversary Edition* featuring *Pac-Man* only is available and is included on the companion CD-ROM!

Atari's arcade titles

Atari has taken a long, somewhat strange trip through the years. Virtually synonymous with the term *arcade*, the Atari company has been split, has been bought and sold many times, and has finally been purchased by Infogrames (www.atari.com/). The company known as Atari today bears little resemblance to the classic Atari company that produced so many excellent arcade video games, but it remains committed to the home game playing market. As the company went through its changes they produced many titles for home use that are still available today. The first set of titles are those published under the Infogrames/Hasbro/Atari umbrella as shown in Figure 14-6.

FIGURE 14-6: A collection of Atari arcade titles.

Titles ™ or ® and courtesy of Atari Interactive, Inc. © 2004 Atari Interactive, Inc. All rights reserved. Used with permission.

Some of the titles are compilations that are re-creations of original games, and some are sequels to original titles with enhanced game play and graphics. Available titles include the following.

Atari arcade compilations

Atari produced several compilations of arcade titles for the PC. This includes *Atari Arcade Hits* Volume 1 and 2, with six games each, and the *Atari Anniversary Edition* comprising all the material from the previous two CDs. Games in these packages include *Tempest, Missile Command, Super Breakout, Asteroids, Centipede, Pong, Asteroids Deluxe, Battlezone, Crystal Castles, Gravitar, Millipede,* and *Warlords*. Gameplay on these titles is amazingly faithful to the original considering they were not emulation projects, but also includes an enhanced mode. For instance, you can choose to play *Tempest*, or the enhanced mode which gives you *Tempest Tubes*—the same game play with a new set of screens to conquer. The CDs come with a host of very nice extra features, including desktop themes, and features the Atari Archive. The archive has images from Atari history and video clips of interviews with Atari founder Nolan Bushnell. The extra material is what distinguishes this from running an emulated version of the game and makes good "eye candy" dressing for your cabinet's desktop and screen savers. The CD is packaged with a nice graphical interface (Figure 14-7), but the games and archive material are also individual applications, meaning you could launch them with your own front end. The Anniversary Edition version installs completely to the hard drive and does not require the CD, making it particularly arcade cabinet friendly.

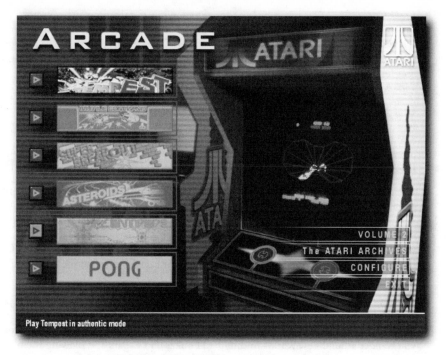

FIGURE 14-7: *Atari Anniversary Edition*—Volume 1 opening screen.

Atari remakes

In addition to packaging reproductions of original Atari arcade classics, Atari/Infogrames also produced a series of remakes for their titles. These are games whose basic premise is the same as the original but with enhanced 3D graphics bearing little resemblance to the original. They also feature enhanced game play with new strategies, enemies, power-ups and the like, with new story lines to complement the new features. As a rule these games are all fun to play but are more complicated than the classics from which they derive. These titles are not designed with arcade cabinets in mind, and though they can be made to work, you will need to add support for extra keys (such as Enter and Esc). Players looking for the original titles will not find them here. Players looking for something new to try will find much to tempt them here. Atari, under the guise of Infogrames, also produced remakes of arcade classics from other manufacturers such as Namco and Konami. I have included all the arcade classic remakes under this section. They are all available online or in retail stores.

- *Asteroids* — *Asteroids* is a remake of an Atari title that was created by Activision. Game play is faithful to the original, with enhanced graphics and sound being the most notable differences. Choices of different ships with different characteristics, new enemies, and new weapons round out the enhancements to this classic title.

- *Break Out* — *Break Out* is a sequel to the original popular game in which you paddle a ball against a stack of bricks, knocking the bricks off one by one until they are all gone. It's now a traditional tale of paddle meets girl, paddle loses girl to evil paddle and gets thrown in jail, paddle has to break out of jail and rescue girl. After spending a few minutes learning the controls (which are customizable), I gave it a test and quickly became addicted. I was pleasantly surprised at how much I enjoyed the game.

- *Centipede* — In classic mode, you play a somewhat familiar game of *Centipede* except the screen and graphics have been converted to 3D graphics mode. Game play is otherwise essentially the same as the classic. In adventure mode you play out a story line in a 3D interactive world. Roaming through each level, your job is to shoot the invading centipedes and a whole host of new bugs while saving houses and citizens of your world.

- *Combat* — *Combat* is an interesting adaptation. Originally, *Combat* was a two-player tank game for the Atari 2600 home game console. Every Atari 2600 shipped with *Combat*, and you're likely familiar with the name. This version has had the usual enhancements made, with 3D graphics and interactive worlds. Your tank is actually a hovercraft, and your object, like in the classic, is to shoot or be shot. The unusual thing about this CD is it comes with an unannounced Atari 2600 emulator called Stella and includes the Atari 2600 ROMs for *Combat* and *Combat2*.

- *Dig Dug Deeper* — This remake is particularly well done, enhancing the original with 3D graphics and extra eye candy while remaining remarkably faithful to the original. Unlike some of the others, game play is almost exactly the same as the original. As Dig Dug, you wander around new worlds finding bad Pookas and Fygars and blowing them up (literally) with your inflating pump or dropping rocks on their heads. New power-ups and different types of rocks, such as ones that explode, enhance game play and distinguish it from the classic without deviating so far as to make it an entirely different game.

- *Frogger* — The new *Frogger* and the sequel *Frogger 2*, from Konami and Infogrames, are another set of sequels worthy of their originals. Basic game play is similar to the original, yet enhanced with many different levels and multiplayer fun. The controls are simple enough to function well with an arcade cabinet, although you will still need an Enter and Esc key.

- *Galaga* — The remake of *Galaga* starts out faithful to the original with enhanced graphics but quickly moves on to advanced levels with a heads-on display and 360 degrees of movement. Controls are more sophisticated than the original but are still within the capabilities of an arcade cabinet's control panel.

- *Missile Command* — *Missile Command* is another well-done enhancement of the original. The graphics are stunning, and game play is true to the spirit of the original. The first wave starts out at a moderate pace, then the game quickly advances to faster and harder levels that will leave you gasping for air. Controls are well suited for an arcade cabinet.

- *Pac-Man* series — Infogrames and Namco have released three titles in this series: *Pac-Man All-Stars*, *Ms. Pac-Man Quest for the Golden Maze*, and *Pac-Man Adventures in Time*. They can be purchased separately or in a combination pack. All three are delightful additions to the franchise, sporting updated 3D enhanced game play while sticking primarily to their original roots. Most of them can be played with a single joystick, with two additional buttons needed for *Adventure in Time*. The graphics are good, the game play is good, and these make fun additions to an arcade cabinet.

- *Pong* — *Pong* is a game you won't find emulated, as there are no microchips in the original *Pong* to emulate. *Pong* was designed with good old-fashioned electronic circuitry. This version is similar to the original in that you have a paddle knocking a ball toward an opponent, but the similarity ends there. The graphics are much enhanced from the original, the sound effects are fun, and it has penguins. How can you go wrong with a game that has penguins? Simple yet addictive game play and basic controls make this a good candidate for an arcade cabinet.

- *Q*bert* — This game is another extremely well done upgrade to the original. It features a classic mode that is obviously a re-creation and not emulation but is so close to the original that the minor differences do not detract at all. The enhanced playing modes include mazes that are much more geometrically disorienting, as they are rendered in 3D with depth instead of flat 2D, but that only adds to the fun of the game play. Simple controls make this a good choice for an arcade cabinet, but like the original you'll need a joystick mounted diagonally instead of square.

- *Warlords* — I have to confess that I was never a fan of *Warlords* in the arcade. Nonetheless, the game play in classic mode on this remake is faithful to that original and fans will be happy with it. The enhanced mode, however, made a believer out of me. Beautiful graphics, with flying dragons and fiery fireballs (is that redundant?) menacing you while ominous music plays in the background, make Warlords a good addition for anyone who has spinner controls on their arcade cabinet.

All of the Atari branded remakes are fun games to have and play. Some of them, such as *Dig Dug*, *Q*bert*, and *Warlords*, are very faithful to the original classics. Others such as *Break Out* and *Pong* are good games in their own right but not terribly close to the original. One title worth mentioning that isn't from Atari comes from an arcade company called Midway:

- *Midway Presents Arcade's Greatest Hits 2* — Midway and GT Interactive collaborated to produce a collection of arcade authentic titles for the PC. Titles include *Blaster*, *Joust 2*, *Splat*, *BurgerTime*, *Moon Patrol*, *Root Beer Tapper*, and *Spy Hunter*. These titles are faithful re-creations of the originals, and the keys are configurable, making it a good addition to a cabinet. Unfortunately, this title is out of print, but you can still find it on eBay and used gaming stores. If you can find a copy it's well worth your while to pick it up.

Digital Leisure's laser disc arcade games

One final genre of arcade classic remakes is brought to us by Digital Leisure (www.digital leisure.com/), a company you were introduced to earlier in this chapter. Digital Leisure specializes in PC ports of laser disc arcade games. All of them feature incredible graphics (see a shot from *Dragon's Lair* in Figure 14-8), with game play virtually identical to the original.

FIGURE **14-8: Dirk hides from the dragon in** *Dragon's Lair.*
Photo courtesy of Digital Leisure, Inc.

Games available from Digital Leisure include the following:

- *Dragon's Lair* — The original classic from Don Bluth studios that set the bar for all laser disc games that followed. Take the part of Dirk the Daring as you try to rescue Princess Daphne from the clutches of the evil dragon Singe! If you pick up no other laser disc title for your cabinet, pick up this one.

- *Dragon's Lair II* — Happily ever after doesn't last long for Dirk and Daphne, as the evil wizard Mordroc kidnaps Daphne, leaving Dirk no choice but to rescue her again. This is an excellent follow-up to the first game.

- *Space Ace* — Following on the success of *Dragon's Lair*, *Space Ace* is another title from the creative forces of Don Bluth studios. In this title you play Ace, who must rescue his girlfriend Kimberley from the clutches of the evil commander Borf!

- *Hologram Time Traveler* — Originally a title in the arcades that used a new technology to display 3D images without requiring 3D glasses, this title has been ported to the PC by Digital Leisure (albeit requiring glasses this time). In this game, you play Marshall Gram, the daring adventurer who must travel through time to rescue Princess Kyi-La from the evil scientist Vulcor! Are you noticing a trend here? When do the princesses get to rescue the men? At any rate, this was another smash arcade hit that has been brought to the PC.

- *Mad Dog McCree I and II* — These titles are laser disc–based shooting games that were very popular in the arcades. Ported to the PC, these games are compatible with the Act-Labs USB light gun. Play the hero and rescue the town sheriff (yes, and his daughter too) from the wicked Mad Dog McCree. Do you have what it takes?

Other titles from Digital Leisure are also available, though the previous listed titles are the most popular arcade conversions. They carry several other shooting titles, all compatible with the Act-Labs light guns. The games often come in both CD-ROM and DVD-ROM formats, with fans typically preferring the DVD-ROM versions. Most arcade cabinet builders will pick up *Dragon's Lair*, *Dragon's Lair II*, and *Space Ace* as the most popular titles of the genre. Digital Leisure conveniently has a collection of these three games available.

Shareware and Other Great Games

Gaming in modern day times centers around incredible 3D graphics and 3D interactive worlds. Many of these games are a lot of fun, but sometimes not enough attention is paid to good old-fashioned game play. Somewhere between the arcade classics of yesterday and the 3D immersive gaming worlds of today lies a collection of freeware and inexpensive shareware games with incredible game play produced by classic gaming fans. Some of these games will make great additions to your arcade cabinet! You can find these games at a variety of places on the Internet. I'll list some of the places you can look for such games as recommended by members of the Build Your Own Arcade Controls (BYOAC) Web site. You can always find the most up-to-date list on the arcade games page at www.arcadecontrols.com/arcade_games.shtml.

One interesting possibility if you have an arcade cabinet with online Internet access is the Shockwave Online Arcade Classics (www.shockwave.com/sw/actiongames/arcade_classics/) page. There are ten titles online: *Defender*, *Defender II*, *Spy Hunter*, *Rampage*, *Joust*, *Root Beer Tapper*, *Robotron*, *Sinistar*, *Bubbles*, and *Satan's Hollow*. These games were developed for the Shockwave folks by the programming team of Digital Eclipse (www.digitaleclipse.com/), who is responsible for many arcade classic recreations and emulations. These games are free to play.

Other places to try:

- **Epic Games** (www.epicgames.com/) is the maker of games such as *Jazz Jackrabbit* currently available from Epic Classics (www.epicclassics.com/). *Jazz Jackrabbit* is an old favorite that gets plenty of play time on the Project Arcade cabinet. It's a game similar to *Sonic the Hedgehog*, where Jazz Jackrabbit runs lickety split around various worlds fighting evil turtles, jumping, shooting, and flying around.

- **PoMPoM Games** (www.pompom.org.uk/index.htm) has *Mutant Storm,* a title that is a popular hit among the arcade cabinet crowd.

- **MegaGames** (www.megagames.com/) lists a *huge* collection of freeware games to try.

- **Armegatron** (http://armagetron.sourceforge.net/tron.html) is a *Tron* lightcycle clone featuring single and networked multiplayer action with configurable controls.

- **Classic Game Remakes** (www.classic-game-remakes.com/) maintains a list of popular freeware remakes of classic arcade, console, and computer games.

- Finally, don't forget the power of Google (www.google.com/). A search for "freeware PC arcade games" will lead you to hours of possible games to try!

Many people will discount freeware or shareware games as not being worth the effort. Those people are clearly missing the mark. Some of the best game companies started out producing freeware and shareware games, and many talented programmers continue that tradition today. There are many gems waiting out there for you to find!

Summary

Emulation is probably the most compelling reason to have a personal arcade machine. There's nothing quite like playing a real arcade game inside a real arcade cabinet. Although there are thousands of possible games that can be played this way, at present legal issues only make playing a small percentage feasible. Other games fill the gap, including commercial arcade titles patterned after classic arcade games. Some of them are extremely well done, such as *Dig Dug Deeper* and *Q*Bert*, while others are fun but substantially different from the originals. Finally, sometimes overlooked are the wealth of excellent games available as freeware or shareware titles.

Though it might not seem like it, you've reached a challenging point in the creation of your arcade cabinet. Many people get to the point where games are playable and stay there for months enjoying the fruits of their labor. That's okay, but you're not quite finished yet! Coming up in the next chapter, I'll talk about the various things you can do to dress up and finish off your cabinet. It's okay if you want to run another game of *Pac-Man* first though, I'll wait!

Buttoning Up the Odds and Ends

I n reaching this chapter you've come to a bit of a crossroads. If you've been following along, your cabinet or controller project is built and playable. You can stop here, and many people do just that. Some people stop temporarily to enjoy the fruit of their labors, and for some this is about as far as they'll go.

I really encourage you to keep at it, though. With just a few more steps, you can move from a good project to a great one, with lighting, artwork, protective covering, a working coin door — in short, all the things that make a real arcade machine! Those are some of the subjects I'll be covering in this chapter. I thoroughly enjoyed writing this chapter — this part is going to be fun!

Decorating the Cabinet

You can decorate your cabinet in many different ways, from the simple to the incredibly complex. Chapter 18, "Online Places to Go," has some examples of cabinets with very nice artwork you may wish to look at while you read this chapter. In this section I'll take a look at the various parts of the cabinet that are typically decorated and how you might go about decorating them.

Artwork philosophies

You should take a moment to stop and think about the artwork you want for your cabinet. Is your cabinet going to have a specific theme, such as re-creating a particular classic arcade cabinet? Are you going for an overall montage look, reminding people of all the classics from the past and present? Maybe you'd be happy with a theme from a particular genre, such as a fighter-themed cabinet (a popular choice among fans of recent arcade titles). Or, perhaps you don't have a particular theme in mind at all and just want something that looks nice? Keep these thoughts in mind as you read the rest of this section.

Something to consider, no matter what theme (or lack thereof) you choose, is the cabinet as a whole and not just as individual sections. A color-coordinated cabinet with matching joystick and button colors can look very appealing. A cabinet with individual pieces that don't match probably won't have the impact you hope for. Consider a cabinet with a particular classic arcade machine theme. A marquee associated with the character's name (for example, "PacMAMEA"), related graphics on the side, and controls with a matching color theme will tie the cabinet together nicely. Would that cabinet be as appealing with unrelated artwork on the marquee, side, and control panel? You'll notice I don't declare anything right or wrong here — once again, it's a personal opinion and yours is the only opinion that ultimately matters (unless you have to face the spouse test)!

Typically the best looking cabinets fall into one of two categories. For those in the first, a particular arcade theme is chosen and followed as the cabinet is decorated. Characters from the original games and their color schemes adorn the cabinet. The second set of cabinets tend to have a more abstract look, usually with minimal character graphics or no character graphics at all. Color choices for the controls, overlay, paint and t-molding tie the cabinet together. Both types of cabinets can look very nice.

Finding artwork

Finding artwork for your cabinet is not difficult at all. There are many resources at a range of budgets available to you. From rolling your own to having something custom designed and printed for you, I'll cover the options in the next few sections.

The forums

A great place for you to start is the artwork forum of the Build Your Own Arcade Controls (BYOAC) Web site at www.arcadecontrols.com/. Whether you're creating your own and need technical assistance and feedback or you're looking for help getting artwork for your cabinet, this forum is a great place to visit.

For those of you who are creating your own artwork, you'll find valuable tips and helpful folks to aid you. I'm frequently amazed, not only at the caliber of talent that is exhibited on this forum, but also at the willingness of people to share their expertise with others. It's not unheard of for one person to post a message indicating they're looking for help making a particular kind of graphic for their cabinet, only to have someone else volunteer to make it for them shortly thereafter! Please do not enter the forum expecting someone to do that every time, however; such offers are gifts of time and talent and shouldn't be taken for granted. It's also fairly common to see someone present a work in progress and then receive constructive criticism that ultimately makes the work better.

You can also find people on the forum who are willing to take on custom work for you under a private arrangement such as for a fee or trade. Again, however, most people do so as a sideline, so patience and politeness are the keywords of the day. The artwork you'll see later in this chapter on the Project Arcade cabinet was created by one such individual and turned out great! Whatever level of assistance you're looking for, the artwork forum is a good stop.

Making your own

Making your own artwork for your cabinet can be as fun and rewarding as building the rest of the cabinet itself. You can either start completely from scratch or find pre-existing artwork and modify it for your purposes. Both choices can turn out looking great! Success depends on knowing what your ultimate goal is before you begin and selecting your tools and settings appropriately.

Raster versus vector

Before you begin, you should understand the difference between *raster*-based graphics, and *vector*-based graphics. A raster-based graphic, such as the JPEG files included on the CD for all the photos in the book, is composed of tiny dots, or pixels. For instance, a simple square might consist of a ten-dot by ten-dot grid of red pixels that produces a red square. If a set of red and black alternating squares form a game board, it would consist of a large collection of different-colored pixels arranged in a manner to produce the game board.

A vector-based graphic on the other hand is composed of a series of mathematically described lines that form shapes. For instance, that simple ten-by-ten dot square might be described as follows: *Start here. Draw a line to the second corner, then the third, then the fourth, and finally back to the first corner. The shape created is colored red.* The specific mathematical formula used is likely different than the simple way I've described it here, of course, but the basic principle applies. Instead of laying the image out bit by bit, the image is described. The computer knows how to turn the image description into the square you see on the screen and displays the square for you. This square is a single shape in the image. For the game board, each square is an additional shape, so a simple two-by-two board would consist of four described shapes.

Why is the difference between raster and vector images important? Choosing one graphic type over the other makes a difference when it comes to *scaling*. Scaling is the process of making a graphic image bigger or smaller than the original. Scaling an image is problematic for raster graphics and is where vector graphics shine. When you make a raster image larger or smaller, you have to add or remove pixels to the image respectively. A 10-by-10 square that is expanded to a 20-by-20 square is now missing 10 pixels per row that have to be filled in. For a single-colored square that's easy enough, but what about an image with angles, curves, or different colors? How do you know which pixels to add or remove and in what color? The computer will make an educated guess for you based on what the nearby pixels look like. However, no matter how good the program is, when you expand a raster image you'll get noticeable jaggies, or pixelization. That's the effect you see when a straight line appears as a stair-step instead of a smooth surface. Vector-based graphics do not suffer from this problem, as the lines describe the same shape and relative position on the image no matter how big or small it's resized. The square is still described as proceeding from one corner to the next until the square is drawn; the corners are just farther apart. A complex vector-based image has many shapes in it, but the principle remains — the shapes are just made larger or smaller without any pixelization effects. You can see an example of the difference in Figure 15-1.

FIGURE 15-1: Left, raster star shape and blow-up. Right, vector star shape and blow-up.

In the top-left corner of the figure is a star drawn in raster mode using Paint Shop Pro. In the top-right corner is the exact same figure in the exact same dimensions drawn in vector mode. They look basically the same. Underneath each star is a small section that has been expanded 1800 percent for illustrative purposes. The raster side has noticeable jaggies, and the color gradation can be seen as a series of color changes instead of a smooth progression. The vector side looks just as smooth at 1800 percent as it does at its original size, with the color changes still progressing smoothly. You may wish to view this image on the CD to get the full effect.

The same issues seen in the star example will be seen when resizing any raster image. Generally, you can resize a raster image downwards without too much noticeable effect (it's there, you just can't see it), while resizing upwards more than ten percent or so will produce noticeable defects. Graphics programs will perform some tricks to make it less visible, such as anti-aliasing, adding pixels of lighter color to smooth out the jaggies (visible in Figure 15-1). However, all the efforts made by the computer to render the new image will still not completely hide the defects. Ultimately, you do not want to work with raster graphics if you intend to resize them.

Unfortunately, unless you start from scratch, most of the artwork you'll find to use or modify for your cabinet will be in a raster format at a particular size. Does that mean you can't use it if you need the image at a different size? Not necessarily! There's a process of converting a raster to a vector image called, appropriately enough, *vectorizing*. That's the process of taking a raster image, identifying all the various shapes that make it up, and then tracing lines to match. Take a two-by-two checkerboard for instance. If you visualize it as a collection of four shapes (four squares), you can select the corners of the squares and trace lines for each square. Once you've traced over the whole raster image, the layer of lines and shapes you've created from your tracing is now in vector format! Most images aren't easy squares of course and converting a complex raster image into a vector image can be difficult, but it's possible, with patience, to convert any raster image into a vector. There are even programs that will automatically vectorize an image, but the general consensus is that the quality is sub-par and manual tracing is the best way to go.

As far as the output of raster versus vector graphics goes, there's no difference. Once your image is in its final form, converting it to a raster image, if necessary, will have no undesirable consequences, beyond that of a larger file size than the same vector-based image. Converting from a vector image to a raster image is as simple as telling the computer what file format to use and saving it. The file format you use for output will largely be dictated by where and how you get it outputted. For an on-screen image, a JPEG is a likely candidate, but a printed copy will depend on the needs of the people doing the printing for you.

The person who created the artwork for the Project Arcade cabinet, Tom Van Horn, has produced an excellent tutorial (`www.arcadecontrols.com/files/Miscellaneous/VectorTutorial_v1_3.zip`) for people interested in getting started with vector graphics for their cabinets. It covers the basics of raster versus vector graphics, how to create and manipulate vector shapes, the process of converting raster graphics to vector, and how to get your artwork printed. Many people with no prior experience have picked up the tutorial and a raster graphic and, in a day or so, have turned out quality resizable vector graphics for their cabinets. I learned a lot from Tom's tutorial and highly recommend it!

Tools

Before you get started you'll need to pick your tools. The Paint Shop Pro program included on the CD (trial version) is a great package to use and is capable of working with both raster and vector-based images. Other packages mentioned by members of the artwork forum include:

- **Adobe Illustrator** — This program, from graphics company powerhouse Adobe, appears to be the hands-down favorite for working with vector graphics. Adobe Illustrator is the program used in the tutorial mentioned in the previous section.

- **Adobe Photoshop** — A powerful graphics editing suite, Photoshop is the default tool of the majority of graphics artists and represents the raster side of the Adobe house. A popular process is to create vector graphics in Illustrator then import them into Photoshop at the appropriate size in order to use the powerful image-manipulation tools that Photoshop has available.

- **Corel Draw** — Another vector graphics program known for its powerful capabilities.

- **Sodipodi** — Sodipodi (`www.sodipodi.com/`) is an open-source vector graphics program currently under early stages of development. Versions exist for Unix/Linux and Windows.

- **The Gimp** — Gimp (`www.gimp.org/`) stands for Gnu Image Manipulation Program and is a powerful open-source, raster-based graphics tool. Versions exist for Unix/Linux and Windows.

Graphics tips

When you start working with graphics, there are a few tips that will help you produce nice results that are consistent from your screen to final output.

Start by considering color. How hard can using colors be — red is red, blue is blue, right? Not necessarily. There are different systems used to create color depending on the media it is intended for. Monitors use a three-color RGB (red, green, blue) scheme. Most commercial printers use a four-color CMYK (cyan, magenta, yellow, black) scheme. A full description of color theory is beyond the scope of this book. However, what's important to know in a nutshell is that the appearance of an image described in RGB will probably vary somewhat from that of an image described in CMYK. RGB colors are additive — light shines through the colors to your eye, and colors are made by adding different intensities of red, green, and blue. CMYK works the opposite — light reflects off the colors to your eye, and colors are made by subtracting different intensities of cyan, yellow, magenta, and black.

The important point to grasp is that what you see on your screen is not necessarily what you'll see when it is printed out. It'll likely be close, but the shades of color may vary. There are fewer colors possible with CMYK than with RGB. Some paint packages will show you a preview of what you can expect when an image is printed. For instance, in Paint Shop Pro, choose File-Preferences-Color Management.

Some programs, such as Adobe Illustrator, allow you to work natively in CMYK. However, RGB color tends to be more vibrant and gives you a broader range of colors to work with. Conventional wisdom seems to be that you should work in RGB mode and convert to CMYK if needed. Do you *need* to convert to CMYK? That depends on where you're printing your image. If you're printing it on your own printer the answer is likely no. If you're taking it to a professional printer, consult with them and ask them what file formats and color model they prefer. Matching your format to their preferences is your best bet for accurate printing.

Another point to consider is the resolution of your image. DPI stands for "dots per inch" and literally means how many pixels there are for every inch of graphic. Fewer dots per inch result in a lower-quality image, while a higher DPI produces a better-quality image but with a corresponding increase in file size. The sweet spot for a balance between image quality and file size seems to be 300 DPI. Lower than that and there really isn't enough data in the image for great results. Good results are possible at a DPI lower than 300, but they probably won't be as good as a higher DPI. On the flip side, resolutions higher than 300 DPI are probably overkill and not worth the extra space required. I wouldn't recommend using more than 300 DPI unless your print shop specifically asks for it. At something like 600 DPI, a single graphic can take up an entire CD!

It is possible to convert from a lower to a higher DPI, but the results are suboptimal. The program you're using must add extra pixels that weren't there before and, no matter how good a guess it makes, the resultant image won't be as good as if the image were produced at a higher DPI to start with. Your best bet is to create your graphics at the higher resolution. If you're importing graphics from another source you don't always have that option, so the rule of thumb is to simply keep it as close to 300 DPI as you can and not worry about the numbers too much. Remember that these graphics are going on an arcade machine, not in the Louvre!

Another consideration is that you will be much happier working in your graphics program in layers. The way layers work in a graphics program is that each element in an image can be on a particular layer that can be turned on or off. In Tom's vectorizing tutorial, for instance, he recommends a separate layer for the hair, shirt, face, and so forth of the character being vector-ized. With all layers turned on you can see the entire image. When you're concentrating on a particular feature, turning off the layers you don't need allows you to only see the one you're working on. If you make a mistake, for instance a slip of the mouse that draws a line across the screen, you've only done something to that layer and the rest of the image is safely hidden away. Layers have a hierarchy where the top layer always shows, the second layer only shows where the first layer has no material, and so on. This makes it easy to create complex images a chunk at a time.

Finally, it's not a bad idea to have bleeding edges around your image. These "bleeders" allow for variances in print sizes that sometimes occur. If you need exactly a 10-inch-wide marquee and the name of your cabinet exactly fills those 10 inches, you won't be able to use the image if it comes out at $10^{1}/_{2}$ or $9^{1}/_{2}$ inches. However, if your 10-inch image with the name of your cabi-net includes some black space around the text, then you'd be okay. If it's too big, you just trim off the black edging as needed. If it's too small, you have a nice black border. Of course, if there's too much variance, then it simply needs to be reprinted. Also, your graphic has to look good with a bleeder edge for this to work. Something with bright colors might look boxed in with a black border. You'll have to make that judgment as you design your graphics.

Printing

I'll give some specific tips on printing for each item in the sections below. There are some gen-eral pointers to bear in mind when it comes to getting your artwork printed professionally.

- The success of your printout depends in large part on the print shop's understanding of what you're trying to achieve. The more they know about your project, the better they will be able to help you decide on materials and printing techniques.

- If possible, take a proof of what the artwork should look like. If you are getting a large piece of *side art*, print a copy on a regular-sized sheet so that the printer knows the pro-portions and color tones that are expected.

- If you don't know what the printer needs, save multiple formats of the image on a CD. Better yet, contact the printer in advance, explain your project, and find out what file for-mat they'd prefer. If you can't produce it in that format, ask them if they can take another and if there's a conversion fee.

- Ask about UV resistant inks. Ultraviolet light can cause ink to fade over time. UV resis-tant ink is designed to avoid that problem. Usually used on products that are expected to be outdoors, it can sometimes be used on other materials.

- Some printers will want to charge you an up-front setup fee in addition to regular print-ing costs. This isn't necessarily price-gouging. Setup can include modifying your image's color tones so the final product from their CMYK print process matches the color of your RGB printed proof. If you're faced with a setup fee, ask them what it entails. Ask if they can guarantee a close color match if they don't mention a setup process.

- Some printers, particularly large chains, may refuse to print well-known images that you don't own the copyright to, such as a picture of Darth Vader on your marquee. Print shops have encountered legal problems by ignoring copyrights and are rightfully cautious. If this happens to you, ask them specifically what portion of the graphic is a problem and what alterations are necessary to print the artwork. Bear in mind they're not going to risk losing their business for one print job, so if you do not agree with the alterations you will not be able to get your material printed there.

- Take a tape measure and a copy of the proof with you when you go to pick up your product. Compare the colors and make sure it was printed at the right size and proportion before you walk out of the store. Mistakes, unfortunately, seem to be fairly common at some of the larger chains so make sure you're getting what you paid for.

Internet resources

The Internet is a great place to find artwork that can be used on your cabinet project. Much of it is copyright protected, meaning you should consult the owner for permission to use it unless they've already explicitly given it. Many art sites have disclaimers along the lines of "free for personal use, commercial use requires a negotiated arrangement." Other images, such as those produced by publicly funded projects like NASA, are free for commercial or personal use. If in doubt, consult the terms of the Web site on which you find the artwork.

Some of the favorite sites for arcade cabinet builders seeking arcade-themed artwork include the BYOAC Web site, Oscar Controls' art gallery, and the Mametrix Reloaded (a collection of vector-based artwork) among many others. You can also find great artwork for cabinets at non-arcade-oriented Web sites, such as deviantArt.com and even eBay! Between both sets of sites, you should be able to find good artwork for side art, control panels, marquees, and desktop wallpaper. You can even find arcade-style fonts for creating your own logos.

You'll find clickable links to the previously mentioned Web sites and many others on the companion CD-ROM. You'll also find control panel artwork ready to use on the CD-ROM, courtesy of Oscar Controls.

Commercial vendors

Another excellent choice for artwork for your cabinet is commercial arcade shops. They sell a mixture of NOS and reproduction artwork for arcade cabinets that will work just as well on a home-built arcade machine as a real arcade machine that's being restored. Prices vary considerably, depending on whether or not a piece of artwork is original or reproduction and how scarce the material is. Expect to pay in the $20 to $40 range for marquees and up to as much as $200 or so for good side art, although it can sometimes be found for considerably less.

NOS: Stands for "New Old Stock" and refers to material that is unused from the day it was made, that is, old stock from several years ago. It is from the manufacturer, with the same colors and material used as the original machines. NOS artwork was usually either produced by the manufacturer as replacements for damaged artwork or as conversion kits for arcade operators (to turn a Donkey Kong into a Donkey Kong Jr. for instance). Reproduction artwork is art that has been re-created from the original. It attempts to faithfully reproduce the original and, for the most part, succeeds. However, quality can vary depending on the materials used.

Some shops will sell a piece of reproduction artwork that's been silk-screened while others may sell a similar print that is from an inkjet printer. Silkscreening is how original arcade artwork was produced and is generally of a higher quality and durability. Inkjet prints have been known to fade over time, although technological improvements have changed that for high-end printers.

In some cases, an inkjet print may be the only available option. As a rule, if both options exist, purchase the silk-screened print. You'll be happier in the long run. Don't hesitate to purchase an inkjet print if no other option is available, however.

On the CD You'll find a clickable list of commercial arcade artwork vendors on the companion CD-ROM.

Every effort was made to verify the merchandise and customer service reputations of the vendors listed on the companion CD-ROM. Other vendors may or may not be reputable. Before purchasing from them, you should seek opinions about the quality of their workmanship from the rec.games.video.arcade.collecting (`http://groups.google.com/`) newsgroup—caveat emptor!

The marquee

Your cabinet's marquee is one of its most noticed features. Glowing from the light behind it, the marquee can attract attention from across the room. Having a nice marquee can really set your cabinet off and make it noticed!

Obtaining a marquee

You have two options for obtaining a marquee—you can make one yourself or use one of the many ready-to-print marquees available on the Internet. Even if you wish to design your own, you might want to use one of the finished marquees on the Internet as clipart or as a starting point. Remember the graphics tips mentioned earlier in the chapter if you choose to create your own. Also bear in mind that a marquee, unlike the rest of the artwork on your cabinet, will be lit from behind. Dark and vibrant colors will work better than a marquee with a lot of white and light coloring.

Places you can find marquees to print or modify for your own include:

- The Build Your Own Arcade Controls (BYOAC) Web site, `www.arcadecontrols.com/`, has marquees available for download in the artwork section. Also, many individuals who have made their own marquees are happy to share. You can find these by browsing the list of cabinets on the Web site (included on the CD-ROM) and by reading the artwork forum.

- Oscar Controls (`www.oscarcontrols.com/`) includes several marquees in their online galleries, some of which are included on the companion CD-ROM.

- The Classic Arcade Game Art archive at `www.arcadecollecting.com/` includes a big collection of marquees from classic arcade games.

- Massive Mame at `www.mameworld.net/massive/` has a very nice collection of marquees that have been used by many home arcade cabinet builders.

Printing the marquee

You have three options for printing your marquee. You can print your own, you can take it to a print shop, or you can have it done by an online shop specializing in printing marquees. Of the three, the online shops are highly recommended, although all three methods can be used successfully.

If you are going to print your own, be sure to use the best materials possible. A good photo-quality paper with photo-quality ink is your best bet (most of today's inkjet printers have these options). I was concerned at first that a piece of photo paper would be too opaque and not allow light through, but in test prints it actually worked fine. In fact, it allowed too much light through (which I'll show you how to solve in the next section). Once I solved that issue, I was pleasantly surprised with the results. However, unless you have the means to use large paper, you'll end up printing your marquee on more than one page and having to piece it together. No matter how careful you are, it's likely that you'll see the seam when it's back-lit.

Retail print shops can print marquees for you as well. Print shops have printers and material that allow them to print your marquee full sized on a single sheet. If you choose this route, make sure your print shop has back-lit material available. This is a semi-opaque film like material designed to be lit from behind. If you want to spend some money on your marquee, you can try to find a print shop that will screen print it onto Plexiglas for you. That is likely to be expensive, however. Either way, be sure to review the pointers in the printing section earlier in this chapter if you choose to use a retail print shop for your marquee.

My best recommendation is that you choose to use one of the online print shops that cater to arcade cabinet builders. At the time of this printing, there are three in operation:

- **ClassicArcadeGrafix.com** — Located appropriately enough at www.classicarcade grafix.com/, this company has artwork (including marquees) for many classic arcade games. These graphics would look great on a home arcade cabinet. They also have a selection of MAME marquees and artwork and will print custom marquees as well. All their products have a 10-day satisfaction guarantee and a 50-year fade protection warranty!

- **EMDKAY** — EMDKAY Marquees (www.emdkay.net/) is probably the best-known marquee shop in the home arcade cabinet community. As a rule, reviews of the marquees customers have received from them have all been positive. They offer a collection of MAME, personalized, and classic arcade game marquees. They will also help you design a marquee or accept a custom marquee from you for printing.

- **MAME Marquees** — As the name might suggest, MAME Marquees (www.mame marquees.com/) specializes in printing marquees for home arcade cabinets. They have several marquees available to choose from and will print your customized design as well. They offer a 30-day money-back guarantee on their marquees, and have received positive reviews on the BYOAC message forums.

All three of these online shops are clearly interested in the home arcade cabinet business. All have good customer feedback, a wide range of products, and a willingness to work with you for a custom design. Prices are approximately the same, and you are likely to be satisfied with choosing any of these three sources.

Light things up

Of course, a marquee looks much more impressive when lit from behind. Part of the fun of having a great marquee is the glow it gives off. Lighting your marquee is a simple matter really. An inexpensive, regular white fluorescent light behind the marquee works well and is recommended. Be careful if you choose another type of lighting. Ultraviolet (black-light) can produce a very nice effect, but is likely to fade your artwork over time. You'll also occasionally see a real arcade machine with a regular light bulb illuminating the marquee, but heat becomes a serious concern. The light bulb will not spread the light across the marquee evenly so you'll have a center bright spot, and the heat from the bulb may discolor the marquee. Stick to a regular fluorescent light, roughly the size of the marquee, and you'll be happy. Pay attention to the length of the power cord when you purchase your light. An extra long cord is preferable. Unfortunately I missed this when purchasing my light and ended up using an extension cord — not a major catastrophe.

You may run into a couple of problems lighting your marquee, particularly if there's a lot of lighter color. The light from behind may be too bright, washing out the colors of your marquee. You can solve this in a couple of ways. The first is to simply print two copies of the marquee and mount them together. The extra marquee will help diffuse the light so the colors show up darker and richer. If your marquee has areas that look good with bright light but also has black areas that appear grey due to excessive lighting, you can fix that as well with a second marquee. Instead of an exact duplicate of the first marquee, only print the dark areas on this second marquee, and leave the rest of it white. The light will pass through the white area without too much dimming, while the light passing through the two layers of dark area will be much more dimmed.

You can also sandwich a single marquee between two layers of Plexiglas/Lexan and leave the paper backing on the inside piece. This will diffuse the light nicely as well. If your Plexiglas doesn't have a white backing (the one purchased for Project Arcade used a clear-blue plastic backing) then you can substitute an appropriately sized sheet of white paper behind the marquee. Also, mind where the light is mounted in relation to the speakers. Don't put the light behind the speakers, thereby casting shadows on the marquee.

Mounting the marquee

Mounting your marquee involves two steps. The first step is finding a way to get the marquee to remain flat when placed on the cabinet. If you are fortunate enough to have a marquee that's been screen-printed onto glass or Plexiglas then it's already rigid and you have this base covered. Most marquees, however, are printed on the back-lit material recommended in the previous sections. This is flexible like paper, so a way needs to be found to keep it rigid. The easy way to do this is to sandwich the marquee between two thin layers of Plexiglas and treat the three layers as a single marquee. No adhesive is necessary.

Once you have a rigid marquee, the next step is finding a way to mount it to the cabinet. Happ Controls (http://www.happcontrols.com/) sells a PVC marquee retainer in ten foot lengths that you can cut to size and use. Alternatively you can find angled aluminum material in various sizes at any hardware store. Both are pictured in Figure 15-2.

The Happ Controls marquee retainer is a U-shaped, curved affair that sticks out approximately $\frac{1}{2}$ inch from where it rests against the marquee. It is easily cut with a hacksaw, is easy to drill holes in, and comes in black, which matches most cabinets. The angled aluminum material is a bit harder to work with but is preferred by some cabinet builders because it is lies flat against the marquee instead of the U-shape of the Happ Controls marquee. The aluminum cuts with a hacksaw and can be drilled with the proper bit. Unless you prefer the metal appearance, the aluminum will need to be painted. Use a primer designed for metal or lightly sand the aluminum with a fine grit to help the paint adhere to the metal.

FIGURE 15-2: Left, Happ Controls marquee retainer. Right, angled aluminum.
Used by permission of Happ Controls.

If your cabinet top or speaker shelf is angled, like the speaker shelf on the Project Arcade cabinet, then the angled aluminum may not work for you because it is rigid and will flex the marquee. Other options in that case include using a ceiling-grid retainer, which will be a bit more flexible, or the Happ Controls marquee retainer.

To mount the marquee, predrill two or three holes in your marquee retainer of choice and the speaker shelf. I prefer to clamp the marquee retainer in place and drill through both retainer and wood at the same time to ensure the holes line up. Be careful! Don't place the holes so the marquee retainer is snug against the wood. That doesn't leave any room for the marquee! Place the marquee or a similar-sized piece of Plexiglas in the proper spot and then place the marquee retainers to ensure proper spacing. Repeat for the top marquee retainer and cabinet top. Voila, your marquee is mounted!

Project Arcade's marquee

The Project Arcade marquee was designed by Tom Van Horn, who created the vector graphics tutorial introduced earlier in this chapter, and printed by the folks at EMDKAY Marquees on thick photo paper with long-life archival inks. It's sandwiched between two sheets of Lexan and held in place with a Happ Controls marquee retainer below and a piece of angled aluminum above. The marquee is absolutely stunning as you can see in Figure 15-3 (be sure to see the color version on the companion CD-ROM), and is arguably one of the most attractive features of the cabinet!

FIGURE 15-3: The Project Arcade marquee, unlit above, lit below.
Used by permission of emdkay.net and Tom Van Horn.

Side art

Next to your marquee, the other item that really draws attention to your cabinet is the side art. The side art on the cabinet is your best opportunity to get creative because of the sheer volume of space you have to work with. There are basically three camps when it comes to side art. Many people will simply place a center graphic somewhere in the two-feet-squared range in the middle of the cabinet. Others will use much more of the available space by using a banner-sized graphic, or, more rarely, something that fills the entire side. Others simply choose not to use any side art at all or to leave the decision for a later date. A cabinet really looks better with some sort of side art applied, so I wholeheartedly recommend you give it a whirl!

Haven't we been here before?

Much of what you need to consider for side art is the same as what you've already read about for the marquee. The same considerations apply for the settings you use when creating the graphics, and you can find artwork and entire side art pieces at the same places. The three vendors who cater to the home arcade cabinet business for marquees also sell side art with the same variety and quality available. This time, ClassicArcadeGrafix.com (www.classic arcadegrafix.com/) was chosen to print the side art for Project Arcade. Whichever vendor or method of printing you choose, there are a couple of differences between printing side art and printing marquees that you should bear in mind:

- **Lighting** — Unlike the marquee, the side art is not going to be lit from behind. This means you can use lighter colors without worrying about them being washed out.

- **Size** — Compared to the marquee or control panel overlay, there is a lot more area to work with. You may want to consider making your lettering and characters larger so they can be seen more easily from farther away, but that's not always the best choice. Once again it comes down to a personal preference, but either way it's something to consider.

- **Material** — Your best choice for material to print side art on is adhesive-backed vinyl. Not all print shops carry adhesive-backed vinyl, so if you're printing your own you may need to go with a non-adhesive-backed vinyl. Other materials can be used but may not be as durable as the vinyl. See the next section, "Applying Side Art," for some ideas when using other materials.

Applying side art

The best advice I can offer you for applying your side art is to consult the place you had it printed. They should know the particulars of the material being used and the best method for applying it. However, if they do not have a recommendation for you , two popular methods are given here. ClassicArcadeGrafix.com provides explicit instructions on applying side art .

If you're using a vinyl that does not have an adhesive backing, you'll need to supply your own. The recommended method is to pick up a can of spray adhesive (3M Super 77 is the most popular choice), spray the back of the side art, and apply it using one of the aforementioned methods.

If you're using a nonadhesive material other than vinyl, then you'll need to apply spray adhesive as well. In addition however, you should also protect the artwork in some fashion. Good results have been reported with spraying the artwork with a clear acrylic coat. Some people spray the artwork before it's applied, while others coat it after it's on the cabinet. Both methods seem to work equally well. Several coats are suggested for maximum protection of the artwork. A wise word of caution comes from Oscar Controls. Before spraying a clear coat, allow the adhesive to totally dry for a couple of days or so. Sometimes the adhesive can leak fumes through the artwork that aren't really noticeable to you but that can interact with the spray acrylic and cause bubbling. After waiting a couple of days that problem generally does not occur. Consult your printer before applying a clear coat to make sure they do not have any cautions against it.

Spray-soak application method

This method of applying side art to a cabinet is very popular in the arcade-collecting community. The basic premise is to position the artwork with the adhesive exposed and slide the artwork around until it's perfect instead of trying to get the artwork perfectly positioned the first (and only) chance you have. The way you do this is by first spraying the side of the cabinet with mildly soapy water. This prevents the adhesive from sticking as you position the artwork. Carefully peel the backing off the artwork to avoid stretching it and place it on the cabinet. When you have it in position, carefully squeegee the water out (so as not to damage the side art), and the artwork then sticks. You should work from the center of the artwork out to the edges to make sure no bubbles develop. If you do develop a bubble (and that's common even with the most careful of installations), use a small pin at the base of the bubble (not in the middle) to pop the bubble gently. Then carefully press the air out. Squeegee the side art several times to make sure all the water is out. You may find it easier to use this method with the cabinet temporarily lying on its side. Don't lay it on its side with the monitor in it!

Hinge application method

The other popular method is the hinge process. A variant of this method is recommended by ClassicArcadeGrafix.com and is shown in Figure 15-5. The basic premise of the hinge method is that you place the graphic on the cabinet with the backing still attached, line it up perfectly, then place masking tape horizontally across the middle so the artwork is hinged from top to bottom. Gently pull the top part down and remove the section of backing from the top down to the hinge. To avoid damaging the graphic, I suggest cutting the backing off in the air when you have it pulled off (you'll need a helper) rather than trying to score the backing while still attached to the artwork. Carefully begin to lay the artwork back down on the cabinet, starting with the sticky part closest to the hinge. Use the squeegee method to work the artwork onto the cabinet, from the center out to the edges. This lets you work any bubbles out. If any bubbles persist, use the pin method to gently pop them (at the base!) and work the air out. Once the top is attached to the cabinet, remove the masking tape, lift the bottom, and repeat the process with the bottom half.

In Figure 15-4 you can see the variant of the hinge method recommended by ClassicArcade Grafix.com and used on the Project Arcade Cabinet. The general premise is the same, but instead of placing the hinge in the middle the hinge is placed at the top of the artwork. Then the entire backing is pulled off, and the artwork is gently rolled back onto the cabinet using a squeegee as described above.

FIGURE 15-4: Applying the artwork.

Project Arcade side art

The side art for Project Arcade was once again designed by graphics artist Tom Van Horn. ClassicArcadeGrafix.com (www.classicarcadegrafix.com/) printed the artwork and did an outstanding job. Not only were the end results excellent, but they pointed out corrections that needed to be made to the original artwork. The black used on the outer edges of the artwork had a slight tint to it that looked fine on-screen by itself but would have contrasted with and shown up visibly when applied against the black paint of the cabinet. A quick correction and the artwork was printed and on its way. The only thing I might do differently next time is to consider a larger-sized graphic, but I'm not completely sure. Installed, the *side art* looks great (Figure 15-5)!

FIGURE 15-5: Project Arcade cabinet with custom side art installed.
Used by permission of ClassicArcadeGrafix.com and Tom Van Horn.

Control panel artwork

Your control panel artwork is equally as important as the other artwork on your cabinet. Unlike the marquee and side art, however, the control panel artwork is seen up close and is what you'll spend the most time looking at other than your bezel. As usual, there are different opinions about what makes good control panel artwork. Some people prefer a minimalist approach, with a few discretely placed graphics, maybe an overall background graphic, and perhaps some labels and arrows around the controls. Others prefer a full-body graphic covering the entire panel, with arcade characters and a lot of action. My personal preference is the former, as I find too much activity on the control panel distracting. Many people prefer the other point of view, however, and, once again, to each their own.

Note Applying artwork to your control panel obviously needs to be done without any controls installed. If you followed the suggestion in Chapter 6 and held off installing controls or skipped ahead to this chapter then you're in good shape now. If not, you'll need to spend a few minutes removing the controls from the control panel top now.

We've definitely been here before!

The same general considerations for the graphics that apply to the marquee and side art apply to the control panel artwork also. There are a few points to mention however. Artwork for the control panel is usually referred to as the control panel overlay (CPO). CPOs can be found at many of the same locations as referred to previously, including two of the three online vendors in the industry (Mamemarquees.com and ClassicArcadeGrafix.com). Control Panel Overlays are normally printed on the same adhesive-backed vinyl material as side art. If necessary, you can also use non-adhesive-backed vinyl with a spray adhesive to attach it to the control panel. You do not need to cover it with a spray acrylic, however, if you intend to protect it with a Plexiglas covering as discussed in the next section, "Covering the Control Panel."

If you intend to place arrows and labels on your control panel artwork, you'll need to be very careful to make sure the graphics line up precisely with the template you used to drill your holes. Another easy method is to use a background graphic that doesn't have specific arrows and labels on it. Then, print the directional arrows and labels separately and place them on the control panel graphic in the appropriate place when the overlay is applied and the holes laid out. This is the method used for the Project Arcade control panel. This only works if you're going to cover the control panel with Plexiglas to hold the graphics down.

Some people choose to use contact paper, or a plain Formica or vinyl overlay on their control panel. This is a simple solution that can look very nice, if somewhat plain. If you use contact paper you can get various patterns for a bit of pizzazz, but you'll need to cover it with Plexiglas because it isn't very durable.

Covering the control panel

Because your control panel gets the most contact with hands and drinks and such, you may want to protect the artwork from getting dirty or damaged. It may seem like this section is out of order as I haven't talked about applying the artwork on the panel yet, but you should work out the control panel protection before the artwork is applied. This is to protect the artwork from mishap while you're working on the protective covering.

Do you want to cover the panel?

While looking at the classic arcade machines in my collection, I noted that the majority of them had nothing covering the control panel overlay. A couple of them were in nice condition, albeit fairly dirty from years of use. The majority of them, however, were ripped and damaged from heavy use in arcades. A few of the machines had a thin Plexiglas cover over the control panel, and those control panels still had nice conditioned artwork although the Plexiglas was a bit beat up.

So you need to decide how, if at all, you intend to protect the control panel overlay on your cabinet. If you're likely to have your arcade cabinet in a controlled environment with only friends and family playing it, you might be just as happy not bothering with a cover over your control panel. Regular cleaning and TLC may keep the control panel looking nice. On the other hand, you never know when accidents are going to happen no matter how careful you and your friends and family are with the cabinet. A layer of protection over the control panel is cheap insurance, particularly if the control panel artwork was difficult or expensive to produce. If your control panel has a simple and inexpensive covering on it without artwork, you're probably okay not doing anything special to protect it. At worst, you may need to replace it down the road. However, if your control panel overlay has artwork or was difficult or expensive to produce, then I strongly recommend a layer of Plexiglas to protect it.

Note

I refer to Plexiglas and Lexan quite a bit in this book and in this chapter particularly. Those are brand names of sheets of acrylic plastic. In all cases I'm using the brand names as generic terms. Any quality acrylic plastic will do. Plexiglas is more durable than Lexan but cracks easier. Lexan is easier to work with without fear of cracking, but is more susceptible to scratches. Other brands exist as well—consult the shop you purchase it from about the properties of the material and the best way to work with it.

Working with Plexiglas, Lexan, and other acrylic plastic

Working with Plexiglas can be tricky. If you apply too much pressure or speed as you're drilling holes, the Plexiglas will probably crack. Murphy's Law says that the Plexiglas will not crack until you're drilling the very final hole! If you don't use the proper technique, cutting it to size can also be frustrating, causing chips and splinters at the edges that can hurt and look horrible (Figure 15-6).

Caution

Working with Plexiglas can be messy, nasty work. Your drill will cause the Plexiglas to melt a bit, putting off acrylic fumes. You don't want to breathe this stuff more than you have to. Make sure you have plenty of ventilation and wear safety gear, including a mask!

With proper techniques however, you can get good results without too much effort other than the time taken to do it right. There are basically three steps to working with Plexiglas: cutting it to shape, drilling holes, and smoothing edges.

Note

Getting the hang of working with Plexiglas can take a few tries. I strongly suggest working with a scrap piece of Plexiglas to get the feel for it before you start cutting and drilling on the one you want to keep. Don't start working with your Plexiglas until you've read this entire section through once!

With the right tools, cutting Plexiglas is easy . A fine-toothed circular saw or high-speed rotary tool can be used but may be overkill. First, with the backing still affixed, place the control panel top over the Plexiglas and line it up so major edges are flush with one another. By lining up the big edges, you minimize the amount of cutting required. Clamp the Plexiglas to the top, and mark the Plexiglas where it will need to be cut. Remove your control panel top and put it aside.

FIGURE 15-6: This Plexiglas was improperly cut, causing a rough edge.

Next, place the Plexiglas on a piece of scrap wood at least large enough to support the length to be cut, if not the entire sheet. Clamp a straight-edge along the first line to be cut with the bulk of the straight-edge covering the part of the Plexiglas you're going to use. This will protect it against slips. Make sure the wood backing, Plexiglas, and straight-edge are clamped firmly together in a sandwich (Figure 15-7).

Using a sharp utility knife (the place you bought the Plexiglas should have a knife designed for cutting acrylic), score the line to be cut several times. *Go slowly but firmly — too fast and you risk slipping and fouling the straight line!* You want to score the plastic about one-third of the way through. Then for good measure, I suggest flipping the Plexiglas over, clamping the straight edge back down on the same line, and scoring the back a few times. Not everyone does the scoring on the back, but I find it can make things easier. Flip the Plexiglas back over so the original side is up.

Now place the Plexiglas, with the deep cut side up, between two pieces of wood so the main piece is supported and the excess is hanging into the air. Clamp the two pieces of wood and Plexiglas together firmly — the scored cut should be precisely at the edge between the two pieces of wood (Figure 15-8). With a smooth, firm motion, place downward pressure on the excess Plexiglas. It should cleanly snap off where you scored it. For a big piece, work from one side to the other, snapping as you go. If things go properly, you have a nice, clean, smooth edge!

FIGURE 15-7: Straight-edge, Plexiglas, and wood sandwich.

FIGURE 15-8: Lined up and ready to snap off.

Before you remove the clamps, carefully inspect the edge of the Plexiglas. If you find a spot that isn't smooth, you can easily sand it flush with the rest of the cut while it's still sandwiched. Take a fine-grit sandpaper and gently sand across the rough edge until it's smooth.

It may take a couple of tries before you get it right, but, once you have the knack of it, it's very easy to get smooth cuts with this method. The trick is to score it repeatedly and to go slowly. In Figure 15-9, you can see a comparison of a sheet that was scored only twice and then snapped without a top sandwich layer and a sheet that was cut following the method described.

FIGURE 15-9: Top, improper method. Bottom, smoothly cut the right way.

Now that you've got the edges cut, you need to drill holes in the Plexiglas for the joysticks, buttons, trackball, and other controls. Drilling Plexiglas is prone to problems if it is done improperly. If it is done carefully, however, good results are easy to achieve. The key is the speed and pressure applied. If you place too much pressure or try to use a high speed, you are prone to crack the plastic. If you use a slow to medium speed, with only a moderate amount of pressure, drilling through Plexiglas isn't likely to cause cracks. Figure 15-10 shows two holes drilled in Plexiglas. One was drilled slowly and the other was drilled at full speed with firm pressure, causing a crack.

FIGURE **15-10: Below, slowly drilled hole. Above, cracked hole.**

You may notice that the *good* hole in Figure 15-10 is fuzzy around the edges. That's because when you drill Plexiglas, you're melting it as much as you're drilling it. The fuzzy stuff around the edges is the plastic shavings that melted and then solidified again. They scrape off easily, leaving a clean hole behind. Drilling through Plexiglas is much easier with the right tools and techniques. A good forstner bit makes drilling button holes very easy. In fact, I was surprised at how easy making holes in Plexiglas was with my forstner bit (Figure 15-11). Thanks to Kendrick Childers for the tip on choosing a forstner bit! Special drill bits that are designed with a gentler point for drilling acrylic can also be purchased .

For the trackball, you should use a properly sized hole saw. Carefully drill the pilot hole until the hole saw touches the surface. Then put the drill in reverse and slowly apply *gentle* pressure. Your goal is to melt the hole away with the teeth on the hole saw working in reverse instead of biting into the plastic and possibly cracking it. You can also use this reverse-drilling technique with a regular bit if you don't have a forstner bit. Patience is the keyword here — this will take a while and you don't want to force it along. You may not need to reverse-drill with the hole saw depending on the particular properties of your acrylic. I recommend testing a scrap piece first. Predrill a pilot hole big enough to fit the hole saw's drill bit, then slowly start the hole saw in the proper direction to see if the acrylic cracks. If not, you're in luck and can drill your Plexiglas panel the easy way, albeit very carefully!

FIGURE 15-11: A smoothly cut button hole next to the forstner bit.

For the carriage bolt holes, you'll want to make the hole slightly bigger than the square block at the head of the bolt. Normally, in wood, you drill a hole the same size as the shaft of the bolt. When fastening the nut onto the bolt, the square block crunches into the wood holding it tight. You can't do that with Plexiglas, so you'll need to make your hole just big enough to accommodate the square block while still being hidden by the top head of the bolt. For a standard ¼-inch carriage bolt, a ⁵⁄₁₆-inch drill bit will work.

Now that you know how to cut and drill your Plexiglas, it's time to go ahead and work on your real control panel cover. First, go ahead and cut your Plexiglas to the proper dimensions of the control panel top. Now, if you haven't predrilled the holes in your control panel top then you can use my favorite method. Place your control panel template, created back in Chapter 6, between the Plexiglas and scrap wood so the template lines up perfectly with the edges of the Plexiglas. If you're using the Project Arcade template then now is a good time to print it out if you haven't yet. Make sure you have it printed out to scale — if necessary, you can print it in sections and carefully tape them together. Clamp the wood, template, and Plexiglas together and double-check that all the edges line up properly. Now you can use the template that you see through the Plexiglas to drill your holes perfectly (Figure 15-12). Don't forget to drill the holes for any carriage bolts needed for joysticks and trackballs, and double check the required size of hole for any spinners or special controls. Remember that if you're using a trackball plate with no visible bolts, you don't need to drill bolt holes in the Plexiglas, only the wood!

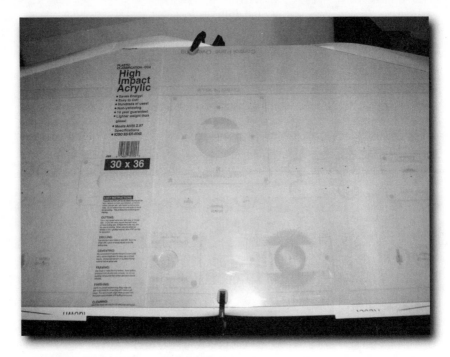

FIGURE **15-12: The first of many holes drilled.**

Once you've drilled all your holes, you can discard the template. If you haven't drilled the holes in your control panel yet, your Plexiglas cover is now the perfect template for drilling holes in your control panel top! Clamp the template to the control panel and drill away, using regular wood-drilling techniques. Voila, a perfectly matched control panel and Plexiglas cover!

If you pre-drilled the holes in your control panel top, then you can use a similar technique now. Place the Plexiglas between a piece of scrap wood and your control panel top. Make sure the Plexiglas and control panel top are oriented the same way they will be on the control panel box, that is, you don't want to drill one side of the Plexiglas then try to flip it over to place it on the control panel top — the holes won't match up. Firmly clamp everything together and then use the control panel top's holes as your template for drilling the Plexiglas. Once again, a perfectly matched control panel and Plexiglas cover!

Note What about any extra holes to fasten the Plexiglas to the control panel top? In most cases, the joystick bolts and button lips should be enough to hold it firmly in place. If that is not the case, you can drill a couple of small holes for tiny screws as needed. I do not recommend doing so unless necessary.

The last step is to go over all the cuts and drilled holes and to make sure they are smooth. You don't want jagged edges tearing your control panel overlay or injuring someone. Use a knife to trim away jaggies left from drilling and then gently sand sharp edges with a fine grit sandpaper. Remember to wear a mask when sanding—you don't want to breathe Plexiglas fibers!

Applying the control panel overlay

Applying your control panel overlay is easy enough. Use a similar technique as followed for applying side art. If you're using the wet technique, make sure you're not working over electronics. For example, if you've already drilled the holes in the control panel top and it's resting over your control panel box, the hinge technique may be easier.

Before you apply your overlay, I need to remind you about making sure your control panel has a flush surface if you plan to use a Plexiglas cover. Without a cover, your joystick dust covers can just rest above the graphic. With a Plexiglas cover, however, you need to rout out enough space so your dust covers lie beneath the graphic. Make sure you put them in before you lay down the vinyl. You also might consider having the dust cover on top to hide the hole in the Plexiglas, although real arcade machines all bury the dust cover beneath the graphic and leave the hole exposed. Either way, the one thing you can't do is have the dust cover between the Plexiglas and the graphic. Also, make sure your trackball plate is routed flush with the control panel surface before you apply the graphic. In a nutshell, your control panel top has to be smooth before you can apply a Plexiglas cover to it.

If your control panel overlay has graphics on it that have to line up with your controls, such as directional arrows around the joysticks, then you should verify that everything lines up properly before applying the overlay. You can use your Plexiglas cover as an easy way to do this. If everything lines up then you're in great shape—carefully apply the overlay using the method of your choice. If for some reason your overlay doesn't line up, you have a difficult choice to make. If it's not significant, you may choose to ignore the problem. Alternatively, you'll need to re-do the graphic or, in the worst case, redrill your holes in your control panel top and Plexiglas.

If all has gone well, you now have your control panel overlay properly placed on the control panel top. All that remains is to pierce the control panel overlay at the holes in the control panel top and either trim away the overlay or fold the excess into the holes. If you're using a Plexiglas cover then go ahead and place it on top now. Congratulations! You've now got your control panel ready to install/reinstall the controls!

For the Project Arcade cabinet, I elected to try my own hand at designing artwork. I chose a simple space-type background that I tweaked a bit in Paint Shop Pro and then applied the Project Arcade logo to it. The graphic was printed at a local chain print shop on non-adhesive vinyl and applied to the control panel with 3M Super 77 spray adhesive. I then covered the panel with Plexiglas. It turned out very nice (Figure 15-13)!

FIGURE 15-13: The Project Arcade control panel.
Used by permission of Tom Van Horn.

Bezels

The bezel is the shroud or glass covering that goes over your monitor. Its purpose is to look attractive while hiding the insides of the monitor and cabinet that would show around the edges without it. Some bezels are part of the glass covering the monitor while others are plastic or foam inserts that rest between the front glass and the monitor.

In the *Protecting your cabinet* section that follows later in this chapter, I recommend placing a sheet of glass over the monitor area to protect the insides of the monitor and cabinet. You can create a bezel for your cabinet by placing artwork or black paint around the inside edge of the glass, thereby masking the parts of the cabinet around the monitor that you don't want people to see. You can also get a glass or Plexiglas screen printed with your artwork at some print shops. If you choose to do this, prepare to spend a bit of money and remember that you want the artwork on the inside of the glass to protect it. That means it has to be reverse printed (which your print shop will be able to handle). A lot of people simply get artwork printed on paper or vinyl and then sandwich the artwork between the monitor glass and another layer of something rigid behind, such as a sheet of Plexiglas or a stiff posterboard backing. I do not recommend gluing your artwork directly to the glass because it is easy to make a mistake and the adhesive may show on the glass. By the way, under the glass covering of the monitor is a great place to put instructions for your cabinet!

In addition to, or as an alternative to, using the monitor glass cover as a bezel, I highly recommend a bezel directly surrounding the monitor itself. Happ Controls makes an easy-to-use black plastic bezel in a variety of sizes that fits directly on the monitor (Figure 15-14). The center open area is sized to fit your monitor, while the plastic surrounding the opening is oversized so you can trim it to exactly fit your cabinet's opening. Happ also sells a foam bezel.

FIGURE 15-14: A 27-inch bezel from Happ Controls.
Used by permission of Happ Controls.

Many people also choose to make their own bezel. Any dark, rigid material, such as poster board or cardboard, can be assembled into a bezel. Most homemade bezels are square, flat, and fit around the frame of the monitor. That works fine, but the Happ Controls bezel is flared out and rests on the outer edges of the monitor tube itself, providing a bit more coverage than a flat bezel. If you combine either of these monitor bezels with a smoked glass cover over the monitor area, players will not be able to see the cabinet's insides while still being able to see the monitor's picture (which is the ultimate goal).

You can find full-sized, pre-made bezel artwork at a couple of places on the Internet. The BYOAC (www.arcadecontrols.com/) artwork page has one displaying MAME across the top that you can have printed or modify. Zakk's Massive MAME page (www.mameworld.net/massive/) has an absolutely gorgeous bezel graphic along with some artwork you can use to create your own.

You can purchase bezels from many of the arcade parts shops listed in Appendix A, "Where to Find Arcade Parts for Your Project." They carry both generic black bezels and also NOS and reproduction bezels for many classic arcade games, in glass, Plexiglas, and cardboard. In addition, Mamemarquees.com and ClassicArcadeGrafix.com both sell bezels designed for home arcade cabinets. Mamemarquees.com also has a design-your-own kit where you choose the placement of graphics on the bezel and send it to them to print.

Instruction cards

You may know where and how everything on your arcade cabinet works, but your guests won't have your detailed knowledge. You can help them out by creating and strategically placing an instruction card or two on the cabinet. The best place to put an instruction card is under the monitor glass on your bezel. Occasionally, some people will place an instruction banner along the top of their control panel. To each their own — if you decide to use an instruction card let the rest of the cabinet's appearance guide you when choosing where to place it.

Creating your instruction card is a matter of spending some time in a paint program such as Paint Shop Pro. Pick a font with a good arcade or video game theme (*Internet resources* earlier in this chapter) and go to town. With a nice border and a couple of arcade characters, some simple instructions can look very nice on the cabinet and be helpful to boot! You can find some instruction cards already made at many of the resources listed earlier in this chapter. However, because everyone's cabinet is a bit different, the instruction cards are not likely to be useful to you. They can, however, make great starting points and inspiration for your own.

Lighting Effects

Next to the artwork on your cabinet, the lighting effects can really grab attention and look great. The areas that people normally light up include the coin-door return buttons, trackball, pushbuttons, and marquee. You can, of course, get much fancier with lighting, including lining parts of the cabinet with glow-wire, using black-lights (but don't forget their possible fading effect on artwork), and other ideas. Those kinds of things are left as an exercise to the reader, but if you're interested in them you might want to do a Google search on "case mods," which will bring up links relating to modifying computer cases (try www.coolight.com/ as a starter).

I've already discussed lighting the marquee, and I'll cover lighting the coin-return buttons in the coin-door later in this chapter. The one thing I want to cover in this section is how to light up the various things on the control panel. If you have many things on the control panel you want to light up, you can elect to use the simple method of placing a small fluorescent light inside the control panel box. Even a small one will take up a lot of room, though, and may put light where you don't want it. You could use small light bulbs — that's often done underneath trackballs. In fact, most trackballs have a kit you can add to them that allows you to illuminate them by mounting a light bulb underneath. However, light bulbs generate unwanted heat that can warp your trackball and tend to burn out when you least want them to. Is there a better way? Certainly! The lighting method of choice in the arcade cabinet-building community is to use light-emitting diodes, or LEDs.

LED technology has come a long way in recent years, and a new class of LEDs has come out called super-bright LEDs. These generate a powerful but focused beam of light and make great illumination sources for arcade controls. Different LEDs require different voltages, so hooking them up becomes an issue to consider. Most off-the-shelf LEDs don't come in convenient 5 and 12-volt sizes, which means you can't just directly hook them up to the power available in the cabinet. Too much power will burn out the LED, while not enough will make it dim. Most LEDs use less than 5 volts, so by adding a resistor in line with the LED you can reduce the voltage to what's needed. LEDs will last for years and draw so little current that you can run dozens of them off a PC power supply without making it blink.

In addition to mounting LEDs under items that are normally illuminated, some cabinet builders are going so far as to hack their normally opaque pushbuttons with LEDs lighting them (another wonderful idea from PacMAMEA, www.1uparcade.com/). A small hole is drilled underneath the button, and an LED is inserted so it doesn't interfere with the mechanics of the button but still has the LED leads exposed so they can be wired. This allows even normal buttons to have a glow effect! You can also find illuminated pushbuttons (using light bulbs or optional 12-volt LEDs) at arcade supply houses, and occasionally on eBay you can find the coveted Atari-style, light-up cone buttons, although the latter are rare.

One other popular thing to do with LEDs is to hook them up to your keyboard encoder in place of the Caps-Lock, Num-Lock, and Scroll-Lock LEDs. The Hagstrom KE72, MK64, and I-PAC encoders all have hookups on them for the keyboard LEDs. MAME will flash these LEDs at certain times to mimic the behavior of real arcade games. For instance, several arcade games flash the one-player start button when a single quarter is inserted and both the one- and two-player start buttons when more quarters were inserted. For this reason, some cabinet builders like to place LEDs under their player 1 and player 2 start buttons or place the LEDs directly in the control panel just for appearance. File this under the "great eye candy" category!

Carsten Wessels (whom you'll meet again in the "Inspirational Projects to See" section in Chapter 18) has a tutorial on his Web site (www.retrospieler.de/e-led-r.html) explaining the electronics of hooking up LEDs and figuring resistor values. Oscar Controls' Web site also has a tutorial (www.oscarcontrols.com/led/index.shtml) on connecting LEDs including using super-bright LEDs with the I-PAC, which natively only supports regular LEDs due to available power. Both have allowed us to include the tutorials on the companion CD-ROM!

Recently, another category of super-bright LEDs has hit the market. These come in various colors (red, blue, green, white, and UV) and are designed to be connected straight into a PC power supply taking 12 volts. These are meant for the case modding community to light up the insides of their computer cases, but credit goes to Zakk from the Massive MAME Web site (www.mameworld.net/massive/) for realizing their potential for arcade controls. Marketed under a variety of names, these come in kits ready to plug straight into a power supply and have mounting mechanisms that make it easy to point them precisely where they need to shine.

You can find super-bright LEDs at these locations among others:

- www.glowire.com/
- www.coolight.com/
- www.svcompucycle.com/
- www.superbrightleds.com/

Light effects add great eye candy value to an arcade cabinet, and super-bright LEDs are a great way to achieve it. The Project Arcade cabinet has a super-bright LED illuminating the trackball, as you can see in Figure 15-15. Things you can do with illumination are limited only by your imagination!

FIGURE 15-15: Happ Controls trackball with super-bright LED attached.
Used by permission of Happ Controls.

Protecting the Cabinet

You've put a lot of effort into building and decorating your cabinet so far. Now would be a good time to give some thought to ways you can protect the cabinet from damage. There are a few specific areas you'll want to protect, many of which have already been discussed but I'll recap here:

- **Control panel overlay** — An acrylic plastic cover over your control panel artwork will look nice and add years to the life of your control panel artwork.

- **Side art** — Side art printed on durable material like vinyl probably does not need additional protection. Less durable material can be protected with a spray acrylic so long as the printed material is compatible with the acrylic and won't bleed.

- **Cooling** — Cooling the cabinet is another item you probably don't have to worry about. If you notice that the temperature inside is climbing too high then a fan or two like that shown in Chapter 13 should do the trick.

- **Monitor area** — Whether you have a decorated bezel of some kind, you should put a protective sheet of glass or Plexiglas over the monitor area to protect the insides and keep inquisitive fingers out. Smoked glass $1/4$-inch thick looks particularly nice and will hold up very well. The glass can be mounted by placing small strips of wood appropriately around the monitor area for the glass to rest against. A small locking strip of wood or mechanism of some kind should be placed on the outside of the glass to prevent it from tipping out accidentally.

The bottom corners of your cabinet are another area you might want to consider protecting. Arcade supply houses like Happ Controls sell corner protectors designed to do just that. These are triangular plates of metal that attach to the corner with screws. If your cabinet is prone to frequent moving you may want to consider these, otherwise they are probably not necessary.

T-molding is the final protective item you will want to think about for your cabinet. Many people consider T-molding decorative, and it certainly is that. In fact T-molding comes in many colors, just to match the overall artistic theme of your cabinet. However, T-molding also serves the important purpose of protecting the edges of your cabinet from being bumped and damaged.

Installing T-molding is easy if you've properly routed the groove for it (as discussed in Chapter 2). T-molding is called that because it looks exactly like a T when viewed straight on. The horizontal part of the T is what shows, and the vertical part is what fits into the grooves in the cabinet edges. The T-molding should fit into the grooves snugly; you may need a rubber mallet to gently tap it into place. If it requires a lot of effort then your grooves are too small (or, like the Project Arcade cabinet, you got a bit frisky with the paint and need to clean out the grooves). If your grooves are too big for your T-molding, you can fix it into place with a bit of glue as you work it into place in the grooves. Of course, you'll have to hold it or clamp it while the glue sets.

The tricky part of T-molding is working around corners. Because you end up with double the amount of T-molding on corners (the front face and the top face both share a small portion of the groove at the corner), the vertical part of the T needs to be trimmed. Cut two or three small, triangular notches out of the vertical part of the T as shown in Figure 15-16 for a slight angle and a large notch for a 90-degree angle. Then work the T-molding around the corner. Be careful, T-molding plastic cuts easily, and it's very easy to accidentally slice through the face of the T-molding.

You can find T-molding in a variety of colors and sizes at most arcade parts shops, like Happ Controls and these specialty stores:

- www.t-molding.com/
- www.t-mold.com/
- www.outwater.com/outwater.html

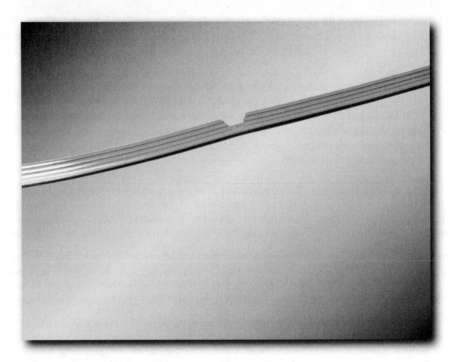

FIGURE 15-16: Notching T-molding to go around a corner.

Other Odds 'n' Ends

Almost there! Here are just a couple more miscellaneous odds and ends to pay attention to when putting together your arcade cabinet.

The coin door

If you've decided to include a coin door in your arcade cabinet, now is as good a time as any to mount and hook it up. Adding the coin door adds a touch of arcade cabinet authenticity that looks great!

A coin door looks great and can make a fun piggy bank to boot. However, the moment you charge someone to play a game on your machine you may be running afoul of local laws regarding running coin-operated machines without proper license to do so. Also, the license under which you've obtained software and arcade ROMs likely doesn't allow operating them for profit. A coin door is for looks and entertainment value only!

Mounting the door

Mounting the door into the hole you cut in the front of the coin-door panel is straightforward. Fit the coin door into the hole and then attach the mounting brackets to the screw holes in the door. As you tighten them down, the coin door will fit snugly against the outside of the panel. Don't over-tighten them or you'll start to bite into the wood. Figure 15-17 shows the coin door mounted into the Project Arcade cabinet. Normally there's a metal container that mounts to the bottom of the coin door that holds your coin bucket. For a home arcade cabinet I elected not to use a mounted container. I simply place the coin bucket on the bottom of the cabinet to catch any coins the kids throw in.

FIGURE 15-17: The Happ Controls over-under coin door mounted.
Used by permission of Happ Controls.

Lighting the returns

The coin-return buttons have lights behind them, and lighting them up adds a very nice effect! If you are using the bulbs that came with the coin door you'll need to check their voltage rating. Some bulbs are rated at 5 volts, some at 6, and some at 12. If you have bulbs rated at 5 or 12 volts, you can power them directly from the PC power supply in your cabinet (using the wiring block that you attached the voltage to earlier in the book). If not, you'll need to provide the proper power, either with a separate transformer or by using resistors with the voltage available in the cabinet as described earlier for LEDs.

What a lot of people prefer to do is to replace the bulbs with super-bright LEDs as introduced earlier in the chapter. However, Happ Controls makes this even easier with a drop-in replacement for the bulbs that ship with their coin doors. These replacements are either single or three-cluster LEDs that run off of 12 volts and come in a variety of colors. I chose to replace the regular light bulbs from the Project Arcade's coin door with the white cluster LEDs (Figure 15-18). They get power easily from the 12-volt supply in the cabinet and are very bright, making the coin return look great! Because they fit into the mounting sleeve that is designed to attach at the right spot on the coin door, they are easier to use than other LEDs that have to be fastened in place some how.

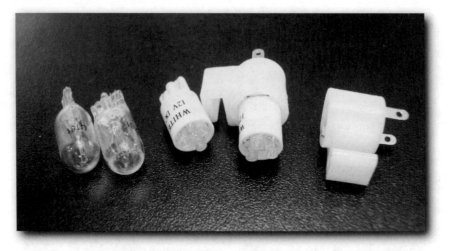

FIGURE **15-18: Regular light bulbs and the three LED super-bright cluster replacements.**
Used by permission of Happ Controls.

Connecting the coin-ups

You can connect the coin mechanisms to your interface so that inserting a quarter into the cabinet really generates a coin-up in your emulator or game. Remember the earlier caution about charging people to play your games though! If you'd like to hook them up (and for the fun of the realism I recommend it, just keep a bucket of quarters nearby for people to play) all you need to know is that they work with a familiar microswitch. The quarter (or token) rolls through the coin mechanism and is either rejected as an improper coin or is accepted and falls through the bottom of the mechanism into the coin bucket. At the last part of the coin mechanism, there's a wire that's pressed down as the coin rolls by. When the wire is pressed down, it activates a microswitch (Figure 15-19). Simply connect the microswitch to the same place you have your coin-up buttons on your control panel to make both of them functional at the same time!

FIGURE **15-19: Close-up of the microswitch on the coin mechanism.**
Used by permission of Happ Controls.

Powering the cabinet

"Scottie, I need more power."

"I'm giving you all she's got sir!"

"Darnit Scottie, I *need* more power!"

Well, the *Enterprise* might have had power issues, but your cabinet won't! I've already covered the low-voltage power inside the cabinet, making 5 volts and 12 volts available for miscellaneous lights and such. What about powering the whole cabinet, however? You could just mount a power strip in the cabinet and turn everything on one by one, but where's the fun in that? This is an arcade cabinet, right? Don't they turn on with a single button?

It used to be that if you wanted the single-button power-on effect you had to work with high-voltage wiring. People would hack power switches so they could extend them to a different location. I cannot at all recommend that as there are now commercial, off-the-shelf solutions that achieve the desired results. Leave working with high-voltage electricity to the electricians.

Caution

Up until now, other than the monitor, everything discussed for your arcade cabinet has been low-voltage stuff. The main power to the cabinet, however, is high voltage. Once again, you need to be careful—do something incorrectly and you can be hurt or killed! The author and Wiley Publishing emphatically recommend that you *do not* do any high-voltage wiring hacking for your cabinet, and that, instead, you use the safe off-the-shelf solutions that are available.

What home arcade cabinet builders need is a way to power up their entire arcade cabinet with a single button without having a bunch of power cords exiting the cabinet. This is easy enough with the Project Arcade plans because of the open back. Simply mount your power strip conveniently near the opening in back, plug all your equipment into it, and turn everything on with a flick of the strip's power button.

What if you don't have an open back, however, or don't want to have to reach in the back to turn it on? If your PC has the ability to power on with a keystroke (which many computers do; check the system setup on the PC), then you can power the entire cabinet up by pressing a single arcade pushbutton! What makes this work is a clever power strip (Figure 15-20) from a company called Bits Limited (`www.smartstrip.net/`).

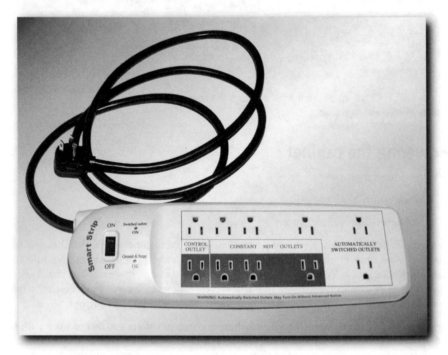

FIGURE 15-20: The power strip from Bits Limited.
Used by permission of Bits Limited.

The Bits Limited power strip has three different kinds of outlets on it. The first is a control outlet. You plug your PC into that. The other outlets are relay outlets. Everything else goes into those. The last outlets are regular power outlets that you probably won't use. The control outlet senses when whatever is plugged into it is turned on. When it realizes something's been turned on, it turns power on to the devices in the relay outlets. Turn on your computer, and your monitor, speakers, and marquee all come powering on as well! All you need to do is include a button somewhere on the cabinet that's connected to your encoder and generates the right keystroke needed to power on your computer. Some computers will power on with the space bar, some with another keystroke or perhaps even a mouse button. Consult the documentation or the system settings on your computer to see if this applies to you and what keystroke is needed. Sears sells a smaller power outlet that is similar, but it plugs directly into the wall so you'll need to run cords out of your cabinet to the wall, somewhat defeating the purpose. The power strip from Bits Limited works great and has an adjustable sensitivity for the different power requirements of control devices. Bits Limited acted in direct response to requests from the arcade cabinet community and added a model of their power strip that had a black power cord instead of the default white. They also offered free upgrades to their customers who had purchased earlier versions without the sensitivity adjustment capability. Clearly, a sign of a company eager to please their customers!

Summary

Wow! For being a chapter involving odds and ends, there was a lot of material to cover! I hope you had as much fun working through this chapter as I had writing it. From having a functional but unadorned cabinet, you've now progressed through lighting it up, applying artwork, protecting the vulnerable parts, and powering everything up. Now it not only plays games like a real arcade machine, it looks and acts like one too. You also got to play with power tools again! What a great chapter! What else could there be to talk about?

Well, if you've made it this far without anything going wrong, congratulations! Unfortunately, I had a stumbling block or two as I was putting everything together, and the odds are that you may have run into one somewhere along the line as well. In the next chapter, I'll take a look at where you can go for help and what to do if you get stuck. There are still many exciting things to look at in the rest of the book, so carry on to Chapter 16!

Like the Concept but Not Sure You Have It in You?

part

V

Stuck? Frustrated? Out of Quarters?

It's inevitable. Like the way a younger relative puts you to shame on a game you thought you were the master of, sooner or later a problem may get the better of you. No matter how good your plan or how skilled you are, you're likely to come to a point in your cabinet building where you need some help. Even the mad scientist had Igor! Where can *you* go for help building your arcade cabinet? Right here! I'll start by pointing out a few troubleshooting tips for commonly encountered problems and then move on to places you can go for extra assistance if needed. Read on!

Troubleshooting Tips

Getting stuck can be incredibly frustrating. The most important thing to remember is not to panic. I had my share of problems when I put together Project Arcade, and everything turned out not only well but outstanding in the end. Whatever challenge or hurdle is in front of you, it's likely that some-one has dealt with it before. There's no way to predict exactly what issue you might run into. However, several problems seem to come up time and again, and I'll try to help you out with those. Start your way out of your problem with these basic troubleshooting tips. Some are common sense, and some are specific to issues that have come up before in these kinds of projects.

Cabinet-building conundrums

Most cabinet construction issues fall into the common sense category. It's important to spend some time here and get everything right. Computer, controls, and software issues can all be dealt with at any time. Your cabinet, however, will be difficult if not impossible to tweak once it's all put together. The following are some common pitfalls you may encounter and possible solutions.

Minor wood fitting and placement issues

This is a likely problem, particularly with angled cuts. If the problems are minor, then a bit of cosmetic touchup is likely all that you'll need. I ran into this problem building Project Arcade. My angles weren't perfect, and I had a visible gap between the back angled piece and the upper back piece. Once I applied wood putty and paint, the gap could not be seen (see Figure 16-1). While I was focused on that part of the project it was extremely frustrating, but once I patched it and moved on to other areas I realized it didn't matter at all. I was stressing about something that no one but I was likely to ever see, much less notice that it was patched, even if they did see the back of my cabinet. Lesson learned: *Don't let minor cosmetic issues bother you.*

FIGURE 16-1: Close-up of back panels with no visible gaps.

Major wood fitting and placement issues

Hopefully you won't run into a major problem. If you do, however, you have several options. If the problem doesn't affect the structural soundness of the cabinet, you can disguise the problem. If it does affect the stability of the cabinet, you'll need to take steps to correct it, even if it means buying new wood and rebuilding a section. For instance, I originally misplaced the monitor shelf by about an inch or so (Figure 16-2). I could have simply added an additional strip of wood to cover the huge gap and/or disguised it with the monitor bezel. However, I elected to remove the shelf and replace it properly. It was painful to have to undo and redo it, but the cabinet is better off for having been done correctly. Lesson learned: *It's better to bite the bullet and do it over than to live with a major defect.*

FIGURE 16-2: Monitor shelf too high and recessed in the cabinet with huge gap.

Painting problems

Your paint job may or may not be a major issue to you. If you're going to have your cabinet in a dimly lit basement game room, it's probably not worth worrying too much about it. If your project is going to be the centerpiece of a brightly lit family room, however, then a good paint job can make or break the appearance of the cabinet. If you're having problems getting it to look the way you want, double-check these tips:

- Make sure you're using the right paint and tools. Generally, a latex semi-gloss is the paint of choice for MDF-based cabinets. Also, not all rollers/brushes are made alike. Make sure the tools you use are meant for the paint you're using and the finish you're after. A builder's grade paint roller will not give you the best results on your cabinet's surface! The folks at your paint store can help you out if you're not sure.

- Proper surface preparation is key. Make sure you've applied a layer or two of primer and that you're sanding the surface smooth between coats of primer and paint. If you're after a really smooth finish, don't be afraid to sand it almost down to the next layer with fine-grit sandpaper. Multiple thin coats of paint will yield better results than fewer and thicker layers. Don't overlook the appeal of a slightly textured surface, however. It can look just as nice as a mirror smooth surface and is much easier to achieve.

- Don't rush the painting. Use nice smooth strokes while you are painting and take your time. Then make sure you leave enough time for the surface to totally dry between coats of paint. Read the drying times for your paint and stick to them. Don't be afraid to take a couple of days for the entire paint job.

Lesson learned: *Using the right material and tools and taking the time to do the job properly will yield much better results than trying to hurry this step along using the wrong material and tools.*

Problems getting tools to cooperate

Trying to accomplish something when you don't have the right (and working) tool for the job is incredibly frustrating. My best example of this is attempting to cut the groove for t-molding without a slot cutter bit. My buddy and I tried using a Dremel rotary tool first. It was extremely slow and almost burned up the tool. Next, we tried a router with a straight cutting bit. It was fast enough but essentially impossible to guide in a straight line (due to the narrow edge of the wood, we weren't able to use a straight-edge guide). Finally, my slot-cutting bit arrived in the mail. Using it, I was able to easily and accurately cut perfectly straight grooves in very little time. I was literally able to work about ten times as fast with about one-quarter of the effort. Sometimes you have no choice and simply have to work with what's available. However, if you have the option then buy, rent, or borrow the proper tool for the job in front of you. There is simply no acceptable substitute for having the right tool for the right job. Lesson learned: *Using the right tool for the right job isn't just a cliché; it will save you time and frustration in the long run.*

Gain a fresh perspective

If all else fails, take a break and come back to it later. It frequently amazes me that what seemed insurmountable after a long and frustrating work session is easily solved when you look at it after taking a break. Consider getting a second opinion at that time from a buddy as well. The problem I had with the monitor shelf seemed insurmountable at first but was simple enough to resolve the next day. Lesson learned: *Building a cabinet shouldn't be a race. Taking a break and coming back with a fresh perspective is much easier than trying to brute-force a solution when you're frustrated.*

Software snafus

Setting up your computer and games is likely to throw up an occasional stumbling block as well. Much of what you'll put into your arcade cabinet is pieced together from multiple sources and not from a single software solution. That means it's possible that you'll run into issues getting everything working together properly. Here are a few tips to help you stave off software snafus.

Identify the culprit

The first step in resolving a software problem is identifying where the problem lies. A blank screen that appears when you launch a Multiple Arcade Machine Emulator (MAME) game through the Dragon King front end could be a problem with the emulator, the front end, the ROMs being used, or something else entirely. Where do you start troubleshooting? Start with a process of elimination. The game should run straight from the emulator without the front end, so try that. If running it manually in MAME works but running it with Dragon King does not, then something has gone wrong with the front end. If it won't work in the emulator directly, then there's no point in even looking at the front end. If you have another computer, try running the emulator and ROM on that system. If it works there and not on your cabinet computer, you've probably got a configuration or driver issue. If it won't work on either computer, then the ROM may be corrupt or emulation of that game may not be working yet. Lesson learned: *Identifying the root of the problem is the first step toward fixing it.*

Check your paths

Probably the most common issue that comes up with emulators and front ends is using incorrect directories (also known as folders) or not specifying them properly. Emulators have to know where the ROMs for the games you want to play are, and front ends have to know that and where the emulator is as well. Most assume a standard set of defaults. For instance, the assumed default for MAME is C:\MAME for the emulator and C:\MAME\ROMS for the ROMs. If you're using different directories, make sure you've configured the emulator and/or front end appropriately. Several front ends tested while writing this book assumed that they were installed in the same directory as MAME. I ran into this while testing because I used separate subdirectories for each front end to keep things cleaner. Obviously, those front ends that need to be in the same directory as MAME wouldn't work. It took me some head scratching and consultation on the message forums to figure that out because that requirement wasn't always clearly documented. Lesson learned: *Pay attention to the directories used when installing your software, and make sure that what you have configured or what the software requires matches what you actually have.*

Just the FAQs, ma'am

If you're having problems with a specific emulator or front end, see if there's a FAQ on the software's Web site. FAQ stands for Frequently Asked Questions, and if there is one, then it might have the answers you're looking for. MAME's FAQ can be located at www.mame.net/mamefaq.html. Lesson learned: *The problem you have may have already been addressed by the software developers; take a look.*

Come back to it later

Sometimes with emulation and gaming software, giving up *temporarily* is the right thing to do. The problem may be one that's not solvable with the tools available to you at the time. Particularly with emulation software, remember that you're usually not purchasing an off-the-shelf commercially supported product. Emulating another hardware and software system is complex, and first efforts often come with bugs. In fact, those bugs may be known and documented at time of software release or shortly thereafter. For instance, the MAME Testers Web site (www.mametesters.com/) was created specifically to help identify bugs in MAME and to track their statuses. This is a good place to check if you're having a problem with a specific MAME game. If there's a known bug, you have two choices — wait for a new version to hopefully correct it or, in the case of open source software, you might consider looking at the code and helping to fix it. Either way, emulation software often gets updated with a host of bug fixes after its release. This also applies to front ends, operating systems, and hardware drivers. Lesson learned: *Sometimes a problem with a particular piece of software simply can't be solved. With thousands of other games available, learn when a problem isn't worth further troubleshooting efforts and mark it for a return visit when the software's been updated.*

Update everything

If you're having a problem you can't figure out, make sure every piece of software involved is up to date. A sound issue in an emulator could be a fault in the emulation or it *might* be a problem with older sound card drivers. Display problems? Make sure you have the latest version of your video drivers and Direct-X from Microsoft installed on your system. Making sure all your software and all hardware drivers are fully up to date can save you time troubleshooting. However, there is one instance where you might want to take the opposite advice: Because MAME is a documentation project first and foremost, later versions of MAME sometimes break (temporarily) games that worked in earlier versions. Reverting to an earlier version is sometimes the easiest way to resolve a particular game problem. Lesson learned: *The problem you're facing may be solvable simply by updating (or in rare occasions, reverting to an earlier version of) the software you're using.*

Getting Help

If a bit of extra time and the previous troubleshooting tips didn't work, then it's time to ask for help. Fortunately, you have many resources available to you. There are many online resources dedicated to this crazy, wonderful hobby. I'll introduce you to some of the best places to get help in this section.

How to get help, and how not to

By picking up this book and thinking about or actually building your own arcade cabinet, you've joined a select but growing group of retro-gaming enthusiasts. By conservative estimates, there are a few thousand home-built arcade machines out there, and more are being built every day. This means that, although you may have found a unique idea to try, for the most part the path you're traveling has been walked upon before. One of the signature marks of this hobby is the overwhelming number of people who donate time, effort, and money (by financing a product or hosting a Web site) to help others join the fun. These people have documented, photographed, and self-published via Web sites and message forums their contributions to the hobby for all to share.

These are all wonderful resources you can turn to for help. However, this also means a bit of effort is warranted on your part when you seek answers. Newcomers to the hobby are always welcomed enthusiastically, but it is important that you've taken advantage of the available resources to try to find your answer. For instance, a request such as this is likely to find many helpful answers: *"I've searched the Web site and message forums, but I am still unclear on this point. How do you mount the marquee at the top of the arcade cabinet without screwing holes into it?"* On the other hand, a request along the lines of this next one is more likely to get a curt reply to read the available documentation (or to be ignored) than anything else: *"Need someone to explain to me step by step how to build an arcade machine. E-mail it to me. Thanks."* Almost every aspect of this hobby has been documented in some fashion, so take the time to read about it first. Not only are you likely to find your answer that way, but even if you aren't, you'll be able to ask more specific questions than a general cry for help.

If you do need to ask for help, use the public forums whenever possible as compared to E-mailing someone directly. There are several advantages to doing so. Instead of relying upon a single person to help you, by posting in a public forum you allow for the possibility of hundreds or thousands of people being able to assist you. Also, many people who have some public presence in this hobby (such as the first one to create a rotating control panel) can receive hundreds of E-mails weekly. Personally speaking, it sometimes takes me more than a week to respond to E-mails that come to my public E-mail addresses. By posting to a public forum you can often get an answer in minutes or hours instead of days. Finally, and probably the most compelling reason to ask for help publicly, is that the question you're asking is one that someone else is probably wondering about as well. By getting a good discussion going on the question and possible answers, that information will be available to the next person in the future. That's truly the strength of the Internet at work!

Helpful Web sites

You can find many excellent Web sites relating to the emulation and arcade cabinet-building communities. Most of the sites are dedicated to a particular aspect or genre of the hobby. For instance, just about every emulator and front-end program has a home Web site, as referenced when introduced in this book.

On the CD You'll find a clickable list of these Web sites on the companion CD.

You can also find a few Web sites that are broader in scope and should be on your list of places to go to for more information and assistance:

BYOAC

A great place to get help is the Web site that was the spark behind writing this book, the Build Your Own Arcade Controls FAQ at www.arcadecontrols.com/. Until the second edition of this book comes out (I can dream!), changes and updates from the time of this printing will make their way to the Web site. You'll find how-to instruction guides, hardware reviews, utilities and multimedia downloads, and a several-thousand-member active user community at BYOAC. BYOAC is also the home to the comprehensive examples database, listing and linking to more than 700 arcade cabinet and joystick console projects at the time this book goes to press.

Unquestionably the most active sections of the BYOAC Web site are the message forums. This is where you can go to meet and discuss arcade cabinet-related issues with other like-minded folk. Message forums at BYOAC include the following:

- **Main forum** — This forum contains the bulk of the discussions at BYOAC. Anything that doesn't fit into a dedicated forum goes here. Frequent topics of conversation here occasionally spin off a dedicated forum. Help for anything from building arcade cabinets to discussing arcade controls to purchasing components can be found here.

- **Buy/Sell/Trade** — As the name suggests, this is a marketplace for people to buy, sell, or trade anything related to arcade cabinet building. Commercial vendors are welcomed here. Need help finding a rare part? This forum is for you.

- **Software** — This forum is primarily devoted to front-end programs, emulators, juke boxes, and other arcade cabinet-related software topics.

- **Monitor/Video** — This forum is for discussing all things related to monitors and video cards. This is one of the first forums that grew out of repeated discussions in the main forum.

- **Audio/Jukebox/MP3** — This is a forum for the discussion of speakers, sound cards, juke boxes, MP3s (legal only please!), and all things audio related.

- **Project Announcements** — This forum is a place to announce new projects in the works, brag about your continued progress, and get feedback while you're still working on your project.

- **Artwork** — Looking for artwork for your cabinet or willing to provide it to others? Seeking comments on artwork you've created? Post about it here!

- **Consoles** — A forum for bringing arcade cabinet-building concepts to the world of game consoles such as the Xbox and PlayStation.

With more than 16,000 topics of discussion as of the time of this writing, you're likely to find that just about any issue you're having problems with has already been discussed here. If not, feel free to start a new topic of discussion. Chances are it won't be long before you're on the way to solving your problem!

MAMEWorld

MAMEWorld (www.mameworld.net/) dubs itself as the largest MAME resource on the net, and with good reason. Not only is it an absolutely wonderful emulation news site, it also hosts a plethora (and that's really the appropriate word here) of sections and specialty sites devoted to MAME. Granted, MAME is not the only thing you're able to play on your cabinet. However, almost every emulation cabinet out there does run MAME, so quality MAME help is good to find. Among the dozens of sites hosted by MAMEWorld are the DOS MAME support site, Zakk's wonderful Massive MAME Project, Easy MAMECab, and EmuAdvice. DOS MAME (www.mameworld.net/dosmame/), as the name implies, will help you configure your cabinet's computer with DOS and MAME. Massive MAME (www.mameworld .net/massive/) is a must visit, with some 20 or so emulation cabinets to the Web master's credit. You'll find artwork for your cabinet, how-to articles, and much more at Massive MAME. Easy MAMECab (http://easymamecab.mameworld.net/) has specific DOS and arcade monitor advice. Finally, EmuAdvice (www.mameworld.net/emuadvice/) is an older Web site devoted to helping you get started with emulation. It has since been replaced with the next Web site, but it still has much useful information if you're running older emulators.

easyEmu

easyEmu (www.mameworld.net/easyemu/) is another excellent Web site to visit for assistance with setting up and running emulators. Along with MAME support, easyEmu has guides and tutorials for another dozen or so emulators and utilities. The guides and tutorials are particularly handy for some older emulators that are no longer in development or supported but are still choices you may want to consider.

Newsgroups

Usenet newsgroups are another wonderful Internet resource you can turn to for help. A newsgroup is a discussion forum that is not hosted in any one central location but instead is decentralized across the Internet. Messages in a particular newsgroup are copied from server to server, and to access them you simply need access to a server that carries the newsgroup you're interested in. It used to be that your Internet service provider had to carry the newsgroup you wanted to read or you were out of luck. However, these days you can access newsgroups online through Google Groups (`http://groups.google.com/`). There are three groups of particular interest to arcade cabinet enthusiasts:

- **RGVAC — Rec.Games.Video.Arcade.Collecting**
  (`http://groups.google.com/groups?q=group:rec.games.video.arcade.collecting`) is a newsgroup dedicated to discussions about real arcade machines and collecting them. It is *not* an appropriate place to discuss emulation-related topics and matters specific to home arcade cabinets. There is much overlap, however, between a home arcade cabinet and a real classic arcade cabinet. For instance, discussions on repairing arcade monitors or painting techniques for arcade cabinets are certainly on target.

- **RGVAM — Rec.Games.Video.Arcade.Marketplace**
  (`http://groups.google.com/groups?q=group:rec.games.video.arcade.marketplace`) is a place to discuss buying, selling, and trading items related to arcade collecting. This is a good group to keep an eye on for cheap arcade parts and the like. Topics are often cross-posted to RGVAC as well, but that should really be avoided to keep the noise level there down.

- **AGM — Alt.Games.MAME**
  (`http://groups.google.com/groups?q=group:alt.games.mame`) is dedicated to discussing all things related to MAME, the Multiple Arcade Machine Emulator. Topics range from running MAME to building arcade cabinets for use with MAME.

It's time to bring up the warning about the wild nature of the Internet again. You'll find the best and worst of people on the newsgroups. In addition to wonderfully on-topic discussions and useful information, you'll find an occasional profane or hate-filled posting. Filter it out and the newsgroups are a must-visit resource.

Giving Back

Okay. So you've done your planning and gotten started. You've probably made mistakes, skinned your knuckles, or perhaps thought of something unique and brilliant. Hopefully this book or one of the many projects out there has inspired and helped you. Finally, you're faced with the results of your efforts, a beautiful home arcade cabinet! Are you done?

Maybe not — you might want to consider *one more thing* when it comes to your arcade cabinet project. Presumably the wonder you've created came about with the help and advice of others. Wouldn't it be great if you could give some of that back to the community now that you're an arcade veteran yourself? You can! Being a community, there are a few ways you can help out the next person trying to reach arcade cabinet happiness. Document what you've done, what you've learned, what you'd recommend, and what you'd avoid! Don't forget what it was like when you were just getting started. Someone else is just beginning, and they could use all the help you're able to give!

Build a Web site

Start by considering a Web site. It doesn't have to be anything terribly fancy, although once you've mastered an arcade cabinet project putting together a nice Web page should be no challenge at all. If you took my advice in Chapter 1, then you've already got the makings of a Web site in the construction diary you've been keeping. Even if you haven't kept track as you went along, reconstructing the basic steps probably won't prove too difficult. A Web page with some good photos of your project, along with a description of anything particularly complicated or unique about your cabinet, makes a great addition to the arcade cabinet-building community.

If you have an Internet connection, then chances are your Internet service provider has given you some Web space on which you can host your arcade cabinet project. If not, you can find several Web hosting companies willing to host your site for free in exchange for placing ad banners on your site. You can also ask on the message forums; occasionally someone there is willing to host an ad-free site for you.

Join the BYOAC community

If a Web site is outside the scope of things you're up for then consider becoming an active member of the BYOAC community. Even if you do put up a Web site, we'd love to see you join us online. Becoming an active posting member of the message forums at www.arcade controls.com/ is sure to give you a great feeling, and helping someone with a problem is good karma! Aside from the regular message forum postings, there's a semi-regular group that meets in the BYOAC chat room (graciously hosted by Internet provider Datasync, www. datasync.com/) every evening Monday through Friday. You'll find the chat room linked off the message forums at the BYOAC Web site. Hope to see you there!

Summary

Building an arcade cabinet and using emulation software on it is a bit of an adventure into the unknown. Although the hobby has begun to mature and has evolved from the sparsely documented beginning days, there's still a lot of new territory being covered. It's an interesting time to be involved in the hobby, but recall the curse "*May you live in interesting times.*" Fortunately, if you run into uncharted waters there are several resources you can turn to for help. Software Web sites, newsgroups, and online discussion forums are great places to turn to when you run across a stumbling block. Do your homework first, and you'll find many people and places happy to help you along your journey to arcade Nirvana!

Building an arcade cabinet is the ultimate expression of this hobby. However, not everyone wants to go the full distance at first or put in all the time and effort. Some people are just interested in a better way to play games than the keyboard, and are looking to buy their way to arcade Nirvana rather than build their own. That's okay, and is what I'll present to you in the next chapter.

Buying Your Way to Gaming Nirvana

Building an arcade control cabinet is an incredibly rewarding experience. It can also be a costly one — in terms of both time and money spent. Some people report building full-sized arcade cabinets for a few hundred dollars, but most will spend somewhere between $1,000 and $1,500 (or more) when all is said and done. This includes the costs of tools, mistakes, and other "first-time" expenses. If you're planning to build more than one, the costs usually go down based on lessons learned and tools obtained for the first. If you're only planning on building one cabinet, for the same amount of money, you might consider purchasing something in kit form that will take you a day to build instead of days and weeks. You have a lot of great choices if you'd like to go this route! Of course, you can also find preassembled cabinets in the $3,000-plus range if you want top of the line! I'll take a look at some of the offerings here and point you to the rest online. Check your wallet, and dig in!

in this chapter

☑ Kits

☑ Arcade Controllers and Cabinets

☑ Game Console Controller Adapters

Note Where available, I will provide pricing for products listed here that is current as of time of writing. However, take this with a grain of salt. With a lot of competition, you may see prices begin to drop. Also, some vendors may be willing to customize their offerings for you, which will allow you to save some money on items you'd prefer to supply yourself such as the computer. If one of the kits or machines interests you, but you have sticker shock, it never hurts to ask!

Kits

Kits are a great compromise between building your own from scratch and buying an arcade cabinet fully assembled. Normally, I shy away from hardware reviews in a book format because the information gets dated so quickly. (Reviews can be found online at the Build Your Own Arcade Controls [BYOAC] Web site if you'd like to read more.) However, all the kits in this section were sent to us for a hands-on review so I'll go ahead and share the results here. The kits were placed into the hands of my buddy Mark. Mark is an arcade enthusiast who has never delved into building his own arcade controllers or cabinets before (other than a brief stint with the router while building Project Arcade) and, as such, made a perfect test case for the ease and completeness of these kits.

Some comments apply to all the kits in general. Assembly of the three upright cabinets and one cocktail cabinet took a full day, which means any of these kits can be built within a few hours. If you have assembled any furniture in kit form before, such as bookshelves available at any department store, then these kits will look familiar. As a rule, all of the packages were heavy so arrange to have a buddy to help you with the lifting. Quality varied from plain but serviceable furniture to top-of-the-line "Wow I gotta have that!"

Space constraints only allow for one picture at most per kit or cabinet included here. On the companion CD-ROM, I've included several shots of each item, where available, so you can get a really good look at them.

Arcade Depot cocktail kit

Arcade Depot (www.arcadedepot.com) sent a cocktail kit for review (see Figure 17-1). Initial impressions were in the "wow" category. The kit came in two, incredibly well-packed boxes. The cardboard boxes were framed inside with wood boards and had plenty of packing material inside. The cocktail glass had no less than 25 rubber bumpers placed on it with packing material, and the box was clearly labeled not to lay it flat. Needless to say, everything arrived in perfect condition!

FIGURE 17-1: The Arcade Depot cocktail kit (assembled).
Used by permission of Arcade Depot.

Assembling the kit went quickly. Printed instructions included many pictures, and instructions were detailed and complete. Tricky points along the way were anticipated and pointed out, which helped to avoid problems. The cabinet is constructed of plywood, dowel pins, and wood glue with a few screws and brackets thrown in for extra support. The control panels are a tad small as befits a cocktail cabinet, which normally houses games with a single joystick and a few buttons, but a third and larger control panel option is available for the side. The control panels are made of metal and are available as blanks with pre-drilled holes in a standard pattern or with customized pre-drilled holes, depending on your needs. We were very impressed with the quality of the kit. You will need a screwdriver and a variety of clamps for optimal construction.

The only question left after constructing the cabinet is how to mount the monitor. The hinged door is meant for cabinet access only and will not support the weight of a monitor. You will have to determine your own method for installing the monitor, computer, and joysticks. Depending on the options selected at time of purchase, prices for the kits range upward from $200. The kit pictured in Figure 17-1 is available for approximately $310.

This is a great little kit and is very reasonably priced. Arcade Depot also sells preassembled cocktail cabinets, including a replica *Ms. Pac-Man* cocktail cabinet complete with inside electronics and cabinet graphics.

HanaHo ArcadeWerX

HanaHo may not be a familiar name if you are new to the home arcade cabinet hobby, but, if you're an arcade veteran, then you're familiar with their work. They have been building arcade cabinets for arcade manufacturers for 30 years, such as the Dragon's Lair cabinet among many others. HanaHo *knows* arcade cabinet building, and it shows! They sent one of their ArcadeWerX mini cabinet kits for us to build (www.arcadewerx.com). It was packed extremely well and made it to us in great shape. The assembled cabinet is shown in Figure 17-2.

The instructions included for assembly are very well documented and include many construction pictures. There were no ambiguous points so mistakes were easily avoided. There are a lot of wrist-killing screws and bolts in this kit and use of a power screwdriver is highly recommended. The kit is constructed from 3/4-inch, Melamine-laminated wood with a black finish and matching black t-molding. HanaHo includes several nice touches in their kit, such as the professionally made ArcadeWerX marquee, locking front panel (keys are taped to the back; remove before assembling!), and a Number 3 Phillips Bit. Everything in the kit spoke of the quality that comes from years of experience.

FIGURE 17-2: The ArcadeWerX mini cabinet.
Used by permission of HanaHo Games.

The cabinet does not come with a control panel. It is designed to work with the HotRod control panel from HanaHo (shown later in this chapter), or you can build your own to fit the space provided. This makes a great kids' cabinet (see Figure 17-3) or a sit-down cabinet. Adults will not want to play on it for long periods of time standing up because it will grow uncomfortable. However, HanaHo also sells an optional stand you can add that raises the cabinet by 10 inches.

The ArcadeWerX sells for $600. When you apply the included full-sized side art and light up the marquee, you have a great looking mini arcade cabinet! This cabinet is destined for the kids' playroom and is sure to be a favorite for years to come.

FIGURE 17-3: My children look over their new ArcadeWerx cabinet.
Used by permission of HanaHo Games.

SlikStik arcade cabinet

Big. That's the very first impression you get when the packages from SlikStik arrive at your door. The next impression is "heavy." This is one solid package! SlikStik (who also sells the Tornado spinner you were introduced to in Chapter 4) sent us their arcade cabinet kit to look at (www.slikstik.com). At the risk of sounding like a broken record, "wow!" (see Figure 17-4).

Protecting the kit was obviously well-thought-out. For instance, all the cabinet parts have a plastic film over them to protect the finish. The Styrofoam packaging was damaged in several places, but the packaging did its job, and the cabinet parts were unscathed. No instructions are included with the cabinet because they are available online after you purchase it. The instructions are in PDF format and include many pictures and details. Once the instructions were downloaded and printed, Mark got to work.

FIGURE **17-4: The SlikStik arcade cabinet.**
Used by permission from SlikStik.

At several points during the construction, Mark was heard to exclaim at the quality of what he was assembling. This is a full-sized arcade cabinet somewhat similar in design to the Project Arcade plans. It assembles much like self-assembly furniture with insert and twist locking cam latches. Some self-assembly furniture feels rickety and fragile. Lest I give you the wrong impression, rest assured that the assembled SlikStik cabinet is a solid, durable beast. It was apparent during the assembly process that much attention was paid to the overall design of the cabinet. Quality is not a concern here! Nice touches with this cabinet include a coin door, speaker grill covers, marquee holder, and hidden keyboard drawer among others. The cabinet does not include a control panel, but it is designed to work with the various control panel models SlikStik sells (shown later in this chapter).

Having been in business for a few years, SlikStik is a relative newcomer to the arcade cabinet community, but its product line continues to impress. This is the third product from SlikStik to make its way to us, and all have been top-of-the-line quality products. The arcade cabinet kit is available in the 27-inch model we received for $1,100 and an even bigger 33-inch model! As I showed this review to my buddy Mark, he instructed me to add another "wow" here at the end! You would be hard-pressed to find a better arcade cabinet — in kit or assembled form — than the SlikStik arcade cabinet.

X-Arcade Machine cabinet by Quasimoto

Wrapping up the roundup of arcade cabinet kits is the X-Arcade Machine from Xgaming (www.x-arcade.com/htm/cabinet.shtml). This cabinet is actually made by a company called Quasimoto (www.quasimoto.com), which markets its products through resellers like Xgaming instead of directly to customers.

We got off to a bad start with this cabinet. Unfortunately, the packaging was not up to the rigors of shipping, and our unit arrived with a broken front door. We had some missing hardware (screws and washers) and incomplete directions. We also damaged the decorative trim when moving it across the carpet, and the cabinet assembly seems less sturdy than the others. That's the bad. The good is that we liked the overall design of the cabinet and would have been favorably impressed with it had the execution been better. The cabinet comes with a 1-year warranty so, if you have any problems, Xgaming will work with you to resolve them.

The overall concept of the X-Arcade Machine is very nice. It's an attractive cabinet with a Euro-style curved back and sleek black styling (no, it's not a car). This cabinet seems catered to fans of game consoles (like the Nintendo Game Cube and such) because it varies somewhat from the standard arcade cabinet mold. There are shelves behind the bottom door to house game consoles, and the top area behind the marquee is exposed instead of enclosed. The snazzy looking header doesn't light up, but it can be instead flipped back to reveal the equipment stored up there (such as a game console). The header is made of an opaque mesh so it's a great place to put a speaker.

Quasimoto put some very nice touches in the design of the cabinet, such as the adjustable mounting brace on the monitor shelf to accomodate different-sized monitors or televisions. The monitor area will hold up to a 27-inch display, which is plenty big for as close to the action as you get. The cabinet also includes a power strip that mounts out of the way behind the unit, and the rounded enclosure in the back means all the cords are hidden from view except the single power cord to the wall outlet. Very nice!

The kit is the only one I received that includes a control panel, the X-Arcade joystick. The cabinet is available for $1,100, which includes free shipping and the joystick console, or you can elect to buy it without the console for $950. Overall, the X-Arcade Machine gets good marks for concept and appearances, but more attention needs to be paid to quality control. We've alerted the manufacturer as to the issues we encountered. Check online at the Web site (www.arcadecontrols.com) to see if there are any updates regarding this cabinet. The X-Arcade Machine by Quasimoto, in full working order, would make a decent addition to a family or kids' game room. Fill it with a couple of game consoles, VCR/DVD player, and a 27-inch television, and go to town.

Arcade Controllers and Cabinets

If building a kit isn't your cup of tea, you can purchase a ready-to-play setup from a variety of places instead. Both desktop arcade controllers and arcade cabinets are available.

You can find pictures of many of the controllers and cabinets listed in the following sections on the companion CD-ROM.

Desktop arcade controllers

You can find a lot of people making and selling desktop arcade controllers. Many people make them one-at-a-time and customized to your specifications. A list of those would be impossible and out-of-date almost immediately, but, if you'd like to find them, you can look on the BYOAC message forums and the `alt.games.mame` newsgroup. These can make great additions to a game room, and I would not hesitate to consider one just because they do not have a company behind them. However, the backing of a company usually means a certain level of support and speed so be aware of all the factors (ask) before you purchase.

There are also several companies doing business that make arcade controllers every day as a normal part of business. Space constraints limit complete reviews, but you can find many of these products reviewed online. Check the reviews page on the BYOAC Web site (`www.arcadecontrols.com`) for up-to-date links to reviews. Some of the places you can look for arcade controllers include:

- GameCab (`www.gamecab.com`) sells a variety of customizable arcade controllers starting at $120 and ranging up to $500 or so. The controllers use either KeyWiz or I-PAC encoders, and options include Oscar Control spinners and Imperial trackballs.

- HanaHo (`www.hanaho.com`) was the first company to get into and *stay* in the home arcade controller business. They sell a very popular arcade controller called the HotRod, which is a two-player controller with one stick and seven buttons per player. As a bonus, the controller ships with a CD collection of 14 licensed ROMs from Capcom! HanaHo has fired the first shot in a possible price war by dropping the price to $100.

- SlikStik (`www.slikstik.com`) sells an amazing home arcade controller. Hands down, it is the biggest control panel available and comes in a variety of configurations ranging from $250 to $700. Their four-player control panel has to be seen to be believed! They are the manufacturers of the Tornado Spinner introduced in Chapter 4. In addition to the standard range of colors and joysticks, they also have stainless steel joysticks available for a unique look!

- Treyonics (`www.treyonics.com`) is a relative newcomer to the home arcade market. Treyonics has been getting attention for the quality of their Devastator II arcade controller. Most recently, *Maximum PC* magazine gave it their highest rating, and they are a notoriously tough crowd to please. The controller comes with two joysticks (one is a top fire), a handful of buttons per player, a trackball, a spinner, and a lifetime warranty for $400.

- Xgaming is another big presence in the home arcade market with their popular X-Arcade (`www.x-arcade.com`) line of arcade controllers. They make a single- and a two-player unit with one joystick and eight buttons per player. The signature selling point of the X-Arcade units is their customized encoder interface. The X-Arcade is capable of connecting not only to a PC, but, with the right adapter sold by the company, it can also connect to PlayStation, Xbox, GameCube, Dreamcast, and Macintosh systems. Xgaming has stated their commitment to continue to come out with adapters for new game consoles as they are introduced, making the one-time investment in the X-Arcade one that will continue to pay off. The X-Arcade sells for $150 with one adapter, and extra adapters are available for $20 to $30.

Full arcade cabinets

Just like arcade controllers, there are many people who would be happy to build you a custom arcade cabinet. The same caveat applies. There's nothing wrong with buying from an individual as long as you realize you are buying from an individual and not a company. The BYOAC forums and the `alt.games.mame` newsgroup are both good places to find someone willing to build you a cabinet. Often, you can find someone local to your area and save a bit on shipping costs.

There are also many companies that would be happy to sell you an arcade cabinet. Be prepared for sticker shock; these cabinets are not usually cheap. Bear in mind you're not only paying for the materials, but you're also paying for the time and labor you are not having to spend. This is a very fluid market right now with new vendors coming onto the scene and others dropping off. Some of the companies listed subsequently are known, stable sources for arcade cabinets (such as HanaHo and Game Cabinets, Inc.). Others are relatively new to the market but appear to be promising. Before buying, be sure to check current status, references, and feedback on the BYOAC forums and `alt.games.mame` newsgroup.

- ArcadeShopper.com (`www.arcadeshopper.com`) defies easy categorization. An online arcade business, they sell an eclectic collection of arcade cabinets and kits. See their Web site for current offerings and prices.

- Custom Arcades (`www.custom-arcade.com`) is another relative newcomer to the home arcade cabinet community and has an exciting host of cabinets available. They are the only vendor at the time of this writing selling a sit-down driving cabinet that I am aware of, dubbed the Roadrage. Prices start at $1,800 for the countertop model complete with computer and range up to $6,000 for the awesome racing cabinet.

- Dream Authentics (`www.dreamauthentics.com`) sells a variety of pre-built arcade cabinets outfitted with SlikStik control panels. Prices range between $3,000 and $6,000 and include computer, monitor, controllers, and sound system.

- Game Cabinets, Inc. (`www.gamecabinetsinc.com`) was referenced earlier in Chapter 2 for the cocktail cabinet construction plans they sell. They also sell pre-built cocktail cabinets that have been well-received by those who have purchased them. The current shipping model is a three-controller cocktail cabinet available in a black marble or cherry wood finish for $3,999.

- HanaHo (`www.hanaho.com`), of course, is the juggernaut of the home arcade cabinet business. In addition to the ArcadeWerx cabinet kit mentioned earlier in this chapter, they sell three preassembled cabinets as well in their ArcadePC line. They have a mini cabinet, full-sized deluxe, and cocktail model available. These cabinets use their popular line of HotRod controllers with extra options like a trackball and additional 4-way joystick. The ArcadePC and HotRod products have been getting great reviews for a while now. As pointed out in the ArcadeWerx review, building arcade cabinets has been HanaHo's business for 30 years — a pedigree no other cabinet vendor can boast. Prices range from $4,000 to $6,000 and include a PC with 50 licensed Capcom game ROMs.

Using an arcade machine

It has probably occurred to you that it might be simpler to convert a real arcade machine into a home arcade cabinet. Why hasn't anyone thought of that before? Well, the obvious answer is that they have. Roughly half of the home arcade cabinets submitted to the BYOAC database are converted arcade cabinets. This can be a great way to go and can be done fairly inexpensively. There are a few things to know if you're considering going this route.

Note

Before you obtain and start to convert a real arcade machine into a home arcade cabinet, *please* read Appendix B, "The Great Debate — Preserving Versus MAMEing the Past." This is an emotional issue — believe it or not — and you should know what you're getting into before you leap. Many beautiful and irreplaceable arcade treasures are being destroyed by well-meaning but uninformed people. Read Appendix B, and avoid becoming one of them!

Finding a cabinet

You can find cabinets to use for a home arcade cabinet conversion at a variety of locations. The best place to find a cabinet to use is at an arcade auction. If you haven't been to an arcade auction yet, and one is near you, I heartily recommend you go. They're a lot of fun to experience at least once. You'll encounter a warehouse full of classic and modern arcade cabinets, a row or two of pinball machines, and a variety of other gadgetry from arcades and pubs like pool tables, air hockey tables, slot machines, and so forth. Sometimes, you'll get a machine that sells for a third of its value. Other times, you'll see a beat-up clunker go for more than twice what it should. You never know what will happen at an arcade auction!

Normally at an auction, there's an area affectionally(?) referred to as "dead row." These are machines that have seen much better days. Some have damaged cabinets (steer clear), and others have all of their parts and artwork stripped but are otherwise structurally intact. These are the machines for you to keep your eye on. Often, they'll sell for as little as $1 because operators just want to get rid of them and would rather not have to haul them back home. With a structurally sound "throw-away" cabinet as a starting point, building your own arcade cabinet can be really easy!

Several arcade auction companies exist and hold auctions around the country every few months. You can check the following Web sites to see if an auction is coming near you!

- Super Auctions (www.superauctions.com)
- US Amusement Auction (www.usamusement.com)
- Auction Game Sales (www.auctiongamesales.com)

Converting a cabinet

Converting a real arcade cabinet to a home arcade cabinet is not any different from the techniques already discussed in this book with one exception that I'll get to in a moment. Having been in use in an arcade for its entire life, the cabinet is likely to need some minor repairs. A bit of wood putty, glue, and some new screws can do wonders for its stability. You'll want to clean the cabinet thoroughly at a minimum and probably will want to sand, prime, and paint it unless it has salvageable artwork on it. (You *did* read Appendix B, right?)

If there are any salvageable parts left in it that you don't want, post a message on the `rec.games.video.arcade.collecting` newsgroup to see if anyone needs them to restore a cabinet they're working on. You can either sell the part to them, or, in the true spirit of the collecting group, give it to them for the cost of shipping. Even if it looks damaged or unusable, post a message anyway. It might have that one small part on it that someone needs to bring an old friend back to life.

The one exception to a conversion being like building your own cabinet is if you are converting a cabinet that has a working game in it. Instead of hacking things apart inside the cabinet to make it talk to your computer, you can make the computer talk the arcade cabinet's language! There's a conventional standard used in many arcade cabinets called "JAMMA." JAMMA stands for Japanese Amusement Machine Manufacturers' Association and references a standard electrical hookup for monitors, speakers, and control panels. By taking advantage of the fact that JAMMA is a standard, an interface can be made that takes a PC's inputs and outputs and connects them to the JAMMA hookups in the arcade cabinet.

Because you've put an interface between the JAMMA hookups and the computer, you haven't had to modify the arcade cabinet in the slightest. You've simply unplugged the arcade cabinet's game circuit board and replaced it with your computer. You now have a home arcade cabinet with very little effort at all! If at any point in the future you want to sell the cabinet, all you have to do is plug back in the original circuit board, and it's back to its original condition. Of course, by choosing this route, you've elected to use the arcade cabinet as-is with the joysticks and buttons that it came with. You *could* add extra buttons and controls, but you're then back to the regular old method of hacking the cabinet.

You can follow this method in one of two ways. You can decide to build the interface yourself, make the wiring harness, and deal with the issues involved in using an arcade monitor as described in Chapter 12. There's a great Web site that pioneered this concept called the PC2JAMMA project at `www.mameworld.net/pc2jamma/`. Full details on how to build the PC2JAMMA interface are available there.

Building the PC2JAMMA interface can be a fun project, but, until Ultimarc came upon the scene, it was the only way to achieve the desired results. However, Ultimarc now has an adapter available called the J-PAC (`www.ultimarc.com/jpac.html`). It has the same basic functionality of its popular I-PAC encoders, but it also adds the hookups for JAMMA cabinets, including circuitry designed to work properly with an arcade monitor. With a functioning JAMMA arcade cabinet and a J-PAC, you can switch back and forth between a home arcade cabinet and a working real arcade cabinet in minutes!

Note   Do you like the idea of being able to switch back and forth? For the ultimate in switchable games, take a look at the MultiJAMMA kit from `www.multigame.com/jamma.html`. This kit allows you to plug several JAMMA arcade boards into a single JAMMA arcade cabinet and switch back and forth at the press of a button. Add your PC2JAMMA- or J-PAC-enabled PC to the mix, and make your arcade cabinet into an über-arcade cabinet!

Game Console Controller Adapters

You've got one more piece of arcade gaming fun to learn about. Entire generations have been brought up on video game consoles such as the Super Nintendo, Sega Genesis, Nintendo 64, Dreamcast, and the Sony PlayStation line. Rather than an arcade cabinet with a joystick and buttons, to them, video gaming is best done with a handheld console controller with directional pad and mini buttons. There's a whole genre of games that works well with these types of controller that aren't really any better with a joystick than they are with a keyboard.

Do you have a favorite game console controller that you'd like to use with your computer gaming? Of course, by now, you realize that, when I bring a subject like this up, it's because there's a way to get the best of both worlds! For some time now, clever game players have been building adapters and hacking game console controllers to work with personal computers. Like many things that start as home-brew hobbies, commercial adapters are now available that will connect many different controllers to your computer's USB port. You can find such adapters at many locations on the Internet. The ZTNET store (www.ztnetstore.com) is one good place to start. It sells products that connect Nintendo 64, Playstation, Dreamcast, and other console controllers to your PC. Importer Lik-Sang (www.lik-sang.com) is another online store where you can purchase such adapters, and you can also do a Google search on "PC console controller adapter" to find yet more!

 Even though there are commercial adapters to do the work for you, some of you might be thinking of building your own console controller adapter. Space doesn't permit including it here, but we've included some information on the companion CD-ROM to get you started!

Summary

Building a home arcade cabinet is an incredibly rewarding and fun experience. However, it can take more time, effort, and money than you may be willing or able to devote. If time and effort are not on your side, then you have a wide range of arcade controllers and cabinets that you can purchase. Some even come with licensed game ROMs that you can't get anywhere else! Alternatively, if all you're after is something better than the keyboard without spending more than a few dollars, a game console controller adapter makes a great addition to a computer gaming setup.

For every field of endeavor, you can find those projects that stand out above the rest. In the next chapter, I'll introduce you to some of the most inspirational controller and cabinet projects that have come through the BYOAC project database so far. You've done a lot of reading and work in the last 17 chapters. The next one's just for fun!

Online Places to Go

Now that you've got the bulk of the book behind you (unless you skipped ahead, which is okay), you've probably got a really clear understanding of how this all goes together. You may have a partially or completely finished project and be thinking of a second, or you might be reading the whole book before you plunge in. Either way, this is a great chapter to read next! I've gathered some inspirational projects for you to look at and some online resources for diving deeper into the hobby. Think you've seen it all? Think again, and dive in!

Inspirational Projects to See

Every Project Arcade creation is someone's dream. Most projects reach the point of having a playable home arcade machine, with more to do *later* on the horizon. You might have a complete cabinet, but might not have full artwork or a specific control, like a flight yoke, installed yet. That's the trap I mentioned earlier in the book, when work stalls because the machine is playable. There's absolutely nothing wrong with that; the whole point is to have fun with it. Any working home arcade machine or controller that you've built with your own hands is a great achievement! Still, however, some home arcade projects transcend the merely great to achieve awesomeness — projects that can truly be considered works of art. These are the projects that inspire us in our drive to create the *perfect* home arcade machine.

Upright arcade cabinets

Statistically speaking, you are probably most interested in examples of unique upright arcade cabinets. There are well over 500 examples of upright arcade cabinets listed in the Build Your Own Arcade Controls (BYOAC) database. The following are a handful of those that stand out from all the rest.

Note Some figures have been slightly altered for copyright reasons while still maintaining the integrity of the picture as a whole. You can see the original, unaltered images on the appropriate Web sites.

1UP's PacMAMEA

The PacMAMEA arcade cabinet (www.1uparcade.com) is probably the most acclaimed home arcade cabinet project of all. The brainchild of Rob Meyers, known online as 1UP. PacMAMEA (see Figure 18-1) is both aesthetically pleasing and a marvel of engineering, with a simple Pac-Man yellow theme, rotating control panels, and almost every type of arcade control imaginable.

FIGURE 18-1: 1UP's PacMAMEA arcade cabinet.
Used by permission of Rob Meyers.

One of the design goals with the PacMAMEA cabinet was to create as authentic an arcade cabinet appearance as possible. It started with yellow laminate for the sides, which produced a very nice arcade cabinet finish without the hassle of painting. Next, using Photoshop and high-resolution arcade artwork found on the Internet, 1UP created custom side art and control panel images. These were then printed at a local print shop on their large-scale printers. The side art was coated with spray acrylic to protect it, and the control panel overlays were covered with ⅛-inch Lexan. The marquee was printed on backlit film and sandwiched between two layers of Lexan. LED and glowire lighting (available at www.glowire.com, among other places) completes the effects used to create a classy yet eye-catching authentic arcade cabinet!

The rotating control panel setup used in PacMAMEA is probably its most distinctive and commented-upon feature. The cabinet sports three panels; one panel is active while the other two are rotated into the cabinet body. The three panels include a standard compliment of joysticks and pushbuttons as well as a removable *Star Wars* flight yoke, removable force-feedback arcade guns, Tron style trigger-grip joysticks, a trackball, and an Oscar Controls spinner. The controls are interfaced to an Ultimarc I-PAC, an Opti-PAC, and a Microsoft SideWinder Dual Strike game pad. 1UP was the first person to note that the Microsoft SideWinder Dual Strike game pads used 5K potentiometers and could be used to hack analog-style arcade controls.

The PacMAMEA Web site is fairly well detailed, and emphasis is placed on the special projects in the cabinet, including the flight yoke and gun hacks and removable modular base for the same. There is sufficient detail on the Web site to enable you to design your own version of the cabinet, and detailed plans will be available for purchase in the near future.

Note   Prominent features of the PacMAMEA arcade cabinet: rotating control panels, analog control hacks, attractive artwork.

Carlos' Centipede

Carlos' Centipede cabinet (`www.retrospieler.de`) is another blend of arcade beauty and technical innovation. The cabinet is a from-scratch-built replica of an Atari Centipede cabinet complete with reproduction artwork, swappable control panels, and a motorized rotating monitor (see Figure 18-2).

FIGURE **18-2: Carlos' Centipede cabinet.**
Used by permission of Carsten Wessels.

The cabinet pieces were cut out on a professional CNC router, which produces very nice results. Reproduction Centipede artwork from Arcadeshop Amusements (www.arcadeshop.com) was applied to the white background, producing a look virtually identical to the original. The marquee was replicated from a scanned image and printed on backlit paper. If it were not for the custom controls, you would be hard pressed to tell the difference between this cabinet and a real Centipede arcade machine.

Demonstrating the principle that sometimes simpler is better, Carlos originally had an all-in-one control panel design but then switched to a classy-looking swappable control panel approach instead. Controls are interfaced to an Ultimarc I-PAC and Opti-PAC through an easily disconnected cable that allows quick control panel swapping. The first control panel has only a single joystick and four buttons, which suits the majority of classic arcade-style games that will be primarily played on the cabinet. The player 1 and 2 start buttons are lit with LEDs that will flash in some games in the Multiple Arcade Machine Emulator (MAME), replicating the behavior of the original machines. Carlos includes a nice tutorial on his Web site on how to connect the LEDs.

Although the artwork on the cabinet is very nicely done, the project's biggest claim to fame is probably the automatic motorized rotating monitor. Cannibalized from an actual production arcade machine, the rotating monitor mount will automatically rotate the monitor from horizontal to vertical and degauss the monitor when it does so. Carlos caps the project off with a custom-designed front end that will eventually tell the monitor mount to rotate when needed, making it truly 100 percent automated! Detailed measurements and plans are available on his Web site to help you if you'd like to re-create this cabinet, although finding another motorized rotating monitor mount will be a trick!

Note   Prominent features of Carlos' Centipede cabinet: impressive replica cabinet and artwork, automated rotating monitor.

Frosty's Arcade

Frosty's arcade cabinet (www.arcade.tomvanhorn.com) is yet another example of the lengths you can go to when creating a home arcade cabinet. Thomas Van Horn, a.k.a. Frostillicus or Frosty online, is the creative genius behind the Project Arcade marquee and side-art graphics you saw in Chapter 15. His talent shows in the quality of the cabinet he has created. Based on a modified version of the PacMAMEA project, this cabinet sports custom-designed graphics and a rotating control panel (see Figure 18-3).

The marquee and side art for this project were created in Adobe Illustrator by Tom, based largely on characters from fighter-style arcade games. Each of the three control panels has a different themed overlay inspired from different genres of arcade games. The quality of the graphics is one of the items that really sets this cabinet apart from others. Tom has put together a popular tutorial on how to create quality arcade artwork available online at (www.arcade controls.com/files/Miscellaneous/VectorTutorial_v1_3.zip). The cabinet itself is a two-piece design, meaning the top can be separated from the bottom for easy maintenance and moving!

FIGURE 18-3: A look at Frosty's Arcade.
Used by permission of Thomas Van Horn.

The three rotating control panels boast a collection of standard joysticks and buttons, a Tron trigger stick and spinner, a trackball, dual rotary joysticks, and Atari cone start buttons. The controls are interfaced to an Ultimarc I-PAC and Opti-PAC, and the rotary joysticks are connected to a rotary interface made by Druin. Each panel is oriented toward a specific set of games, such as the trackball panel that includes Tron-inspired artwork, the trackball, and the trigger-grip joystick. The start buttons, the Tron joystick, and the translucent trackball are lit from beneath with LEDs, which adds to the eye-candy appeal of this cabinet.

Distinctive features of this cabinet include the rotating control panel, the custom-designed artwork, and the two-piece design. Plans are available for download for this cabinet and include details on how the top and bottom parts are connected.

Note Prominent features of Frosty's Arcade: impressive artwork, rotating control panels, two-piece design.

GSXRMovistar's Arcade

GSXRMovistar's arcade cabinet project (www.runriot.pwp.blueyonder.co.uk/arcade) shows not only how it's possible to produce an aesthetically pleasing appearance without being a graphics artist, but also how to fully document the construction of your cabinet. The cabinet is actually a work in progress at the time of this writing, with a completed control panel and partially completed cabinet (see Figure 18-4).

FIGURE 18-4: GSXRMovistar's completed control panel and work-in-progress cabinet.
Used by permission of Andrew D. Baker.

The artwork for this project is very well-done, with a blue space type of theme carried on throughout the control panel, marquee, side art, and background for the front-end program. Rather than design it totally from scratch, GSXRMovistar was able to find a suitable image on the Internet. After asking the creator for approval, he modified the image to suit his needs and produced an overall theme that is frequently commented upon by BYOAC members. This is a great example of how you can come up with quality artwork for your project without being a graphics artist yourself!

This project is also an excellent example of planning and flexibility. It started by designing the control panel and cabinet in a graphics program. The control panel was designed as a standalone unit and was constructed first. The cabinet was designed as a two-piece unit, making the entire design a modular three-piece system that's easily moved. By having the design in a digital form, the creator was able to change the design on the fly as circumstances dictated.

Both the design of the control panel and the physical dimensions of the cabinet changed as work progressed. For instance, GSXRMovistar created a mockup of the control panel using cardboard, as recommended earlier in the book, and realized upon testing that the layout was not what he'd hoped for. This was easily corrected in the cardboard and the design was then updated.

The cabinet uses an assortment of standard joysticks and pushbuttons, a trackball, and an Oscar Controls spinner. These are interfaced to an Ultimarc I-PAC and Opti-PAC, with additional control available via two PlayStation game pads and a PlayStation-to-USB converter. A 21-inch VGA computer monitor completes the cabinet's hardware. Stand-out features of this project include the modular design, pleasing artwork theme, and an extremely well documented Web site detailing the steps of construction. Plans for this project are not currently available.

Note Prominent features of GSXRMovistar's Arcade: eye-catching artwork, modular construction.

Roswell 88201

The Roswell 88201 arcade cabinet, built by Craig Schaible (www.ourvictorianhouse .com/CraigsArcade/Roswell 88201/Roswell.html), holds a special place in the BYOAC examples database. It was one of the first projects to break away from the standard look and feel of basic black home arcade cabinets way back in the stone age of this hobby (1999). It is also the first cabinet to feature swappable control panels and an overall artistic theme encompassing the entire cabinet.

When this cabinet was built, keyboard encoder interfaces were expensive and largely unknown to the small arcade cabinet-building community. Most control panels at the time used keyboard hacks with the assorted issues that came with them. Craig, however, used the programmable PowerRamp game pad from Act Labs (no longer available, but the PowerRamp MITE successor is available at www.act-labs.com) to interface his controls. Controls include a standard set of joysticks and buttons, a trackball, and a Twisty-Grip spinner.

Other than the uniqueness of the design at the time, the most distinctive feature of this cabinet is the artwork used to decorate it. The entire cabinet has a space theme from the marquee to the cabinet artwork to the customized front end. The cabinet artwork is a wrap-around mural of the moon's surface purchased from Environmental Graphics (www.egproducts.com). The bezel has stars painted on it, and the green and white colors of the controls compliment the artwork in a striking manner. Craig's use of wallpaper to cover his cabinet appears to be unique among arcade cabinet builders.

Note Prominent features of the Roswell 88201 arcade cabinet: unique wallpaper artwork, original swappable control panels.

Supercade

Jeff Allen's Supercade (www.cybercoma.com/supercade) is one of those projects that, when seen, elicits statements along the lines of, "I wish I had built that!" Sporting an attractive appearance and a full compliment of arcade controls, including a light gun, the Supercade stands out as one of the most often commented upon home arcade cabinets (see Figure 18-5).

FIGURE **18-5: The Supercade.**
Used by permission of Jeffrey Forester Allen.

The Supercade has a really tasteful and distinctive theme. The cabinet is painted black with red t-molding and grey control panel overlays. Each player's controls are a different color scheme and the joystick and buttons match. Other than the marquee, there are no graphics anywhere on the cabinet. It's a perfect example of how a cabinet can look attractive without requiring any artwork. The marquee was modified from a design available for download from Massive MAME (www.mameworld.net/massive) and printed on backlit material at a local print shop.

The controls are where this cabinet really shines. Instead of rotating or swappable control panels, Supercade uses a double-decker control panel to accomodate all the different controls used on the cabinet. The lower panel has joysticks and buttons for four players and a single trackball in the middle. The upper panel includes a trigger-grip flight stick, a spinner, and an 8-way joystick. The 8-way joystick is used with restrictor plates from Oscar Controls to turn it into a 4-way-straight or 4-way-diagonal joystick. The controls are interfaced to KE-72 and ME-4 encoders from Hagstrom Electronics. An Act-Labs light gun with a holster inset into the front control panel rounds out the controls on this cabinet. Plans are available for this project, but the author notes that they are not exact measurements and should be used as guidelines instead of cookbook instructions.

Note Prominent features of the Supercade: Unique double-decker control panel, pleasant *graphics-free* design.

Other inspirational uprights

The rest of these projects are cabinets that have one or two features that really stand out, or are just overall examples of well-made home arcade cabinets. I'll take a brief look at each.

Jubei: Rob's Arcade Cabinet

Jubei (http://cmdrtaco.net/cabinet) is the creation of Rob Malda, better known as CmdrTaco, the founder of the Slashdot (www.slashdot.org) Web site. This cabinet is a derivative of the LuSiD design used in building Project Arcade and has a few interesting features. The front of the control panel is rounded instead of angled, and the overall size of the cabinet is narrowed a bit. It was constructed from birch plywood, stained, and then finished with black t-molding. The rounded front, wood stain, and t-molding produce a nice furniture effect. The computer runs on Linux and is accessible on a wireless network, which allows maintenance of the system without opening the cabinet. At the time of writing, a picture was unavailable, but you can see the cabinet on its Web site.

Note Prominent features of Jubei: stained wood, wireless LAN, Linux operating system.

MrSalty's Arcade

MrSalty's Arcade cabinet (www.mrsalty.net) is another pioneer in the home arcade cabinet-building community. The cabinet is a converted Defender cabinet that was rescued from an original arcade conversion gone bad. It uses a KE-24 keyboard encoder from Hagstrom Electronics and a Happ Controls trackball-to-mouse interface kit to connect the various controls. Along with four swappable control panels, this project was one of the first to include a rotating arcade monitor. The Web site has a very detailed write up of how the rotating monitor mount works, accompanied by many pictures.

Note Prominent features of MrSalty's Arcade cabinet: four swappable control panels, manually rotating monitor.

Rick's MAME Projects

Rick's MAME Projects (http://home.carolina.rr.com/rmartinko/mame.htm) are a set of four arcade cabinet conversions whose biggest claim to fame is the extremely pleasing artwork used with a similar purple flame theme running throughout all of them. These machines use a mixture of Ultimarc interfaces and arcade monitors and run DOS 6.22.

Note Prominent feature of Rick's MAME Projects: impressive artwork.

Scott's Unicade

Scott's Unicade (http://home.austin.rr.com/shumate/unicade/index.htm) is a nice two-player cabinet modeled after the Neo-Geo series of arcade machines (see Figure 18-6). Aside from being an overall nice cabinet, its most notable feature is the use of a framework made up of 2×4 boards. This makes the cabinet extremely durable and stable, at the expense of added weight. Design measurements for the cabinet, including framework, are available at the Web site.

Note   Prominent feature of Scott's Unicade: internal 2×4 wooden framework.

FIGURE 18-6: Scott's Unicade cabinet.
Used by permission of Scott Shumate.

Yet Another MAME

Yet Another MAME cabinet (`www.robboweb.com/mamecab`) by Rob Bischoff is an eye-pleasing example of a converted arcade cabinet (see Figure 18-7). It features custom graphics, a full compliment of arcade controls, and Ultimarc interfaces. The cabinet uses a 25-inch arcade monitor and runs in Windows 98 DOS mode with Advance MAME and Advance Menu. This cabinet is a great illustration of what a home arcade cabinet can look like with a bit of effort.

Note   Prominent features of Yet Another MAME cabinet: attractive appearance and artwork.

FIGURE **18-7: The Yet Another MAME cabinet.**
Used by permission of Rob Bischoff.

Cocktail arcade cabinets

Another popular genre of arcade cabinets is the cocktail cabinet. The BYOAC Web site database includes approximately 60 cocktail-style arcade cabinets. I've highlighted three of them in the following:

Class of 81

The Class of 81 cocktail cabinet (www.oscarcontrols.com/cocktail) is a real cocktail arcade cabinet converted by Kelsey Schell, owner of Oscar Controls. The cabinet started life as a Ms. Pac-Man/Galaga Class of 81 Reunion cabinet that was damaged before it was ever put out in the public. Kelsey rescued it just before it was thrown out and repaired and converted it into the home cocktail arcade cabinet shown in Figure 18-8.

FIGURE **18-8: Converted Class of 81 cocktail arcade cabinet.**
Used by permission of Oscar Controls.

The cabinet is a good example of what a traditional classic cocktail arcade cabinet looks like. Kelsey's goal when putting this cabinet together was to keep it as close to the original as possible. The broken side panel was re-created and replaced, and authentic touches like backlit Plexiglas panels lighting the players' controls were added. Vents for cooling were cut with a router in a grill pattern, as shown in Chapter 15. Controls were kept simple, with only two joysticks and two buttons per player. Arcade speakers were used for sound, and a pair of cheap PC speakers were hacked for the volume control and connection. An 18-inch arcade monitor rounds out the package.

This cabinet is a very nice example of the beauty of simplicity. It is not a cabinet you will want to build if you are looking for a single cabinet that will play every possible game. It is an excellent choice for a second or limited-purpose cabinet that will fit into a living room or game room quite nicely. Because this was a restored original cabinet, plans are not available.

Note Prominent features of Class of 81 cocktail cabinet: simple design, hacked PC speakers.

Gemini Project

The Gemini Project (www.skum.org/gemini) is another cocktail cabinet by Kelsey Schell of Oscar Controls. This project was built from scratch and designed to be a two-player cabinet (see Figure 18-9).

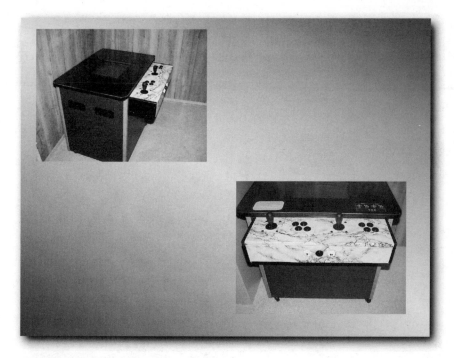

FIGURE 18-9: The Gemini Project.
Used by permission of Oscar Controls.

This cabinet is another fairly simple project that turned out well. The controls consist of a single joystick and four buttons per player, with a couple of coin-up and administrative buttons on the front of the control panel. The monitor is a 17-inch VGA monitor placed on its back, which fortunately showed no signs of magnetic distortion. The PC nature of the monitor was disguised by simply coloring the white plastic with a black marker, which proves that sometimes the easiest solution is best.

The goal of this cabinet was to be aesthetically pleasing enough to pass the *spouse test* and to be placed in the main living space. To this end, the controls for both players were placed side-by-side on a single control panel, which saved space and somewhat minimized the arcade cabinet appearance. The cabinet is covered by a custom-cut glass table top surface with various arcade graphics, a custom instruction card, and a button map underneath for atmosphere. A coat of hunter-green paint and prefinished wooden trim complete the cabinet.

The cabinet was apparently a success and was allowed in the living space. Graphics files and AutoCAD plans of the cabinet are available on the Web site should you wish to give a cabinet like this a try.

Note   Prominent feature of the Gemini Project: side-by-side two-player control panel.

MameHAC

MameHAC, the MAME Home Arcade Cocktail (www.arcadepinball.com/basement/ mamehac), is the creation of Eric Seeds. Eric has the distinction of being one of the very first people to create (or at least to document the creation of) a home arcade cabinet with the creation of MameHAM, the MAME Home Arcade Machine. MameHAC is his second venture into home arcade cabinets (see Figure 18-10).

FIGURE **18-10**: MameHAC — The MAME Home Arcade Cocktail.
Used by permission of Eric Seeds.

MameHAC deviates from a standard squared cocktail cabinet because it has one end flared out into three angled panels. The center panel houses a coin door and administrative buttons and the other two each house a steering wheel. Controls on two other sides of the cabinet include a trackball panel with three buttons and a single joystick with three buttons. Controls are interfaced via a Microsoft SideWinder gamepad hack and an Ultimarc Opti-PAC interface. Administration on the cabinet is done through a wireless keyboard.

The VGA monitor inside the cabinet was painted black to disguise the PC origins, and the plastic housing cannot be seen underneath the cabinet's smoked glass cover. The monitor can be manually rotated to place it in the proper orientation for whichever side of the cabinet you occupy (as dictated by which set of controls you need to use).

Note | Prominent features of MameHAC: dual steering wheels, manually rotating monitor.

Desktop arcade controls

Not everyone has the space or inclination to go with a full-sized arcade cabinet. Standalone desktop arcade controls are very popular; 150 or so examples are listed in the BYOAC database. The following are a few that stand out as inspirational examples:

BlackBox MacMAME Controller

The BlackBox MacMAME Controller (www.control-click.com/blackbox) is a simple desktop controller designed to work with a Macintosh computer. This controller is a fine example of a relatively inexpensive and simple desktop arcade control setup. It features two joysticks and ten buttons interfaced through an Ultimarc I-PAC in USB mode. It was constructed out of $^3/_4$-inch wood, painted black, and covered with a Plexiglas overlay. Directional arrows around the joysticks set it off with a distinct arcade touch without being overly distracting. This controller demonstrates that arcade happiness can be achieved simply and with relatively little effort. Something like this makes a fine starter project or gift.

Note | Prominent feature of BlackBox MacMAME Controller: simplicity in action.

MAME32QA Controller

The MAME32QA Controller (www.classicgaming.com/mame32qa/controller/controller.htm) is the creation of John Hardy, IV, one of the members of the MAME32 development team. It was inspired by the BlackBox MacMAME Controller and is another example of a simple yet elegant solution (see Figure 18-11).

The controller is designed to be a single-player controller and features two joysticks and six buttons interfaced to an Ultimarc USB I-PAC. The buttons and joysticks are black, and the control panel overlay is a nice green-to-black gradient. The shiny Lexan protective cover sets off the controller nicely. The Web site detailing the construction is well done and points out a few setbacks encountered along the way. This is another good example of a simple personal arcade controller.

Note | Prominent feature of the MAME32QA Controller: simple, elegant single-player controller.

FIGURE **18-11: The MAME32QA Controller.**
Used by permission of John Hardy, IV.

Mr. Emulator 2

The Mr. Emulator 2 arcade controller (www.cp-lighting.co.uk/mame) is a stunning example of a modern elegance. It may seem strange to describe an arcade control panel as elegant, but in this case the term fits. This is one of my favorite examples of a standalone desktop arcade controller (see Figure 18-12).

The controller features controls for two players with one joystick and seven buttons each, a trackball with three mouse buttons, and an Oscar Controls spinner. The controls are interfaced through an Ultimarc I-PAC and the spinner is connected via USB.

The most unique feature of this controller is notable right away—the top and sides are covered with a brushed stainless steel overlay. The stainless steel is accented with black t-molding, joysticks, and buttons. Add a stainless Oscar Controls spinner knob and a white trackball and you end up with a functional modern day piece of art! I am really impressed with how classy this controller turned out and will attempt to duplicate it myself one day. Plans for this controller are not available.

Note

Prominent features of Mr. Emulator 2: stainless steel overlay, striking monochromatic appearance.

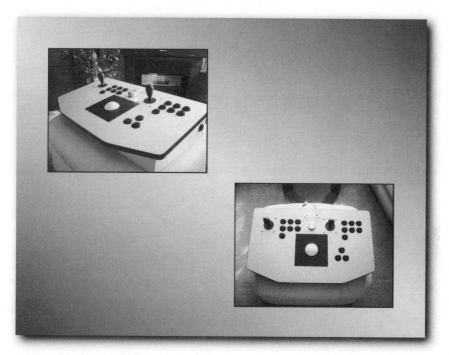

FIGURE 18-12: The Mr. Emulator 2 arcade controller.
Used by permission of Dave Penfold.

Other arcade projects

No matter how you try to classify arcade projects, there's always someone who breaks the mold. Several *build-your-own* projects defy easy categorization into upright cabinets, cocktail cabinets or desktop controllers. Some of the more interesting of such projects are highlighted here:

Domesticated Arcades

Domesticated Arcades is the Web site of Donald Brown, a man gifted with woodworking skills and an imagination to match. He has put together several projects that might loosely be called arcade cabinets that are definitely worth browsing if you're thinking of trying something a little different.

Coffee Table Arcade

The Coffee Table Arcade is an interesting contraption. Start by picturing a living room with an ordinary coffee table in front of a sofa. Company's over and everyone's having a quiet discussion over tea and biscuits (I'm not English; just trying to set a tone. Work with me here...). Suddenly the host announces, "Who wants to play a game of *PacWrestle-DeathMatch*?" and throws back the top of the coffee table, revealing a bright red and blue set of arcade controllers that pop up ready to play! You've just been introduced to the Coffee Table Arcade (see Figure 18-13).

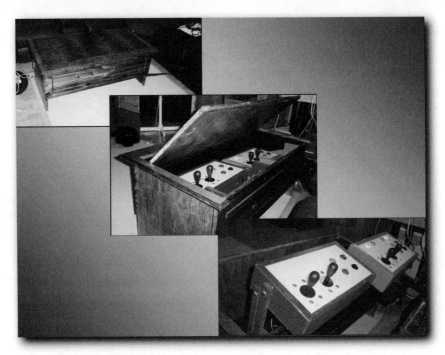

FIGURE **18-13: The Coffee Table Arcade: closed, opened, and ready to play.**
Used by permission of Donald Brown, © 2004 Domesticated Arcades.

The Coffee Table Arcade is a fairly attractive normal piece of furniture at first glance. It's constructed of pine board and birch plywood that has been stained a dark walnut. The top of the coffee table lifts up and folds down into the cabinet. Inside are two separate controllers that pop up from within the cabinet for game play. They are painted red and blue, respectively, and have Formica covering on the tops. Two sticks on each side of the controllers keep them in the proper orientation as they pop up and are used.

Each controller has two joysticks and four buttons. The right controller also has the coin-up and start buttons for both players. Because the two controllers are separate units, the interface is located inside the coffee table cabinet itself and not in the controller boxes. Long cables connect the various controls to an Ultimarc I-PAC that is mounted next to the computer inside the cabinet. The controllers rest above the computer inside the coffee table when they are put away. The cabinet does not have a monitor and is connected to a large-screen television for gaming.

This is an impressive piece of work, even more so because it only took three weekends to produce. Plans for the Coffee Table Arcade are available for $20 from the GameCab Web site at
www.gamecab.com/Arcade%20Plans.htm.

Note   Prominent feature of Coffee Table Arcade: arcade controls disguised inside coffee table furniture.

Living Room Arcade and Secret Arcade

Two other projects from Domesticated Arcades really stand out—the Living Room Arcade (Mark II, at www.eamontales.com/livingroom) and the Secret Arcade (www.eamontales.com/secretarcade). These were two more attempts at building an arcade gaming platform that wouldn't be obvious as such and would fit into a household living room. Both projects look like regular furniture wardrobes or cabinets when closed (in fact, one is actually an off-the-shelf wardrobe kit) and have a nice stained wood finish and brass handle work (see Figure 18-14).

FIGURE 18-14: The Secret Arcade (left) and the Living Room Arcade (right).
Used by permission of Donald Brown, © 2004 Domesticated Arcades.

However, when you open them up the fun is revealed! The Secret Arcade contains a full-sized open-front cabinet with a fold-down control panel, flat-screen monitor, and hookups for not only a computer but video game consoles as well (see Figure 18-15).

The control panel in the Secret Arcade is a three-sided rotating unit similar to the designs of cabinets introduced earlier in this chapter. One face includes the arcade controls designed for two players, with one joystick and four buttons per player interfaced to an Ultimarc I-PAC. The second face has a membrane keyboard and trackball mouse glued to it for computer control. The third face is blank and is used for game console controllers when playing those machines.

FIGURE **18-15:** The Secret Arcade opened with control panel lowered.
Used by permission of Donald Brown, © 2004 Domesticated Arcades.

Topping the Secret Arcade off is a color scrolling LED sign that takes the place of a marquee. Altogether, the Secret Arcade contains enough gaming fun and eye candy to make anyone happy, neatly wrapped up in an unimposing piece of furniture. Nicely done! Plans for the Secret Arcade are not available, but the author believes enough information exists on his Web site to create your own.

The Living Room Arcade cabinet (Mark II, because the first attempt was universally rejected as looking like a *pregnant armoire*) has a similar set of surprises in store when it is opened (see Figure 18-16).

The single-sided control panel pulls straight out from the cabinet to reveal a two-player selection with one joystick and two buttons each. The pull-out panel is 18 inches deep, providing enough space so that you are not sickeningly close to the screen. Controls are interfaced to the computer through an Ultimarc USB I-PAC. The rest of the lower half of the cabinet contains drawers and storage for a mini keyboard and trackball mouse, game consoles, and the computer. Plans for this cabinet are available for $25 from Game Cabinets, Inc. at (www.gamecabinets inc.com/plans.html).

Donald's first attempt at woodworking (since high school) was building a cocktail cabinet following plans from Game Cabinets, Inc. It was during this construction that the ideas for the

Secret Arcade were born. He's provided some words of encouragement for those who might be thinking of following in his footsteps. "My strengths in woodworking are that I'm willing to try anything, and I'm willing to create scrapwood." Words to live by and certainly in keeping with the Project Arcade spirit! Donald's other projects can be seen at his main Web site, www.eamontales.com/arcades.

Note Prominent feature of Living Room Arcade and Secret Arcade: innovative placement of arcade controls inside ordinary appearing household furniture.

Happy Hour :: Bartop MAME

The Happy Hour :: Bartop MAME cabinet (www.skum.org/bartop) is another creation from the owner of Oscar Controls. It is a countertop cabinet with the control panel and monitor packaged in a compact cabinet (see Figure 18-17).

The Happy Hour cabinet has a clean and pleasing appearance; it is painted white with bright green t-molding, joystick, and buttons. Arcade graphics are discreetly placed on the corners of the control panel and back side corners of the cabinet, with green lettering and a logo on the top and back, respectively. A black bezel with the name of the cabinet in green lettering completes the look.

FIGURE 18-16: Inside the Living Room Arcade cabinet.

FIGURE 18-17: The Happy Hour :: Bartop MAME cabinet.
Used by permission of Oscar Controls.

The control panel is a simple affair, with a single joystick and three player pushbuttons. Mini buttons were added for coin-up and start functions and provide functionality without taking up much of the limited real estate on the control panel. A detachable remote control box was added with a power-on button and administrative buttons to control MAME. When removed, the cabinet can be played but not administered, which is perfect for party settings! All controls are connected to a keyboard hack inside the cabinet.

The Happy Hour :: Bartop MAME cabinet is a good example of what can be done with limited space and a small monitor. A countertop cabinet is a great addition to a game room with a wet bar or anywhere that has space constraints. Plans and graphics used on the cabinet are available for download from the Web site.

Note   Prominent features of the Happy Hour :: Bartop MAME: countertop form, remote power, and administrative control.

MiniMAME

The MiniMAME cabinet (www.minimame.com) by Chris Cowherd looks at first glance like a nice but ordinary upright arcade cabinet similar to 1UP's PacMAMEA introduced earlier — that is, until you see the cabinet next to something else for perspective (see Figure 18-18).

FIGURE **18-18: The MiniMAME cabinet next to a car.**
Used by permission of Chris Cowherd.

The MiniMAME cabinet is in fact patterned after the PacMAMEA cabinet, but it is scaled down to suit a child. The creator has two different versions shown on his Web site: one standing 40-inches tall, and one standing 48-inches. The cabinets are constructed from MDF sections, laminated a Pac-Man yellow, and trimmed with black t-molding. A small monitor or television is used for the display, and controls and interface are left as an exercise for the reader.

The cabinet plans are available for download from the Web site, including full-sized templates for the side panels. I personally think this is a *great* idea and have one in the works for my own children. Any children with a mini arcade cabinet in their room will be the envy of all their friends!

Note   Prominent feature of the MiniMAME: upright cabinet shrunk to suit a child.

UncleT's Mom's Arcade

UncleT's Mom's Arcade by Todd Rosen is one of those Übergeek arcade cabinets that pushes the hobby further than it's gone previously. It's a sit-down arcade driving cabinet with multiple driving and flying controls (see Figure 18-19).

FIGURE 18-19: UncleT's Mom's Arcade.
Used by permission of Todd Rosen.

The cabinet features six control panels that rotate horizontally around the cabinet, featuring steering wheels, joystick controls, and even a coveted Star Wars–style flight yoke. The controls are interfaced through Microsoft SideWinder Dual Strike hacks as described earlier in the book. Todd tops the cabinet off with multiple gear shifters mounted on the right-hand side, adjustable driving pedals, and a rotating monitor that doubles as the family television. This cabinet is an incredible feat of engineering!

Note   Prominent features of Mom's Arcade: sit-down driving cabinet, horizontally rotating control panels.

Great Places to Get More Information

Still thirsty for more? Got an inspiration for something brand new? There are some excellent online resources you can visit to get more information and to help you on your way. This is an eclectic collection of places around the Internet with information relating to arcade collecting and home arcade cabinet construction. A lot of people migrate to collecting real arcade and pinball machines after constructing one or two home arcade cabinets (and vice versa). Both are fun and fascinating hobbies with a lot of overlap between the two. Even if you're only interested in one, you can still learn a lot from the other. I'll even sneak in a couple of game console links as well.

Caution

Make sure you've had something to eat and have a drink nearby. The following collection of links can lead to a Web surfing coma—a condition where you suddenly realize you've been Web surfing for days without coming up for air and suddenly keel over comatose. Occasionally, interventions by a spouse or loved one may be necessary. Enjoy!

- **Randy Fromm's arcade school** (www.randyfromm.com) — Randy Fromm is a video arcade machine technical expert and magazine writer and has numerous how-to repair articles to his credit. He runs the Randy Fromm arcade school where you can go for a five-day intensive education on repairing arcade machines. For those who cannot make it to a training session, video tapes and books are available on his Web site. These tapes and books are highly recommended to people who want to learn more about what makes video games tick and how to repair them!

- **The Real Bob Roberts** (www.therealbobroberts.com) — Bob Roberts' Web site is primarily known as a great place to get arcade parts inexpensively. Aside from that, however, his site has a big collection of technical and how-to articles that are highly recommended.

- **Arcade Gameroom Design Information** (http://members.cox.net/jmccorm) — Now that you've built a home arcade machine or two, what are you going to do next? No, a visit to Disney World isn't in order; it's time to build a real game room! This Web site is an attempt to walk you through things to consider when you put together a personal game room, and it makes a great visit.

- **Blacklight carpeting** — No game room is complete without blacklight reactive carpeting like that found in arcades and movie theaters. You can find this carpeting online at these Web sites:

    www.valuecarpetonline.com/carpet-black-light.htm

    www.newmillenniumcarpets.com/fluorescent.htm

    www.kidcarpet.com

- **Newsgroups and mailing lists** — You've already been introduced to rec.games.video .arcade.collecting (RGVAC), alt.games.mame (AGM), and rec.games.video.arcade.marketplace (RGVAM) as good places to go to for help. They're also great groups to read just to learn more about the hobby (reachable at Google Groups, http://groups .google.com). In addition, two other great resources are the Vectorlist and Rasterlist mailing lists for the discussion of vector-based and raster-based arcade machines, respectively. Signup information and past archives can be found at www.vectorlist.org.

- **The Basement Arcade** (`www.basementarcade.com`) — This is one of the premier arcade collecting sites on the Web. Aside from a great arcade collection and technical info, it is home to one of the biggest collections of interesting arcade links on the Web.

- **Videotopia, "The Exhibit of the True History of Video Games"** (`www.videotopia.com`) — This is a traveling museum of classic arcade game history. The exhibit consists of between 60 and 85 arcade games from the original Computer Space to modern side-by-side racing games. The Web site has an online mini version of the exhibit you can visit.

- **Arcadecollecting.com** (`www.arcadecollecting.com`) — This site is not only a great place to find artwork, as introduced in Chapter 15, it's also a repository of technical information and tips!

- **The Arcade Restoration Workshop** (`www.arcaderestoration.com`) — This site is a must visit for anyone working on old arcade machines. It is absolutely chock full of tips, tricks, articles, photo tutorials, and links related to arcade machine collecting and repair. Highly recommended!

- **VAPS, The Video Arcade Preservation Society** (`www.vaps.org`) — This site is dedicated to organizing arcade collectors into a group. Post your collection in their database, and look for like-minded fellows in your area that are accepting visitors!

- **Clay Cowgill's Multigame.com** (`www.multigame.com`) — This site is an interesting visit. He sells various kits and adapters for real video games, for instance, a few that turn individual games into multi-games. These would go well next to a home arcade cabinet. There are also several good technical articles on the site, such as how to powder coat arcade parts, which gives a very nice and hard paint-like finish.

- **Al's Arcade** (`www.alsarcade.com`) — This is another good stop on the Web for arcade collecting information.

- **Roger's Classic Arcade Tips and Tricks** (`www.classicgaming.com/rcatt`) — Now that you have an arcade cabinet running your favorite arcade games, what do you need (besides a game room to put it in)? Tips and hints on how to win, of course! Visit this site for those.

- **ePanorama.net** (`www.epanorama.net/documents/joystick` — Tomi Engdal's collection of technical information about joysticks is an absolute must visit for those interested in joysticks from all manner of computer and game systems.

- **Stephan Hans** (`http://home.t-online.de/home/stephan.hans/tricks.htm`) — Stephan Hans is one of the pioneers of the home arcade cabinet hacking hobby. The site hasn't been updated in a while, but still has pertinent technical information on hacking keyboards and joysticks.

- **GameSX.com** (`www.gamesx.com`) — This site is one of my favorites on the Web. There isn't a game console or arcade contraption they're afraid of taking apart and documenting. Highly recommended!

- **APPOLO's Arcade** (`www.appolo.com`) — This site is another regular stop on the Web for arcade collectors. Items of note include several arcade-related tutorials and a collection of paint codes for matching paint on classic arcade machines.

- **Kevin Steele's Retroblast** (`www.retroblast.com`) — This is a favorite among home arcade cabinet and emulation fans. Kevin has a series of reviews of products in the field that are good reads before you buy. Be sure to visit the articles link to see the construction of his personal arcade cabinets!

- **Arcade Fever** (`http://arcadefever.com/wifesperspective.htm`) — This site will be a good visit on the Web for any arcade collector because of all of its other content, but it's the "wife's perspective" that is on my must-visit list. It details one wife's story of dealing with her husband's other woman, Ms. Pac-Man. It's very funny and no introduction to arcade collecting would be complete without it!

- **Xiaou2's home on the Web** (`www.homestead.com/xiaou2/arcade.html`) — This is a collection of arcade control hacks and custom designs. He was one of the first to come up with a concept for a rotating control panel, with an incredible *six*-panel rotating design. The project hasn't taken off to a full cabinet yet, but the ideas and homemade controls (including a wooden Star Wars flight yoke) on his site are a must read.

The Project Arcade Finale

Still need that last bit of convincing that building an arcade cabinet is something you can or want to do? Consider the author of this book and the Project Arcade cabinet. Before I started this whole thing, I'd never built anything more complicated than a cheap screw-together bookshelf kit. I'd tinkered with arcade controls, put together the BYOAC Web site, and gathered all the information you hold in your hands now — but I'd never actually built a complete cabinet from scratch. I had a cabinet I was going to convert and knew that if others had done it then I could too, but I had been in the *getting started* mode for two years and hadn't made any progress. Then the opportunity to write this book came along, and over the course of a few months I was able to start from a pile of wood and create my own dream arcade machine.

It's my creation. I made it with my own two hands. The cabinet's big and shiny. The smoked glass over the monitor rests perfectly over the monitor area, protecting the huge 27-inch monitor and hiding the mysterious depths of the cabinet beneath. The blue t-molding sets off the custom marquee and side art perfectly. A collection of multicolored arcade controls lie in a custom-designed field of stars beneath a shiny protective overlay. My buddy's reaction when he sees the cabinet is the icing on the cake. It lights up, makes noise, and plays anything I put on it. There's not another arcade cabinet exactly like it anywhere in the world. Turn off the lights, put on some music from the 80's, turn on the cabinet, and you're instantly sent back to your teenage years, spending all your time and money at the local arcade. Finally, there's that magic moment — select a game, insert a credit, and start playing! Would I do this again? You bet! There's nothing else quite like the feeling of owning and playing your very own, custom-built, home arcade machine. If I can do it, you can, too! It is with some amount of pride that I present to you the Project Arcade cabinet (see Figure 18-20)!

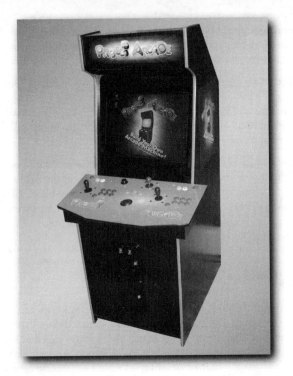

FIGURE 18-20: The Project Arcade cabinet, ready to play!

Summary

Some very talented people have built many different types of arcade machines that are a cut above the ordinary. Some started with already existing skills, while others picked up tools for the very first time and dug in. The one thing they have in common is something you share as well — a dream and the desire to see it come to fruition. I hope the projects highlighted here have inspired you for your next (or first) project! Perhaps you'll see *your* project here in future revisions.

Congratulations are now in order — you've reached the end of the book! The appendices that follow include a few footnotes and details that are well worth reading, but for the most part you've seen all that I have to show you. I hope you've learned a thing or two and have successfully created your very own arcade machine! Creating the Project Arcade cabinet as I wrote this book was an extremely rewarding experience personally, watching it unfold from a few lines on paper and a pile of wood to a fully functioning home video arcade machine.

Hopefully your experience has been just as good and you won't stop here. There's always room for a second machine and personal arcade controllers make great gifts! This hobby is truly in its infancy, having come into existence primarily in just the last five years, although a few pioneers were tinkering with it many years before that. The next few years are sure to get more exciting — why not be part of it? Come join us on the newsgroups and at my Web site, Build Your Own Arcade Controls at www.arcadecontrols.com. Hope to see you there.

Thank you for reading my book. I hope you enjoyed it!

Where to Find Arcade Parts for Your Project

You can find good-quality arcade parts from many locations. Arcade parts vendors are broadly broken down into three categories: direct from manufacturer, purchases from resellers, and purchases from used markets. Like any shopping trip, price, quality, and availability should be your guides as to where to buy.

Direct from manufacturer is almost always guaranteed to be a satisfactory transaction but tends to be the most expensive option. They are usually more geared toward selling to large arcade shops and resellers than they are to individual customers. However, they'll often have sales and specials that can't be found anywhere else, so I would always check with the manufacturers before buying.

Resellers tend to be the easiest transactions at good prices. They are geared toward selling to individual customers and are usually active in the collecting community. Purchasing from them is a good way to find what you need and give something back to the community in a small way. Selection is sometimes smaller than the manufacturers can offer, however. Service levels tend to be high.

The used and after markets are where you can find some incredible deals and out-of-production rare parts to use. However, every purchase in this market comes with a *caveat emptor* (buyer beware) attached. Check feedback for anyone you're doing business with in the used market before you purchase.

In the following section you'll find resources listed under category (direct, reseller, used). Sometimes the distinction between manufacturer and reseller is blurry, so I've placed them where they seem to fit best. You can find other vendors by searching online as well. Happy shopping!

On the CD You'll find a clickable cross-reference chart on the CD-ROM listing arcade parts and sellers, arranged by part. Need a pushbutton? Click the pushbutton link and see a clickable list of all the vendors who sell pushbuttons. No typing required!

Buying Direct

- **3tronics** — www.3tronics.com, manufacturer of Multiple Arcade Machine Interface (MAMI) keyboard encoders and external volume control for arcade cabinets.

- **Betson Imperial** — www.betson.com/MainDept.asp, large manufacturer and distributor of arcade parts.

- **Druin's Rotary Interface** — http://connect.to/rotary, manufacturer of rotary joystick encoder interface.

- **GameCab.com** — www.gamecab.com, manufacturer of StarWars style flight yoke and reseller of arcade parts and cabinet plans.

- **Hagstrom Electronics** — www.hagstromelectronics.com, manufacturer of keyboard encoders and optical encoders.

- **Happ Controls** — www.happcontrols.com, large manufacturer of arcade parts of all types and other arcade-related materials.

- **KeyWiz** — www.groovygamegear.com, manufacturer of KeyWiz keyboard encoders; also sells arcade parts and joysticks customized for home arcade cabinet builders.

- **MK64** — www.mk64.com/ron, manufacturer of the MK64 keyboard encoders.

- **Oscar Controls** — www.oscarcontrols.com, manufacturer of arcade spinners, joystick restrictor plates, and optical interface.

- **SlikStik** — www.slikstik.com, manufacturer of arcade spinners and stainless steel joysticks.

- **Ultimarc** — www.ultimarc.com, manufacturer of I-PAC keyboard, Optic-PAC optical encoders, and ArcadeVGA video card; also sells arcade parts and joysticks customized for home arcade cabinet builders.

- **Wico** — www.wicothesource.com, large manufacturer and reseller of arcade parts.

Buying from Secondary Vendors

- **Arcadeshop Amusements** — www.arcadeshop.com, reseller of arcade parts and arcade artwork.

- **Centsible Amusements** — www.centsibleamusements.com, reseller of arcade parts and artwork, including leaf joysticks.

- **Coin-Op Yellow Pages** — http://randyfromm.com/amusements/yellowpages, a listing of arcade-related vendors hosted by Randy Fromm.

- **Game Cabinets, Inc.** — www.gamecabinetsinc.com, reseller of arcade parts and manufacturer of arcade cabinet plans and cocktail cabinets.

- **James Games** — www.jamesgames.biz, reseller of arcade parts and emulation cabinets.

- **Massive MAME** — www.mameworld.net/massive, Canadian reseller of Oscar Controls products.

- **Mike's Arcade** — www.mikesarcade.com, reseller of arcade parts, artwork, and manufacturer of various arcade game kits as well as arcade circuit board repairs.

- **The Real Bob Roberts** — www.therealbobroberts.com, reseller of arcade parts; very popular choice among Build Your Own Arcade Controls (BYOAC) community members.

- **Video Connection** — www.videoconnect.com, reseller of new and used arcade parts, including hard to find leaf joysticks and rotary joysticks.

- **X-Arcade** — www.x-arcade.com, seller of arcade joysticks and parts used in their desktop arcade controllers.

Buying from Used Markets

- **Auctions** — Real arcade auctions are a good place to look for arcade parts. A throw-away broken down arcade cabinet (*please* read Appendix B) can be a great place to get coin doors, joysticks, and buttons. Usually they're picked over by the owner before being dumped, but a lot of times you can find great deals that someone else wouldn't look twice at if you're willing to put in the time to clean them up. Auction locations can be found online at these Web sites:

  - **Super Auctions** — www.superauctions.com
  - **US Amusement Auction** — www.usamusement.com
  - **Auction Game Sales** — www.auctiongamesales.com

- **BYOAC forums** — The Bring Your Own Arcade Controls buy/sell/trade message forum (www.arcadecontrols.com) is a great place to find arcade parts, including special runs of items designed for home arcade cabinets.

- **eBay** — http://listings.ebay.com/listings/list/all/category13718, eBay's coin-op arcade category is a great place to find rare or cheap arcade parts. Don't get caught up in a buying frenzy and pay too much though!

- **RGVAC/RGVAM** — The rec.games.video.arcade.collecting and rec.games.video .arcade.marketplace (http://groups.google.com) newsgroups are another good place to find arcade parts at a good price, although patience is required.

The Great Debate—
Preserving Versus
MAMEing the Past

It seems like such a good idea at first thought. Building a home arcade cabinet is a lot of fun, but it can be a good bit of work. Why not take an already existing arcade cabinet, strip out all the stuff you don't need, and turn it into your home arcade cabinet? It can be really cheap—throw-away cabinets go for a dollar at arcade auctions; nice cabinet shells with artwork and monitors can go for $100 to $150. It's easy—instead of building from scratch you simply have to clean it up and you're ready to go. What's not to like? What's the big fuss about?

Most likely you picked up this book due to happy memories of time spent in an arcade, feeding quarters into some machine that you were determined to beat or get a high score on. Maybe you missed the heyday of the arcades and would like to get a glimpse of it now. Either way, most of us are trying to re-create a part of the past that we can visit whenever we wish. That seems harmless enough. What's the great debate about then? The issue is this:

Please don't destroy that past as you attempt to re-create it!

Classic arcade cabinets—Tron, Star Wars, Galaxian, and so on, are a dying breed. They suffer from the ravages of time and conversion to other games. Some will sit in a leaky warehouse until the elements turn them into kindling. Other beautiful classic arcade cabinets will get converted into some mindless fighting game (with apologies to fighting game fans) when the original stops making money. The problem is that classic arcade cabinets represent a finite resource. The arcades of yesterday are just that—a thing of the past. Barring a scattering of reproduction projects, these classic cabinets cannot be replaced. As if these problems were not bad enough for classic arcade cabinet fans and collectors, suddenly home arcade cabinets (often referred to as Multiple Arcade Machine Emulator [MAME] cabinets for the emulator most often used on them) started popping up. No one begrudges someone building a personal cabinet from scratch. However, every time a classic arcade cabinet is converted to a home arcade machine, somewhere someone cringes now that there's one fewer cabinet available to collectors.

To an arcade collector, modifying a classic arcade cabinet is akin to chopping down old growth redwood forests. The people doing so may have the legal right to their actions, but they are doing a disservice to humanity. Granted, the degree of the problem is certainly different! Hacking apart an old Robotron cabinet won't cause environmental problems or displace animals (except, perhaps, a family of mice). It will mean, however, that there's one less Robotron cabinet in the world. That same cabinet could be some collector's *holy grail*—the one item they're looking for to complete their collection. Even if the cabinet is in bad shape, someone probably has the parts and desire to rebuild it and restore it, if only they had the cabinet.

On the other hand, there are a bunch of not-so-classic cabinets, generic cabinets, and the aforementioned already-been-mutilated (converted) cabinets out there. Those are much better candidates for conversion to a home arcade cabinet than a nice classic cabinet. Yes, they usually mean more work for you than a cabinet that's in nice condition. That's a small price to pay for entering the classic arcade community. You don't *have* to destroy a classic arcade cabinet to get the convenience of using an already constructed cabinet for your project.

If you must use a classic arcade cabinet for your home machine (which is, after all, totally within your rights as owner of the cabinet), please consider a few limitations. Use a PC2JAMMA conversion, so that the original woodwork and artwork are kept intact. Restore what needs TLC instead of slapping black paint on it and putting up a customized logo. If you're going to remove parts, sell or give them away instead of junking them. That way, the classic cabinet still exists, and its parts can go to help another classic machine live again.

There's room for both home arcade cabinet builders and classic arcade collectors along the road to arcade nirvana. Many arcade cabinet builders end up becoming collectors as well. MAME led me to discover using real arcade controls, which in turn led me to my current collection of seven real arcade cabinets, two pinball machines, and an air hockey table! Many arcade collectors also end up adding an emulation (MAME) cabinet to their collection as well. A little consideration for both camps goes a long way. Enjoy your new hobby, and thank you for considering the impact of your choices on the arcade collecting community!

What's on the CD-ROM

appendix C

This appendix provides you with information on system requirements, using the CD, and the contents of the CD that accompanies this book. The most current information can be found in the ReadMe file located at the root of the CD.

System Requirements

Make sure that your computer meets the minimum system requirements listed in this section. If your computer doesn't match most of these requirements, you may have a problem using the contents of the CD. Your PC must meet the minimum requirements for the version of Windows you're running in order to operate the CD. Individual programs on the CD have varying requirements; see the relevant chapters in the book or ReadMe files with each program.

The CD should work with Windows 9x (preferably Windows 98 or later), Windows 2000, and Windows XP. It may work with Windows NT.

For Windows 9x, Windows 2000, Windows NT4 (with SP 4 or later), Windows Me, or Windows XP

➤ PC with a Pentium processor running at 120 MHz or faster

➤ At least 32 MB of total RAM installed on your computer; for best performance, we recommend at least 64 MB

➤ Ethernet network interface card (NIC) or modem with a speed of at least 28,800 bps

➤ A CD-ROM drive

For Linux

- PC with a Pentium processor running at 90 MHz or faster
- At least 32 MB of total RAM installed on your computer; for best performance, we recommend at least 64 MB
- Ethernet network interface card (NIC) or modem with a speed of at least 28,800 bps
- A CD-ROM drive

Using the CD with Windows

To install the items from the CD to your hard drive, follow these steps:

1. Insert the CD into your computer's CD-ROM drive.
2. A window will appear that gives you the following options: Install, Browse, Links, and Exit.

   Install. Gives you the option to install software from the CD-ROM.

   Browse. Allows you to view the contents of the CD-ROM in its directory structure.

   Links. Opens a hyperlinked page of Web sites.

   Exit. Closes the autorun window.

If you do not have autorun enabled or if the autorun window does not appear, follow the steps below to access the CD.

1. Click Start ➪ Run.
2. In the dialog box that appears, type **d:\setup.exe**, where *d* is the letter of your CD-ROM drive. This will bring up the autorun window described above.
3. Choose the Install, Browse, Links, or Exit option from the menu. (See Step 2 in the preceding list for a description of these options.)

Using the CD with Linux

To install the items from the CD to your hard drive, follow these steps:

1. Log in as root.
2. Insert the CD into your computer's CD-ROM drive.

3. If your computer has Auto-Mount enabled, wait for the CD to mount. Otherwise, follow these steps:

   a. Command line instructions: At the command prompt type:

   ```
   mount /dev/cdrom /mnt/cdrom
   ```

   (This will mount the "cdrom" device to the mnt/cdrom directory. If your device has a different name, then exchange "cdrom" with that device name — for instance, "cdrom1".)

   b. Graphical: Right-click on the CD-ROM icon on the desktop and choose "Mount CD-ROM" from the selections. This will mount your CD-ROM.

4. Browse the CD.

5. To remove the CD from your CD-ROM drive, follow these steps:

   a. Command line instructions: At the command prompt type:

   ```
   umount /mnt/cdrom
   ```

   b. Graphical: Right-click on the CD-ROM icon on the desktop and choose "UMount CD-ROM" from the selections. This will mount your CD-ROM.

Using the CD with the Mac OS

To install the items from the CD to your hard drive, follow these steps:

1. Insert the CD into your CD-ROM drive.

2. Double-click the icon for the CD after it appears on the desktop.

3. Browse the CD.

What's on the CD

The following sections provide a summary of the software and other materials you'll find on the CD.

All chapters

Color figures. Every chapter folder on the CD-ROM includes full color versions of the figures used throughout the book.

Web links. This book includes over 300 links to useful Web sites. The companion CD-ROM includes a Web-enabled listing of these links, organized by chapter. As you read the material in the book, you can keep this listing on your screen for handy access.

Shareware programs are fully functional, trial versions of copyrighted programs. If you like particular programs, register with their authors for a nominal fee and receive licenses, enhanced versions, and technical support. *Freeware programs* are copyrighted games, applications, and utilities that are free for personal use. Unlike shareware, these programs do not require a fee or provide technical support. *GNU software* is governed by its own license, which is included inside the folder of the GNU product. See the GNU license for more details.

Trial, demo, or evaluation versions are usually limited either by time or functionality (for example, some will not allow you to save projects). Some trial versions are very sensitive to system date changes. If you alter your computer's date, the programs will "time out" and no longer be functional.

Software

All installable programs throughout the book referenced as on the CD-ROM will be found in this folder. Specifically:

Adobe Reader. The Adobe Reader is needed to view certain files on the CD-ROM.

Paint Shop Pro evaluation. A 30-day evaluation (fully functional) of the Paint Shop Pro version 8 software used in the creation of Project Arcade.

Ghost Keys. A utility by John Dickson you can use to test keyboard hacks and keyboard encoder configurations.

Linux Joystick Driver. A driver for using joysticks on Linux-based computers.

Spybot. Software designed to protect your computer from spy-ware and other intrusive programs.

Dragon King. An emulator cabinet front-end program by Howard Casto.

MAMEWah. Another emulator cabinet front-end program by Steve Lilley-Hopkins.

VNC. Freeware remote control software that enables you to control the computer in your arcade cabinet from another system.

MAME32. The Windows GUI-based version of MAME, the Multiple Arcade Machine Emulator.

Return of Arcade demo. A demonstration version of the Return of Arcade software from Microsoft.

Chapter 1

Examples database. The examples database is a Web-enabled listing of over 750 "Project Arcade" style projects. Clicking on a link in the examples database will launch the home page on the Internet of the project in question.

Chapter 2

Project Arcade Plans. The design plans for the Project Arcade cabinet, based on the original design by Sean Hatfield (LuSiD).

Ultimate Arcade II Plans. These are an alternate set of plans you can use to build an arcade cabinet, provided courtesy of The Mame Room at www.mameroom.com/.

Chapter 3

No CD-ROM content is included beyond color figures for Chapter 3.

Chapter 4

Arcade Stupidity spinner plans. A Web-based guide to building your own spinner controller from old hard drive parts, including video clips.

Gearhead Labs spinner plans. Another Web-based guide to building a spinner from scratch.

Twisty Grip spinner plans. Yet another Web-based tutorial on constructing a spinner from parts available at any hardware store.

Chapter 5

PacMAMEa gun hack. How to hack a Microsoft Sidewinder Dual Strike game pad to connect arcade gun controllers to your computer.

PacMAMEa Star Wars hack. A guide on hacking the Microsoft Sidewinder Dual Strike game pad to an Atari Star Wars flight yoke controller.

DDR Homepad. Instructions on creating a Dance Dance Revolution style dance pad to connect to your computer.

Jude Kelly's Star Wars controller. A link to a Web site with instructions for hacking an Atari Star Wars flight yoke to your computer.

Twisty Grip yoke animations. Video clips of the Twisty Grip flight yoke in action.

Chapter 6

Interactive Control Panel Designer. A Web-based utility for designing control panels.

PacMAMEa rotating panels. This is a portion of the PacMAMEa Web site, explaining how to create rotating control panels.

Paint Shop Pro evaluation. A 30-day trial (fully functional) of the Paint Shop Pro version 8 software used in the creation of Project Arcade.

Templates. Layout and mounting templates of different arcade controls you can use when creating your control panel. A full scale version of the Project Arcade control panel template is also included.

Yoke mounting platform. Instructions from the PacMAMEa Web site on constructing a mounting platform for a Star Wars flight controller.

Chapter 7

Starbase 74 soldering tutorial. A Web-based tutorial demonstrating how to successfully solder and avoid problems.

Chapter 8

Keyboard hacking guide. How to hack a keyboard by Marshall Brooks (Tiger-Heli). Includes information on specific keyboards that have been successfully used in arcade cabinets.

Chapter 9

Oscar Controls DPDT switch tutorial. Instructions courtesy of Oscar Controls on how to connect a trackball and spinner to a single mouse hack using a dual-pole-dual-throw switch.

Chapter 10

Microsoft Sidewinder Dual Strike hack. Web-based instructions from PacMAMEa on how to hack the Microsoft Sidewinder Dual Strike game pad to analog arcade controls.

Chapter 11

Klipsch speaker mounting templates. To-scale mounting templates for the Klipsch ProMedia 2.1 speakers.

Virtual Music Jukebox. A trial version of a jukebox-based MP3 music file player.

List of jukebox links. A Web-enabled list of jukebox programs. Clicking the links will direct you to the home pages of the various programs.

Oscar Controls speaker amplifier hack. Instructions from Oscar Controls on how to use car or arcade speakers with PC-based speaker amplifiers.

Oscar Controls volume control hack. Information from Oscar Controls on how to build a remote volume control for your arcade cabinet.

Chapter 12

No CD-ROM content is included beyond color figures for Chapter 12.

Chapter 13

No CD-ROM content is included beyond color figures for Chapter 13.

Chapter 14

StarROMs Project Arcade Web site. A link to the special Project Arcade section of the StarROMs ROM selling service.

Chapter 15

Carsten's LED tutorial. A Web-based tutorial on how to connect LEDs to your arcade cabinet project.

Oscar Controls joystick graphics. Artwork you can place around joysticks on an arcade control panel, courtesy of Oscar Controls.

Oscar Controls marquees. More artwork from Oscar Controls, this time meant for the marquee of your arcade cabinet project.

Links to artwork resources. A Web-enabled list of free resources for finding artwork for your arcade cabinet project.

Links to commercial artwork resources. Another Web-enabled list of commercially available arcade cabinet artwork.

Chapter 16

Helpful Web links. Web-enabled listing of emulation and arcade Web sites and newsgroups.

Chapter 17

Arcade Depot pictures. Photos of the cocktail cabinet kit from Arcade Depot.

HanaHo ArcadeWerx pictures. Photos of the ArcadeWerx arcade cabinet kit from HanaHo.

HanaHo HotRod photos. Pictures of the HanaHo HotRod desktop arcade controller.

SlikStik cabinet pictures. Photos of the SlikStik arcade cabinet kit.

SlikStik classic console photos. Pictures of the SlikStik desktop arcade controller.

X-Arcade console pictures. Photos of the X-Arcade and X-Arcade Solo desktop arcade controllers.

Chapter 18

Project Arcade photos. Pictures of the completed Project Arcade cabinet.

Troubleshooting

If you have difficulty installing or using any of the materials on the companion CD, try the following solutions:

- **Turn off any anti-virus software that you may have running.** Installers sometimes mimic virus activity and can make your computer incorrectly believe that a virus is trying to infect it. Be sure to turn the anti-virus software back on after you've finished the installation.

- **Close all running programs.** The more programs you're running, the less memory is available to other programs. Installers also typically update files and programs; if you keep other programs running, installation may not work properly.

- **Check the ReadMe:** Please refer to the ReadMe file located at the root of the CD-ROM for the latest product information at the time of publication.

If you still have trouble with the CD-ROM, please call the Wiley Product Technical Support phone number: (800) 762-2974. Outside the United States, call 1(317) 572-3994. You can also contact Wiley Product Technical Support at www.wiley.com/techsupport. Wiley Publishing will provide technical support only for installation and other general quality control items; for technical support on the applications themselves, consult the program's vendor or author.

To place additional orders or to request information about other Wiley products, please call (800) 225-5945.

Index

Continued

C

Continued

Continued

Continued

Continued

Wiley Publishing, Inc.
End-User License Agreement

READ THIS. You should carefully read these terms and conditions before opening the software packet(s) included with this book "Book". This is a license agreement "Agreement" between you and Wiley Publishing, Inc. "WPI". By opening the accompanying software packet(s), you acknowledge that you have read and accept the following terms and conditions. If you do not agree and do not want to be bound by such terms and conditions, promptly return the Book and the unopened software packet(s) to the place you obtained them for a full refund.

1. License Grant. WPI grants to you (either an individual or entity) a nonexclusive license to use one copy of the enclosed software program(s) (collectively, the "Software") solely for your own personal or business purposes on a single computer (whether a standard computer or a workstation component of a multi-user network). The Software is in use on a computer when it is loaded into temporary memory (RAM) or installed into permanent memory (hard disk, CD-ROM, or other storage device). WPI reserves all rights not expressly granted herein.

2. Ownership. WPI is the owner of all right, title, and interest, including copyright, in and to the compilation of the Software recorded on the disk(s) or CD-ROM "Software Media". Copyright to the individual programs recorded on the Software Media is owned by the author or other authorized copyright owner of each program. Ownership of the Software and all proprietary rights relating thereto remain with WPI and its licensers.

3. Restrictions On Use and Transfer.

   (a) You may only (i) make one copy of the Software for backup or archival purposes, or (ii) transfer the Software to a single hard disk, provided that you keep the original for backup or archival purposes. You may not (i) rent or lease the Software, (ii) copy or reproduce the Software through a LAN or other network system or through any computer subscriber system or bulletin- board system, or (iii) modify, adapt, or create derivative works based on the Software.

   (b) You may not reverse engineer, decompile, or disassemble the Software. You may transfer the Software and user documentation on a permanent basis, provided that the transferee agrees to accept the terms and conditions of this Agreement and you retain no copies. If the Software is an update or has been updated, any transfer must include the most recent update and all prior versions.

4. Restrictions on Use of Individual Programs. You must follow the individual requirements and restrictions detailed for each individual program in the What's on the CD-ROM appendix of this Book. These limitations are also contained in the individual license agreements recorded on the Software Media. These limitations may include a requirement that after using the program for a specified period of time, the user must pay a registration fee or discontinue use. By opening the Software packet(s), you will be agreeing to abide by the licenses and restrictions for these individual programs that are detailed in the What's on the CD-ROM appendix and on the Software Media. None of the material on this Software Media or listed in this Book may ever be redistributed, in original or modified form, for commercial purposes.

5. Limited Warranty.

   (a) WPI warrants that the Software and Software Media are free from defects in materials and workmanship under normal use for a period of sixty (60) days from the date of purchase of this Book. If WPI receives notification within the warranty period of defects in materials or workmanship, WPI will replace the defective Software Media.